MW01490844

YEATS THE EUROPEAN

THE PRINCESS GRACE IRISH LIBRARY SERIES

YEATS
THE EUROPEAN

edited by
A. Norman Jeffares

Princess Grace Irish Library: 3

BARNES & NOBLE BOOKS
Savage, Maryland

Copyright © 1989 by The Princess Grace Irish Library, Monaco
'Lily Yeats, W. B. Yeats, and France' © 1989 by William M. Murphy

All rights reserved

First published in the United States of America in 1989
by Barnes & Noble Books, 8705 Bollman Place, Savage, MD 20783

Library of Congress Cataloging-in-Publication Data

Yeats the European.

(The Princess Grace Irish Library series ; 3)
Proceedings of a conference held at the Princess
Grace Irish Library in Monaco.
Includes index.
1. Yeats, W. B. (William Butler), 1865-1939 – –
Knowledge – – Europe – – Congresses.   2. Yeats, W. B.
(William Butler), 1865-1939 – – Knowledge – – Literature
– – Congresses.   3. English literature – – European
influences – – Congresses. 4. Europe in literature
– – Congresses.   I. Jeffares, A. Norman (Alexander
Norman), 1920-   . II. Series.
PR5908.E87Y44   1989   821'.8   89-7015
ISBN 0-389-20875-2 (alk. paper)

Originated and published in Great Britain
by Colin Smythe Limited, Gerrards Cross, Buckinghamshire

Produced in Great Britain
Phototypeset by Crypticks, Leeds,
and printed and bound by Billing & Sons Ltd., Worcester

CONTENTS

ILLUSTRATIONS

OPENING ADDRESS BY
H.S.H. PRINCESS CAROLINE

This international conference entirely devoted to the Irish poet William Butler Yeats is something special because the son and daughter of the poet are with us today, sharing the literary interest.

I would like to greet the outstanding scholars who are taking part in this Seminar, especially the Conference Chairman, Professor Jeffares.

This Library has now become a mature institution of scholarship, enjoying the approval and support of many universities all over the world.

I wish you full success in your discussions and I look forward to a volume of proceedings emerging from your debates to be published in the Princess Grace Irish Library Series.

To mark the special nature of our Conference, I hereby unveil the bust of the great Irish poet, which has been donated to the Library by the sculptor Kees Verkade.

I declare the Conference open.

THE IDÉAL SÉJOUR

still loftier than the world suspects
Browning

Ever since the morning of Thursday 8 April 1982 — I remember it so well! — when Mark Mortimer of Paris took me high up to Roquebrune-Village, and still higher up along tortuous mountain roads, to its churchyard in order to show me the Dulac Unicorn plaque, my obsessive dream had been to have an international Yeats Conference organised in the Principality of Monaco.

It had been only the day before that Her Serene Highness Princess Grace had spent the whole afternoon and evening — nine solid hours! — listening attentively to us Joyceans celebrating that other Dubliner's centenary. But the Irish Library did not at that time exist in Monaco, and this Yeats conference idea was nothing more than a wild dream — or a utopia — or was it an intuition of the large-scale cultural activities in the English language that were soon to come to the Principality?

The moment the Princess Grace Irish Library became a reality — on 20 November 1984 — I more than knew that the International Yeats Conference was slowly but certainly on its way. What preceded it were two introductory events, to break the ice: one was devoted to the scrutiny of a very recent edition of Joyce's *Ulysses* that its Editor wanted to pass on as dogma (which was not very wise!); the other gathering was entirely devoted to a possible definition of the impossible concept of Irishness . . .

But a Yeats event was *autre chose*: it was the focal point. After all, W. B. Yeats had lived, written, socialised, and died at a stone's throw from Monaco in a place more than symbolically called — by a Joycean coincidence — Hôtel Idéal Séjour! Could one recreate that *idéal séjour* fifty years later? Having known Derry Jeffares for just under a quarter of a century — his scholarly attachment to WBY, his enterprising spirit, his quick and most accurate decision processes and, above all, his worldwide network of scholarly contacts — I was more than certain that a pleasurable reconstruction

xi

of what Yeats had felt and experienced about continental Europe
was feasible through him, and through him only.

So Derry took over with the promptitude, confidence, and
inventivity that is his hallmark. It was very easy to work with
him: he sent out the invitations; I received the replies. He drafted
the academic programme; I and the Library's Trustees took care
of the social programme and everything else that a four-day international conference entails. When it came to chairing, Derry and
I chaired jointly: I was keeping the good timing, and he was
keeping the good mood; and it was the most satisfying tandem
chairing that I have ever experienced. We had become a team to
such an extent that it never even occurred to me to thank him at
the end of the day for all he had done for us. And when somebody
from the audience drew our attention to this omission, it suddenly
dawned on me that, deep down inside, Derry was by now one of
the house and the essentially pleasurable and highly evocative
nature of our *séjour* was largely due to him.

The presence of Yeats's children enhanced our family feeling,
and pre-war evocative connotations; I wish to thank Senator
Michael Yeats and Miss Anne Yeats for their very active participation throughout. I also wish to thank Sir David and Lady Orr for
accepting our invitation to attend.

And then, one sunny morning His Serene Highness Prince
Albert of Monaco casually walked into the conference hall right
in time to listen to the talk on Ezra Pound and then to my friend
Bernardo expounding volubly on Lady Gregory.

In a word, it has been *un idéal séjour* for all of us.

C. George Sandulescu
Series Editor
Monaco, 16 June 1988

YEATS THE EUROPEAN

Address by the Conference Chairman, A. Norman Jeffares

When I suggested the theme of *Yeats the European* for this conference in Monaco in the Princess Grace Irish Library, the activities and well-being of which are so graciously presided over by Her Serene Highness Princess Caroline, I had in mind the possible advantages of setting Ireland's greatest poet within a larger framework than the one with which he is usually linked. And so the distinguished company of Yeatsian scholars and critics invited to this conference have been asked to consider one of the finest poets of our century in a European context.

Though Yeats spent most of his life on Europe's two major offshore islands he himself was in no way intellectually insular. Completely Irish, he fought throughout his life to give his country's literature a European poise. He found much of his inspiration in the complex interlinked legacy of tradition and thought, of literature and art, that is every European's heritage.

Yeats celebrated Irish places and their legends, then he realised Ireland's Celtic heritage and set himself to revitalizing the stories and personages of Irish mythology: Oisin and Niamh, Conor and Deirdre, Cuchulain and Emer, Diarmuid and Grania . . . But he also knew an even older European tradition: the classical literature of Greece and Rome. He came to this through the English poets, quoted freely to him by his father, the artist John Butler Yeats, as the two of them took the train from Howth to Dublin and walked together through the city streets, the one to his studio in York Street, the other to his nearby school in Harcourt Street. Tennyson and Arnold had linked Lincolnshire and Oxfordshire with Greece and Rome, as Shelley, early a dominant influence on the youthful Yeats, had matched his fine knowledge of Greek literature with the reds and yellows of Italy. Small wonder, then, that Pallas Athene, Helen of Troy and Hector, Catullus and the Roman Caesars are as at home in Yeats's poetry as the heroic figures of Irish mythology and history.

There were many other European elements: the Hebraism and Christianity of the Bible re-echo in Yeats's work more often than may be generally recognized. He absorbed medieval allegory from Spenser and first learned about Dante in conversations with Olivia Shakespear. Indeed conversations often stimulated him into deeper knowledge of his intellectual heritage. With Edwin Ellis he explored the visionary work of Blake. Arthur Symons translated the symbolists for him — Verlaine, Mallarmé, Maeterlinck and, of course, Villiers de l'Isle Adam. Later Iseult Gonne introduced him to the French poets, Jammes and Peguy. And his wife translated many authors for him, including Benedetto Croce.

There was always his devouring interest in the occult, in magic and mysticism, fuelled by his awareness of, say, Jacob Boehme and Emmanuel Swedenborg. Later Nietzsche, Descartes, Kant and Hegel were to hold his attention. Indeed as he grew older his deepening interest in philosophy nearly led — but luckily only nearly — to Plato and Plotinus bidding the Muse go pack. Then came his excited discovery of those eighteenth century Irish writers he regarded as his intellectual ancestors: Swift, Goldsmith, Berkeley and Burke, all of them nurtured in the traditions of Greece and Rome, and Goldsmith particularly cognisant of current European thought since he had made his unorthodox tour of the continent and explored its intellectual life.

Yeats, too, had come to know the European mainland. Paris stimulated his interest in symbolism, though his visits there were largely to see Maud Gonne. In 1907, however, Italy provided him with artistic and spiritual refreshment when, with Lady Gregory and her son Robert, he saw the glories of Florence, Milan, the steep streets of Urbino, the green shadow of Ferrara wall and the mosaics of Ravenna. Lady Gregory had read him Castiglione's *The Book of the Courtier* and now he saw for himself, fresh from disillusionment caused by serving the needs of his 'fool-driven land', what enlightened Renaissance patronage could do for the creation of great art.

His own achievement was recognised by the award of the Nobel Prize. In Stockholm with his wife to receive the prize he appreciated more European links with the past, describing the Swedish King as like an old country gentleman able to quote Horace and Catullus.

Yeats's visits to Europe continued, arranged by his wife as a means of getting him away from the stress of life in Ireland to the healthgiving sunshine of Sicily and the stimulus of seeing its mosaics. Rome with the Vatican galleries and the Sistine chapel

entranced him. He visited Milan, Algeçiras, Cannes and Rapallo
— 'the little town described in "The Ode on a Grecian Urn" '. The
medieval tower the poet had bought in 1917 and restored as a
summer residence no longer suited a man liable to bronchial
troubles; after a few winters in Ireland it seemed wise to find
periods of peace and warmth in visits to Rome, Majorca, then to
Menton and finally, in November 1938, to Cap Martin where he
died in January 1939.

Europe made Yeats free of its intellectual traditions and its
physical beauty. In return he gave us poetry, prose and drama
intertwined with the European past, often full of foreboding for
the future, but also of delight in and praise for the present — as
we here today praise the establishment of this Princess Grace
Irish Library, its name and contents commemorating the past of
Monaco with its recent beautiful and dignified Irish enrichment
— something, however, like the literature, art and music it serves
and preserves, to be summed up in the old Greek phrase, κτῆμα
ἐσ ἀεί, a possession forever.

WHEN YEATS SUMMONED GOLDEN CODGERS TO HIS SIDE

ALASDAIR D. F. MACRAE

During his speech in the debate on divorce in the Senate in 1925, Yeats, who was indulging in some historical background, was interrupted by An Cathaoirleach: 'Do you think we might leave the dead alone?' Yeats replied: 'I am passing on. I would hate to leave the dead alone.'[1] In his poetry the dead are certainly not neglected; Yeats is an invoker, a summoner, a mobilizer: 'Bid a strong ghost stand at the head'; 'I summon to the ancient winding stair'; 'O sweet everlasting Voices, be still'; 'Swear by what the sages spoke'. He invites, he commands, he prays, he begs pardon, and throughout all of his poetry a force of direct address gives a sense of drama and intimacy. As he calls his witnesses, we the readers, a jury of critics, watch. What is Yeats attempting to prove?

My primary concern here is to ask why Yeats summons the dead in his poetry and why in different phases of his career he uses different figures from the past. To talk of 'the dead', however, is to muddy the water because the figures Yeats invokes are often mythical and, therefore, in Yeats's view immortal. In a great deal of criticism and teaching of literature in universities it has been taken for granted that poets employ mythical material. Students now often see no reason why such a practice should be tolerated and demand to know why a contemporary poet cannot cope with the contemporary world in contemporary terms. Yeats himself anticipated their demand and traced it back to the nineteenth century: 'It was only with the modern poets, with Goethe and Wordsworth and Browning, that poetry gave up the right to consider all things in the world as a dictionary of types and symbols and began to call itself a critic of life and an interpreter of things as they are.'[2] His choice of examples of this modern tendency seems bizarre and, although some of Wordsworth's Lyrical Ballads might illustrate his theory, he would surely have found Whitman a more suitable exponent. Partly, no doubt,

1

because of his father's insistent materialism, Yeats felt obliged to
justify the more etherial aspects of his early poetry and in letters
and essays he tried to explain his poetic practices. There is a
wonderful passage in Schiller's play *The Piccolomini*, translated by
Coleridge, which can serve as a foundation for Yeats's own use of
myth:

> The intelligible forms of ancient poets,
> The fair humanities of old religion,
> The power, the beauty, and the majesty,
> That had their haunts in dale, or piny mountain,
> Or forest by slow stream, or pebbly spring,
> Or chasms and wat'ry depths; all these have vanished;
> They live no longer in the faith of reason!
> But still the heart doth need a language, still
> Doth the old instinct bring back the old names,
> And to yon starry world they now are gone,
> Spirits or gods, that used to share this earth
> With man as with their friend; and to the lover
> Yonder they move, from yonder visible sky
> Shoot influence down: and even at this day
> 'Tis Jupiter who brings whate'er is great,
> And Venus who brings everything that's fair.[3]

'Still the heart doth need a language', and, for a language to
communicate, its terms must be validated by previous use
whereby the personal became public. Even, or specially, Ezra
Pound who wanted to 'Make it new' found himself driven into an
historical and mythical allusiveness of a density beyond anything
to be found in Yeats. It may be that the very Modernist aggression
and daring of Pound, Joyce and Eliot forced them to display a
knowledge of the past superior to that of their traditionalist
contemporaries.

For Yeats, it was not simply a matter of finding an intelligible
language for his heart although this aspect is often passed over
too glibly by critics eager for more intellectual motives. He states
a belief in *Autobiographies* when he writes: 'Because those imaginary people are created out of the deepest instinct of man, to be
his measure and his norm, whatever I can imagine those mouths
speaking may be the nearest I can go to truth.'[4] In his early poetry,
however, up to and including *In the Seven Woods*, symbolist,
esoteric and nationalist intentions are intermeshed. According to
himself, it was only after he read Standish O'Grady's books that,
'I turned my back on foreign themes, decided that the race was

more important than the individual, and began my *Wanderings of Oisin*.[5] During the 1890s his knowledge of Celtic mythology and the Irish sagas increased and his conviction grew stronger that only native material could satisfy his various aspirations. In 'The Celtic Element in Literature' (1902), he asserts that

> Literature dwindles to a mere chronicle of circumstances, or passionless fantasies, and passionless meditations, unless it is constantly flooded with the passions and beliefs of ancient times, and of all the fountains of passions and beliefs of ancient times in Europe, the Slavonic, the Finnish, the Scandanavian, and the Celtic, the Celtic alone has been for centuries close to the main river of European literature.[6]

The reiterated protestation of passion makes the whole contention sound hollow and the essay is too easily derived from the grandiose claims of Ernest Renan and Matthew Arnold. Nonetheless, Yeats's commitment to Irishness was very fierce and was proclaimed in almost everything he wrote in this period. Much later, in 1927, he could still insist to Sturge Moore that all his theories of art depend on 'rooting of mythology in the earth', reminding us of his rhetorical question in *Autobiographies*: 'Have not all races had their first unity from a mythology that marries them to rock and hill?' (p. 194). His espousal of Irish mythology precluded what he called 'an international art' which could garner stories and symbols where it pleased and, in his evangelical fervour, he believed Irish writers who had been forced into foreign service would willingly return to devote their talents to the study and promotion of Irish history and legend.

Alongside his wish to find in Celtic myth the spoor of his symbolist, esoteric and nationalist quarries, Yeats introduced a complicating notion derived from his theory of Masks. Not only had the myths to provide archetypal symbols for the Anima Mundi, symbols with which we could identify and which prefigure and reflect our hopes and fears, and loves and hates, but they had to provide symbols antithetical to us.

> Nations, races, and individual men are unified by an image, or bundle of related images, symbolical or evocative of the state of mind which is, of all states of mind not impossible, the most difficult to that man, race, or nation; because only the greatest obstacle that can be contemplated without despair rouses the will to full intensity.[7]

Although the development and formulation of his theory of Masks takes place after the turn of the century, the evidence is there in the earlier poetry that he was already experimenting with roles and counter-selves. It is also true that as his knowledge of the theatre became more extensive, so his ideas about dramatic character and his ability to create characters outwith his ordinary self both advanced. However, too often it seems to me mythological schemes and epics are seen as straightforward reflections of the society out of which they arose; and what we encounter in Yeats is not a mythology shaken down and established after centuries of association with rituals but a devised fiction based on fragments of broken and compounded stories. When Dorothy M. Hoare worries anxiously that he may not have allowed the sagas to emerge clearly because his dreams realigned and muffled them, she is quite right but she is mouthing a truism about literary creation. Yeats's admired predecessor, Sir Samuel Ferguson, was an antiquarian and he had a scholarly interest in recovering intact as much as he could of early Ireland; what motivated Yeats's poems, however, was not antiquarianism but something more private and psychological. When Yeats re-embodied Fergus or Oisin or Cuchulain or Aengus in his verse, the meaning they have in a poem is only in part to be explained by any reference to a source document. In 1909, in a letter to Robert Gregory, he asserts that he has 'no instincts in personal life' and for all his talk of passion and instinct in his essays of the 1890s, his literary cunning is evident in the poetry of that decade.

'The Song of Wandering Aengus' stands as an example of how complicated and cunning Yeats's treatment of myth can be:

> I went out to the hazel wood,
> Because a fire was in my head,
> And cut and peeled a hazel wand,
> And hooked a berry to a thread;
> And when white moths were on the wing,
> And moth-like stars were flickering out,
> I dropped the berry in a stream
> And caught a little silver trout.
>
> When I had laid it on the floor
> I went to blow the fire aflame,
> But something rustled on the floor,
> And some one called me by my name:
> It had become a glimmering girl
> With apple blossom in her hair
> Who called me by my name and ran
> And faded through the brightening air.

> Though I am old with wandering
> Through hollow lands and hilly lands,
> I will find out where she has gone,
> And kiss her lips and take her hands;
> And walk among long dappled grass,
> And pluck till time and times are done
> The silver apples of the moon,
> The golden apples of the sun.

In *A New Commentary on the Poems of W. B. Yeats*, Professor A. Norman Jeffares provides a wealth of information relating to possible sources for the poem and to other uses of similar mythical materials. The poet's own note on the poem when it appeared in *The Wind Among the Reeds* (1899) is a curious pot-pourri:

The Tribes of the goddess Danu can take all shapes, and those that are in the waters take often the shape of fish. A woman of Burren, in Galway, says, 'There are more of them in the sea than on the land, and they sometimes try to come over the side of the boat in the form of fishes, for they can take their choice shape.' At other times they are beautiful women; and another Galway woman says, 'Surely those things are in the sea as well as on land. My father was out fishing one night off Tyrone. And something came beside the boat that had eyes shining like candles. And then a wave came in, and a storm rose all in a minute, and whatever it was in the wave, the weight of it had like to sink the boat. And then they saw that it was a woman in the sea that had the shining eyes. So my father went to the priest, and he bid him always to take a drop of holy water and a pinch of salt out in the boat with him, and nothing could harm him.'

The poem was suggested to me by a Greek folk song; but the folk belief of Greece is very like that of Ireland, and I certainly thought, when I wrote it, of Ireland, and of the spirits that are in Ireland. An old man who was cutting a quickset hedge near Gort, in Galway, said, only the other day, 'One time I was cutting timber over in Inchy, and about eight o'clock one morning, when I got there, I saw a girl picking nuts, with her hair hanging down over her shoulders; brown hair; and she had a good clean face, and she was tall, and nothing on her head, and her dress no way gaudy, but simple. And when she felt me coming she gathered herself up, and was gone, as if the earth had swallowed her up. And I followed her, and looked for her, but I never could see her again from that day to this, never again.'

The county Galway people use the word 'clean' in its old sense of fresh and comely.[8]

The poem was first published in 1897 with the title 'A Mad Song' and it might as well have kept that title for all the help commentators seem to have derived from this lengthy note. Over the years it has remained one of Yeats's most popular poems but many critics have been remarkably coy in their comments on it. Perhaps, as Yeats suggested about the symbolism in *The Wanderings of Oisin*, the symbols should enter our minds by a process of easy osmosis. According to legend, Aengus, the god of love, youth and beauty, became infatuated with a girl who appeared to him only in dreams. Eventually, when Aengus was pining away, she was identified as Caer, encountered in her other form as a swan, and the two found happiness together. Near Aengus's home (what we now call Newgrange) was a sacred grove of hazel trees growing over a pool in which was to be found the salmon of wisdom. The salmon was made wise by eating the sacred hazel nuts and if a person could catch the salmon and eat it he partook of the wisdom. We know from other references that Yeats associated Maud Gonne with apple blossom because she was standing next to a vase of it on their first meeting in 1889 and we also know from elsewhere that he considered the moon as symbolic of imagination and the sun as symbolic of reason. Even without resorting to so much information imported from beyond the page, even allowing for the oddity of a god of love and youth suffering failure in love and the blight of age, the central pressure of the poem is clear. It is an exploration of unachieved aspiration. The fire is in his head from the beginning and it is the fire which drives him to fish in the dawn, a time of day associated with revelation in Yeats's poetry. The metamorphosis of the fish into the girl who knows his name prolongs the quest. In the last stanza Aengus expresses a fierce determination or desperation to achieve unity and wisdom through finding the elusive girl. Yeats escapes from the private and the idiosyncratic by invoking the generalized and emblematic elements of the mythical Aengus: the passion is human, the terms of expression are divine, the usual combination in nympholepsy.

The Green Helmet and Other Poems, published in 1910, has no reference to a figure from Irish mythology and Yeats now talks in terms of Homer, Helen and Olympus. What happened in the years between 1904 and 1910 which can explain this shift in loyalties? The contrast is obvious between the attitude expressed at the beginning of the early phase and the attitude expressed in 1908. In 1889 Yeats contended that, 'Cosmopolitan literature is, at best, but a poor bubble, though a big one. Creative writing has always a fatherland'.[9] In 1908 he allows, 'All literature in every country is derived from models, and as often as not these are foreign models, and it is the presence of a personal element alone that can give it nationality in a fine sense, the nationality of its maker.'[10] The most striking note in *The Green Helmet* poems is of bitterness and disappointment:

> In this blind bitter land
> My barren thoughts have chilled me to the bone
> On the day's war with every knave and dolt
> But was there ever dog that praised his fleas?
> The seeming needs of my fool-driven land

In the opening decade of the new century Yeats wrote very few poems and much of his time was devoted to writing plays and managing the Abbey Theatre which opened in 1904. In the previous year Maud Gonne had married the 'drunken, vainglorious lout', Captain MacBride. 1907 saw the death of John O'Leary and the riots at the Abbey when Synge's *The Playboy of the Western World* was produced. The poet's father emigrated to the United States in 1908 and in 1909 Synge died and Lady Gregory came near to dying. In 1910 his uncle George Pollexfen died. He had quarrelled with previous allies, Arthur Griffith, George Russell and George Moore. Personally, poetically, and publicly, particularly with regard to his efforts for an Irish cultural nationalism, he felt he had come to an impasse or, worse, had taken a wrong road which had led him into a wilderness in 'this blind bitter land'. His disenchantment with Ireland seemed almost total at times and comes out in his indignation

> at the fumbling wits, and the obscure spite
> Of our old Paudeen in his shop.

His earlier faith that the literary wild geese would return to Ireland and help to create a new nation, conscious and proud of its past, vigorous and spiritually minded, was broken:

> Romantic Ireland's dead and gone,
> It's with O'Leary in the grave.

A tour of Northern Italy in 1907 with Lady Gregory and her son Robert caused him to see the Renaissance in a new light. Earlier, it had seemed to pose a threat to his claims for a distinctively Irish culture but visits to some of the Italian cities, particularly Urbino and Ravenna, and some study of Renaissance writings, particularly Castiglione's *The Courtier*, showed that there was much for him to learn from outside Ireland. If Ireland was to continue to be bullied by an 'unmoral bourgeoisie' who favoured the tawdry and the temporal, then, according to Yeats, the only wise course of action for aspiring writers was to live abroad from the age of eighteen to twenty-five. It is significant that after a gap of seven years in his *Autobiographies* the two extracts from his diary of 1909 should be called *Estrangement* and *The Death of Synge*.

The nature of his poetry had to be scrutinized; it did not square with the situation in which he now found himself. In a letter to George Russell in April 1904 he castigates much of his earlier writing:

It is sentiment and sentimental sadness, a womanish introspection . . . As often happens with a thing one has been tempted by and is still a little tempted by, I am roused by it to a kind of frenzied hatred which is quite out of my control . . . I cannot probably be quite just to any poetry that speaks to me with the sweet insinuating feminine voice of the dwellers in that country of shadows and hollow images. I have dwelt there too long not to dread all that comes out of it. We possess nothing but the will and we must never let the children of vague desires breathe upon it nor the waters of sentiment rust the terrible mirror of its blade.[11]

The language of this self-flagellation is not entirely lacking in indulgence. It was only two years earlier that he wrote a nauseating letter to James Joyce commending him on such poems, according to Stanislaus Joyce, as the Villanelle, later to be included in *A Portrait of the Artist as a Young Man*: 'Your technique in verse is very much better than the technique of any Dublin man I have met during my time. It might have been the work of a young man who lived in an Oxford literary set.'[12] The only question to be asked about the Villanelle is whether it is a dreadful pastiche or a good parody of the kind of poem by Yeats against which he himself revolted when he sought a 'less dream-burdened will' in his verse. His practical work in the theatre and his first tour of the United States in 1903 with forty lectures to deliver probably contributed to his new inclination towards hard edges, clarity and verbal economy in poetry. In preparing his *Collected Works* (eight volumes) for the press in 1908 he had to reconsider all that he had written and in the same year he met Ezra Pound who encouraged him to get rid of what he called 'emotional slither' and abstract words.

In particular, he revised some of his ideas about myths. In 1900 in a letter to George Russell he mentions one change: 'I avoid suggesting the ghostly (the vague) idea about a god, for it is a modern conception. All ancient vision was definite and precise.' In the plays where he continues to use Celtic myths there is a sharper definition in the characterization and the language than there was in his plays up to the end of the century. Celtic myth, however, disappears from his poetry for a number of years. Apart from the factors outlined above, there is one special reason for his neglect of Celtic allusions and his adoption of Greek ones. It centres round his feelings for Maud Gonne and is crucial to the way in which he wishes to present her in the poems. One of his most elaborate descriptions of her occurs in *Autobiographies*:

There was an element in her beauty that moved minds full of old Gaelic stories and poems, for she looked as though she lived in an ancient civilization where all superiorities whether of the mind or the body were a part of public ceremonial, were in some way the crowd's creation, as the entrance of the Pope into Saint Peter's is the crowd's creation. Her beauty, backed by her great stature, could instantly affect an assembly, and not, as often with our stage beauties, because obvious and florid, for it was incredibly distinguished, and if — as must be that it might seem that assembly's very self, fused, unified, and solitary — her face, like the face of some Greek statue, showed little thought, her whole body seemed a master-work of long laboured thought, as though a Scopas had measured and calculated, consorted with Egyptian sages, and mathematicians of Babylon, that he might outface even Artemisia's sepulchral image with a living norm.[13]

To begin with, he places Maud Gonne in a Celtic context of 'old Gaelic stories and poems' but as his description continues she becomes more foreign and detached and she is finally identified with measurement and the impersonal finish of Greek art. There is nothing intimate, comely or sentimental about her beauty, rather something removed, cold and even frightening. Yeats saw her, as he saw Helen of Troy, as emblematic of an historical turn away from soft, yielding qualities towards a cold and destructive direction. Later, in *A Vision*, he describes Helen:

She came before the mind's eye elaborating a delicate personal discipline, as though she would make her whole life an image of a unified antithetical energy. While seeming an image of softness and quiet, she draws perpetually upon glass with a diamond . . . For all the languor of her movements, and her indifference to the acts of others, her mind is never at peace. She will wander much alone as though she consciously meditated her masterpiece that shall be at the full moon, yet unseen by human eyes, and when she returns to her house she will look upon her household with timid eyes, as though she knew that all powers of self-protection had been taken away, and that of her once violent primary tincture nothing remained but a strange irresponsible innocence . . . Is it because she desires so little, gives so little that men will die and murder in her service?[14]

In the *Green Helmet* poems, Maud Gonne does not appear in her own person but through the magnifying glass of Yeats's wish to see her emblematically. She is elevated in her characteristics of 'sternness', 'strength', 'strangeness', 'fiery blood', 'A woman Homer sung'. He concedes that her presence and conduct have debarred him from writing the kind of verse that moved readers emotionally in his earlier period. 'Reconciliation' is a precarious, brittle poem but the poem in which Maud Gonne's mythologization is most complete is 'No Second Troy'.

> Why should I blame her that she filled my days
> With misery, or that she would of late
> Have taught to ignorant men most violent ways,
> Or hurled the little streets upon the great,
> Had they but courage equal to desire?
> What could have made her peaceful with a mind
> That nobleness made simple as a fire,
> With beauty like a tightened bow, a kind
> That is not natural in an age like this,
> Being high and solitary and most stern?
> Why, what could she have done, being what she is?
> Was there another Troy for her to burn?

As is so common in Yeats's poetry from now on, the rhetorical assertiveness is held as a suspended drama by the repeated questions. The opening question really consists of two questions: should she be blamed for causing him misery, or should she be blamed for infecting ignorant men with a revolutionary violence? Lines 6-10 develop the imagery of destructiveness through her identification with fire and a drawn bow. The words 'courage', 'nobleness', 'beauty', 'high' (one of Yeats's favourite adjectives), 'solitary' and 'stern' are mounted against 'misery', 'ignorant', 'little', 'an age like this'. The unnatural is her nature. The heavy stresses on the obvious rhyme words play against the syntax uncoiling through the lines and lead to the final question. But is 'another Troy' Yeats with his misery or Dublin with its streets? And is the title a defiant answer to that question?

It might seem, despite what I have argued, that Yeats could just as easily have used the doom-bearing Deirdre for his mythical enlargement of Maud Gonne; and would such a manoeuvre not have been more indigenous and a natural development of Maud Gonne's identification with Cathleen in *The Countess Cathleen* and her success in the leading role of *Cathleen ni Houlihan* (1902)? After all, in 'The Rose of the World' Deirdre and Helen seemed to co-exist and Helen became the definite figure in 'The Sorrow of Love' only after Yeats's redrafting of the poem for the new edition of 1925. Such a late revision of the poem surely supports my contention that he wished categorically to associate Maud Gonne with Helen and not with a Celtic figure. Looking forward, we are aware that Helen comes to blur into her mother Leda as the poet traces Greek civilization *ab ovo* and Maud Gonne even becomes Pallas Athene.

Responsibilities (1914) is the first fully cosmopolitan collection in terms of the mythical figures called into play by Yeats. The word 'mythical' now has to include all creatures who are given a fixed character in the drama of the poet's work: King Guaire, Helen, the Magi, Parnell can all be made into Olympians. Even the living are not exempt from his mythologizing process. Characters from Celtic mythology re-emerge in this collection but Yeats seems careful to avoid the misty dreaminess of, for example, *The Shadowy Waters* and, instead, promotes a comical and eccentric quality in the Celtic figures. For more serious matters, he, like his new found model, Guidobaldo of Urbino, seeks wisdom 'By sucking at the dugs of Greece'. It appears in 'The Coat' that he disowns his previous disguises and adoptions:

> I made my song a coat
> Covered with old embroideries
> Out of old mythologies
> From heel to throat;
> But the fools caught it,
> Wore it in the world's eyes
> As though they'd wrought it.
> Song, let them take it,
> For there's more enterprise
> In walking naked.

As has often been pointed out, Yeats may have dispensed with certain ornate garbs but he certainly does not walk naked in his later poetry. He may become a 'tattered coat upon a stick' but the tatters are carefully chosen and artfully arranged. Although Celtic myths play only a small part in *The Wild Swans at Coole* and *Michael Robartes and the Dancer*, we feel that he is free from obligations or inhibitions as to whence he selects his emblems and even European civilization is not to be a boundary.

I thought constantly of Homer and Dante, and the tombs of Mausolus and Artemisia, the great figures of King and Queen and the lesser figures of Greek and Amazon, Centaur and Greek. I thought that all art should be a Centaur finding in the popular lore its back and its strong legs . . . Had not Europe shared one mind and heart, until both mind and heart began to break into fragments a little before Shakespeare's birth?[15]

Section VI of the rather overlooked 'Upon a Dying Lady', written in respect for Mabel Beardsley, is an example of the new global reach:

Her Courage

When her soul flies to the predestined dancing-place
(I have no speech but symbol, the pagan speech I made
Amid the dreams of youth) let her come face to face,
Amid the first astonishment, with Grania's shade,
All but the terrors of the woodland flight forgot
That made her Diarmuid dear, and some old cardinal
Pacing with half-closed eyelids in a sunny spot
Who had murmured of Giorgione at his latest breath —
Aye, and Achilles, Timor, Babar, Barhaim, all
Who had lived in joy and laughed into the face of Death.

The 'pagan speech' of symbol has been cultivated and extended and the 'monuments of unageing intellect' will be sought wherever they are:

I have prepared my peace
With learned Italian things
And the proud stones of Greece,
Poet's imaginings
And memories of love,
Memories of the words of women,
All those things whereof
Man makes a superhuman
Mirror-resembling dream.   ('The Tower')

Like the 'mummy wheat' ('On a Picture of a Black Centaur by Edmund Dulac') which according to reports had been found in excavations of ancient Egyptian tombs and could still be planted and bear wheat, like the bodies of holy men and women who, centuries on, 'exude/Miraculous oil' ('Oil and Blood'), the mythical from another time and another place can resurrect in us. *A Vision*, finished in 1925, is Yeats's attempt to define the contribution made to the pattern of change by the persons and events of the drama which is history; their meaning is in their endless recurrence.

Such is the proliferation of mythical materials in *The Tower* and later collections, and such is the mingling of periods and consciousnesses, that it is sometimes difficult to locate the persona and to ascertain the source of the myth. How the Seven Sages see Berkeley, Swift, Goldsmith, and Burke, although their comments bristle with topical details, extracts these men from a full historical context. Byzantium becomes a condition of the mind. When we approach 'Among School Children' through the two songs from the play *Resurrection* and 'Leda and the Swan', can we accept or allow Yeats's dream of Maud Gonne as Ledaean? Is the identification of the actual with the mythical, of Leda and Helen's stories with a 'trivial event/That changed some childish day to tragedy' for Maud Gonne, permissible or in the worst possible taste? (Compare Sylvia Plath's running together of personal events with extermination in the Nazi concentration camps.) When the poet writes, 'And I though never of Ledaean kind/Had pretty plumage once', is he, even jocularly, associating himself with the divine swan? Perhaps it is not surprising that he cannot know 'the dancer from the dance'. However, *A Woman Young and Old*'s eighth section, 'Her Vision in the Wood', is a wholly successful fusing of the actual and the mythical, the immediate and the visionary. Section VIII has, of course, its context in the whole sequence but in itself it contains a rich drama couched in a range of suggestive references. Whether the 'wounded man', the 'beast-torn wreck', is identified as Diarmuid or as Adonis makes little difference; in fact, the blurring of the two substantiates Yeats's reading of myth and the poem in the end returns to the mysteries of human emotion:

> they had brought no fabulous symbol there
> But my heart's victim and its torturer.

In rage and 'grief's contagion' the woman is enabled to see through the vision, through 'a thoughtless image of Mantegna's thought' to her present self.

In 1918 a disgruntled Yeats had written 'The Leaders of the Crowd', a poem of self-defence:

> They must to keep their certainty accuse
> All that are different of a base intent;
> Pull down established honour; hawk for news
> Whatever their loose fantasy invent
> And murmur it with bated breath, as though
> The abounding gutter had been Helicon
> Or calumny a song. How can they know

Truth flourishes where the student's lamp has shone,
And there alone, that have no solitude?
So the crowd come they care not what may come.
They have loud music, hope every day renewed
And heartier loves; that lamp is from the tomb.

Despite his declaration in a letter to Lady Gregory in 1900 that
'One must accept the baptism of the gutter', and a repeated line
of argument that 'wisdom comes of beggary' ('The Seven Sages'),
that Solomon 'grew wise/While talking with his queens' ('On
Woman'), Yeats returns over and over again to the image of the
scholar in a solitary tower searching for wisdom in the books of
earlier cultures: the lamp of knowledge and truth shines from the
past. In the final ten years of his career, however, his manner of
using the past and its sages, heroes, paragons, demonstrates a new
flexibility and a wide variety of tone. This development fortunately
coincides with the virtuosity of his syntax (his 'passionate syntax')
in the late period. Perhaps his new attitude to his material necessitated a change in syntax; perhaps it was the other way round.
Last Poems makes much use of motifs derived from Irish mythology,
folklore and history but not in any exclusive way. Often the Irish,
the Greek and Renaissance elements seem interchangeably available to the poet.

'The Statues' and 'News for the Delphic Oracle' are sometimes
lumped together by critics as similarly indigestible conglomerates
of Yeats's System. Actually, they are very different from each other.
In 'The Statues' an extraordinarily condensed analysis is offered
of the contending ideologies and their iconographies which
struggled for supremacy in European civilization and still do.
Again, for Yeats, the commanding quality of Greek culture was its
insistence on measurement, discipline, precision, on an abstract
art that contained (in both senses of the word) the vaguenesses
and confusions of life and, thereby, repulsed 'All Asiatic vague
immensities'. Again, for Yeats, the abstract or what seems the
dead can be the distillation of life for the living:

Pythagoras planned it. Why did the people stare?
His numbers, though they moved or seemed to move
In marble or in bronze, lacked character.
But boys and girls, pale from the imagined love
Of solitary beds, knew what they were,
That passion could bring character enough,
And pressed at midnight in some public place
Live lips upon a plummet-measured face.

In the final stanza he reverts to a connection between Greek thought and something he senses in Irish thought, a connection which, if actualized, could transform the contemporary world:

> When Pearse summoned Cuchulain to his side,
> What stalked through the Post Office? What intellect,
> What calculation, number, measurement, replied?
> We Irish, born into that ancient sect
> But thrown upon this filthy modern tide
> And by its formless spawning fury wrecked,
> Climb to our proper dark, that we may trace
> The lineaments of a plummet-measured face.

He seems to have rid himself of his fears in the early 1900s that Irish myths were a seductive dream world. In the final phase of his career he returns with greater fondness and obvious personal involvement to the fate of Cuchulain. In his dramas he always did remain faithful to his Irish sources and it may be that it is because of his experiments with Irish myths in the plays that, at this late stage, he can utilize the Irish material with such confidence in his poems.

'News for the Delphic Oracle' manifests something of Yeats's freedom in handling the Immortals:

> There all the golden codgers lay,
> There the silver dew,
> And the great water sighed for love,
> And the wind sighed too.
> Man-picker Niamh leant and sighed
> By Oisin on the grass;
> There sighed amid his choir of love
> Tall Pythagoras.
> Plotinus came and looked about,
> The salt-flakes on his breast,
> And having stretched and yawned awhile
> Lay sighing like the rest.

The 'News' of the title announces something surprizing, something unpredicted (even by the Delphic Oracle). F. A. C. Wilson, in *W. B. Yeats and Tradition* (1958), p. 218, suggests that the opening of the poem could be a mimicking of the popular song 'The Groves of Blarney'; I think this parallel points correctly to the tone adopted by Yeats. I would go further than Wilson, who reverts to a scholarly staidness in his analysis, and suggest that Yeats is mocking his own earlier dealings with the Immortals.

'Golden' and 'silver', 'great water' and 'wind' have not been absent
from his earlier poetry and his Celtic Twilight was loud with
'sighing'. The colloquialisms of 'codgers', 'man-picker' and
'stretched and yawned awhile' detract from any expected solem-
nity. The poem concludes with an unbuttoned vision of the
mythical characters:

> Foul goat-head, brutal arm appear,
> Belly, shoulder, bum,
> Flash fishlike; nymphs and satyrs
> Copulate in the foam.

Like 'The Statues' and 'News for the Delphic Oracle', 'The
Circus Animals' Desertion' was probably written within a year of
Yeats's death. It is often read alongside 'Under Ben Bulben' as the
poet's final testament and a retrospective survey of his career. The
actualities of the poem do not provide adequate evidence to
support this interpretation.

THE CIRCUS ANIMALS' DESERTION

I

> I sought a theme and sought for it in vain,
> I sought it daily for six weeks or so.
> Maybe at last, being a broken man,
> I must be satisfied with my heart, although
> Winter and summer till old age began
> My circus animals were all on show,
> Those stilted boys, that burnished chariot,
> Lion and woman and the Lord knows what.

II

> What can I but enumerate old themes?
> First that sea-rider Oisin led by the nose
> Through three enchanted islands, allegorical dreams,
> Vain gaiety, vain battle, vain repose,
> Themes of the embittered heart, or so it seems,
> That might adorn old songs or courtly shows;
> But what cared I that set him on to ride,
> I, starved for the bosom of his faery bride?

> And then a counter-truth filled out its play,
> *The Countess Cathleen* was the name I gave it;
> She, pity-crazed, had given her soul away,
> But masterful Heaven had intervened to save it.

I thought my dear must her own soul destroy,
So did fanaticism and hate enslave it,
And this brought forth a dream and soon enough
This dream itself had all my thought and love.

And when the Fool and Blind Man stole the bread
Cuchulain fought the ungovernable sea;
Heart-mysteries there, and yet when all is said
It was the dream itself enchanted me:
Character isolated by a deed
To engross the present and dominate memory.
Players and painted stage took all my love,
And not those things that they were emblems of.

III

Those masterful images because complete
Grew in pure mind, but out of what began?
A mound of refuse or the sweepings of a street,
Old kettles, old bottles, and a broken can,
Old iron, old bones, old rags, that raving slut
Who keeps the till. Now that my ladder's gone,
I must lie down where all the ladders start,
In the foul rag-and-bone shop of the heart.

What it is like is a rewriting and expansion of 'Alternative Song for the Severed Head in *The King of the Great Clock Tower*', written some four years earlier. The opening stanza expresses his despair of finding a theme on which to write and suggests that 'till old age began' he had a wealth of subjects. Professor Jeffares in his *New Commentary on the Poems of W. B. Yeats* glosses 'My circus animals' as 'Yeats's early work' but this is not quite what Yeats says in this stanza. True, what he writes about in section II is his early work, but this particularity seems, to me, one of the oddities of the poem. There is no reference in the poem to any of his work written after the *Green Helmet* collection and all the allusions are to Celtic motifs. It is difficult to be precise about when Yeats felt that old age began but surely he could not discount everything he had written during the preceding thirty years. Is he suggesting that 'Themes of the embittered heart' and the 'counter-truth' explored in *The Countess Cathleen* remained as the poles and axis of all his work? At its conclusion, the poem is firmly in the present tense but the ladder by which he arrived there seems curiously deficient in rungs. As with his unending revision of his work and his anxiety that before the tribunal of the sages he may have little to offer in his defence, is he again worrying

about the Irish base on which he had made his first stand? 'The
Man and the Echo' voices a similar disquiet. Earlier in 'Per Amica
Silentia Lunae' he had written:

Communication with Anima Mundi is through the association of
thoughts or images or objects; and the famous dead, and those of whom
but a faint memory lingers, can still — and it is for no other end that, all
unknowing, we value posthumous fame — tread the corridor and take
the empty chair.[16]

Yeats's involvement with mythological strands was not something peculiar to him. Innumerable books on mythology and
cultural anthropology were written around the turn of the century.
The first volume of Frazer's *The Golden Bough* appeared in 1890, the
twelfth and final one in 1915. Freud and Jung wrote much of their
seminal work in the same period and it was probably difficult for
a writer to avoid the pull of these minds. What emerges in any
study of Yeats is how problematic such terms as myth and symbol
are. Ezra Pound, in an essay on Arnold Dolmetsch in 1918, offers
a common-sensical theory of the origins of myths:

The first myths arose when a man walked sheer into 'nonsense', that is
to say, when some very vivid and undeniable adventure befell him, and
he told someone else who called him a liar. Thereupon, after bitter
experience, perceiving that no one could understand what he meant
when he said that he 'turned into a tree' he made a myth — a work of art
that is — an impersonal or objective story woven out of his own emotion,
as the nearest equation that he was capable of putting into words.[17]

Yeats, however, would grant more solidity to the myth, something
more than one person could create or grasp. Study of the mythical
is enlightening but also humbling:

Any one who has any experience of any mystical state of the soul knows
that there float up in the mind profound symbols, whose meaning, if
indeed they do not delude one into the dream that they are meaningless,
one does not perhaps understand for years. Nor I think has anyone, who
has known that experience with any constancy, failed to find some day,
in some old book or on some old monument, a strange or intricate image
that has floated up before him, and to grow perhaps dizzy with the
sudden conviction that our little memories are but a part of some great
Memory that renews the world and men's thoughts age after age, and
that our thoughts are not, as we suppose, the deep, but a little foam upon
the deep.[18]

His apprehension of the great Memory widened and deepened through his career and his extension from Ireland to Europe was only part of this enlargement. Edwin Muir, the centenary of whose birth falls this year, took a similar route of self-expansion from

> My childhood all a myth
> Enacted in a distant isle
>
>   ('The Myth')

to wider shores of place and time:

> Into thirty centuries born,
> At home in them all but the very last,
> We meet ourselves at every turn
> In the long country of the past.
> There the fallen are up again
> In mortality's second day,
> There the indisputable dead
> Rise in flesh more fine than clay
> And the dead selves we cast away
> In imperfection are perfected,
> And all is plain yet never found out!
> Ilium burns before our eyes
> For thirty centuries never put out,
> And we walk the streets of Troy
> And breathe in the air its fabulous name.
> The king, the courtier and the rout
> Shall never perish in that flame;
> Old Priam shall become a boy
> For ever changed, for ever the same.
>
>   ('Into Thirty Centuries Born')[19]

YEATS AS A EUROPEAN POET: THE POETICS OF CACOPHONY

HELEN VENDLER

Before he became a European poet, Yeats was an English poet, then an Irish poet. As we know, he began as an English poet. He said in late life,[1]

All my family names are English, and . . . I owe my soul to Shakespeare, to Spenser, and to Blake, perhaps to William Morris, and to the English language in which I think, speak, and write . . . [;] everything I love has come to me through English. (*EI*, p. 519)

To the end of his life, Yeats wrote what we may call English poems, poems in which there is no trace of anything but the English tradition. Yeats's country-house poems, many of the love poems, and almost all of the elegies reveal the English harmonies that compose the foundation of the Yeatsian style. Such poems display what Seamus Heaney has referred to, not uncritically, as Yeats's 'vitreous finish'.[2] And though Denis Donoghue has wittily said that Yeats 'invented a country, calling it Ireland',[3] it is not so often said that Yeats had to invent himself as Irish poet. Yeats himself said as much, however, when, in his 'General Introduction for my Work', he traced the original dialectic of love and hate within himself. The love of England had come first, with the love of England's poets; the hatred of England came second, with the awakening of his political consciousness. Writing of what he calls the English 'persecution' of the Irish, and of what he calls the English 'wars of extermination' against the Irish, he says, 'There are moments when hatred poisons my life and I accuse myself of effeminacy because I have not given it adequate expression . . . My hatred tortures me with love, my love with hate'. (*EI*, p. 519) In setting himself against those of his fellow-writers who recommended an Irish literature in Gaelic, Yeats said unrepentantly that 'no man can think or write with music and vigour except in his mother tongue . . . Gaelic is my national language, but it is not

20

my mother tongue'. (*EI*, p. 520) And for all his efforts to render his poetry Irish — by inserting in it Irish proper names, Irish themes, and an Irish landscape — the harmonies of his earlier 'Irish' poetry are often those of Tennyson, Browning, Rossetti, and Morris.

Yeats did not escape imitativeness of English poetry until he began to incorporate into his lyrics the lessons of his work in the theatre. When his work became terse and conversational, it took on the contour of his own speech instead of the contours of the speech of his English masters. That personal contour, together with the conscious Irishness of the 1914 volume *Responsibilities*, mark Yeats's maturity as an Irish poet.

It was not until the publication of *The Wild Swans at Coole* in 1919 that we can genuinely call Yeats a European poet. In becoming a European poet — an identity superadded to his identities as English and Irish poet — he had deliberately to think of writing in an international style. This was not to be the style of international socialism, which he hated as a style of the 'point of view' (*EI*, p. 511), but the style of a European consciousness. I want to suggest here both the early and the ultimate consequences in style of that search for a European consciousness.

Yeats's investigation of what a European style might be was of long standing. In his 1902 essay on Spenser, he looked longingly back to what he called 'the Anglo-French nation', veiling his own quarrel with the mercantile Protestantism of Ireland in representing it under the guise of the quarrel between the older 'Anglo-French' nation of Chaucer and the 'Anglo-Saxon nation' arising, in Spenser's time, under the Puritans:

This [Anglo-Saxon] nation had driven out the language of its conquerors, and now it was to overthrow their beautiful haughty imagination and their manners, full of abandon and wilfulness, and to set in their stead earnestness and logic and the timidity and reserve of a counting house.
(*EI*, p. 365)

We are not surprised, in this account, to be told that Shakespeare and Spenser are 'of the old nation', nor that 'our poetry . . . has been a deliberate bringing back of the Latin joy and the Latin love of beauty'. (*EI*, p. 378)

In 1902, Yeats concealed, under the rubric of recuperation of Latin beauty, the deep feelings of inferiority to Europe that any proponent of Irish culture would have felt at the beginning of the century. There was no concealing such feelings when his art went public. In the 1919 essay, 'A People's Theatre', they are boldly faced, as he defends himself, ostensibly to Lady Gregory, for seeking European helpers and London audiences:

How shall our singers and dancers be welcomed by those who have
heard Chaliapin in all his parts and who know all the dances of the
Russians? Yet where can I find Mr Dulac and Mr Rummel or any to match
them, but in London or in Paris, and who but the leisured will welcome
an elaborate art or pay for its first experiments? (*E*, p. 256)

Yeats certainly feared that he would have to mount his plays in
London or Paris rather than in Dublin, that he would become in
fact a European rather than an Irish playwright. (We may see
Beckett's career as the fulfilment of the destiny Yeats at least
momentarily envisaged for himself.) But with a look homeward
to Ireland, Yeats said in the same open letter to Lady Gregory, 'My
rooks may sleep abroad in the fields for a while, but when the
winter comes they will remember the way home to the rookery
trees'. (*E*, p. 256-257)

We might pause for a moment to ask what it might mean to call
Yeats, as Edward Engelberg did, 'the last of the great European
poets'.[4] In an obvious sense, Yeats was necessarily 'European',
not only because of the Celtic settlement of Ireland, but because
of the Christianizing of Ireland in the Middle Ages and its
Anglicizing in the Renaissance. Any English poet, in one sense,
is a European poet, since English poetry arises in part from
European models which poets investigate and depend on. Yeats,
however, was 'European' in his early verse in another way: he
was already seeking European models for Irish patriotism, and as
early as 1887 he had found in a Hungarian hero of 1848, Ferencz
Renyi, an exemplary figure, if an unnerving one (Renyi's patriotism costs him his sanity). (*P*, pp. 505-509) It is typical of Yeats's
European' side that he would not choose a patriotic model from
England's other colony, the United States: he did not regard
Ireland as a 'new' nation casting off its conqueror, but rather as an
old nation reclaiming its origins from an usurper.

Yeats may be considered a European poet in part, too, because
of his frequent trips to Paris and his residence in London. He found
in France and England the contemporary avant-garde he could not
find in Ireland, and he was more conscious of its experimentation
than his Irish predecessors had been. The theosophical movement,
too, itself European in origin, brought him into European, rather
than purely British, thought. (We should recall here that Yeats
did not stop at Europe in his poetic evolution, but went on to
investigate the Islamic and Asian worlds as well in experiments

that I cannot treat here.) What can be said about Yeats as a European is that in his continental sources, in his presumption of an eventual European audience for his work, and in his religious and cultural pursuits (not least his interest in architecture and painting), Yeats was bound to experience his own mentality, from the beginning, as a European one.

None of these assimilations, however, was without difficulty. Poetry is by its nature the most language-bound of the arts, and sometimes, in consequence, the most national. The separatist energies of the Irish literary movement were considerable, and Yeats faced political opposition in asking for an Irish culture that embraced other than Irish models. Late in life, when he described Byzantium as the ideal city — where East meets West, the old meets the new, Christianity meets the classical, and philosophy meets art — Yeats defined, one might say, Dublin as he would have had it be, and Irish art as it might become. That such an image could occur only in a historical fantasy points to the real difficulties Yeats found when he imagined himself as a European poet. What he was to discover was that an eclectic thematic syncretism alone, of the sort we see in the early experiments with Indian or Hungarian materials, would not suffice. In the long run, the rag-and-bone shop of his European mind would exact a style as disharmonious as its long-assembled contents. Not all the work of Yeats the European poet is cacophonous; but it was Yeats the European, not Yeats the English or Irish poet, who discovered the necessity for cacophony in the service of imaginative truth.

In his early poetry, Yeats's motives for cultural inclusiveness were religious and political, rather than stylistic, ones. Believing with Blake that everything possible to be believed is an image of the truth, he gathered together Celtic, Christian, European, classical, Asian, and Indian materials without any very clear idea of the poetic consequences of combining them. He took to simply listing his desired ingredients, as in 'The Sacred Rose' he listed the Magi with Concubar and Cuchulain, or as in 'The Rose of the World' he coupled Troy and Usna's children.

But by 1919, when Yeats publishes *The Wild Swans at Coole*, he has come to realize that themes entail style. He becomes aware that instead of an all-purpose nostalgic nineties style enfolding Troy, India, Cuchulain, and the Magi, he must find, so to speak, a Greek style for Troy, a Babylonian style for the Magi, an Irish style for Cuchulain — or, failing that, a style that juxtaposes these plural cultural markers while acknowledging — by the evidence of rhythm, language, stanza-form or image — the culture-shock

produced by bringing Troy and Usna's children into one poetic
room. And, committed to preserving a historical sense, he wishes
to retain — even to foreground — the shock, to avoid absorbing
all culture into a single embracing style. 'Pound's conception of
excellence', he says 'is of something so international that it is
abstract and outside life. . . . I can only approach [a] more distant
excellence through what I inherit, lest I find it and be stricken
dumb.' (*E*, p. 294) The 'traditional attitudes' that Yeats wished to
integrate into his poetry — and he cites Sophocles, Shakespeare,
the Old Testament, and the literature of 'modern Europe' as
among his sources (*E*, p. 295) — are not simply gathered up and
used, but rather must be 'hammered into a Unity'. '[I] see myself',
he said, 'set in a drama where I struggle to exalt and overcome
concrete realities perceived not with mind only but as with the
roots of my hair.' (*E*, p. 302)

Because it is in *The Wild Swans at Coole* that we see Yeats deciding
to be, in the full sense, a European poet, I will dwell on that
volume, looking only briefly, at the end of this essay, at the
ultimate stylistic consequences of Yeats's Europeanness. In *The
Wild Swans*, Yeats is enormously aware, at any given moment, of
the style in which he is working. He is composing with and
against his two basic norms — that of classical Greek and Latin
poetry and that of English lyric. When we look through *The Wild
Swans* we notice, with some uneasiness, that 'perfect' lyrics exist
side by side with lyrics exhibiting difficult prosody, slant
rhymes, and either odd stanzas or no stanzas at all. It is easy
enough to perceive that the openly experimental poems are
destroying or adjusting old stylistic forms in favour of new ones,
but we are less likely to see — though it is there to be seen even
in the title poem — Yeats's stylistic questioning of his 'perfect',
'English', style. Again, the epigrams contained in *The Wild Swans*
show us Yeats making himself into a Greek or Roman epigrammatic
poet, but the brevity, bitterness, symmetry and wit of the classical
and European epigrammatic style take on in this volume a Yeatsian
modulation. 'On Being Asked for a War Poem', for example,
though it presents itself as a public epigram, borrows its rhyme
scheme from the sestet of the Petrarchan sonnet; and into the
Roman plainness and chiastic force of 'An Irish Airman Foresees
his Death', there intrude two lines of Yeatsian arabesque:

> My country is Kiltartan Cross,
> My countrymen Kiltartan's poor.
>
> (*CP*, p. 133)

In the most striking case in this volume, we can see Yeats's double allegiance to the European and native traditions, and the dilemma of style he therefore faces, in the two formal elegies for Robert Gregory, the one, 'Shepherd and Goatherd', a pastoral eclogue by Virgil out of Spenser, the other, 'In Memory of Major Robert Gregory', a mimetic English poem with Irish references. And yet 'Shepherd and Goatherd' is made unclassical by its inclusion of an esoteric Yeatsian afterlife, while 'In Memory of Major Robert Gregory', a more interesting poem, is equally made untraditional by its conscious questioning of elegiac decorum, and by its modernist play among genres. The poem is successively an epithalamion *manqué* (as Yeats hopes to find a fit welcome for his bride), a symposium *manqué* (as Yeats names the guests, all dead, he wishes he could introduce to his bride), an elegy for those vanished friends, an elegy for Gregory (the most recently dead), and an apology for silence, as Yeats finds himself robbed of any heart for speech. These Chinese boxes of intention make this poem a modernist aesthetic inquiry into genre-production and into decorum, as Yeats undoes, in the course of his reflection, all the successive genres he proposes to employ. Both elegies are experiments, in the end, in varieties of decorum; but Yeats cannot write an elegy for Gregory that might combine the European classical allegory with modernist mimetic speech: his strategy here is to keep his inheritances separate.

In *The Wild Swans*, Yeats is still visible wanting to be an Irish poet as well as a European or English one. However, among the purely Irish poems only one — 'The Fisherman' — is fully achieved, probably because it, and it alone, faces squarely the stylistic problem posed by the absence of an audience for poetry in Ireland. Realizing that the only Ireland for which a poet can ever write will always be an imaginary one (Yeats was no Utopian), Yeats sharply opposes in this poem two styles — a satiric one for Irish actuality, a Platonic one for the Ireland of the mind. The two coexist in a cacophony, two irreconcilable musics that the poem cannot resolve into one. This juxtaposition of two mutually incompatible styles fits the two contrasting adjectives Yeats borrowed from his father to govern his aesthetic at this moment — 'cold' for ethical judgment, and 'passionate' for ethical yearning: 'I cried', says Yeats, writing of his imagined fisherman,

> Before I am old
> I shall have written him one
> Poem maybe as cold
> And passionate as the dawn.   (*CP*, p. 146)

From this moment on Yeats realizes that a poem can, through cacophony, hold in a single thought reality and justice. It can also hold, through style, several competing realities; and it is this realization which enables Yeats finally to become a European poet.

We have seen, in this volume, Yeats as English poet, as classical poet, and as Irish poet. (We can also see him here as the writer of an Italian canzone in 'Broken Dreams'; as an Arabist in 'Solomon to Sheba'; and as a Dantesque system-builder in 'The Phases of the Moon' and 'Ego Dominus Tuus'.) But there are several poems in this volume that wish to speak in a fully 'European' or even 'world-cultural' voice, and I want to consider this aesthetic choice on Yeats's part against the alternatives — to be an English poet, to be an Irish poet — that were among his options. In his poems (good or bad) as a European poet or world poet, Yeats tends toward historical and geographical allusiveness, sometimes casually — as in the elegy on Mabel Beardsley where he refers in one breath to Grania and Diarmuid, 'some old cardinal', Achilles and Tamerlane — but more often systematically, as in the last 'world-cultural' poem of this collection, the poem that closes the volume as confidently as 'The Wild Swans at Coole' had opened it.

This is 'The Double Vision of Michael Robartes', and we might recall, as we come to it, some of Yeats's unpublished notes of 1919 quoted by Richard Ellmann.[5] In these notes, Michael Robartes speaks, saying that he has lived 'among men who could not understand their own philosophy reshaped to the needs of my European mind'. That 'European mind' was Yeats's own, reshaping what he believed to be the inner thought of Ireland into a European vocabulary, but encountering difficulties of assimilation. 'The Double Vision of Michael Robartes' is, stylistically speaking, a seriously divided poem. In the first part, Michael Robartes has a vision which espouses determinism, in the second a vision espousing free will, and in the third he gives thanks for the second vision, in which he has seen the European Sphinx and the Asiatic Buddha, with a dancer dancing between them. The scene of both visions, deterministic and free, is the rock of Cashel, as though Yeats were declaring that in becoming a world-poet he did not intend to forsake his Irish origins. The poem attests to his difficulties in finding appropriate styles for the two visions and the subsequent thanksgiving. The first vision is inscribed in one style; the second vision and thanksgiving are in a second style.[6] There is no third style representing a fusion of the two visions in rhyme and personnel, and this absence suggests that a more accurate title for the poem might be 'The Two Visions of Michael Robartes', rather than the assimilative title as we now have it. The 'European mind' has not yet found a single 'European' style.

In the volume *The Wild Swans at Coole* Yeats plays with Irish, English and European genres, using Irish, English, European and Asian symbols, intermixes mythological with contemporary events, heaps up linguistically incompatible lists of names, and takes an intellectual position superior to all the historical cultures which he plunders and remakes at will. But we can see, in the extreme stylistic and philosophical dualism of 'The Double Vision of Michael Robartes', on the one hand, the smooth historical assimilations (possible only in Paradise) of 'Upon a Dying Lady', on the other, Yeats's inability to find as yet a style fully compatible with his thematic heterogeneity. It is at this time easier for him to sequester his styles in separate poems, as in the two elegies for Robert Gregory, or at least to keep them separate within the one poem, as in 'The Fisherman' or 'The Double Vision of Michael Robartes'. He has, it is true, reproved the insularity of both English and Irish verse by incorporating foreign material, and has been enabled by that material to make a gesture against both the homogeneity of English literature and the nationalism of the Irish literary tradition. But he has still not found a European style.

Yeats's career as a 'European' poet after 1919 could occupy us for a long time. It contains strange political moves, like his 1926 proposal for an Irish body modelled after the French Academy (*L*, p. 716) or like his proposal in the introduction to 'The Resurrection' that modern man should choose between Lenin, Pope Pius X, and himself. (*E*, p. 394-395) 'Today', he said in the introduction to *The Words upon the Window-Pane*, 'imagination is turning full of uncertainty to something it thinks European, and whether that something will be "arty" and provincial, or a form of life, is as yet undiscoverable'. (*E*, p. 343) What I would like to insist on is his discovery, following upon that uncertainty, of a variety of styles appropriate to a mind trying to contain in itself all of European historical and imaginative reality, classical and modern — and not trying merely to contain, but also to judge, to 'hold in a single thought reality and justice'. (*V*, p. 25) The judicial aspects of style become increasingly important in the later work, though they had been present to Yeats's mind as early as 1901, when he wrote:

Moses was little good to his people until he had killed an Egyptian; and for the most part a writer or public man of the upper classes is useless to this country till he has done something that separates him from his class. We wish to grow peaceful crops, but we must dig our furrows with the sword. (*E*, p. 83)

Becoming a European poet at a moment of extreme Irish nationalism after the Easter Rising was just that act of swordplay. I want, however, to take as my first example of the ultimate consequences of the 'European style' Yeats's single most offending act as a European poet. When, in 1935, he published the blasphemy and cacophony of the second and seventh of his 'Supernatural Songs', he offered stylistically violent versions of his hope that in repudiating a mechanical industrialism 'Europeans may find something attractive in a Christ posed against a background not of Judaism but of Druidism, not shut off in dead history, but flowing, concrete, phenomenal'. (*EI*, p. 518) In these songs, Yeats's alter ego, the pre-Patrician Celtic hermit Ribh, denounces as 'an abstract Greek absurdity' the all-male Trinity that St Patrick has come to preach. Against Patrick, Ribh declares that all genuine trinities, no matter whether we find them in natural or super-natural stories, are sexually-constituted, consisting of 'man, woman, child (a daughter or a son)'.[7] Both of these 'supernatural' songs are written in Trinitarian tercets, rhyming aaa; but these tercets, unlike the theologically correct egalitarian pentameters of Dante, are rhythmically irregular and full of Browningesque grotesquerie. Ribh declares that

> Natural and supernatural with the self-same ring are wed.
> As man, as beast, as an ephemeral fly begets, Godhead begets Godhead,
> For things below are copies, the Great Smaragdine Tablet said.

The seventh song celebrates a sexual trinity in which God is at once father, mother, and the engendered child-cub:

WHAT MAGIC DRUM?

> He holds him from desire, all but stops his breathing lest
> Primordial Motherhood forsake his limbs, the child no longer rest,
> Drinking joy as it were milk upon his breast.
>
> Through light-obliterating garden foliage what magic drum?
> Down limb and breast or down that glimmering belly move his mouth and sinewy tongue.
> What from the forest came? What beast has licked its young?

ever heard of cohabit: Plotinus and Niamh, Oisin and Peleus, the Holy Innocents and the Golden Codgers, Pythagoras and Pan, satyrs and Thetis. The ages of man organize the scene, but not successively or in an orderly way. Instead of a calm and level grove, we see a bay, a cliff, a cavern, and a grassy bank. The rude rhythms and the ruder final rhyme stand musically for that cacophonous and therefore 'intolerable' music of Pan — intolerable because in that music all homogeneous cultural gravity and suavity, whether classical, English or Irish, are sacrificed.

The poem ends with one of Yeats's last self-portraits, in which he casts a farewell glance at himself in the person of Peleus, a foolish blinded adolescent lover in the toils of a more calculating and conscious mistress. Peleus is about to beget Achilles upon Thetis:

> Slim adolescence that a nymph has stripped,
> Peleus on Thetis stares.
> Her limbs are delicate as an eyelid,
> Love has blinded him with tears;
> But Thetis' belly listens.
> Down the mountain walls
> From where Pan's cavern is
> Intolerable music falls.
> Foul goat-head, brutal arm appear,
> Belly, shoulder, bum,
> Flash fishlike; nymphs and satyrs
> Copulate in the foam.
>
> (*CP*, p. 324)

This poem is all the more European for being based on a painting by Poussin. In embracing a European mentality, Yeats foregrounded the psychic incoherence it necessarily brought into his verse — the intolerable music of allness, under the aegis of Pan rather than Orpheus, in which the cultural baggage of the years accompanies the emotional accumulation heaped at the foot of the heart's ladder.[9]

'We writers are not politicians', Yeats wrote in 1921 to AE, 'the present is not in our charge but some part of the future is. Our speech will not make it very happy, but it will be even less happy than it might be perhaps if we are silent on vital points'. (*L*, p. 667) One of those 'vital points' was the future of a poetry of nationalist sentiment or nationalist censorship of imagery. The claims for such a poetry had been made by the Young Ireland movement, and it was against such claims that Yeats had asserted himself in

1908, pointing out that songs and ballads of the Young Ireland movement were almost all 'imitations of the poetry of Burns and Macaulay and Scott', and therefore more Scottish and English than properly Irish. He continued with a definition of a truly national literature from which he never swerved:

All literature in every country is derived from models, and as often as not these are foreign models, and it is the presence of a personal element alone that can give it nationality in a fine sense, the nationality of its maker. It is only before personality has been attained that a race struggling towards self-consciousness is the better for having, as in primitive times, nothing but native models, for before this has been attained it can neither assimilate nor reject. It was precisely at this passive moment, attainment approaching but not yet come, that the Irish heart and mind surrendered to England, or rather to what is most temporary in England; and Irish patriotism, content that the names and opinions should be Irish, was deceived and satisfied. It is always necessary to affirm and to reaffirm that nationality is in the things that escape analysis. We discover it, as we do the quality of saltness or sweetness, by the taste, and literature is a cultivation of taste. (*E*, pp. 233-234)

It is perhaps not accidental that Yeats sketched his last bravura self-portrait as a European poet in Monaco, a small observation post from which to watch the great European nations:

Here in Monte Carlo, where I am writing, somebody talked of a man with a monkey and some sort of stringed instrument, and it has pleased me to imagine him a great politician. I will make him sing.

The politician — who could be, as the song says, English or Irish or European — sings of his conversion away from action to song. He represents, of course, Yeats's abandon of the late fantasy of actual politcal power in favour of 'sweet music'. Here, cacophony is predicated not only of the sound of music ('an old foul tune') but also of the appearance of the singer, with his monkey and his lute:

> With boys and girls about him,
> With any sort of clothes,
> With a hat out of fashion,
> With old patched shoes,
> With a ragged bandit cloak,
> With an eye like a hawk,
> With a stiff straight back,
> With a strutting turkey walk,
> With a bag full of pennies,

> With a monkey on a chain,
> With a great cock's feather,
> With an old foul tune.
> *Tall dames go walking in grass-green Avalon.*

(*E*, p. 452-453)

Behind this inventory we hear earlier Yeatsian phrases: 'a coat/ Covered with embroideries', 'the yellow-eyed hawk of the mind', 'that straight back and arrogant head', 'Malachi Stilt-Jack am I', 'Brown Penny', 'a great peacock/With the pride of his eye' (*CP*, pp. 125, 147, 300, 331, 96, 119). This is the cacophony of echo, the old-age music of self-parody.

In embracing a poetics of cacophony, Yeats was perhaps only following the immemorial path by which poets discover, after their first youth, that beyond the beautiful there lies the interesting, that within the beautiful there must occur the ugly. But his way of following that path was to decide that he would become a poet of a world wider than the English and Irish settings to which he had been born. The oddity and even stridency of his attempts to write as a European are evidence of the difficulty of that aim, now as then. Nothing that Yeats said or did in politics could equal, as a revolutionary gesture, the attempt to write poetry as a citizen of the world. In his reformulation of poetry for his era, he brought Irish verse (as Joyce brought Irish prose) out of insularity and into European culture, out of self-indulgence and a fearful nationalism into high intelligence and linguistic manumission.

YEATS'S FRANCE REVISITED

PATRICK RAFROIDI

Surely one of the most hilarious stories of the Celtic Revival is that of the composition of Yeats's and Moore's *Diarmuid and Grania* as related by George Moore in *Hail and Farewell*.

'I'll try to write within the limits of the vocabulary you impose upon me', Moore had told Yeats, 'although the burden is heavier than that of a foreign language . . . I'd sooner write the play in French.' A very imprudent thing to say:
That night I was awakened by a loud knocking at my door, causing one to start up in bed.
'What is it? Who is it? Yeats!'
'I'm sorry to disturb you, but an idea has just occurred to me.'
And sitting on the edge of my bed he explained that the casual suggestion that I preferred to write the play in French rather than in his vocabulary was a better idea than he had thought at the time.
'How is that, Yeats?' I asked, rubbing my eyes.
'Well, you see, through the Irish language we can get a peasant Grania.'
'But Grania is a King's daughter. I don't know what you mean, Yeats, and my French—'
'Lady Gregory will translate your text into English. Taidgh O'Donoghue will translate the English text into Irish, and Lady Gregory will translate the Irish text back into English.'
'And then you'll put style upon it? And it was for that you awoke me?'[1]

To prove that he did start writing the play 'if not in French', as he modestly puts it, 'in a language comprehensible to a Frenchman', Moore then quotes five pages of his homework,[2] which must be a genuine part of the first version since as far as I can see, they do not translate any passage kept in the final text.[3] Reading such quite felicitous phrases as these for instance:

GRANIA: J'ai entendu un bruit. Quelqu'un passe dans la nuit des rochers . . . Le jour est pour la bataille et pour les perils, pour la poursuite et pour la fuite; mais la nuit est le silence pour les amants qui n'ont plus rien qu'eux mêmes.

I wondered whether — without waiting for Yeats to do so — Moore had not already put 'style' upon the discourse — Yeats's style, of course, of which this would be a pastiche. In which case, if Moore had not given up the scheme, Yeats would deserve an indirect mention alongside those Irish writers who, like Wilde in the case of *Salomé*, or like Beckett, have contributed to two different literary traditions. An amusing thought.

Funnier still is the fact that when *Diarmuid and Grania* (written only in English), had been performed (the first night was on 21 October, 1901 at the Gaiety Theatre and the music by no less a composer than Elgar), Yeats, as well as Moore — the accusation was, of course, less unexpected in the case of the novelist responsible for *Esther Waters* and *The Mummer's Wife* — should have been abused for their French brand of immoral *naturalisme*.[4]

Now naturalism, *à la Française*, is not exactly the most striking trait of Yeats's aesthetic creed or practice. Nor are nature and reality what he seems to have sought either in our country or in our culture.

Yeats, for an Irishman of his time, was an exceptionally frequent visitor to Paris from 1894 onwards, with first hand knowledge of several quarters and hotels — the Hôtel Corneille, near the Luxembourg, where he met Synge, for instance — but nowhere in his works, not even in *The Adoration of the Magi*, does the feeling of the French capital appear as it does — to return to him — from the very start of George Moore's *Confessions of a Young Man*.

We all know the great, grey and melancholy Gare du Nord at half past six in the morning; and the miserable carriages, and the tall, haggard city. Pale, sloppy, yellow houses; an oppressive absence of colour; a peculiar bleakness in the streets. The ménagère hurries down the asphalt to market; a dreadful garçon de café, with a napkin tied round his throat, moves about some chairs, so decrepit and so solitary that it seems impossible to imagine a human being sitting there. Where are the Boulevards? Where are the Champs Elysées? I asked myself; and feeling bound to apologise for the appearance of the city, I explained to my valet that we were passing through some by-streets and returned to the study of a French vocabulary.[5]

In his unpublished novel, *The Speckled Bird*, Yeats does not even remember the place names, and, when he does, can shift them at will in space as well as in imagination:

He [Michael, the hero] had noticed that a certain place in his father's park was like a shady place under beech trees in the Bois de Boulogne. One day he tried to imagine himself in the Bois de Boulogne, saying to himself that the ornamental waters lay in such a direction, the —— gate in such another. Then the fancy took him to imagine that he was in the Bois de Boulogne trying to imagine himself in the place that was so like it, at home in Ireland.[6]

The only realistic sketch I can think of is a *scene d'intérieur* whose main characters are Verlaine 'in a little room at the top of a tenement house in the Rue Saint Jacques' (and this already looks more like Dublin than Paris), 'sitting in an easy chair, with his bad leg swaddled in many bandages', his middle-aged mistress who kept canary birds and chromolithographs scattered among nude drawings, and 'a singular visitor, a man, who was nicknamed Louis XI, . . . who had not shaved for a week, and kept his trousers on with a belt of string or thin rope, and wore an opera hat, which he set upon his knee, and kept shoving up and down continually while M. Verlaine talked'.[7]

Yeats had a sense of observation all right, but he was not interested in cities. Nor, outside Ireland, in landscape or seascape. And yet he must have known the French coast pretty well, given the number of visits he paid to Normandy, at Colleville sur Mer where Maud Gonne lived, or his later stays near Fréjus (1927-8), in Menton and at Cap Martin. But he does not 'see' anything. Even the visual splendour of Mont Saint Michel is but the occasion of an abstract meditation on 'the substantiation of the soul' which gave the monks 'for a thousand years the miracles of their shrine and temporal rule by land and sea'.[8] Like his master, William Blake, Yeats wants to see 'through' things and it takes Valéry's *Cimetière Matin* to make him mention midday light or sea waves.[9]

For Yeats, France was definitely a Spanish inn — where he found what he had brought, and his reading of French authors — apart from the symbolists who walked in the same direction — tells us more about his own preoccupations than about their actual achievements, and this holds true for his views on Hugo as well as on Péguy, on Balzac or on Huysmans.

Yet, like all great minds, Yeats was thoroughly inconsistent and perhaps, after all, although he attacked naturalism even where it was not to be found (in Proust, for instance[10]), he may have been, at least unconsciously, attracted by that facet of the French mind as he was by the expression of peasant reality. He, of course, had to protect John Millington Synge, but it was in defence of a version of Molière's *L'Avare* by Lady Gregory that he took the following rather un-Yeatsian stand against 'the old dislike of farce' shown by 'parvenus' who 'shudder at all that is not obviously and notoriously refined'.[11]

And it is not totally unlikely that Gallic influences may have joined forces with unrequited lust and the ancient spirit of the Gaels to shape some of his poems; Villon, for instance, whose 'Ballade des Pendus', comes to mind in 'A Man Young and Old':

> We should be hidden from their eyes,
> Being but holy shows
> And bodies broken like a thorn
> Whereon the bleak north blows . . . [12]

or whose 'An Old Woman's Lamentation' — to use the title of Synge's translation[13] — heralds the Crazy Jane series.

My last remark in the first part of this paper as well as some of my material (although the unorthodox views are my own) I have borrowed from the — unfortunately still unpublished — doctoral dissertation which Margaret Stanley wrote under my supervision and defended in 1977.[14] This study provided a survey of a thoroughly tilled field but which, of course, needs a postscript at least on Yeats's fortunes in France during the last decade.

Leaving out papers published in incestuous periodicals, we seem to get a scant harvest in as far as plays in translation are concerned, but all stage versions are not published: Pierre Leyris's *Purgatoire*, produced at the Théâtre de Poche, Montparnasse in April 1987, has not yet appeared, as far as I know. *L'Alphée* for November 1980 has Alain de Gourcuff's translation of *A Full Moon in March*,[15] *L'Herne* (1981) that of *The King's Threshold* by Yves de Bayser and of *The Cat and The Moon* by Jacqueline Genet and Elizabeth Hellegouarc'h.[16]

Both *L'Alphée* and *L'Herne* also contain French renderings of poems, by François Xavier Jaujard in the former,[17] by Jean Briat and others in the latter,[18] a task which earlier translators such as Yves Bonnefoy and René Frèchet have carried on elsewhere.

The *Cahier de l'Herne*, with its 451 pages in 4°, its articles by well-known scholars, its translations, its bibliography of French Yeatsiana, is by far the most comprehensive book to have appeared on Yeats in France in the last few years. It has been edited by Jacqueline Genet to whose devotion we are also indebted for the translation of six volumes of prose[19] — she is currently working on John P. Frayne's collection.

Unlike most books — whether good or not — from university presses, Mrs. Genet's has been a commercial success: Yeats's reputation in this country has never been more secure.

YEATS AND EUROPEAN CRITICISM

DENIS DONOGHUE

On 15 July 1902 John Quinn sailed from New York on his first trip to England and Ireland. By the end of August he had met Lady Gregory, Douglas Hyde, George Moore, W. B. Yeats, Edward Martyn, T. W. Rolleston, and several other writers. When he went back to New York in September, he sent Yeats a batch of Nietzsche, including his own copy of *Thus Spake Zarathustra* and copies of *The Case of Wagner* and *A Genealogy of Morals*. He may also have sent him a copy of Thomas Common's selection of Nietzsche called *Nietzsche as Critic, Philospher, Poet and Prophet* (1901); but that is not certain. In any event, by the end of the year, Yeats was deep in Nietzsche, 'that strong enchanter', as he called him in a letter to Lady Gregory from Woburn Buildings: 'Nietzsche completes Blake and has the same roots — I have not read anything with so much excitement since I got to love Morris's stories which have the same curious astringent joy.'[1] In the following months his thoughts were almost entirely Nietzschean. On 14 May 1903 he wrote to AE, sending him a copy of *Ideas of Good and Evil*:

I am no longer in much sympathy with an essay like 'The Autumn of the Body', not that I think that essay untrue. But I think I mistook for a permanent phase of the world what was only a preparation. The close of the last century was full of a strange desire to get out of form, to get to some kind of disembodied beauty, and now it seems to me the contrary impulse has come. I feel about me and in me an impulse to create form, to carry the realization of beauty as far as possible. The Greeks said that the Dionysiac enthusiasm preceded the Apollonic and that the Dionysiac was sad and desirous, but that the Apollonic was joyful and self sufficient.[2]

In a letter of the following day to Quinn, Yeats said much the same thing, but he added that

I have always felt that the soul has two movements primarily: one to transcend forms, and the other to create forms. Nietzsche, to whom you have been the first to introduce me, calls these the Dionysiac and the

38

Apollonic, respectively. I think I have to some extent got weary of that wild God Dionysus, and I am hoping that the Far-Darter will come in his place.[3]

I shall make a comment or two about Yeats's recourse to Nietzsche in 1902 and 1903, but I want to note the happy coincidence by which, in the summer of 1903 or — if Professor Jeffares's dating of the occasion is right — 1904, Lady Gregory read to Yeats from Castiglione's *Book of the Courtier*, in Hoby's translation of 1561, and sometime later made him a present of the book. Yeats was much taken by Castiglione's images of power and patronage, and by the force of personality — the *sprezzatura* or nonchalance — which Castiglione's imagery seemed to offer. I gather that Castiglione's repute is under some shadow at the moment; or at least that Northrop Frye has found it possible to refer to 'that pathetic figure Castiglione, explaining how essential grace was to the ideal courtier who would serve his prince, yet writing against a background of Machiavelli's political vision, the campaigns of Julius II, the French invasion and the sack of Rome'.[4] But this reference seems to issue from an understanding of grace as a fragile merit, a quality of bearing which men used to think of as effeminate. It seems clear that grace, as Yeats construed it from Castiglione, was entirely compatible with vigour. Indeed, Hoby translates *sprezzatura* as 'recklessness', and Opdycke gives it as 'nonchalance': in either version, the force issues from conjunctions of power and intelligence which survived, at least in Yeats's eyes, the sack of Rome. When he visited Venice, Ravenna, Urbino, Ferrara, Milan, and Florence in April 1907 with Lady Gregory and her son Robert, he found that force exemplified alike in palaces and frescoes.

Indeed, my first comment is that there is kinship and no incompatibility between Nietzsche, Castiglione, and the other major book which impressed Yeats at the same time, Plutarch's *Lives*, in Sir Thomas North's translation of 1579. They are all concerned with power and personality, the relation between will and deed, the individual and the social context in which he lives and acts.

For a second comment I have to go somewhat roundabout. I think it is generally agreed that Yeats's access to a distinctly European body of images and ideas began with his work, his partner being Edwin Ellis, on the edition of Blake; because the commentary on Blake obliged both men to make themselves reasonably erudite on neo-Platonism in its several forms. I would

favour holding this lore separate from Yeats's second mode of
access to European thought; that is, his sense of the Symbolist
movement in poetry, especially the theory of Symbolism which
he learned mainly from Arthur Symons, and the practice from
Mallarmé. It is well to keep these apart, without making the
separation complete, because they correspond to a distinction
which Paul de Man proposed some years ago between the epistemologies of symbol and emblem.

In *The Rhetoric of Romanticism* De Man argued that Yeats's early
books veer between two quite distinct affiliations. On the one
hand, the conception of imagery, in many of Yeats's early poems,
does indeed place him within the general European tradition of
symbolism, such that a reference to Baudelaire is appropriate.
This affiliation is predicated upon what De Man calls 'the
ontological supremacy of the natural object'. Language can
mediate between mind and matter because it partakes of both. In
such a poem as 'Ephemera' the natural objects alluded to — stars,
yellow leaves, 'a rabbit old and lame' — are details in a landscape
and are there chiefly for that reason. If their associations are
communal or otherwise shared, they become symbols, but they
continue to have their meaning by nature, or at least by long-
established kinship between people and the lands on which they
have lived. On the other hand, according to De Man's argument,
in such a poem as 'The White Birds', the images have given up
all pretense of being natural objects and they have become something else. Meteor, star, lily, rose, and the white birds have their
meaning not from a real or imagined landscape but from a pattern
of relationships between the images themselves. De Man calls
these images not symbols but emblems, as Yeats himself did but
not consistently. Yeats made the same distinction, without
emphasizing it as such, in the essay 'Symbolism in Painting',
where he says upon Blake's authority that emblems have their
meaning 'by a traditional and not by a natural right'.[5] They can
only come from a tradition already poetic, according to which
names are substituted for the things ostensibly named, and a
largely independent meaning adheres to the name in association
with other names. In 'The Philosophy of Shelley's Poetry' Yeats
provided a rudimentary grammar of Shelley's emblems — his
domes and caves and so forth — and assumed that they floated
into Shelley's mind from a storehouse of unconscious memory,
which is as close as Yeats was willing to go to naming the divine
logos. Such emblems arise not from a mind looking hard at an
object or a landscape but from a mind attentive to the tradition in

which it participates with other minds, and holds its meanings in common. The key to such meanings is not found by going outside them to the things in nature to which the words apparently refer; but by staying within the symbolic field of their ancestral and poetic associations. In the epistemology of the symbol, Yeats finds significance in the things to which the words refer. In the epistemology of the emblem he finds a different significance in language as the vessel of divine intellect, the Great Memory: that is the epistemology according to which 'words alone are certain good'.

The distinction between symbol and emblem corresponds to that between the European Symbolism we understand as a late development of Romanticism, and the neo-Platonism which Yeats found diversely in Henry Moore, Blake, and Swedenborg.

De Man argued that Yeats veered or vacillated in the early poems between the two epistemologies: the later poems testify, on the whole, to the defeat of emblem by image; of supernature by nature; of spiritual love by desire. I am persuaded by the distinction he makes, but not by the history he gives it, his sense of the rhetoric of Yeats's later poems. But that is another day's dispute. What I want now to suggest is that it was precisely in an effort to clear up his vacillations between the two epistemologies that Yeats resorted to the different vocabularies provided by Nietzsche, Castiglione, and Plutarch.

I have no doubt that of these the most far-reaching vocabulary was provided by Nietzsche. It was Nietzsche who showed Yeats how he might turn vacillation into an aesthetic of conflict, culminating in the heroic conjunctions of tragedy. It is still a matter of dispute whether the tragic hero of Yeats's later poems, the man who laughs in the face of death, is or is not identical with Nietzsche's Übermensch; the problem is that the übermensch of *Thus Spake Zarathustra* can hardly be regarded as a definite type or psychological figure. But I do not doubt that Yeats in 1903 found Nietzsche's projection of such a man exhilarating, and thought the political consequences might be left to trouble John Butler Yeats, as indeed they did. I would emphasize only the fact that it was clearly a relief to Yeats to find a structure of ideas which accommodated the tragic hero, the Renaissance prince, the personage. Yeats's answer to the secularization enforced by positivist science and economics was not to assert the sacredness of life as such, the form in which a divine will is expressed, but to locate images of sacredness in the individual personage, the hero; a Nietzschean alternative to the Christian saint. Instead of veering,

Yeats could act within the aesthetic of conflict, and give his allegiance to either side in the struggle. Indeed, he could even retain his two epistemologies, holding each for what it was, and administering each upon occasion. I'm thinking of 'Coole Park and Ballylee, 1931' where the first stanza seems to find sufficient meaning in moorhens, otters, Coole Park, and an underground river. But suddenly Yeats says: 'What's water but the generated soul?' The easy answer to this rhetorical question is that water is many things, and is the generated soul only according to neo-Platonism in general and Porphyry in particular. In the first lines of the stanza, water is a natural image, or a symbol if we emphasize any of its shared meanings; but Yeats insists on making it an emblem in the last line of the stanza and finding its meaning in a particular tradition and not elsewhere. I would maintain that it was Nietzsche's imperious way with conflicting principles that showed Yeats how to overcome his perhaps constitutional timidity.

I would also maintain that in moving between Nietzsche, Castiglione, and Plutarch, Yeats took possession of certain themes which could not have issued from the local conditions of an Irish poet. Local conditions could of course admit nearly any degree of meditation, but Yeats's early years in Ireland, his work to call forth an Ireland worthy of the name, did not require the elaborate engagement with the philosophy of history which we find in *A Vision* and the later poems. Did not require it, I mean, at the time. Much later, in the last years of his life, Yeats turned the implications of several philosophies of history upon a country that could hardly be expected to sustain the shock of that interrogation. But in the early years there was no merit in calling upon Hegel and Vico and Nietzsche to define a nationality not yet in being.

It is my understanding that the sense in which Yeats is a European is largely a matter of his dealing with the philosophy of history and a somehow corresponding politics. In this respect, as in nearly every other, he differs from Joyce. Joyce made himself a European upon principle; mainly upon the principle of separating himself from the project of an Irish Literary Revival and a corresponding nationalism; and incidentally in the hope of escaping from Yeats's otherwise inordinate influence. He sought out Ibsen, Aristotle, Aquinas, Homer, and Dante long before he took any interest in current European politics. I agree with William Empson's argument that Joyce was prevented from being an Irish Nationalist by his belief that in Ibsen Europe was going ahead with its own large development. But I think it would have been enough for Joyce to see Europe as the shortest way out of Yeats's shadow. Whatever Europe's large development is supposed to be, it could not have been clear — even with Ibsen's example in view — when Joyce left Ireland in 1904 'to seek misfortune'. Yeats's relation to European thought was a quite different matter: it developed from interests which remained unfulfilled even when the Abbey Theatre was founded and a certain phase in the definition of Irish nationality could be deemed to have been reached. No issue of principle was involved, at least to begin with, but it soon became clear that a critical relation to Ireland might be sharpened by recourse to European interrogations.

It is clear from both versions of *A Vision* and from other evidence that Yeats sought with notable deliberation a philosophy of history: he read the big projects, Hegel's *Philosophy of History* as well as his *Aesthetics*, Vico's *New Science*, and many smaller works, notably Pierre Duhem's *Le Systeme du Monde*, Hermann Schneider's *The History of World Civilization*, Sir William Flinders Petrie's *The Revolutions of Civilization*, Toynbee's *A Study of History*, Croce's *The Philosophy of History*, and an unnamed book by 'the most philosophical of archaeologists', as he calls him in *A Vision*, Josef Strzygowski. I presume the book was *The Origin of Christian Church Art*. I have left the list short, but these works will stand for others. From these books he arrived at a sense of history more Nietzschean than Hegelian. I can't find anything in it which corresponds to Hegel's notion of Absolute Spirit; there is nothing eschatalogical in view. But in any case I seem to find his sense of history according to two paradigms.

He seems to have held, as one paradigm, the idea of society as a civic illusion. In his Journal for 12 February 1909 he writes:

By implication the philosophy of Irish faery lore declares that all power is from the body, all intelligence from the spirit. Western civilization, religion and magic alike insist on power and therefore body and these three doctrines — efficient rule, the Incarnation, and thaumaturgy. Eastern asceticism answers to these with indifference to rule, scorn of the flesh, contemplation of the formless. Western minds who follow the Eastern way become weak and vapoury because they become unfit for the work forced upon them by Western life. Every symbol is an invocation which produces its equivalent expression in all worlds. The Incarnation involved modern science and modern efficiency and also modern lyric feeling which gives body to the most spiritual emotions. It produced a solidification of all things that grew from the individual will. It did not, however, produce the idea of the State; that comes from another evocation,

polytheistic Greece and Rome. The historical truth of the Incarnation is
indifferent, though the belief in that truth was essential to the power of
the evocation. All civilization is held together by a series of suggestions
made by an invisible hypnotist, artificially created illusions. The knowledge of the reality is always by some means or other a secret knowledge.
It is a kind of death.[6]

Yeats might have found that notion in several places, most
conveniently perhaps in certain passages of *The Birth of Tragedy*
and again in Nietzsche's essay 'On Truth and Lie in an Extra-
Moral Sense', where Nietzsche answers the question: 'What is
Truth?' by saying: 'A moving army of metaphors, metonymies, and
anthropomorphisms, in short a summa of human relationships
that are being poetically and rhetorically sublimated, transposed
and beautified until, after long and repeated use, a people con-
siders them as solid, canonical, and unavoidable. Truths are
illusions whose illusionary nature has been forgotten . . . ' But the
further implication of Yeats's entry in the Journal is that while
these civic illusions persist, nevertheless a secret knowledge of
reality is gradually enforcing itself. Presumably the particular
civilization collapses when the secret knowledge spreads sufficiently to deconstruct, as we would now say, the illusions.

   This idea of civilization stayed in Yeats's mind for many years,
but quietly, till it came to the surface under the provocation of *The
Holy Mountain*, which Shri Purohit Swami translated; it was
published with an Introduction by Yeats in 1934, at a time when
Yeats had tired of Hegel and Rousseau and found his sympathies
in harmony with the Upanishads and Indian asceticism. In this
mood he wrote the poem 'Meru':

>   Civilization is hooped together, brought
>   Under a rule, under the semblance of peace
>   By manifold illusion; but man's life is thought,
>   And he, despite his terror, cannot cease
>   Ravening through century after century,
>   Ravening, raging, and uprooting that he may come
>   Into the desolation of reality:
>   Egypt and Greece, good-bye, and good-bye, Rome!
>   Hermits upon Mount Meru or Everest,
>   Caverned in night under the drifted snow,
>   Or where the snow and winter's dreadful blast
>   Beat down upon their naked bodies, know
>   That day brings round the night, that before dawn
>   His glory and his monuments are gone.

The desolation of reality is not merely the dismantling of whatever civilization is in place; it is what the mind comes to when it insists, as it sometimes does, upon living without myth and its illusions. There is an argument, as to whether or not it is possible to come upon such a thing; if only for a reason which Wallace Stevens gave in a similar context, that the absence of imagination has itself to be imagined: nothing is merely given. There is also another argument, put forward some years ago by Frank Kermode in *The Sense of an Ending*, that we would be much wiser if we gave up our myths, the illusions which we have forgotten are illusions, and lived instead upon fictions, consciously projected as such and therefore never to be mistaken for myths. Yeats, in speaking of civilization, seems to be referring to myths and their civic illusions, and to the human desire to be rid of whatever myths are in force. He assumes that at least a few people feel the desire to come to such poverty, and that the hermit on Mount Meru is a man who is not content merely to replace one myth by another.

There is more to be said about the 'Supernatural Songs' of which 'Meru' is the last. Pareto somewhere remarked that history is a cemetery of aristocracies, and the remark has bearing upon these poems. But it is worth noting that Yeats's sympathy with Indian mysticism, in his last five or six years, was genuine but provisional: it could only be notional, given his prior and far more fundamental commitment to every value we think of as confirmed by Nietzsche and Duke Ercole. Indeed, Yeats's Introduction to *The Holy Mountain* includes a paragraph which amounts to a reservation if not a dissent, and the spur in that paragraph is, I think, Nietzsche:

Indifferent to history, India delighted in vast periods, which solemnised the mind, seeming to unite it to the ageless heavens. The Indian would have understood the dialectic of Balzac, but not that of Hegel — what could he have made of Hegel's optimism? — but never cared to discover in those great periods a conflict of civilisations and of nations. Even the Great Year of Proclus, though that is cold and abstract compared with the conception that has begun to flit before modern minds, was impossible to the Indian's imagination. Preoccupied with the seeds of action, discoverable by those who have rejected all that is not themselves, he left to Europe the study and creation of civilisation.[7]

I deduce from this and from certain parts of *A Vision* that in another mood Yeats wanted to understand history in shorter spans of time and subject to patterns which might be recurrent but should not seem timeless:

The historian thinks of Greece as an advance on Persia, of Rome as in
something or other an advance on Greece, and thinks it impossible that
any man could prefer the hunter's age to the agricultural. I, upon the
other hand, must think all civilisations equal at their best; every phase
returns, therefore in some sense every civilisation.[8]

The poem that speaks to this mood is 'The Statues', the only
poem, incidentally, in which the word 'Europe' appears. The
poem has been well read and fully glossed, so I shall take it mostly
for granted, and comment only on those three lines which seem
to refer back to 'Meru':

> Empty eyeballs knew
> That knowledge increases unreality, that
> Mirror on mirror mirrored is all the show.

Such insight is available to one who climbs the holy mountain,
climbing Mount Meru or Everest. It is not immediately clear
what it is doing in this very Western poem. Yeats's point seems
to be that the best thing about Christianity is that it remembers
the civilization it supplanted, and therefore keeps a place for
antithetical emotions, what Yeats in *The Trembling of the Veil*,
recalling William Morris, calls 'the resolute European image
that yet half remembers Buddha's motionless meditation'[9]. It is
quite different from Hamlet's modern speculativeness and
curiosity. Indeed, Yeats — much influenced by Pater's essay on
Shakespeare's kings, attributed it to Shakespeare, on the strength
mainly of his having written *Richard II*: 'He meditated as Solomon,
not as Bentham meditated, upon blind ambitions, untoward
accidents, and capricious passions, and the world was almost
empty in his eyes as it must be in the eyes of God.'[10] As for
Christianity in its official character: Yeats seems to have thought
of it much as Swinburne did, who said that the world had grown
gray with the breath of Christ. But on the other hand Yeats's
Fifteenth Phase, we find, is guarded by Christ and Buddha. Frye
has a nice comment, that

Christ descended into the bottom of the cyclical world — made himself
of no account, as Paul says — and then rose out of it, with a great company
following. Buddha meditated on that deliverance of man from his own
Narcissus image, 'mirror on mirror mirrored', the genuine Hercules in
heaven liberated from his shadow in Hades.[11]

In any case, what Yeats wanted, and summoned in the last stanza of 'The Statues', is another antithetical, neo-Greek profane perfection of mankind, his percursors in this demand being Nietzsche and Pater. I am describing an elaborate circuit, on Yeats's part, by which, starting from the local conditions at hand in Ireland, he extended his art — discursively to begin with, but soon enough in poems — to include considerations distinctively European. His procedure depended upon two axioms, both indeed tendentious. The first is that history is the deeds of great men. Like Pound in the *Cantos*, Yeats thought the historical narrative 'a schoolbook for princes'. In this respect, he is bound to offer scandal to those readers who insist that a true history would be a narrative of the defeated; just as a true account of modern history would be a description of mass society and how it came about. The second axiom is no less tendentious. Yeats assumes that political considerations must be judged by aesthetic criteria. In this, Nietzsche was his most peremptory master, except that as Nietzsche derived the birth of tragedy from the spirit of music, Yeats found his civic criteria in the history of art and, more particularly, of sculpture. In both Nietzsche and Yeats we find the aesthetic valorization of politics.

Many years ago, Donald Davie maintained that three analogies should be invoked in relation to modern poetry: sculpture for Pound, music for Eliot, and theatre for Yeats. I have no quarrel with that argument, but I would point to the significance, for Yeats's last poems, of an evident move from theatre to sculpture as his analogy for the relation between mind and nature, or between power and form.

Indeed, it might be argued that the move to sculpture was on the whole unfortunate, if only because it caused Yeats to forget some of the best insights he had already gained from the analogy of ancient theatres. Northrop Frye has a paragraph which might be quoted in this rather difficult context:

Once a poet finds his art, and it becomes the outward form of his creative life, it loses all real connection with his natural life. Art is not auto-therapy: Morris did not cure his tactlessness by writing romances about people with plenty of tact. The poet, by presenting us with a vision of nobility and heroism, detaches that vision from our ordinary lives. He thus works in a direction exactly opposite to that of the political leader who insists on trying to attach it, and so perverts its nature, as fascism perverted the Nietzschean gospel of heroic virtue into the most monstrous negation of it that the world has ever seen.[12]

I would only add that Yeats was more secure in the distinction
between the natural man and his daimon so long as he had the
metaphors of theatre, drama, and the mask to make the distinction
evident. Sculpture made other intuitions possible, and certain
imperious poems, but did not protect the poet from thinking that
man and poet are one and the same.

VILLIERS DE L'ISLE-ADAM AND YEATS

JACQUELINE GENET

A certain prudence is necessary in the study of the influence of French literature on Yeats's work. In 1915, the poet wrote to Ernest Boyd: 'Of the French symbolists I have never had any detailed or accurate knowledge.'[1] He was indeed far from possessing our language: in his youth, he had assiduously followed the French classes organized by young socialists in an old stable belonging to W. Morris, until his sisters attended them; then he gave up, refusing to be considered as a model student by his family. Anne Yeats gave a confirmation in an interview granted to Marilyn Gaddis Rose in 1964 in which she said that his French was, in her opinion, quite negligible; and, asked about Mallarmé's influence, she answered that it occurred only through translations, adding however that her father read French but not without difficulty.

As regards the translated texts, Yeats recognizes his debt towards Symons who adapted several works of Mallarmé, Verlaine, etc. into English. In *The Symbolist Movement in Literature*, Arthur Symons presented the Symbolists from over the Channel. His study includes articles on Nerval, Rimbaud, Verlaine, Laforgue, Mallarmé, Huysmans, Maeterlinck and Villiers de l'Isle-Adam. *The Symbolist Movement in Literature* was dedicated to Yeats: 'both as an expression of a deep personal friendship and because you, more than anyone else, will sympathise with what I say in it, being yourself the chief representative of that movement in our country'[2] and he adds: 'France is the country of movements, and it is naturally in France that I have studied the development of a principle which is spreading throughout other countries, perhaps not less effectually, if with less definite outlines. Your own Irish literary movement is one of its expressions.'[3] He continues, reminding the reader that he has often discussed these problems with Yeats and, that, so doing, they elaborated together 'a philosophy of art'.[4] Of his debt towards Symons, Yeats was perfectly aware: 'my thoughts gained in richness and in clearness from his sympathy',[5] he declares. Among the French Symbolists, the most obvious influence is undoubtedly that of Villiers to whom Symons devoted several studies. Besides the chapter in *The Symbolist Movement in Literature*, he had written an article in *The Woman's World* of October 24th 1889 and another in *The Illustrated London News* of January 1891.

But before being initiated by Symons, Yeats knew Villiers' play *Axël*: 'I had read *Axël* to myself, or was still reading it, so slowly, and with so much difficulty, that certain passages had an exaggerated importance, while all remained so obscure that I could without much effort imagine that here at last was the Sacred Book I longed for.'[6] In Paris, he had attended a performance of the play; in 1894 the first night marked, in Antoine's opinion, a date in the history of contemporary theatre; its effect was 'to widen the circle of the possible at the theatre'.[7] The poet was deeply moved; thirty years later, he wrote that these symbols became part of himself and for years dominated his imagination and he concluded that he was still dominated.[8] As early as April 1894, he wrote an enthusiastic account in the *Bookman*. Villiers' work was the most important influence among the French Symbolists, even if the two men never met, since Villiers had just died when Yeats arrived in Paris. 'Villiers de l'Isle-Adam, the haughtiest of men, had but lately died. I had read his *Axël* slowly and laboriously as one reads a sacred book — my French was very bad — and had applauded it upon the stage.'[9] Therefore he succeeded in knowing him through his creations and the memories of Verlaine and Mallarmé. In his *Memoirs*, he conjures up his first visit to Verlaine: he eagerly questions him about his poetry, a little about Hugo's and much about Villiers'. Through Verlaine, Yeats learnt of the close friendship which united Villiers and Mallarmé, and it was to listen to the latter speaking of *Axël*'s author that he became bold enough to take part in the 'Tuesdays'.

Affinities existed between the characters and thoughts of the two men. Villiers was Breton, belonging to a family of sailors and priests like Yeats's. He spent a dreamy youth on the beaches and the wild moors; the young Yeats, for his part, took walks on the shores near Sligo and listed to the fishermen's tales. Both, in their early youth, frequented the artistic literary milieus and the esoteric circles. Villiers appears to John Charpentier as 'the very expression of the renaissance of the Celtic soul'[10] and Yeats will be one of the chief promoters of the Irish Literary Renaissance. Both were idealists and symbolist writers. Villiers' influence exercised itself at once on Yeats's prose — *Rosa Alchemica, The Tables of the Law* and *The Adoration of the Magi* — and on his theatre — *The Shadowy Waters*.

Villiers started writing *Axël* towards 1869. At his death, twenty years later, he had not yet put the finishing touch to his text, though the first part was published as early as 1872 and a complete version had been published in 1885-1886. Untiringly taken up and revised, *Axël* represented for Villiers the epitome of this thought. The play is really his will, as Stéphane Mallarmé said. *The Shadowy Waters* had not the same importance for Yeats but was also widely revised. As early as 1894, the poet was working on it and it seems that a version was completed in November of the same year. In 1896 a text was ready for the printer but he corrected it and nothing appeared before 1900. It was a poem in a dramatic form which was performed by the Irish National Theatre Society on 4 January 1904. Then the play was completely rewritten and a new version published in 1906. Still dissatisfied, Yeats revised it for the performance at the Abbey Theatre on 8 December 1906, and this version for the stage was published in 1907. It was towards the same time — 1897 — that *The Secret Rose* appeared and the same year a small volume containing *The Tables of the Law* and *The Adoration of the Magi* with a note, probably by Yeats, informing the readers that these stories were originally destined to follow *Rosa Alchemica* in *The Secret Rose*. In 1925 *Early Poems and Stories* published together the three stories that only a publisher's whim had previously separated.

*   *   *

Yeats and Villiers share the same symbolist aesthetics, essentially idealistic. In his essay on Villiers in *The Symbolist Movement in Literature*, Symons writes: 'The Don Quixote of idealism, it was not only in philosophical terms that life, to him, was the dream, and the spiritual world the reality; he lived his faith, enduring what others called reality with contempt.'[11] *Axël's* character, Master Janus, declares: 'Know, once for all, that there is for thee no other universe than that conception thereof which is reflected at the bottom of thy thoughts.' One already thinks of the influence that Berkeley will have on Yeats later. This idealism implies the break with the world of realities. Since Romanticism, people have been artists by opposition to bourgeois utilitarianism. The Symbolists detest daily platitude. Villiers de l'Isle-Adam in his *Early Poems* (1859) expresses his hatred for the foul century. The responsibility for it devolves on the bourgeois whose stupidity is embodied by Tribulat Bonhomet. When he strangles swans to hear their death-songs, he represents the attitude of the bourgeois

to art. He can see only the material aspect of things; that is why
he gives a boundless importance to money which he uses to
measure every value, even spiritual ones; he hates all forms of
idealism. Many writers of this time seem to share the same hatred
of the bourgeois from *Bouvard et Pécuchet* by Flaubert, Poe's
sarcasms, Baudelaire, up to Yeats's fury against Paudeen.

The real world in which the characters of *Axël* and *The Shadowy
Waters* are plunged is that of corruption. Robbery is the rule: the
Commander would like to kill Axël to take hold of his fortune. And
in Yeats, the Second Sailor declares: 'There is nobody is natural but
a robber'[12] and again: 'I not to get the chance of doing a robbery
that would enable me to live quiet and honest to the end of my
lifetime.'[13] So all of them plot to murder the hero. Commander
and sailors belong to the same world: 'Let us creep up to him and
kill him in his sleep',[14] the latter propose. The theme of treachery
contrasts with that of friendship. To robbery and the desire for
murder, one should add covetousness. In both plays a fabulous
treasure is discovered: the stage directions in *Axël* run as follows:

And here comes forth first a sparkling shower of precious stones, a
humming rain of diamonds and the moment after, a cascade of gems of
all colours, wet with lights, a myriad of brilliants with facets like flashes
of lightning, heavy necklaces of diamonds besides, numberless, fiery
jewels, pearls (IV.1.4).[15]

'We have lit upon a treasure that's so great/Imagination cannot
reckon it'[16] says Aibric in *The Shadowy Waters*. These riches stir the
concupiscence of the sailors on one hand, of the Commander on
the other though he has not seen them himself.

Obsession with gold but also desire for women: the Commander, with a cynic immorality urges Axël to debauchery. When
killing him, the hero exercises the function that Villiers attributed
to himself, that of a soldier of faith fighting to the death the
enemies of the spirit: 'What is the use of knocking about and
fighting as we do' says Forgael's First Sailor, 'unless we get the
chance to drink more wine and kiss more women than lasting
peaceable men through their long lifetime?'[17] Corrupted humanity
expresses itself in a language contrasting with the heroes' lyricism,
whether it is Villiers' prose or Yeats's verse. The slightly loose
speech disappears when the opposites are reconciled and the
heroes have found ideal unity.

When Villiers' hatred becomes aristocratic disdain, again one
thinks of Yeats. 'The basis of the character of Villiers was pride',
Symons writes.[18] In the same way as the French writer protests

against the realistic spirit of his time, Yeats criticized vulgarity and English materialism.[19] Is not dandyism, which he has sometimes cultivated, also a form of this refusal of a positivist world? Both feel the same mistrust towards science. Their revolt against materialistic science has no other equal than their curiosity for the invisible.

* * *

Genuine life therefore situates itself beyond ours. One must get beyond the world of illusory appearances to reach Unity, Love, Beauty, the Absolute. These 'beggars for azure', to quote Mallarmé, go 'Biting on the golden lemon of the bitter ideal'[20] and 'The Bellman' pulls 'The cable to ring the ideal'.[21] This thirst for the absolute is shared by the characters of Villiers and of Yeats. Rémy de Gourmont calls Villiers 'the exorcist of the real and the usher of the ideal'.[22] So one turns from life: 'I flee and I cling to all the casement windows/From which we turn our shoulders to life.'[23] Herodias, in love with purity, refuses herself to life.[24] To Cazalis, Mallarmé advises: 'O my Henry, slake your thirst for the ideal. Happiness down here is ignoble . . . one must have very callous hands to pick it up.'[25]

One finds in Yeats's three prose-stories the same anguish, pessimism concerning life, the same often tragic oddness, the same visionary power as in Villiers. Owen Aherne, Michael Robartes and Yeats himself of whom the fictitious characters are the avatars, conjure up, with their solitary towers or mystic chambers, the character of Axël. Like him, they consider the life of action as inferior to the solitary life. No wonder if, as an introductory epigraph to the volume of *The Secret Rose* stories, there is a sentence by Villiers de l'Isle-Adam. The quotation is part of a reply by Axël to Sara who invites him to live, love and enjoy the riches of the world.

Live? No . . . we have destroyed, in our strange hearts, the love of life — and it is in Reality indeed that ourselves have become our souls. To consent, after this, to live would be but a sacrilege against ourselves. Live? our servants will do that for us.[26]

Later Axël says to Sara: 'I am persuaded that you already do not care any longer, in your conscience, about this miserable lure, which is called "living".'[27] This divorce between life and art is that of Yeats's first works.

The consequence is the liberation of dream. Villiers and Yeats oppose Reason to Imagination which alone accedes to the infinite.

More widely, the symbolist movement is characterized by a reaction against the rationalism and materialism of the Naturalists. Yeats writes in 1897:

The reaction against the rationalism of the eighteenth century has mingled with a reaction against the materialism of the nineteenth century, and the symbolical movement, which has come to perfection in Germany in Wagner, in England in the Pre-Raphaelites, and in France in Villiers de l'Isle-Adam and Mallarmé and Maeterlinck, and has stirred the imagination of Ibsen and D'Annunzio, is certainly the only movement that is saying new things.[28]

One escapes towards flickering, almost unreal landscapes which are presented to us by impressionistic notations in Verlaine's manner. This misty scenery is that of the Celtic Twilight. 'All art is dream', Yeats writes in *Essays and Introductions*.[29] Does Christianity offer the desired shelter? Sara does not only refuse the religious call but all Christianity, even if Villiers avoids explaining himself on the deep reasons which have motivated his decision and therefore abstains from formulating an attack against religion. It is clear however that he criticizes the intellectual and social system of the Church. The Abbess and the Archdeacon are unworthy of the functions they are invested with. Moreover Sara does not accept the ascetic ideal of Christianity, and, eager for intellectual independence, she is not satisfied with a ready-made truth.

Frustrated by religion, the dream feeds on the world of legend. Paganism, a remedy to 'the hideousness and despair of modern life' — then ascribed to Christianity,[30] is haunting many minds. As early as his *Early Poems*, Villiers thinks of faded times with nostalgia. Axël who refuses his time, lives right in the middle of the 19th century, withdrawn in the solitude of his castle, 'I daresay', the Commander says,

this manor, including its inhabitants, seems to me unlikely. I find myself paradoxical. Here one is three hundred years behind, watch in hand. I thought I lived at the dawn of the 19th century? Not so! . . . When crossing this threshold, I discovered I lived under the emperor Henry, at the time of the wars of investiture.[31]

Legend in Villiers often adorns itself with the mystery of the Celtic supernatural. His tale *The Portent* tells about a premonitory vision in a Breton monastery and conjures up Yeats's tales. In the same way, the latter turns towards the half-real, half-legendary civilization of old Ireland in *The Celtic Twilight* stories.

Then imagination seeks truth through esoterism. Occultism is 'the driving nerve and the key of the symbolist movement', Guy

Michaud writes; and again: 'It is the time when . . . [symbolism] looked for its first intuitions, a vindication and a philosophical unity that the occult traditions brought back into favour. The impact was decisive and revealing.'[32] A wave of occultism surged over the French intellectual milieus. 'I was often in France', Yeats writes, ' . . . When I went for the first or second time Mallarmé had just written: "All our age is full of the trembling of the veil of the temple" ' (an expression he chooses for the title of part of his *Autobiography*). 'One met everywhere young men of letters who talked of magic. A distinguished English man of letters asked me to call with him on Stanislas de Gaeta because he did not dare go alone to that mysterious house.'[33] 'There are few poets between 1880 and 1900 who have not yielded at least temporarily, to the temptation of exploring some of the secrets' of esoteric doctrines, according to A. W. Raitt.[34] Baudelaire and Rimbaud were delighted. Mallarmé united magic and poetry. 'I say', he asserted, 'that between the old devices and the spell that poetry will still remain, a secret parity exists.'[35] If it is risky to link his aesthetics to occult theories, one can say nevertheless that he was interested in the efforts of Victor-Émile Michelet who wanted to give a literary form to the ideas of the Cabbala and to whom he wrote: 'Occultism is the commentary of pure signs which all literature obeys, an immediate flash of the spirit.'[36] Nerval attempts, as Yeats will, a synthesis of the Cabbala, Swedenborg, as well as Egyptian, Greek beliefs and Eleusinian Mysteries.

As to Villiers, he was the friend of many occultists: Mendès, Schuré, Huysmans and later Victor-Émile Michelet and Saint-Pol-Roux. He had participated in seances of spiritism. He studied Eliphas Lévi, borrowed from him the eruditions of Janus in *Axël*, for instance. The occult elements of *Isis* (1862) in which he expresses his theory of reincarnation in particular, come, to a great extent, from *Zanoni* by Bulwer Lytton. (*Zanoni* tells the story of two Rosicrucian magi; it is focused on the theme of the guilty initiate who abandons his call through love. The similarity in theme with *Axël* is easily perceived.) In Villiers, occultism is often a means of creating a fantastic universe upsetting daily life. He was also attracted by eastern magic and Hindu and Buddhist beliefs. He encouraged Mallarmé's curiosity for occultism. Symons in these terms sums up Villiers' preoccupation: 'Whether or not he was actually a Kabbalist, questions of magic began, at an early age, to preoccupy him, and from the first wild experiment of *Isis* to the deliberate summing up of *Axël*, the "occult" world finds its way into most of his pages.'[37]

Axël describes occultism in the form of the highest spiritual yearnings and exploits a Rosicrucian theme. Master Janus is the prototype of the Rosicrucian adept. When Sara shows Axël the withered flower she keeps on her breast, the harps in the shade resound with the Rosicrucian song. Janus invites Axël to follow his example: 'Become the flower of thyself! Thou art but what thou thinkest: therefore think thyself eternal' and again: 'thou art the God that thou art able to become.'[38] This is probably the best example of escapism and that to which Yeats was the most sensitive, presented by the means of the symbols of the castle, the treasure, the lamp and the rose for which Axël offers to build 'a mystic place'. 'Spiritualize thy body: sublimate thyself', Master Janus tells Axël.[39]

Rosa Alchemica as well as *The Tables of the Law* and *The Adoration of the Magi* owe much to Villiers and his tales imbued with occultism. I think, Yeats says, that 'Villiers de l'Isle-Adam had shaped whatever in my *Rosa Alchemica* Pater had not shaped'.[40] In the first story the narrator-poet who is waiting to be initiated into the order of the Alchemical Rose discovers

a book bound in vellum, and having upon the vellum and in very delicate colours, and in gold, the Alchemical Rose with many spears thrusting against it, but in vain, as was shown by the shattered points of those nearest to the petals. The book was written upon vellum, and beautiful clear letters, interspersed with symbolical pictures and illuminations, after the manner of the Splendor Solis.[41]

The story takes place in the temple, a square building containing a great circular room. A circle inscribed in a square space, this mandala is the representation of divine powers and the psychagogic image which leads the man who looks at it, to illumination. Michael Robartes tries to persuade the poet to join the Secret Society of the Alchemical Rose. In *The Adoration of the Magi*, three old men are called by a mysterious voice to the bedside of a prostitute, the personification of the present decadent period. She gives birth to a spirit looking like a unicorn. According to M. Cazamian, this tale reminds us of

the conditions and social or moral defects which, on the banks of the Seine, have surrounded the birth of a new ideal, and, by a surprising turn, asserts the relations which link this ideal to the Celtic Renaissance under the aegis of a vague Christianity distant as well as radically orthodox.[42]

If the reading of esoteric works contributes to turning Sara from the Church, if Master Janus, the supporter of occultist teaching, is at the same time the supreme agent of all the dream, if Axël and Sara, without their knowledge, only accomplish the fate to which he has dedicated them, nevertheless the occult speeches often remain vague. The many borrowings from Eliphas Lévi are there to dazzle rather than enlighten and a precise doctrine can hardly be defined. The presentation is as succinct and confused as that of Christian religion. Moreover, Janus asks Axël the very question the Archdeacon had asked Sara: 'Do you accept Light, Hope and Life?'[43] and gets the same negative answer. Two transcendent truths are similarly refused. The second part of 'The Religious World' in *Axël* is entitled 'The Renouncing-Woman' and symmetrically the second part of 'The Occult World', the 'Renouncing-Man'. Similarly Yeats, like the Axël of Villiers, finally gives up hermetism: 'I have turned into a pathway which will lead me from them and from the Order of the Alchemical Rose. I no longer live an elaborate and haughty life, but seek to lose myself among the prayers and the sorrows of the multitude.'[44]

*   *   *

So in *Axël* and *The Shadowy Waters*, we are presented with a quest which is also an escape; and that outside all ideology. Sara and Dectora give up titles and functions: Sara refuses the convent and Dectora royalty. One takes off the veil, the other the crown. Axël resists the temptation of occultism. The place of the action, church and castle on one hand, boat on the other, is isolated and limited; it imprisons the characters, creating a closed atmosphere. Is not the vault of the chapel, even that of the castle, the inverted hull of a boat? Sara flees the convent but finds herself back in the precinct bounded by 'the massive wall'.[45] It is indeed a spiritual escape. It is suggested by the scenery which puts the stress on the distance from real life. *The Shadowy Waters* is bathed in a blurred moonlight, *Axël* in an atmosphere of unreality: everything is performed in the darkness of night. It is almost midnight when the ceremony of the taking of the veil begins; twilight falls when Axël comes back from the hunt, and darkness lasts until the lovers decide to kill themselves. Then only 'the first rays of dawn cross the stained-glass'.[46] Light comes in death.

This quest of the absolute takes place in space — the sea-journey of Forgael and Dectora — or in meditation — that of Axël guided by Master Janus. Villiers' play is the history of two souls, too large for the reality of knowledge and riches and who choose death in order to keep their dream. Then there comes a woman, in the two plays who lures the hero in the manner of the pre-Raphaelite characters: 'Under your nocturnal hair, you are like an ideal lily,

blossoming in darkness'[47] (Axël says to Sara); and Dectora asks
Forgael: 'Bend lower, that I may cover you with my hair'.[48] This
enchantress is a queen: Dectora by her rank — when prisoner,
she plays with her authority as queen, tries to urge the sailors to
mutiny, threatens to commit suicide rather than sacrifice her
pride and liberty — Sara, by her name which means princess in
Hebrew, and by her nobility: 'we are like unknown kings' (IV.1.4).[49]
As to the hero whose name — Axël or Forgael — ends with the
suffix 'El' which means God in Hebrew, he is the divine mes-
senger or the elect, besides being the typical hero, expert in the
handling of the sword: 'He's a good hand with the sword',[50] the
First Sailor of Forgael says. As to Axël, he kills the Commander in
a duel. Women do not disdain weapons either. Dectora catches
hold of the sword and Sara threatens the priest with the axe.
Strength and physical ability also allow them to knock down the
obstacles on the way of the quest. The heroes also find a helping
hand either from their faithful lieutenant in Forgael's case or from
zealous servants for Axël.

To the spiritual quest is added that of a perfect love. But love
must first overcome its contrary, hatred; an unexpected change in
the woman's attitude takes place; first Dectora hates Forgael who
is responsible for her husband's death and the situation recalls
the famous scene in *Richard III* where Gloster woos Lady Anne
whose husband he has just murdered. Dectora exclaims: 'My
husband and my king died at my feet,/And yet you talk of love'.[51]
The first reaction of Sara, caught unawares by Axël when he has
just discovered the treasure, is to shoot him. But the two plays then
become magnificent love-songs. Besides the analogy has been
pointed out between *The Shadowy Waters* and *Elen*, Villiers' drama
in which 'the two heroes . . . in an opium dream, sail towards an
ideal love, in a boat in the middle of a death-landscape'.[52]

This quest escapes time which punctuates the reality of the
world. First the authors underline the distant origins of the
process, conjuring up King Arthur in *The Shadowy Waters*, Axël's
ancestors in Villiers'. In Yeats's play in particular, time seems to
stretch on: 'It is long enough, and too long', the First Sailor says,
'Forgael has been bringing us through the waste places of the
great sea'.[53] We are almost already in that timelessness which the
main characters are seeking.

For they decide to go to the end of the journey which leads
them to death. Aibric who represents the good sense of common
humanity, warns Forgael: 'Whatever has been cried into your
ears/Has lured you on to death'.[54] Death dominates the two plays.

In *Axël*, the Commander, Axël and Sara perish; in *The Shadowy Waters*, Iollan and likewise Dectora and Forgael. As regards the main characters, they commit suicide. Fortune seems to smile on Axël and Sara; they have youth, beauty, intelligence, and that heap of gold which allows them to hope for everything. Now, both have refused asceticism. Then together they undergo the temptation of life in its most alluring manifestations. Axël is the first to react against the charm; he tries to convince the young woman that the quality of their hope does not allow them to stay on earth any longer. Sexual relations would be a degradation of the pure essence of love. The only means to shelter their love is to leave life at the precise moment when they have reached the highest point of spiritual ecstasy. This is really a philosophical suicide. According to E. Drougard: 'Axël is therefore really the counter Gospel, the Gospel of death, standing in front of the Gospel of Life'.[55] Villiers has even been careful to underline their intention, inserting his drama within the liturgical cycle: the work begins at Christmas, at midnight, and ends at Easter, at dawn. Integral pessimism or refusal of all compromise, a noble attempt to defend the rights of dreams?

Similarly Dectora and Forgael sail towards an accepted death. For the absolute love that Forgael looks for does not belong to this world: 'It may be that the dead have lit upon it,/Or those that never lived; no mortal can'.[56] Forgael knows he is taking Dectora to death. Aibric: 'Speak to him, lady, and bid him turn the ship./ He knows that he is taking you to death;/He cannot contradict me.' But what does it matter for Dectora? For her also, love alone counts: 'Have we not everything that life can give/In having one another?',[57] even if the price is death. Dectora: 'I am a woman, I die at every breath'. At the moment of choice, she deliberately renounces life: 'The world drifts away,/And I am left alone with my beloved/ . . . We are alone for ever/ . . . We will gaze upon this world no longer'.[58]

The pallor of the characters clearly shows that they are due to die or that they already belong to another world. Villiers insists on Sara's and Axël's very pale complexion. In a dream, Forgael sees: 'the pale forehead, that hair the colour of burning'.[59] And the two heroines already have their eyes turned towards the beyond: 'Why do you turn your eyes upon bare night',[60] Forgael asks Dectora; and Sara walks towards Axël's castle 'her eyes fixed on the star' which twinkles on the forests.[61]

Death is also immortality. It is the ideal aimed for by the characters. Forgael, Aibric says, looks for 'Some Ever-living woman'.

'The Ever-living' are mentioned several times.[62] At the end of the
play, Forgael says to Dectora: 'Beloved, having dragged the net
about us,/and knitted mesh to mesh, we grow immortal'.[63] As for
Axël, he persuades Sara to choose suicide together; the play ends
on Sara's vision: 'all sparkling with diamonds, bending her head
on Axël's shoulder and as lost in a mysterious delight. Now, since
the infinite alone is not a lie, let us take ourselves, forgetful of
other human words, into our shared infinite'.[64]

The theme of death and resurrection appears in the background
of the two plays by the Romantic harmony of atmospheric conditions and events. Mist wraps *The Shadowy Waters*; this is why
the waters are shadowy. Forgael himself is capable of creating
darkness: 'He has put a sudden darkness over the moon', the
First Sailor says.[65] If the landscape darkens, the characters remain
luminous: 'The scene darkens but there is a ray of light upon the
figures'.[66] It is the twilight of the Gods, death for life and the
access to the felicity of the beyond. The First Sailor hears the birds
singing: 'Happiness beyond measure, happiness where the sun
dies'.[67] Axël opens on the darkness of midnight — 'Christmas
midnight is going to ring' (1.1) — and ends after the heroes'
death, at sunrise, announcing the joy of resurrection.

*   *   *

Yeats's literary gods, Villiers de l'Isle-Adam, Baudelaire, Verlaine,
are magi like Sar Péladan, but magi who, like Yeats, possess,
beside the gift of visions, that of poetic expression. Like them,
Yeats does not separate these occult experiences from the search
for a new aestheticism. Henceforth poetry therefore is not only
a means of expression, but of discovery aiming, for Mallarmé
for instance, at giving 'the orphic explanation of the Earth',[68]
at deciphering the mystery of the world. Such is 'The Book' he
wants to create; his task is like that of the Alchemists. The poet
becomes a seer, imagination an almost divine faculty. The symbol
assumes a very important part for the universe possesses a
symbolical structure which must be deciphered. 'The real is a
suggestive symbol from which, quivering for dream, in its naked
integrity, the first or last idea, or Truth will rise'.[69] Thanks to the
symbol, the poet reaches the infinite, or according to Arthur
Symons' words, apprehends 'an unseen reality'.[70] One is very
near Yeats's conception.

The two plays are essentially symbolist. Music in both cases
opens the door to another world. The Wagnerian structure of *Axël*

has been pointed out. With the *Faust* of Goethe, the musical dramas of Wagner deeply influenced *Axël*, its themes and its whole conception in particular *Tristan and Isolde, The Ring of the Nibelung* but also *The Twilight of the Gods* in which death appears as the only possible escape. Axël by his individualism and his obstinate courage also reminds us of Siegfried. For the organization of the themes, Villiers follows the Wagnerian example; thus in *The Ring of the Nibelung*, human action depends on divine action; in the same way Axël and Sara are guided by Janus' mysterious purpose, though they are unaware of it. The writer also wanted in his play to reach the ideal of the 'total work of art' advocated by Wagner. When a stage direction conjures up harps echoing the Rosicrucian song, we understand that, after the fashion of Wagner, Villiers wanted to have recourse to a musical leitmotiv. Another leitmotiv is the coat of arms of the Maupers and Auersperg families. The Abbess describes it almost at the beginning of the play: 'Of Azure, with a winged Death's head, made of silver, standing out on a septenary of stars likewise, in fess; with the motto written on the letters of the name.'[71]

The reader's attention focuses anew on the coat of arms in 'The World of Passion' before Sara handles it to find the treasure. Therefore it establishes a link between Axël and Sara. It also has a symbolic meaning: the winged Death's head means that man can rise only through death. The field azure stands for the infinite into which the lovers are going to disappear. As to the number seven, its role is well known in mystic thinking. The Sphinxes which support the coat of arms suggest that it has its own secret. As to the two mottoes, they announce Sara's and Axël's fates.

In *The Shadowy Waters*, the sailors are afraid of the magic of the harp: 'any man that listens grows to be as mad as himself'.[72] It is the instrument of Forgael's allurement. He says to Dectora: 'They gave me that old harp of the nine spells/That is more mighty than the sun and moon,/Or than the shivering casting-net of the stars./That none might take you from me'.[73] It allows him to neutralize the sailors who want to kill him: 'He has flung a Druid spell upon the air,/And set you dreaming'.[74] In short, it is a kind of supernatural catalyst subjugating the will of others and allowing Forgael to control the situation. At the moment when Dectora wraps her hair round him — a sexual symbol used by the pre-Raphaelites — at the end of the play, it starts burning — 'the harp begins to burn as with fire'.[75] These flames without fire which already announce those of Byzantium, represent the two lovers' perfect union, sexual and spiritual. The magic ritual is stressed by the repeated use of the number nine; Forgael's harp has 'nine spells';[76] but also the treasures are those of nine nations[77] and Dectora promises to the sailor who will first strike Forgael: 'Nine swords with handles of rhinoceros horn'.[78] Throughout the revisions and performances, Yeats stressed the ritual character of the play. In 1904, he wrote to Frank Fay that *The Shadowy Waters* was 'more a ritual than a human story'.[79]

He also uses the Wagnerian leitmotiv with the recurring image of the birds. They are the incarnations of the dead, purified souls. The First Sailor is aware of it: 'The dead were floating upon the sea yet, and it seemed as if the life that went out of every one of them had turned to the shape of a man-headed bird'.[80] They fly to the West — where the Celtic Tír na nÓg is — while singing: 'Happiness beyond measure, happiness where the sun dies',[81] for they show the way which takes them from the world: 'They are sent . . . to lead men away from the world', the Second Sailor says[82] — and which goes to the place 'of shining woman that cast no shadow'.[83] When Dectora and Forgael meet, they trace endless circles round the mast, thus signalling the importance of the moment, crying premonitory phrases: 'From love and death and out of sleep and waking'[84] where come together the opposites that Forgael perceives on the two arms of the cross, there where the rose stands. Does not the circular flight of the birds trace a rose around the mast, an image of the cross? During the scene of seduction, the birds are there again: 'What are the birds at there? Why are they all a-flutter of a sudden?/What are you calling out above the mast?'.[85] They have a human voice and guide Forgael: 'We have to follow, for they are our pilots;/They're crying out. Can you not hear their cry? There is a country at the end of the world/ Where no child's born but to outlive the moon'.[86] Associated with these birds, the golden net naturally comes to enclose the lovers in the meshes of love, of fate which reconciles the contraries: '. . . neither I nor you can break a mesh/Of the great golden net that is about us'.[87] Like the birds, it is a recurring symbol of that play. One should add the boat which leads men far from the gloom of the passion of physical existence, towards a spiritual regeneration.

But the dominating symbol is undoubtedly the rose and cross combined together. They conjure up the Rosicrucians who look for a perfect spiritual realization. For the members of the brotherhood, the reformation of our knowledge and morals induces us to see God in the world and the world in God. Man participates in both.

The cloister in which Sara is imprisoned has been formerly occupied by the Rosicrucians. She has studied esoterism in Rosicrucian texts where she has surprised the secret of the treasure. Kaspar remembers that there were Rosicrucians formerly in the Auersperg family. In the course of his talk with the magus, Axël mentions the Rosicrucians. Then in 'The World of Passion', Sara comments on the double symbol constituted by the rose picked when she left the convent and the cross-shaped dagger hanging from her belt, while the harps repeat the Rosicrucian song. According to the Rosicrucian symbolism, the rose is divine light, the cross terrestrial suffering. When Sara plucks off the petals of the rose on Axël's forehead, this gesture means that, for the love of a man, she has forsaken spirituality. A few moments earlier, Axël's tears had revived the dead flower; in him the pure spirit is still alive, and when Sara has sung the joys of earth, he will convince her to renounce them in death.

Spiritual perfection, the Yeatsian rose is also aesthetic perfection, worship of imagination and beauty. For Forgael, linked to the cross, it unites contraries and symbolizes joy beyond contradictions: 'The red rose where the two shafts of the cross,/Body and soul, waking and sleep, death, life,/Whatever meaning ancient allegorists/Have settled on, are mixed into one joy'.[88]

The rose adorns the cover of *The Secret Rose*, published in 1897. It is the work of Althea Gyles, a friend of Yeats, and, like him, a member of the Golden Dawn. Her drawing, rather than a flower, shows a bush of a circular shape, so that, in its mazy intertwined branches, the symbolism of the rose and of the tree merge. It plunges its roots in a corpse, for life springs out of death and both are indissolubly united. The three roots join in a single trunk: the search for unity is at the heart of Yeats's preoccupations. One remembers, at the same time as Milton's banian to which *Rosa Alchemica* alludes, the Tree of Life and the Sephirotic Tree. Out of the network of the branches, the faces of two kissing lovers emerge, androgynous figures, symbols of long sought perfection. The androgynous state is that of the primordial Being, still undifferentiated and in alchemy represents the philosopher's stone. The lovers are quite high in the tree, near the divine, near the condition where the body is turned into soul. The three roses which crown the summit of the tree — three by analogy with the three roots — indicate that the tree should be climbed for reunification with the divine principle. These flowers which have four petals arranged like the four branches of a cross, suggest the Rosicrucian symbol of the rose at the centre of the

cross: in this association, the flower becomes the symbol of the
Grail or of the alchemical crucible. In the middle of the drawing,
another rose represents the divine principle at the heart of every
being and at the heart of the universe. It darts the rays of this light
which illuminates the initiate, regenerated man. For the rose is
the celestial dew of redemption. It is the sanctuary at the centre
of the individual and the centre of the work protected by those
tortuous ways which are so many dragons and serpents, symbols
of the enigmatic human complexity. It has been said that the tree
of Althea Gyles could be interpreted like 'a caduceus in which the
two serpents climb around the central rose-cross. The contrary
tendencies symbolized by the two serpents balance each other,
winding around the wand which is here the Rosicrucian rose.'[89]
The rose appears as the conciliator of antinomies, a centre of
equilibrium. It is at the heart of the dynamic forces and contraries
that it unites, and therefore it serves to name the unnamable. The
sky towards which the tree rises and the chthonian world where
it has its roots 'are united by these intertwined snakes, the rose-
tree branches', forming 'a circle which is completed by the lovers'
kiss',[90] a metaphor of the biting of the ouroboros, an image of
totality, as the circumference of the tree is. Thus the mystic and
magic implications of the rose are immediately suggested to the
reader.

There are also symbols common to the two plays which, at the
same time as they suggest the quest, constitute leitmotivs which
contribute to the unity of the drama: the journey for instance.
'The religious world' ends with Sara's escape. Janus wears 'the
garments of a rider always ready for long journeys'.[91] After he has
separated from his mentor, Axël decides to leave the castle. One
of the essential passages in the play is 'the invitation to travel'
sung by Sara. At last the real departure takes place, towards death.
As to *The Shadowy Waters*, the whole play is an endless journey.

*   *   *

Do these symbols possess a dramatic value? Do the two plays get
across? There exist resemblances between the two writers'
theatre, essentially lyrical and symbolic. *Axël*, Symons says, 'is
the symbolic drama, in all its uncompromising conflict with the
"modesty" of Nature and the limitations of the stage. It is the
drama of the soul'.[92] The heir to the Romantic tradition — one
thinks of Hugo and *The Burgraves* — it is at the same time one
of the first manifestations of the new dramaturgy. Villiers has

understood the enrichment that Wagnerian music and dramaturgy brought to a tradition which was declining and he renewed it with great mastery. In his *Autobiography,* Yeats writes that he owes to Mallarmé the elaborate form of the lyrical drama. *The Shadowy Waters* 'in which the singsong of the verse accompanies a symphony in blue, green and gold'.[93] But the reading of *Axël* has also left a deep mark on Yeats's mind.

In the two writers, the plot is so simple that the work resembles a dramatic poem rather than a play. This is what Villiers himself declared in 1885. Though he considered *Axël* as his master work, he did not propose it, so it seems, to any stage-manager. Must we conclude that he intended it exclusively for reading? However he asked the composer Alexandre Georges to write stage-music. Undoubtedly he did not exclude the possibility of presenting his work in a theatre on the pattern of that which had been founded in Bayreuth for the grandiose creations of Wagnerian dramas. Émile Drougard rightly says:

Villiers, whatever he may say, conceived and composed *Axël* for the theatre, in its early form . . . But later he gave up his project . . . As a consequence of this decision, he entirely yielded to his fantasy . . . However his deepest wish was to see *Axël* on the stage . . . He was waiting for an evolution of the theatre, a widening of the scenic conception, admitting contests of philosophical ideas, along with conflicts of passions.[94]

This evolution Yeats also wished for. *Axël* was to be performed at the Théâtre de la Gaîté in 1894. It was like a manifesto of Symbolism at the theatre, a date in dramatic history. We gather that Yeats was extremely impressed; he even tried to have *Axël* performed in London, but in vain. Nevertheless, there remains the length of the play, the slowness of the action. Wanting to compete with Wagner, with no other help than that of accompanying music, Villiers accepted a wager which it was difficult to keep, and it is perhaps wise to conclude with Mallarmé: '*Axël* has been conceived instinctively and without any theory. In the dramatic form, it is one of the great conflicts of mystical thought. Speaking clearly think *Axël* can only decline, if performed in the stage'.[95]

If the plot of *Axël* is long, *The Shadowy Waters* is extremely condensed to one act which limits itself to one action: the meeting of Forgael and Dectora. Nevertheless the philosophical or symbolic themes are really conveyed through dramatic conflict. Forgael speculates on his quest for a mystic experience beyond physical life, at the moment when Dectora's boat looms on the horizon. He is a hero and a man of action, as is proved by the loyalty of his lieutenant, as well as a philosopher-poet. If he represents the spirit yearning after that eternity which is access-ible beyond death, Dectora is human will looking for passion in physical life. The end of the play shows the union of these opposites, therefore a transmutation. United, Forgael and Dectora embody perfect humanity, encompassing at once the desire of man and of woman, one for the other, and the longing for a unique eternal being, a kind of platonician androgyne. In his note of 24 November 1906 in *The Arrow,* Yeats writes: 'Forgael and the woman drifted on alone following the birds, awaiting death and what comes after, or some mysterious transformation of the flesh, an embodiment of every lover's dream'.[96] Therefore the play ends in this atmosphere of tragic joy, dear to Yeats, the triumph of the characters and of art: 'The nobleness of the arts is in the mingling of contraries . . . perfection of personality [and] the perfection of its surrender.'[97]

The characters too do not at all resemble those of the traditional theatre. 'The characters', Symons writes about *Axël*, 'are at once more and less than human beings: they are the types of different ideals and they are clothed with just enough humanity to give form to what would otherwise remain disembodied spirit'.[98] In reality, the characters are in harmony with the drama, huge and hieratical; they stand before us in unforgettable poses, like figures in a dream.

Gradually in Yeats, they assume a mythical dimension. Myth is already in the bud in the very name of Dectora. According to *Cuchulain of Muirthemne* by Lady Gregory, she is indeed Conchubar's sister and Sualtim's wife, ravished on her wedding day by the god Lugh; she mysteriously comes back one year later with a son who is to become the hero of the Red Branch Cycle, Cuchulain. Yeats's Dectora is taken from King Iollan by Forgael; should we by analogy think he is endowed with divine power? Aibric starts a ritual lament for Iollan and Dectora joins the keening. Progressively the immediate past blurs into the mythic past: Forgael's image substitutes itself for Iollan's and the queen thinks she recognizes her dead husband under the features of the living king: Dectora (laughing): 'Why, it's a wonder out of reckoning/ That I should keen him from the full of the moon/To the horn, and he be hale and hearty'.[99] She has passed into the reality of dream, from heroism to myth. Forgael himself rises to a mythic level. His birth is lost in the night of time and takes place in these islands where the old Celtic divinities dance: 'Is it not true/That you were born a thousand years ago,/In islands where the children of Aengus wind/In happy dances under a windy moon'.[100] The characters of Villiers whose experience is more modern, do not reach, despite mystic elements, the mythic dimension of Yeats's.

But the intended perfection of language, the music of speech, the plastic scenery, the strange delicate magic of visions put on the stage make these two plays admirable poems where the symbolic ideal of a fusion between all the arts, music, painting, poetry is magnificently realized. Villiers, Symons writes again, 'choosing to concern himself only with exceptional characters, and with them only in the absolute, invents for them a more elaborate and a more magnificent speech than they would naturally employ, the speech of their thoughts, of their dreams'.[101] Certainly there are the gorgeously lyrical speeches but also silence: a whole act is dominated by the dumb presence of Sara whose single word 'No' is so unexpected and pregnant with meaning that it balances the torrential tirades which it is opposed to. In Yeats, the slow rhythm leading to the final ecstasy, draws the play nearer Maeterlinck's.

*   *   *

If the spectator is so much attracted by the two plays, it is perhaps also because the authors have put in them a great part of themselves: the characters are partly autobiographical. They have the pride of their creators. Axël and Sara are young, beautiful, intelligent, courageous and proud. Axël embodies the dreams of Villiers who attempts to protect himself in the middle of the hostile materialistic society of the 19th century, in the same way as his hero fiercely defends his refuge. But Sara is the feminine equivalent of Axël and Villiers has split into the two roles: the same haughty independence, the same exceptional intelligence, the same occult teaching, the same unsatisfied desires. Similarly Yeats has projected on Forgael and Dectora his desire of escapism, his attraction for occultism and above all his unrequited love for Maud Gonne.

Mainly the two writers proclaim their faith in idealism with an uncompromising eagerness which does not shrink before the ultimate sacrifice. Willing death does not appear as a negative act, the more so as it takes place in a magnificently wrought work of art which constitutes a very positive assertion of love for

Beauty. Villiers and Yeats have created in their respective works a new form of art, that of symbolical drama. It has been rightly said that *Axël* was 'the Bible of the Symbolists'. The American critic Edmund Wilson, in his study *Axël's Castle* has seen in Villiers' drama the key-book of a whole generation.

A CROWDED THEATRE: YEATS AND BALZAC

WARWICK GOULD

... there in the crowded theatre are Balzac's readers and his theme, seen with his eyes they have become philosophy without ceasing to be history.
Essays and Introductions, p. 445

The new version of 'The Vision' is finished ... I could not make Robartes a Buddhist because I required a man whose thought was not too far removed from European tradition to comment upon it ... I had to deal with natural individuality, the individuality of civilisations. My world is Balzac's world.
WBY to Frank Pearce Sturm, 8 March 1934

'The nineteenth century as we know it', said Wilde, 'is largely an invention of Balzac. Our Luciens de Rubempré, our Rastignacs, and De Marsays made their first appearance on the stage of the *Comédie Humaine*. We are merely carrying out, with footnotes and unnecessary additions, the whim or fancy or creative vision of a great novelist.'[1]
'The world is a drama where person follows person',[2] said Yeats, daring to hope that if his 'old fellow students' would 'master what is most abstract' in *A Vision*, 'the curtain may ring up on a new drama' (*AVA* p. xii).
At the heart of both remarks is *theatrum mundi*. Wilde insisted upon it in the service of the aesthetic theory that 'Literature always anticipates life',[3] but for Yeats the trope was not only an aesthetic truism, it was the essence of his occult beliefs.[4]
Between life itself, and philosophies of it, lay for Yeats the poet a distinction ultimately artificial, which might wrongly imply something causative about those abstractions, deduced from life in the first place, and something other than it. The poet had to convey, not 'abstract truth' but 'a kind of vision of reality', as he wrote to his father in 1914, 'which satisfies the whole being'.[5]
The list of books which did not falsify the world grew shorter, and more mythic: Shakespeare, the *Arabian Nights*, Morris (incorporating Homer and the Sagas), probably Dante and perhaps

Don Quixote, and Balzac 'who saved me from Jacobin and Jacobite' (*E & I* p. 447). A short list, but a 'multitudinous' one.[6]

Balzac and Shakespeare, 'concrete' men of phase 20 (with Balzac's *alter ego*, Napoleon[7]) were read for distinct reasons, if not ultimately for different ones. The one was read for his 'wisdom', the other, increasingly, for his 'tragic joy'. The *Comédie Humaine* had the power to startle 'with a wisdom deeper than intellect': it demanded 'an audience of the daring and the powerful'.[8] But Balzac was 'no complete solution' which could 'be found in religion alone' (*E & I* p. 425). And the artist could not allow himself to be too absorbed in religion, particularly in 'Asiatic vague immensities' (*VP* p. 610):

. . . whenever I have been tempted to go to Japan, China or India for my philosophy, Balzac has brought me back, reminded me of my preoccupation with national, social, personal problems, convinced me that I cannot escape from our *Comédie Humaine* (*E & I* p. 448).

Yeats was certainly not the only thinker to be captivated by Balzac's *milieu* — Marx comes to mind — but he might be the least materialist one. 'Wisdom' and inescapable *milieu* were contraries which informed the *Comédie*, which seemed to him to retain its power for a comparatively simple reason. It managed to include its audience into its substance, not by saying '*de te fabula narratur*' but by a theatrical method:

Balzac leaves us when the book is closed amid the crowd that fills the boxes and the galleries of grand opera . . . there in the crowded theatre are Balzac's readers and his theme, seen with his eyes they have become philosophy without ceasing to be history.[9]

This is the fundamental memory to which all of Yeats's accounts of reading Balzac fined down.[10] Balzac's double vision challenged, but also reassured Yeats, particularly upon a late reading. Balzac is there in the 1908-1909 journal, there in 'Per Amica Silentia Lunae', there in both versions of *A Vision*. If Michael Robartes declined the chance to write a commentary on *Louis Lambert* in 1933 (*L* p. 805), and if Yeats in his essay upon that novel ultimately passed up the chance to 'fill the gaps' in Balzac's thought, so as not to 'lose the bull-necked man, the great eater, whose work resembles his body' (*E & I* p. 443), Balzac nevertheless held up well. The drama in which he was 'absorbed' was the important thing. Will, Mask, Husk, cyclical theories of history (this last one has to search for in Balzac) — all the detail in the end seems less significant to Yeats, his own system in place, than that act of vision which had enabled Balzac to discover 'in his own mind, and in the European past, all human destiny' (*Ex* pp. 429-30, cf. *E & I* p. 444).

For Balzac, that mental act, in starving poet, arraigned swindler or great scientist, was the 'Apocalypse that reveals the past'.[11] This kind of vision, which according to Yeats, Balzac shared with Vico and Swift, (*Ex* pp. 429-30), Yeats obviously felt he shared too. For Yeats, the artistic vision of a Balzac or a Dante was of theatrical intricacy and completeness, just as it was manifold in its growth and symbolical ordering. It was sustaining, too, as a life-illusion.

Balzac does not use the word 'vision' of his own conception of his work as Yeats does — and as does Cary's Dante.[12] But there can be no doubt of the visionary intensity and suddenness with which he discovered by some act of 'pénétration rétrospective'[13] the form which his work, written and unwritten, was to take. He crossed Paris in a rush to announce his genius to his sister.[14] He saw the mind as a theatre,[15] just as he saw the world as one: it is the containment of the second trope within the first that provides Yeats with the realization that artistic acts of mind which do not separate philosophy from history are analogues of a greater perception, denied to all but the saint.

A Vision may well have been for Yeats the fulfilment of a long-held and unconscious desire to emulate Louis Lambert or Raphael Valentin by writing his own *Traite de la volonté*, but as the mature if incomplete systematization of his thought it seems preferable not to compare it with these fictional treatments of Balzac's own adolescent ambition, thwarted by the Oratorians at Vendôme, but with that unwritten *Essai sur les forces humaines* with which, in 1834, Balzac had hoped to 'top out' the edifice of the *Comédie humaine*.[16] In his last if not final plan for the whole work, that essay was replaced by a number of different pieces, a Monograph on Virtue, an Anatomy of Universities, a Pathology of Social Life and, finally, a *Dialogue philosophique et politique sur les perfections du XIXᵉ siecle*. A deep student of Balzacian bibliography,[17] Yeats even drafted his own *Vision* as a philosophical dialogue at first, (though his model seems to have been Landor).

MASK

Perhaps the earliest acquaintance with Balzac indicates why Yeats subsequently tended to misprize him, consistently in the direction of a more occult *Comédie*. The more he relied on the solidity of Balzac's world, the more this tendency deepened. Lily Yeats remembered that as early as 1874 John Butler Yeats would tell the three elder children stories as they walked, she remembered 'hearing "The Merchant of Venice" and "The peau de chagrin" in this way'.[18] Oral delivery can only have heightened the awesome effects of Balzac's 'Oriental fancy' in which, as Balzac says, 'Life is represented in a deadly struggle with Desire, the first principle of every passion'.[19] Before 1886 Yeats had read 'a couple' of Balzac novels (*Au* p. 87), and his later memory of Nettleship preferring the 'yellow-backs' to Shakespeare (*Ex* p. 269), suggests that Balzac was discussed in Bedford Park. Then there was, in Theosophical circles, the impact of the Katherine Prescott Wormeley translation of the *Comédie*, especially of the *Études philosophiques* with their introductions on Balzac's occultism by George Frederic Parsons. Yeats would have known of these by 1890.[20]

'At Stratford-upon-Avon' (1901) brings Foedora to mind, the 'coquette, who seems the image of heartlessness' (*E & I* p. 102) in *La Peau de chagrin*. Indeed she is the 'Woman without a Heart' of the second section of that novel. 'Nobody', recalled Yeats, 'had ever heard her sing.' Yet, 'in her singing, and in her chatter with her maid . . . was her true self.' Balzac, Yeats says, 'would have us understand that behind the momentary self, which acts and lives in the world, . . . is that which cannot be called before any mortal judgment seat, even though a great poet, or novelist, or philosopher be sitting upon it'.[21] The incident Yeats recalls he found 'improbable', but unforgettable. In it, Raphael Valentin conceals himself behind a curtain in Foedora's bedroom — it becomes a stage — to observe her all night.

. . . humming a few notes of *Pria che spunti*, the countess entered her room. No one had ever heard her sing; her muteness had called forth the wildest explanations. She had promised her first lover, so it was said, who had been held captive by her talent, and whose jealousy over her stretched beyond his grave, that she would never allow others to experience a happiness that he wished to be his and his alone.

I exerted every power of my soul to catch the sounds. Higher and higher rose the notes; Foedora's life seemed to dilate within her; her throat poured forth all its richest tones; something well-nigh divine entered into the melody. There was a bright purity and clearness of tone in the countess's voice, a thrilling harmony which reached the heart and stirred its pulses. Musicians are seldom unemotional; a woman who could sing like that must know how to love indeed. Her beautiful voice made one more puzzle in a woman mysterious enough before. I beheld her then, as plainly as I see you at this moment. She seemed to listen to herself, to experience a secret rapture of her own; she felt, as it were, an ecstasy like that of love.

She stood before the hearth during the execution of the principal theme of the *rondo*; and when she ceased her face changed. She looked tired; her features seemed to alter. She had laid the mask aside; her part as an actress was over. Yet the faded look that came over her beautiful face, a result either of this performance or of the evening's fatigues, had its charms, too.

'This is her real self,' I thought.[22]

The mask, to the lover, is the coquette, but to Yeats it is the 'real self', proposed to the daily self and revealed in spite of it. Raphael subsequently is puzzled. When the maid enters, Foedora yawns and scratches her head, and seems 'perfectly natural; there was nothing to indicate the secret sufferings or emotions with which I had credited her.'[23]

Yeats recalls the incident from the perspective of the lover behind the curtain. It is a performance in which love 'creates a mask' (*Mem* p. 145). In the 1909 Journal, meditating on the 'wisdom' and 'discipline' of the love of Solomon and Sheba, he develops the idea: in 'wise love each divines the high secret self of the other and, refusing to believe in the mere daily self, creates a mirror where the lover or the beloved sees an image to copy in daily life.'

The doctrine of the mask seems to spring ready made into the 1909 Journal. Its roots in Yeats's experience seems straightforward enough. He lost 'all social presence', became 'rude and, accordingly, miserable' after the 'very ordinary folly of a very ordinary person' and felt the loss of 'self-possession' inexcusable (*Mem* pp. 137-8). The incident seems sufficient to have prompted the reflections which built the doctrine of style and courtesy as the 'sensible impressions of the free mind' (*E & I* p. 253). But the aristocratic virtues of 'Poetry and Tradition', written in August 1907, are Castiglionian, and become the doctrine of the mask only under the impress of the comprehensive reading and rereading of Balzac undertaken in 1908 and 1909. The reading brought back to his mind an old preoccupation with the mask,[24] and showed how it could become the symbol of a new, and not entirely exoteric, doctrine.

The set of 1901 American reprints of the 40 volume J. M. Dent Balzac had been purchased from Bullen in 1905 (*L* p. 449, May 30, 1905), and, slowly at first, references to Balzac begin to mount in Yeats's writings.[25] 'Half-read wisdom' is recovered; surprising self-discoveries result. Between February 1908 and October 1909 the reading is heaviest. By December 27, 1908 he has read '12 or 13 & some of rest years ago'. Balzac's 'philosophy' interests Yeats 'almost more than his drama'.[26] By 21 February, 1909 he has read '30 of the 40 volumes', since 'last summer', and by October 10 he has only four or five left to read. The reading was not uncritical: Balzac's world lay 'under the curse of his own toil'; he granted 'too much to deliberate ambition' and could not give enough credit to 'dreaming and drifting'.[27] A strict diet of Balzac was recommended to potential Abbey authors[28] whose work was not good enough, while a few friends[29] came off badly from comparisons with Balzac's *dramatis personae*.

Yeats's later rereading of the *Comédie* has attracted its commentators[30] but this formative reading has not been examined. From his idiosyncratic numbering of his set, it is possible to trace the very volumes Yeats was reading even when the titles have not remained in his collection.[31] *The Thirteen*, *The Unconscious Mummers* (both frequently cited[32]), *The House of the Cat and Racket*, *A Princess's Secrets* and *La Grande Bretêche* leave their traces on his thought.

In the last named, 'Another Study of Woman' entertains an after-dinner *cénacle*. The intimate friends and enemies hear the young Prime Minister, Henri de Marsay, recall the formative experience, by which he became the 'monster' of statesmanship he knows himself to be. Readers of the more famous novels know him as the dandy and member of the Thirteen whose adventure with 'The Girl with the Golden Eyes' (his own lesbian half-sister) the 'too-prudish' editor or publisher found 'brilliant', but 'inconvenient'[33] for the Dent translations. In *A Distinguished Provincial at Paris*, de Marsay cuts a remarkable figure to Lucien fresh from the provinces and at the Opéra for the first time. There, de Marsay's 'girlish beauty' is 'counteracted by the expression of his eyes, unflinching, steady, untamed, and hard as a tiger's'. With his 'wit and charm of manner' he is 'privileged to be insolent' (*DPP* p. 27); he undertakes sartorial advice for Lucien, as well as the role of second in Lucien's duel with Michel Chrestien, but leaves Lucien's genius to fend for itself (*ibid*, pp. 353, 27).

In 'Another Study of Woman' we hear how this young man reconstructed himself:

'The statesman, my friends, exists by one single quality,' said the Minister, playing with his gold and mother-of-pearl dessert knife. 'To wit: the power of always being master of himself; of profiting more or less, under all circumstances, by every event, however fortuitous; in short, of having within himself a cold and disinterested other self, who looks on as a spectator at all the chances of life, noting our passions and our sentiments, and whispering to us in every case the judgment of a sort of moral ready-reckoner.

'That explains why a statesman is so rare a thing in France,' said old Lord Dudley.

'From a sentimental point of view, this is horrible,' the Minister went on. 'Hence, when such a phenomenon is seen in a young man — Richelieu, who, when warned overnight by a letter of Concini's peril, slept till midday, when his benefactor was to be killed at ten o'clock — or say Pitt, or Napoleon, he is a monster. I became such a monster at a very early age, thanks to a woman.'[34]

The situation de Marsay describes, of being in love with a woman some six years older than himself and of superior social station is one inhabited over and over again in the *Comédie*, and from every possible perspective, especially in the scenes of Parisian life. Raphael and Foedora, Madame de Beauséant and d'Ajuda-Pinto in *Le Père Goriot*, Rastignac and Delphine de Nucingen in the same work, Lucien de Rubempré and Madame de Bargeton, d'Arthez and La Princesse de Cadignan: — in Yeats's words, a 'beautiful high-bred woman' (*Mem* p. 158) is adored by and frequently severed from a younger man, usually of genius. 'It is only a woman's last love that can satisfy a man's first love.'[35] 'High-bred' recalls the women of 'Adam's Curse', 'Baile and Aillinn', 'The Old Age of Queen Maeve' and 'No Second Troy'. One need not emphasize the significance then of those stories in which the disillusion of a young man of genius is slowly annealed through discovery of a beloved's shortcomings. One recalls also the 'incomparable distinction' (*Mem* p. 72) of Olivia Shakespear, herself a devoted Balzacian:[36] the woman of superior status, more wordly but perhaps no less idealistic than her lover, or perhaps much less idealistic, being Balzac's repeated type. But, even in the case of Maud Gonne and her 1898 revelations, there was nothing in Yeats's life to match the education de Marsay (aged seventeen) receives at the height of his ardour for the Comtesse Charlotte, when her infidelity is revealed.

'And you were alone?' — 'Alone,' said she, looking at me with a face of innocence so perfect that it must have been his distrust of such a look as that which made the Moor kill Desdemona. As she lived alone in the

house, the word was a fearful lie. One single lie destroys the absolute
confidence which to some souls is the very foundation of happiness.

'To explain to you what passed in me at that moment it must be
assumed that we have an internal self of which the exterior *I* is but the
husk; that this self, as brilliant as light, is as fragile as a shade — well,
that beautiful self was in me thenceforth for ever shrouded in crape.
Yes; I felt a cold and fleshless hand cast over me the winding-sheet of
experience, dooming me to the eternal mourning into which the first
betrayal plunges the soul. As I cast my eyes down that she might not
observe my dizziness, this proud thought somewhat restored my
strength: "If she is deceiving you, she is unworthy of you!" . . . There is
always a precious ape in the prettiest and most angelic woman!'

At these words all the women looked down, as if hurt by this brutal
truth so brutally stated.

'I will say nothing of the night, nor of the week I spent,' de Marsay
went on. 'I discovered that I was a statesman.' (*LGB* pp. 22-3)

The statesman in private life will, according to de Marsay, soon
recover his self-possession, refuse to drown in self-pity, or to
compromise that recently discovered inner self.

'Cured of . . . my pure, absolute, divine love, I flung myself into an
adventure, of which the heroine was charming, and of a style of beauty
utterly opposed to that of my deceiving angel. I took good care not to
quarrel with this clever woman, who was so good an actress, for I doubt
whether true love can give such gracious delights as those lavished by
such a dexterous fraud. Such refined hypocrisy is as good as virtue . . . I
tried to be the same lover.' (*LGB* p. 24)

Two months later de Marsay casually asks his unfaithful mistress
'When are you to marry the Duke?' In the resulting exchange, he
allows her to find loopholes in his response so as to be able to
escape censure and to turn the blame onto him (*LGB* p. 27). De
Marsay provides for his female audience (the discomfiture of
which Balzac puts to the forefront), an imitation of every twist
and turn of her response to his refusal to blame or to become
angry. They part; she has the moral luxury of believing that she
'still had something to avenge', while de Marsay can feel satisfied
that his retreat has been 'judicious', and that as to his mind

'and heart, they were cast in a mould then and there, once for all, and the
power of control I thus acquired over the thoughtless impulses which
make us commit so many follies gained me the admirable presence of
mind you all know.' (*LGB* p. 30)

The moral cunning and wisdom derived from de Marsay's self-possession, itself derived from his theatrical conception of self, is similar to that carefully won in many of the extracts from the 1908-1909 Journal. Ignoring for the moment[37] the wit and mastery with which Balzac includes de Marsay's audience into his theme by way of instant authentication of his decisions, I turn to some of those Journal passages:

There is a relation between discipline and the theatrical sense. If we cannot imagine ourselves as different from what we are and try to assume that second self, we cannot impose a discipline upon ourselves, though we may accept one from others. Active virtue as distinguished from the passive acceptance of a current code is therefore theatrical, consciously dramatic, the wearing of a mask. It is the condition of arduous full life (*Mem* p. 151).

I choose the most famous of the meditations from the Journal, which goes on to name 'Plutarch's heroes' and modern *poseurs* such as Wilde and Whitman, and of course that Wordsworth who failed to create a second self and was rewarded, according to Yeats, with the admiration of *Spectator* journalists. The process to be observed is the complete assimilation of Balzac, the substitution of 'actual men and women' for Balzac's *dramatis personae*, the complete translation from the contemned world of French journalists to the disdained world of London ones. *A Vision's* system begins with meditations such as this one. During the time Yeats wrote this journal, he read at least 35 of the 40 volumes of the *Comédie*: Balzac's world was a complete and sudden mirror to his life.

Perhaps certain terms have their origin here too: de Marsay's 'husk' and Raphael's 'mask' are metaphors for the occult notions of exterior, divided and perfected selves explored in *Séraphita*, *Louis Lambert* and elsewhere in Yeats's reading. But just as interesting as such source hunting is the example provided elsewhere in the shorter fictions Yeats was reading at that time. In de Marsay's audience is the Princesse de Cadignan, whose own story is the final movement after a remarkable emotional career. She sets out to win the love of Daniel d'Arthez, the indulgently treated projection of Balzac himself. Sublime trickery is successful, and utter concealment becomes necessary. She sends Daniel into a lions' den, the salon of Madam d'Espard, to convince the usual crowd of wits and dandies that theirs is a brother-and-sister relation.

All the guests are of course her former lovers. Their game is to force d'Arthez to reveal by his loyalty that he loves her. He manages to defend her without displaying or revealing feeling.

He chooses to defend woman against man, by indicating that
their fascination with this particular woman comes from their
supressed outrage that she, almost alone of her sex, should
amuse herself among men as men amuse themselves with
women.

> 'We knew before today that your character is as great as your talent,' said
> Blondet. 'You bore yourself just now not like a man, but rather as a god.
> Not to be carried away by one's feelings or imagination, not to blunder
> into taking up arms in the defence of the woman one loves (as people
> expected you to do), a blunder which would have meant a triumph for
> these people, for they are consumed with jealousy of celebrated men of
> letters — ah! permit me to say that this is the supreme height of statecraft
> in private life.'[38]

It is 'as clever as it is difficult to avenge a woman without defending
her' says Nathan (*APS* p. 69). Balzac has further twists in this tale
— d'Arthez is so happy with his sublimely duplicitous Princess
that he is content to throw 'poor words away' and to live without
writing.

Of course, Lady Gregory was *not* the Princesse de Cadignan.
But Blondet's response to d'Arthez is yet another endorsement of
the refusal 'to be swept away, whatever the emotion, into confusion
and dullness' (*E & I* p. 253). In very different circumstances, it
could have been the model for Yeats's attempts *not* to do 'a passionate thing' because of pride, at the time when, while Yeats's Civil
List pension was under consideration, Gosse was so 'insolent' to
Lady Gregory and Yeats became the focus for conflicting loyalties,
not least that to himself (*Mem* p. 252 et seq; also pp. 289–91). By
this time the destruction of 'instinctive indignation' in himself
was complete, and the attempts to either recreate it or to act it
were indecisive and unsuccessful. It was an odd (and to Robert
Gregory, a dismaying) struggle between self-conception and
sincerity. Such manoeuvres had 'made their first appearance on
the stage of the *Comédie humaine*', but this time life would not
quite imitate art.

WILL

During this comprehensive reading of the *Comédie*, Yeats was
inclined to believe that Balzac had over-emphasized the will
(*Mem* p. 158). Critical attention — notably that of Carl Benson —
has been directed to those of the *Études philosophiques* which dwell
on the will. At the time of the late essay *Louis Lambert* Yeats was

again inclined to play down the materialist-occultist conception of the will that had obsessed the young Balzac and found its way into *La Peau de chagrin* and *Louis Lambert*. Yeats's interest was that of the well-informed historian of occult scientific thought, which is to say that he felt that if will could be explained by material science, then it was being explained away.

That early reading of the *Études philosophiques* as occult science needs much more study, but Balzac survived that kind of attention and Yeats's sense of him grew from it. As late as 1934 Yeats was able to claim that 'The *Peau de chagrin* and *Catherine de Médicis* contain my philosophy of History' (*E & I* p. 468; see also *Ex* pp. 429-30 & 393). Yeats at the same time gestured to 'a passage' in *La Peau de chagrin* as having 'started' him in his occult romances and his myth 'in reply to a myth' of progress (*VPl* p. 932). Balzac put the fantastic story *and* the historical romance of Catherine's times into the *Études philosophiques*, and the Hoffmannesque story is rooted in the events on both sides of July 1830. How do these stories of will and power provide a philosophy of history? Identifying the 'passage' as the revelation Raphael has in the antique shop, the hypnagogic vision of the 'melancholy ruins of cancelled cycles'[40] certainly is appropriate to a philosophy in which 'all things fall and are built again' (*VP* p. 566) even if it yet takes some ingenuity to see Vico's *corsi* and *ricorsi* in Balzac, as Yeats felt he could (*E & I* p. 468).

Catherine de Médicis, according to Yeats, is a work in which Balzac is just to the queen, who 'preserved the State personification of the family' against Calvin's 'war of ideas' (*E & I* p. 444). Hers is a 'struggle to keep self-control', she is that 'great tragic person . . . who must display an almost superhuman will' who resists the 'loss of control' (*AVB* p. 268). *La Peau de chagrin* dramatizes the consequence of a surrender of will to a talisman, which provides in consequence of that surrender a stylized destiny. The old Jew catches Raphael ripe for the conclusion of a Mephisthophelean bargain. On the point of suicide, he discovers that 'the most poetic memorials of the material world' become 'a symbolical interpretation of human wisdom' (*WAS* p. 69). The Jew provides the 'great secret of human life', as Heraclitean an axiom as Yeats could have wished:

'By two instinctive processes man exhausts the springs of life within him. Two verbs cover all the forms which these two causes of death may take — To Will and To have your Will . . . To Will consumes us, and To have our Will destroys us.' (*WAS* pp. 32-33)

For Balzac the will is always dynamic and always disruptive. Disorganization on a vast scale can be caused by the rampant will of one man, as Yeats well saw (*E & I* p. 444). Thus Raphael's acceptance is not without its contrary consequences for the old Jew who has sought the 'perpetual calm' of knowledge in order to destroy the destructive forces of will within him. Like the narrator of 'Rosa Alchemica' he had believed he had 'attained everything because I have known how to despise all things'.[41] Ineluctably his fate is caught into opposition to Raphael's as the forces which acceptance of the Talisman unleashes begin to act. He ends in the arms of a prostitute, making love while his feet are growing cold, but happy, for one 'hour of love has a whole life in it', (*WAS* p. 200) he says, recycling Scott, his 'dim eyes peering forth from behind a mask of youth' at Raphael's 'young man's eyes set in a mask of age' (*WAS* p. 198) at a performance of *Sémiramide*.

Raphael and the Jew are contraries, 'dying each other's life, living each other's death' (*AVB* p. 68). 'Measure thy desires, according to the life that is in thee. This is thy life . . .', (*WAS* p. 31) says the Talisman.[42] Self-measurement is an aspect of a central Balzacian activity, the examination of causes, to which the *Études philosophiques* are devoted. In Balzac's words, these are the 'backstage and the machinery' while the *'moeurs* are the play itself'.[43] The philosophy of causes spirals up and away from play and backstage to *principles*, or the author, and it is not just apparent in the overall stratification of the *Comédie*, but is everywhere apparent, from the most minute examination of a financial transaction to the combinations of chance and choice that drive a man in a critical moment to the gambling table. All effects are related to causes in the hidden wires or machinery of the will. It is thus that the *Comédie* is incarnate as a body of fate. Balzac demonstrates this by the 'stylistic arrangement' of the Faustian bargain and possession of the Talisman in *La Peau de chagrin*: in the whole Lucien de Rubempré cycle the divorce of creature from will is expressed in the relationship of Vautrin and Lucien.

With his 'unbounded ambition'[44] and 'poetical temperament', Lucien confesses that he is 'nothing unless a strong inexorable will is wedded to mine' (*LI* p. 329). The 'Devil' and the poet (*AHP* 1, BP pp. 62, 64) form two halves of a 'body politic' in the bargain that Vautrin drives (*AHP* 1, p. 53). The sense that he is but half of an uncompleted whole precedes Lucien's first proposal of suicide: it is a self-assessment made at the critical moment before he meets Vautrin. Unlike the reconstructed man, such as de Marsay, who can balance inner self and husk, a weak man such as Lucien must either become the mummer obedient to an exterior will or go under. It is a mark of Lucien's middling wit that he is not an *'unconscious* mummer' and this is as close as he comes to tragic awareness. Richard Ellmann[45] reads Lucien's seduction by Vautrin as the carefully coded account of a homosexual seduction. It is true that Vautrin does not like women, this we know from *Le Père Goriot*. From that work, too, we know of his predilection for dominating vulnerable young men from the provinces — a dominance Rastignac surmounts. We do not accept at face value his accounts of his 'Spanish' generosity, nor really his protest that he wants a son. Nevertheless he doesn't seek Lucien's body, but his soul: he wants Lucien to serve as puppet in the quest for power, dominance and wealth. Vautrin takes a vicarious pleasure in Lucien's triumph. Lucien's splendours are balanced by Vautrin's austerities, a complementary relation drawn more tightly by Balzac than similar antitheses which enact their contradictions elsewhere in the *Comédie*.

In short, Vautrin's seduction is to offer Lucien an irresistible conspiracy theory of human activity. After Lucien's death, Vautrin is described as a *döppelganger* (*AHP* 2 p. 139); theirs has been a 'compact, in which each is in turn master and slave' and as such unique 'in any one life' (*AHP* 1 p. 97). Vautrin's 'spiritual paternity' (*BHP* 2 p. 139) transcends all family ties, the 'indissoluble' nature of their bond (*BHP* 1 pp. 87-8) is best summed by Vautrin himself: 'I am the author, you are the play; if you fail, it is I who shall be hissed.' (*AHP* p. 90)

Lucien's powers and desires are in fatal disproportion. His fortunes, like Raphael's , appear to change when he is on the brink of suicide. He feels himself sink, like a prince from the *Arabian Nights*, into an undersea world of luxury, but Vautrin's bargain makes him the janissary to Vautrin's Sultanship, the efreet to this genie.[46] The lessons which begin in the coach back to Paris are stern:

'You do not seem to me to be strong in history. History is of two kinds — there is the official history taught in schools . . . and there is secret history which deals with the real causes of events — a scandalous chronicle. Let me tell . . . a little story which you may not have heard . . .'*LI* p. 340).

But we have heard it already, from de Marsay. It is that account of Richelieu choosing to oversleep so as not to be able to warn Concini whose fate was sealed (see above, p. 75), having judged the King implacable.

This secret, or Procopian history will, Vautrin insists, give Lucien the right 'precepts' to live by (*LI* p. 341). Society is composed of fatalists and the 'full force of an individual's will and every action of his life' can be 'brought to bear' in 'one idea' upon them (*LP* p. 343). Lucien accepts this 'poison' apparently as a '*tabula rasa*'. Principles are as nothing, systems political and moral have 'started from one point and reached another diametrically ⁓ opposed; and men have professed one kind of opinion and acted upon another' . . . 'Success is the supreme justification of all actions whatsoever. The fact in itself is nothing; the impression that it makes upon others is everything.' The effective man keeps the 'seamy side of life to himself and is a model of public probity'. Vautrin will accordingly remain backstage, Lucien will strut on 'the great theatrical scene called society'. (*LI* pp. 345-6) The 'law of laws' is secrecy (*LI* p. 348).

Yeats saw the *Comédie* as embodying 'a struggle for survival' in which each character was an 'expression of will', and I suggest that, preoccupied with causes, he too was seduced by Balzac's sense that history could be explained by conspiracies. He once 'intoned' to an uncomprehending Hugh Kingsmill that 'all Nietzsche is in Balzac'. He apparently seemed hurt when Kingsmill could only reply that Nietzsche had found Balzac a 'vulgarian obsessed with money'. For Kingsmill, Balzac 'romanticis[ed] . . . any and every form of power' but he seemed to move Yeats 'deeply' (*I & R* p. 296).

'Belief is the spring of action' (*Ex* p. 400), and belief to Yeats was a concentration of Balzacian will. Unsurprisingly the matter emerges, rampant, in *On the Boiler* :

. . . a hundred men, their creative power wrought to the highest pitch, their will trained but not broken, can do more for the welfare of a people, whether in war or peace, than a million of any lesser sort no matter how expensive their education . . . the Irish masses are vague and excitable because they have not yet been moulded and cast (*Ex* pp. 441-2).

Yeats's theory of history is a theory of action, of 'great men' (as was Louis Lambert's [*S* p. 211]), their greatness defined not as character but as individual will or passion. History is then abstracted to a personal astrological code, by means of which it could seem (in 1930)

a human drama, keeping the classical unities by the clear division of its epochs, turning one way or the other because this man hates or that man loves. (*Ex* p. 290)

It follows that historical forces are those of which the *apparent* agents are frequently but ignorant instruments, a theory, according to Yeats, developed by Balzac's Louis Lambert (*E & I* p. 442). 'Accident is destiny' (*Myth* p. 336), the *dramatis personae* are 'ignorant' that they are on stage.

> What sacred drama through her body heaved
> When world-transforming Charlemagne was conceived?
>
> (*VP* p. 560)

To study these forces is to study 'the seamy side' — Balzac's sense[47] is more pejoratively conveyed in English than in the French *L'Envers de l'Histoire Contemporaine*. But backstage history is both 'plot', and 'a plot'.

Those who read part two of *Illusions perdues* without first reading of Lucien's adventures as a distinguished provincial in Paris might have no reason to doubt Vautrin's description of Lucien as a '*tabula rasa*'. He is a singularly apt pupil, and we should not be surprised to see him at the Opera ball which opens *A Harlot's Progress* with the masked Vautrin lurking in his train, all but unrecognisable from the days at Madame Vauquer's boarding-house to the watching Rastignac, but still a terrible demi-urge (*AHP* 1 p. 21). Lucien has been schooled in the role before, and has discovered that on his own he lacks volition equal to ambition. In Paris for the first time with Madame de Bargeton, he has met the beau monde in the boxes at the Opéra, the demi-mondaines backstage. He quickly opts for the seamy side of success under the influence of Lousteau, for the world of puffery, claque-hiring, wire-pulling, a world which soon found its way into some of the bitter reflections of Yeats's *Samhain* pieces on the Dublin theatre (*Ex* p. 231; *DPP* pp. 108 *et seq.*). Too vain for any unity of being, he will say anything and therefore stick at nothing. He accepts the devil's bargain of journalism and leaves the obscure but noble world of d'Arthez's circle for the instant, dubious world of the string-pullers and reputation-makers (and breakers), the world in which the fluid expression of the will is money, that energy which animates the Parisian milieu as 'some strange unheard-of drama' (*DPP* pp. 152-4; *S* p. 226). Social mobility, an extreme rapidity of events, the crossing of social frontiers, and unprincipled, self-serving and self-perpetuating power make 'his head swim' and give a masque-like quality to much of the action. Journalism is 'a giant catapult set in motion by pigmy hatreds' (*DPP* p. 214), it acts to 'blunt his intellect and sully his soul' (*DPP* p. 189). Lucien has yet to learn its reflexive power, and when it is first proposed, the lesson is in the form of mockery:

Everything is bi-lateral in the domain of thought. Ideas are binary. Janus is the fable signifying Criticism and the symbol of Genius (*DPP* p. 252).

In a century in which politics has become 'a permanent puppet show' (*DPP* p. 256) the journalist is a 'hand to mouth' Machiavelli, his wit can only echo in parody the deeper principles of action Balzac seeks to embody:

Moralists will never succeed in making us comprehend the full extent of the influence of sentiment upon self-interest, an influence every whit as strong as the action of interest upon our sentiments; for every law of our nature works in two ways, and acts and reacts upon us (*LI* p. 248).

Or, as one of the philosophers in the *cénacle* remarks, in the Heraclitean terms the whole novel animates:

In art as in nature, there are two principles everywhere at strife . . . and victory for either means death (*DPP* p. 274).

To Yeats, insisting that consciousness is conflict (*Ex* p. 331), these and other sage saws were incarnated in the *Comédie*: Heraclitus is recalled in the same paragraph of *On the Boiler* as Balzac and Vico (*Ex* p. 430). Journalists' farce pictures d'Arthez's 'philosophico-religious symposium' at work on 'the meaning of life', worrying about paradigms of progress:

They were very hard put to it between the straight line and the curve; the triangle, warranted by scripture, seemed to them to be nonsense, when, lo! there arose among them some prophet or other who declared for the spiral (*DPP* p. 276).

Mockery holds Balzacian speculation in check in the Parisian scenes, but anyone who reads Balzac for his 'wisdom' finds demonstration of such doctrine everywhere. Vautrin is a 'vortex' in the 'river of life' (*AHP* 2 p. 138). Another extraordinary passage comes as Lucien is trapped into either destroying d'Arthez's book in a review or having his own party attack his mistress's failing skill as an actress. He writes the review, but submits it to d'Arthez first. D'Arthez is contemptuous enough to upgrade its venom, but he will not absolve Lucien more than once:

'I look upon a periodical repentance as great hypocrisy,' d'Arthez said solemnly; 'repentance becomes a sort of indemnity for wrongdoing. Repentance is virginity of soul, which we must keep for God; a man who repents twice is a horrible sycophant. I am afraid that you regard repentance as absolution.' (*DPP* p. 343)

How Yeats got from this passage to his celebrated remark to John Sparrow that the 'tragedy of sexual intercourse is the perpetual virginity of the soul' (*LDW* p. 174) is another story.[48] A more sophisticated criticism will eventually chart the hidden roads from such passages in fiction to Yeats's leading concepts and even to his table-talk. Certainly, George Harper's recent *The Making of 'A Vision'* lays enough of the process of the automatic writing before us to compel some more comprehensive examination of Yeats's reading than has yet been undertaken.[49] Classic studies of Yeats's iconographic and doctrinal sources — W. G. Holmes's *The Age of Justinian and Theodora*, for example, or his reading of various neo-Platonic texts — can take us so far. Influence theory, narrow because of its nervous disdain for traditional source study, can take us a little further. But not all symbolical or conceptual arrangement is neurotic and *A Vision*, as Harper makes clear, is constructed out of a kaleidoscopic fragmentation of *two* people's reading. I gesture here only to some of the principles governing *A Vision*'s re-aggregation.

I suggest that Yeats's reading of the scenes of the *Comédie* has been overlooked in favour of the 'sacred books' — *Louis Lambert* and *Séraphita* in particular. The scenes of all kinds, the *Études de Moeurs*, are the *theatrum mundi*, the 'body of fate' in which the forces of will and the concepts of mask and husk are brought to life. They were also the example of Balzac's own 'creative mind' at its greatest stretch. While Yeats could remain argumentative about Balzacian doctrine, he could no more quarrel with Balzac's example than with creation itself. Through him, the wisest man in the world, 'creation itself thought and wrote' (*Ex* p. 271).

CREATIVE MIND

Profound acts of mind necessitated judgment for Yeats. When Blake wrote that 'The Last Judgment is not Fable or Allegory but Vision'[50] he was writing of a picture of that subject, but Yeats could easily have reversed his sentence: Vision *was* judgment. For Blake 'Vision' was 'a Representation of what Eternally Exists.

Really & Unchangeably'. Balzac, for all his rootedness in history and *milieu*, provided enough examples that

> [the human mind] was capable, during some emotional crisis, or, as in the case of Louis Lambert by an accident of genius, of containing within itself all that is significant in human history and of relating that history to timeless reality' (*E & I* p. 440).

Lucien's death vision, and, Yeats might have added, Raphael's vision in the antique shop, were such acts. We recall that Louis Lambert's mind was 'a *camera obscura*' (*S* p. 163), which could concentrate will and thought as 'living forces' (*ibid*, p. 208). For Yeats such deep acts of mental attention were inescapably judgmental; Synge seemed to embody a 'perpetual "Last Day", a perpetual trumpeting and coming up for judgment' (*Au* p. 511). Dante had found 'Divine Justice', 'unpersuadable justice' (*VP* p. 369); *A Vision* attempted in its 'stylistic arrangements of experience' to 'hold in a single thought reality and justice' (*AVB* p. 25). Such an act of mind was 'sacramental', it was the attention Yeats felt God demanded.[51]

Artistic vision then was one aspect only of this supreme attention:

> But body gone he sleeps no more,
> And till his intellect grows sure
> That all's arranged in one clear view,
> Pursues the thoughts that I pursue,
> Then stands in judgment on his soul . . . (*VP* p. 633)

Balzac's Promethean forms of attention — with a little help from caffeine — produced that midnight wisdom, which was as close to religious vision as the artist could allow himself to come. Sanctity was inimical to the artist (*Myth* pp. 333; 337-8), but it was an excellent analogue or ambition as an ideal of attention. Balzac offered over and over again examples of vision in which aesthetic and judgmental acts were inseparable, as in the 'immense clearness of mind, and the swiftness of hand' familiar to authors in the fever of composition 'that accompanied Lucien de Rubempré's last moments, and his medieval vision of Saint-Louis's Palace in its 'pristine beauty' (*AHP* pp. 113-6).

Yeats speculated that filling in 'the gaps' in Balzac's thought would prove that as a schoolboy and while obsessed with his Theory of the Will at Vendôme Balzac had been driven 'to Swedenborg, perhaps to Bonaventura and Grosseteste' (*E & I* pp. 443; 440). All the doctrine now lay 'hidden in his blood and in his nerves' (E & I p. 446). Medieval thought had enabled him to recover some 'perfect accord between intellect and blood', a recovery inspired by an intuitive drive 'more profound . . . than mere speculation' (E & I p. 440). Here as elsewhere, Yeats is trying to prove a link between instinct and the folk mind, between modern man and an all-but-forgotten learning and mysticism. The enquirer could well fill in the gaps in Yeats's thought, but would risk being lost on 'Hodos Chameliontos'.

In the case of Balzac I suggest the matter might be just as profound, and yet vastly simpler than the recovery of the thought of Grosseteste and Bonaventura would necessitate (with all the attendant proof). Balzac's 'wisdom deeper than intellect' is achieved through the internalization and elaboration of what is indeed a mediaeval model, *theatrum mundi*, and Yeats correctly descried the mediaeval character[52] of the effects Balzac could produce from it, which in one place he compares to those of 'Dante . . . or some great mediaeval monk, preaching in Rheims' (E & I pp. 446 and see above, n. 21). The audience he proposes for Balzac, of the 'daring and the powerful', (E & I p. 446) recalls that Ernst Curtius suggests for *theatrum mundi* in the later middle ages: 'God and the heroes of virtue',[53] or, more immediately, that of 'The Grey Rock': the heroes and gods who listened when 'cups went round at close of day' in the *theatrum* of that poem which is indeed the whole terrestrial world — the play both tragedy and comedy, the action happening in the theatre as well as on the stage.

Yeats's emphasis on justice in his system prompts one to ask if the ultimate congeries of incarnations for each individual soul does not represent a comedy. That such a view of the system is compatible with the much quoted remark that we 'begin to live when we have conceived life as tragedy' (Au p. 189) is possible. Yeats's law of karma demands that each of our exits and our entrances be played as though final, that each is its own tragedy of incompletion. Balzac's leading characters, conscious and unconscious mummers alike, rendered grotesque by their particular distortions of will, play similarly tragic roles in an overall *Comédie* with one difference: they have no subsequent chances. A consciousness of this gives some of the great women a lively sense of 'tragic joy'.[54]

Yeats saw *Louis Lambert* (1832) as the 'first sketch' of the *Comédie*. Actually this is not so[55] but Yeats's point is that the work shows both unity and a principle of growth. 'The demonstration of its truth', he wrote, 'is that it made possible the *Comédie humaine*'

(*E & I* p. 444). This principle is *not* a metaphor: '. . . what is true of the work of art is true of the . . . dramatist's own life, and if the work is not to be a closed circuit that first sketch has been shaped by desires and alarms arising from another sketch, made not for art but for life' (*E & I* p. 443). Certain artists, says Yeats 'inherited that sketch in its clearest and simplest form, but Balzac had to find it in his own mind' (*E & I* pp. 443-4).

Those who had 'inherited' the sketch — Fielding, Austen, Scott — achieved less, Yeats seems to be saying. Balzac had laboured to discover in his own mind some overall vision of the *theatrum* in which he was but an actor — there seems to be no other way to read Yeats's thought here. Like Dante, who 'set his chisel to the hardest stone' (*VP* p. 369), Balzac had achieved more because he had mastered a greater 'vision of reality'. So *Louis Lambert* had provided in its philosophical fragments and occult aphorisms and speculations a profound model, to which Balzac had but to add his elaborations:

Then too, always somewhere in the background must lurk Vautrin, Séraphita, the Thirteen. He creates the impossible that all may seem possible[56] . . . And this world of his, where everything happens in a blaze of light, and not the France of the historians, is early nineteenth-century France to thousands all over Europe (*E & I* pp. 444-5).

This world is related via the *Études philosophiques* to 'timeless reality' and that relation was to have been further examined in the *Études analytiques* had Balzac lived. These various levels of abstraction could follow the incarnation already established in the *Études de Moeurs*.

I have tried to suggest some aspects (and some of the terminology) of Balzac's *theatrum mundi*, including mask, will, milieu or body of fate, and the example of his creative mind. 'Principles' and 'Faculties' (*S* p. 278) might have done no more than suggest to Yeats 'hard symbolic bones' (*AVB* p. 24) under the unfinished thought of Balzac. The implication is that Yeats could not resist giving Balzac's system a mighty shove in his own direction. Balzac does not seem responsible for the geometrical and astrological elaboration of the 'system', which surely came 'Out of a medium's mouth' (*VP* p. 439). It seems unlikely that had Balzac lived, the 'great eater . . . the mechanist and materialist' would ever have returned[57] to the occultism of the *Études philosophiques* which survived to tantalize Yeats, and to provide enough apparent philosophical (if not mediaeval) backing to the mediaeval world trope. By contrast, Yeats saw Stendhal and his mirror (*AVA* p. 94; *Myth* pp. 333-4) as representative of all that was 'slight and shadowy' about most modern writing, except Balzac who was with Dante, Villon, Shakespeare and Cervantes (*Ex* p. 275).

'I cannot escape', said Yeats, 'from our *Comédie humaine*'. Each life was rooted in milieu, each was a role in a vast drama, the actor accorded only partial knowledge in a system where 'all knowledge' might be 'biography' (*Ex* p. 397). The basis of creativity was soliloquy, the listening of a self proposed upon a stage, the stage enclosed in the mind that could thus internalize a perpetual play. Balzac offered confirmation that such a mediaeval vision was still viable and could be reached via occult symbologies.

I have mentioned the masque-like effects Balzac achieved: Yeats would perhaps have ascribed them to that creation of the 'impossible' that made 'all seem possible'. Masque — *The Tempest's* masque-like effects will do to illustrate — tends towards moments of discovery, dissolution, vision. *Theatrum Mundi* in 'the deeps of the mind' forces a like revelation. Showing always the will in crisis, Balzac offered to Yeats a further insight, that revelation could occur in the midst of a '*substantial* pageant', not always on a 'baseless fabric'. Yeats extrapolated the lesson into a larger perspective, moving further away from the geology of recorded history than Raphael Valentin, or even Balzac's beloved Cuvier. The destinies of his 'actual men and women' having been pricked upon the Platonic Year, he could be satisfied to find 'but drama' (*Ex* p. 398).

This is not to say that he completed Balzac — as he felt Nietzsche to 'complete Blake' (*L* p. 379) — without falsification. Balzac's world seems to offer a 'steady state' of struggle rather than flux and reflux. Then again, his *Dialogue philosophique et politique sur les perfections du XIXe siecle* sounds like the sort of document that might well have started 'a myth in . . . reply to a myth' of progress (*VPl* p. 932). But there is no doubt that Yeats in *A Vision* abstracted, and expanded, beyond and behind the world of the *Comédie*. His whirling forces typify, their combinations individuate, but on a vaster scale, with an Olympian perspective. Thus even 'Balzac's world' is placed in a succession, each with its own 'one myth' supplied by Yeats, but awaiting perhaps its own secretary for its full individuality to be discernible. Yeats was too absorbed in his own 'drama' to do more than 'touch and pass on' in sketching out his own *Essai sur les forces humaines*, surely a larger, far more bizarre document than Balzac had dreamed of for his own *Études analytiques*.

So *A Vision* is perhaps and in part made possible by the example of the unfinished *Comédie*. But, as a *theatrum mundi*, it is an antithetical example.[58] Yeats contains multitudes, aeons, and, obsessed with Babylonian starlight, observes his actual men and women from a distance. We are never allowed to forget that their stage, crowded as it may be, is surrounded by even greater silent spaces of unrecorded history. It has closer similarities perhaps with the *theatrum mundi* of the *Somnium Scipionis*.[59] Balzac's *Comédie*, although it reaches back to the Paris of Dante (and so seems to embrace the *Divine Comedy* into the *Human Comedy*), takes its solidity from its systematic embodiment of the forces of post-revolutionary France. If it seems otiose to pursue further a contrast between a written *Essai sur les forces humaines* and the many-layered *Comédie* from which an unwritten one should have come, it is worth observing that perhaps the *Comédie* is the 'reality' from which Yeats seeks to extract what he calls 'justice'.

YEATS AND THE 'BOUNTY OF SWEDEN'

BIRGIT BRAMSBÄCK

Adding some fresh material, especially about 'Two Songs from a Play' and its relationship to the Golden Room of the Stockholm City Hall, the present paper is largely based on two previous articles, one 'W. B. Yeats and Sweden', read at a Congress of the International Association for the Study of Anglo-Irish Literature arranged at the University of Graz in 1984, and another 'William Butler Yeats och Sverige' [William Butler Yeats and Sweden], published in *Tvärsnitt* (I, 1986) a Swedish learned journal. My paper takes its title from *The Bounty of Sweden*, the work Yeats published in 1925 after his visit to Sweden in 1923 when he was awarded the Nobel Prize for Literature.[1] This booklet contains two essays, the first 'The Bounty of Sweden', a kind of diary-like description of his and his wife's experiences in Stockholm, and the second, 'The Irish Dramatic Movement', a speech delivered by Yeats to the Royal Swedish Academy on 13 December 1923.

Yeats was certainly aware of visiting the native country of Emanuel Swedenborg, the first Swede by whom he was impressed and who meant so much to his own development, and August Strindberg, who, with Swedenborg, was part of what Yeats meant when he coined the expression 'The Bounty of Sweden'. Yet this phrase refers above all to the Nobel Prize itself and to Swedish art and culture, including the Stockholm City Hall inaugurated in 1923, the same year as Yeats was awarded the Nobel Prize, in itself a significant fact.

Yeats was the second author writing in English to be awarded the Nobel Prize for Literature, Rudyard Kipling being the first in 1907, and Bernard Shaw the third in 1925 (although he did not accept it until 1926). In 1901, when the prizes were given for the first time, Sully Prudhomme was the recipient of the literary prize. Although recent attempts have been made to denigrate the Prizes, they fulfil an international role important to Sweden, and the award of Prizes on Nobel Day, 10 December, can be stated to be the greatest cultural ceremony of the Swedish year.

Yeats's candidature was proposed by the well-known Swedish poet, novelist and critic, Per Hallström (1866-1960), who was the first to make Yeats known in Sweden, through an article in *Edda*, 5, published in Kristiania (Oslo) in 1916. In this Hallström stresses Yeats's role as the founder and central figure of the Celtic Revival or Irish Renaissance Movement, the aim of which was to create a specific Anglo-Irish literature, distinct from English literature, and which was deeply rooted in the rich treasure of Gaelic Ireland but also in English literary tradition. In his article, Hallström praised especially *The Wanderings of Oisin* as well as others of Yeats's early poems, notably 'The Song of Wandering Aengus', in which he felt that Yeats had given 'classical stringency' to the fairy-tale.[2] Although expressing some doubt about a few of the *Secret Rose* stories, Hallström praised some of them, not least for their prose style. He was particularly fascinated by Red Hanrahan, whom he called 'a monumental folk character'. Of the plays down to 1916 Hallström preferred *The Countess Cathleen*, *The Land of Heart's Desire*, *Cathleen Ni Houlihan*, and *The King's Threshold*.

As a member of the Swedish Academy and President of the Nobel Prize Committee for Literature, Hallström had a vantage position in promoting Yeats's candidature for the Nobel Prize, which was announced on 14 November 1923. Yeats was awarded the Prize 'for the elevated inspiration and the sober artistic form of his work through which he was able to make the soul of a people speak' (the original French text read: 'pour son oeuvre d'une inspiration toujours élevée qui, sous la forme artistique la plus sobre, fait parler l'âme d'un peuple').[3]

On 15 November 1923 the Prizes were first-page news in the Swedish newspapers, those of Stockholm in particular, but also in the press of Malmö and Gothenburg. Appreciations of Yeats's work and translations of a number of his poems appeared on that date and later.[4] Yeats was hailed as an Irishman and as more or less the greatest poet of his time. The *Stockholmstidningen* and the *Svenska Dagbladet* were both enthusiastic, *Stockholms Dagblad* a little less so, whereas in the *Dagens Nyheter* a dissenting voice, Torsten Fogelqvist writing under the signature 'T. F-t', was heard. He politely pointed out that, in his opinion, Yeats was a provincial writer, and he regretted the fact that the Prize had been given to an Irishman, and a Nationalist Irishman at that. Yeats would have answered, as he did afterwards in *The Bounty of Sweden*, that he and his generation were working for 'the creation of a literature to express national character and feeling, but with no deliberate political aim'. Yeats did, of course, have political views, yet always strongly objected to literature serving as the handmaid of politics.

There were dissenting voices in England also, who remembering the Easter Rising of 1916 and the Civil War of 1922, did not approve of the Prize being awarded to an Irishman. Sir Edmund Gosse, for example, supported the candidature of Thomas Hardy and later showed his disappointment in the choice of Yeats in his review of *The Bounty of Sweden* in *The Sunday Times*, 26 July 1925. Yeats, however, also had friends and a large number of admirers. Among them was the Swedish Minister in Britain, Erik Palmstierna, who, when the decision was made, wrote a letter inviting Yeats 'to receive the prize at Stockholm'; the Swedish Academy also sent him a letter offering 'to send the medal, money and diploma to Dublin' in the event of his not being able to come to Sweden.

Fortunately Palmstierna wrote down some of his reminiscences of Yeats, both in a newspaper article 'W. B. Yeats. Ett silhuettklipp' ('W. B. Yeats, A Silhouette') in *Dagens Nyheter*, 6 February 1939 — after Yeats's death a number of articles and translations of his poems appeared in Swedish newspapers — and in his essay, 'W. B. Yeats' in *Åtskilliga Egenheter* [*A Number of Eccentricities*].[5] In his friendly and sagacious way, Palmstierna, who himself was a spiritualist and a sympathizer with Swedenborg's doctrines, stated that, whenever he met the poet, be it at the Abbey, in the Swedish Legation at Portland Place, or in a London street, the atmosphere which he experienced was 'always that of winds sweeping the Irish moors, or of the stillness of the waters at Glendalough', or 'sensations such as the light footsteps of "the twilight people" ', and more to the same effect. In Yeats, Palmstierna, moreover, saw 'an imposing figure, a tall bard from the Hills of Tara', 'with strong hands accustomed to harp strings and clashing swords'. His eyes were fascinating as was his subdued voice. He seemed 'as if involuntarily to look into the far distance, one eye looking deeply, dreamily and shyly' — a dreamer's eye.

Palmstierna describes at least five meetings with Yeats, one in a London street when he saw Yeats 'gesticulating and reciting to himself', as was often his habit when composing poems, another in 1923 in Yeats's home in Merrion Square, Dublin: they were in Yeats's kitchen, the dining-room being used for the Cuala Press, discussing 'Swedenborg and Tagore, the incipient materialism in Ireland after the liberation, the history of the Abbey Theatre, the value of words and their power to convey musical impressions'.

Lennox Robinson, who was also there, had plans for staging
Strindberg's *The Father*, plans which do not seem to have material-
ized, at least not at the Abbey where, however, *Crimes and Crimes*
and *The Stronger* had been performed in 1913. Mrs Yeats, whom
Palmstierna refers to as 'a remarkable instrument for the soul',
took part in their discussion of psychical research, and the
evening ended with the performance of one of Lady Gregory's
folk comedies — unfortunately not named.

The last time Palmstierna met Yeats was at the Athenaeum in
London where, 'dressed in brown and blue the poet was reclining
on the sofa under the Apollo statue — quite unperturbed by the
hustle and bustle of the luncheon guests, or by discussions going
on between bishops, learned men and politicians'. Yeats made a
sweeping gesture with his arm and said, 'Surely, there must be
something behind it all', referring to the invisible world. Palmstierna was profoundly interested in occult phenomena and had
written about his experiences through a medium in *Horizons of
Immortality: A Quest for Reality* (1950), which Yeats had read in
manuscript. At the time of their meeting Yeats was about to bring
out the second edition of *A Vision*. According to Palmstierna,
Yeats, after his Stockholm visit, never ceased to admire Sweden,
as is witnessed in *On the Boiler* (1938), in which he states that
Sweden has 'spent on education far more than the great nations
can afford'.[17] Palmstierna also testifies to Yeats's interest in
Strindberg and quotes his words, 'I have always felt a sympathy
for that tortured self-torturing man who offered himself to his
own soul as Buddha offered himself to the famished tiger', words
also found in *The Bounty of Sweden*.[10] We are not told, however,
who the tall beautiful lady was, who spoke to Yeats at the Nobel
Banquet about Swedenborg and asked him about 'this new
religion they are making up in Paris that is all about the dead'
(*Bounty*, 13). It might be added that on their last day in Stockholm,
Yeats and his wife were in fact entertained to tea by one of the
then most famous Swedenborgians in Stockholm, Mrs O. W.
Nordenskjöld, née Georgine Kennedy, who died about two
months later, 75 years old (see *Nya Kyrkans Tidning*, 48:12, Dec.
1923, pp. 151-152, and 49:2, Feb. 1924, pp.19-20).[6]

Malicious tongues in Dublin spread the rumour that the first
words spoken by Yeats when he was told that the Nobel Prize was
awarded him were: 'How much?' The truth is that Yeats doubted
that he would be given the prize, for he answered a journalist in
early November 1923 that he could hardly believe that the Royal
Swedish Academy had ever heard of him and that Hardy was

more likely to be the prize winner. However, once he knew that he would get the prize he was keenly aware of the great honour and wrote in *The Bounty of Sweden* (p. 3): 'I covet honour'. Without hesitation he promised to deliver a lecture to the Academy on the Irish dramatic movement, for he was sure of being able to give a successful one on a subject he knew better than anyone else. Strangely, most of the earlier Literary Prize winners had declined to lecture. When Yeats delivered his lecture on Thursday, 13 December, it met with great approval and was reproduced in its entirety in the press next day, and is printed not only in *The Bounty of Sweden* but also in *Les Prix Nobel en 1923* (1924).[7]

In 1923 the ceremony still took place in the Grand Hall of the Musical Academy. Per Hallström, largely responsible for Yeats's canditature, delivered the speech in Yeats's honour and stressed again what he had said in his *Edda* article in 1916 about Yeats having created a national Anglo-Irish literature, but emphasizing also that the fusion of Gaelic and English traditions in his work had gained him high appreciation in England from the very first, though Yeats did not primarily write for an English audience.

At the Banquet following on the ceremony of the Bestowal of Prizes, Yeats gave a short speech of thanks stating that he owed 'three things' to Scandinavia: Swedenborg, the dramatic literature of Ibsen and Strindberg, and the Nobel Prize.[8] A journalist wondered a little sourly the day after if Yeats might have forgotten that he was in Sweden. Of course he had not forgotten, but most likely he stressed the Scandinavian concept, so as to be able to include Ibsen, whose work for the National Theatre in Norway he admired, even if he did not appreciate everything Ibsen wrote.[9] When preparing for his journey to Sweden, he could not find a single book relating to Swedish literature or history in the Dublin bookshops. The only work from which he could glean any information about Sweden was a biography of Swedenborg, whose *Heaven and Hell, Spiritual Diary,* and *Arcana Coelestia* he had read even before he and Edwin Ellis — who discovered a MS of *Vala* in the British Museum — were preparing their three large Blake volumes between 1889 and 1893, a period when Yeats often had occasion to turn to Swedenborg for the elucidation of obscure passages in Blake. Swedenborg and spiritualism (particularly the form developed by Allan Kardec) remained a lifelong interest to Yeats, and not only his poetry but several of his later plays, and some of his earlier, reveal the significance of Swedenborg's influence. In *Swedenborg, Mediums and the Desolate Places*, written in 1914, we find a survey of Yeats's thoughts on Swedenborg, the man who, after his religious vision in London in 1745, communed with angels and spirits. It might be added that Yeats's own copies of some of Swedenborg's works were heavily annotated by the poet himself (as I saw when consulting these books in the Yeats library in the late 1940s).

In December 1923, two other news items, apart from the Nobel Prizes, attracted the attention of journalists: the inauguration of the new Stockholm City Hall, and, above all, the return to Stockholm of the Crown Prince and Princess after their marriage in London on 3 November. In *The Bounty of Sweden* (p. 14) Yeats refers to this: 'Next day is the entrance of the new Crown Princess, and my wife and I watch it, now from the hotel window [the Grand Hotel], now from the quay side. Stockholm is almost as much channelled by the sea as Venice; and with an architecture as impressive as that of Paris, or of London, it has the better even of Paris in situation. It seems to shelter itself under the walls of a great palace, begun at the end of the seventeenth century' (p. 14). He praises the grandeur of the Royal Palace and 'the tower of the City Hall, the glittering pole upon its top sustaining the three crowns of the Swedish arms'. 'The salvos of artillery' for the Crown Prince and Princess made Yeats 'feel a quickening of the pulse, an instinctive alarm', for he remembered the firing of guns in Dublin the previous winter. One may the more easily understand such a reaction when learning (from an interview in one of the newspapers) that his wife had actually been injured in one shoulder, and that, moreover, as a Senator, Yeats had armed guards outside his house in Merrion Square and that the Free State soldiers sometimes directed their defence from Yeats's windows.[10]

About the reception at the Royal Palace on December 13, Yeats, with his appreciation of ceremony, wrote:

I who have never seen a court, find myself before the evening is ended, moved as if by some religious ceremony, though to a different end for here it is Life herself that is praised. Presently we walk through lines of sentries, in the costume of Charles XII, the last of Sweden's great military Kings, and then we bow as we pass rapidly before the tall seated figures of the Royal Family. . . . One has a general impression of youthful distinction, even the tall, slight figure of the old King himself seems young. (*Bounty* p. 16)

At the Bestowal of the Prizes Yeats himself had made an indelible impression on all those present, including the Royal Family, when, after receiving the Prize from the hands of His Majesty the

King, he walked straight backwards up the steps to his seat without any sidelong movement like the others. He explains this feat as due to his concentrating 'attention upon the parallel lines, made by the edges of the carpet'.

After visiting several art galleries and delivering his lecture on 'The Irish Dramatic Movement' on Thursday, 13 December, the time had come for a visit to the New City Hall on which Yeats wrote a true panegyric in *The Bounty of Sweden* (pp. 28-31). He called it 'the greatest work of Swedish art, and the most important building of modern Europe'. In fact he might have called it 'Italy in Sweden', but its Golden Room actually made him think of Byzantium, and he praised the concerted effort of those who made the creation of the City Hall possible; he mentioned 'the mosaic walls of the "Golden Room"' — which undoubtedly influenced his Byzantium poems — 'the Fresco paintings . . . with their subjects from Swedish mythology', etc. and went on to say that

all that multitude and unity, could hardly have been possible, had not love of Stockholm and belief in its future, so filled men of different minds, classes and occupations, that they almost attained the supreme miracle, the dream, that has haunted all religions. . . . No work, comparable in method or achievement, has been accomplished, since the Italian cities felt the excitement of the renaissance . . . (*Bounty*, pp. 30-31)

In referring to the Stockholm City Hall as 'the supreme miracle, the dream that has haunted all religions', Yeats voiced an idea similar to that expressed by Guy de Maupassant who called La Capella Palatina of the Norman Palace in Palermo 'the marvel of marvels . . . the most astonishing religious jewel of which the human mind may dream'.[11]

Professor Georgio Melchiori is certainly right when, in his outstanding work *The Whole Mystery of Art* (1960), he states that in Stockholm and its new City Hall Yeats saw the symbol of the holy city of art.[12] True, Yeats did not say this in so many words, as he did of Byzantium, but he may certainly have had such an idea in mind when remarking in *The Bounty of Sweden* (p. 29) that the Golden Room carried his mind 'backward to Byzantium', a symbol of art which Yeats depicted with such gusto and love in *A Vision* and to which he gave poetic form in his two famous poems 'Sailing to Byzantium' (1926) and 'Byzantium' (1930).[13]

At least two other poems, 'Wisdom' (which will be dealt with in another connection) and 'Two Songs from a Play', link up in an extraordinary way with Yeats's impressions of the Golden Room.

The first two stanzas of 'Two Songs from a Play' form the opening of his remarkable play *The Resurrection*, and the very first line of this poem runs:

I saw a staring Virgin stand

On revisiting the Golden Room a few years ago, I was immediately struck by the similarity between this line and the central mosaic figure of the staring pagan goddess, the protectress of Stockholm called the Mälar Queen, a name taken from the Lake Mälar which surrounds the City Hall. The Mälar Queen, mysteriously staring into a distant future, holds on her lap the city of Stockholm, or rather the City Hall, a royal sceptre in her right hand and a crown in her left. The artist, Einar Forseth, who drew the sketches and paintings from which the mosaics were worked onto the walls by German artisans, had studied Byzantine art in Italy, not least in Sicily, as well as in Constantinople, and to him we owe the glorious mosaic splendour of the Golden Room.

It seems to me that Yeats's line 'I saw a staring Virgin stand' gives an illustration in words of Einar Forseth's mosaic Mälar Queen. This is not to say that I wish to deny the significance of other mosaics or reject parallels between Yeats's poem and Pallas Athene's role for the poem, as pointed out by the late Richard Ellmann and other critics. On the contrary, here, as Yeats would have said with delight, East and West meet. The Mälar Queen, like Pallas Athene, is City Protectress — a symbol in neo-mosaics of the Swedish national dream at the beginning of this century. There she is in her staring mystery, in the Stockholm City Hall as in Yeats's line, 'I saw a staring virgin stand'. Yet there perhaps the likeness ends, for the poem continues 'Where holy Dionysus died' and develops the idea of the fearful sacrificial death and resurrection of God, first in the shape of Dionysus, whose heart is torn out and carried on Athene's hand, then in the shape of Christ, the odour of whose blood Yeats conjures up in the poem. To my mind, he writes of a religious and metaphysical reality in a symbolical and frightening manner.

Yeats's interest in mosaic art was undoubtedly, like his interest in Swedenborg, lifelong, but with certain intermissions. As Melchiori states, Yeats saw and was impressed by the Ravenna mosaics on his visit, together with Lady Gregory and her son Robert, to Ravenna in 1907, but also before that date he praised the beauty of the Ravenna Baptistery in his story 'Rosa Alchemica', first published in *The Savoy* in 1896. In 1985 I myself had a chance of seeing the mosaics of La Capella Palatina and La Martorana in Palermo as well as those splendid mosaics in the cathedrals of Monreale and Cefalù, places all mentioned in *A Vision*. There is no doubt in my mind that the mosaics in Sicily and those in the Golden Room had a more profound and immediate impact on the later Yeats than the Ravenna mosaics, important as they certainly are. In Sicily he saw the Biblical stories of the Old and New Testaments worked in glorious mosaics and was impressed by the somnambulatory effect the golden background had on him, but he also saw there, as well as in Stockholm, mosaics used for secular purposes in praise of a mundane power. Yeats drew in poetic mosaics his own metaphysical and philosophical view of life and death. It is worthy of notice that after seeing the Golden Room in 1923 and the Sicilian mosaics in 1924, and not until then, did he write his powerful Byzantine poems. Though returning in his old age to Cuchulain, the hero of youth and strength, of life and death, the hero who fought alone against an invading power, he nevertheless turned his back on the Irish-Gaelic-Celtic Land of Youth after his visit to Stockholm and Sicily and embraced the artistic culture of ancient Byzantium which had fascinated him as early as the 1890s. Undoubtedly his visit to Stockholm had a lasting effect on his poetry.

Yeats was awarded the Nobel Prize for the elevated and artistic quality of his work, for his giving a voice to the soul of a people, an evaluation which refers to his entire works, plays included, some written in verse, some in prose, but all having a symbolical and poetic-lyrical dimension. I should like to repeat here what I stated in my study *Folklore and W. B. Yeats* (1984): 'As time passes, Yeats's plays are becoming more and more acknowledged by critics as plays for the theatre, not just as literary works . . . a Dramatic Revival was an important part of the Celtic Revival . . . which Yeats initiated.'[14] As early as 1885, when he was only twenty years of age, he took an interest in dramatic form, and one of his very first aims 'was to bring back poetry to the stage, to create a native drama and a theatre for the people'.[15] Largely because the Irish national theatre that he had created went in a direction which did not appeal to him, Yeats, after 1912, turned to a more aristocratic form of theatre, the Japanese Noh drama, and wrote plays which were chiefly intended for small select audiences; today his plays — with a few exceptions — are but rarely performed, and one may wonder why. However, during his week in Stockholm, the Dramatic Theatre performed his *Cathleen Ni Houlihan* (*Cathleen Houlihans dotter*) on Saturday, 15 December, a performance which he and his wife liked. Since then, however, the only Yeats play which has been given on any Swedish stage, as far as I know, is *The Countess Cathleen* (*Grevinnan Cathleen*). True, his plays from 1916 on have not been translated into Swedish, and it is a *desideratum* that his later plays should be translated into Swedish, and at least some of those modelled on the Japanese Noh performed, for example, *At the Hawk's Well*, *The Only Jealousy of Emer*, *The Dreaming of the Bones*, *Purgatory*, and *The Death of Cuchulain*.[16] A musical and allegorical adaptation of *The Countess Cathleen*, entitled *Irländsk Legend* (Irish Legend) was presented in Stockholm in 1985 by the Opera and the Marionette Theatre. Michael Meschke based his adaptation on the German composer Werner Egk's work.

Yeats rated his work for the theatre as well as his dramatic criticism highly, something that is clear not least from his speech to the Royal Swedish Academy in 1923, which he begins:

. . . I have chosen as my theme the Irish Dramatic Movement because when I remember the great honour that you have conferred upon me, I cannot forget many known and unknown persons. Perhaps the English committees would never have sent you my name if I had written no plays, no dramatic criticism, if my lyric poetry had not a quality of speech practised upon the stage, perhaps even — though this could be no portion of their deliberate thought — if it were not in some degree the symbol of a movement. (*Bounty*, p. 33)

In his speech he further remembered the help he had from Martyn, Synge, Lady Gregory and Annie Horniman; he praised the actors, the speech and the stories of the country-folk, and said towards the end that he wished that 'a young man's ghost [Synge's] should have stood upon one side of [him] and at the other a living woman in her vigorous old age [Lady Gregory]' (*Bounty*, 48-49). With this dramatic Noh effect and some laudatory words about Sweden and her royal family, Yeats ended his Nobel lecture.

Yeats may certainly be said to be one of the greatest twentieth-century poets, and to this might be added that not only did he influence the literary and cultural development of his country, but also the course of its history, as Peter Costello claims in *The Heart Grown Brutal*.[17] Far from being just a provincial writer, as Torsten Fogelqvist would have it in 1923, Yeats is not only of European but of international status, with a central place in world literature. Those who decided to award him the Nobel Prize for Literature in 1923 were certainly right.

A FEW TWIGS FROM THE WILD BIRD'S NEST: YEATS THE EUROPEAN

PETER R. KUCH

'It is remarkable', Russell wrote in *The Irish Statesman* on 22 January 1927, 'that so fascinating a literature as the Irish, in whatever language, Gaelic or English, should never have been discussed as a whole, as a culture.' The study of Gaelic literature, he argued, had not advanced beyond a preoccupation with textual purity and the niceties of translation; while the study of Anglo-Irish literature had come to rest in literary histories like Ernest Boyd's *Ireland's Literary Renaissance* (1916) and Hugh Law's *Anglo-Irish Literature* (1926). What was needed, he declared, was an Arnoldian essay that would offer 'a purely cultural exposition of [the] character, genius, imagination or thought' in all Irish literature, whether written in Gaelic or English.[1]

His challenge went unheeded for five years, until Frank O'Connor asked him to write a foreword to *The Wild Bird's Nest*, a collection of translations from the Gaelic that was about to be published by the Cuala Press. Russell, realizing that this would give him an opportunity to write his desired cultural exposition himself, agreed. He called his foreword: 'An Essay on the Character in Irish Literature'. It is a provocative essay, and successfully delineates some key aspects of Irishness, but its most provocative speculations are those about the Europeanism of Yeats.

Russell begins his essay by remarking that the Irish character has been determined by two factors: that Ireland was never conquered by the Romans, and that it is geographically isolated. The first meant that the Irish were never forced to surrender their 'primaeval culture of imagination' to one of Graeco-Roman origins, while the second ensured that they were able to preserve this culture intact. Thus, for example, while Europe was being disciplined by Aristotelianism, a discipline that was to culminate in modern science with its emphasis on empiricism, Ireland was able to keep intact those mythopoeic modes of apprehension that constituted its 'primaeval culture of imagination'.

'In Irish literature', Russell goes on to argue,

philosophy and science are absent. We never had even a great Irish
theologian. Johannes Scotus Erigena,[2] the one Irishman of intellect
capable of rationalising spiritual nature, went to Europe and became the
greatest of medieval heretics. There were few intellectual influences to
deflect the Irish culture from its natural development . . . [Its] imagination
stormed the heavens. There are in Irish literature many voyages to
heaven world or faery. But there was not as in Europe any rationalising
by philosophy of these heavenly adventures. Philosophy might have
been the net to catch and sustain the spirit in its descent to earth and
keep it from despair at its fall. But the Irish never seem to have made any
attempt to rationalise their vision.

There are, Russell observes, two poles in Irish literature: one
where the visionary imagination rises to Ildathach, the many-
coloured land; the other where the imagination is engaged by
a cold, hard, yet passionate realism. From the first come poems
like 'The Voyage of Bran' and the dialogue between Cormac and
Columcille; while from the second comes poems like 'The Old
Woman of Beare'.[3]
    Yet, though they are apparently opposite in temper, both exhibit
the distinguishing characteristic of the Irish imagination. Neither
in them, nor in the poetry which could be considered to lie
between them, is there a 'trace of the philosophic mind', the
mentality we see to perfection in Wordsworth's 'Intimations of
Immortality' and in so much English and European literature,
where Aristotelianism, or Platonism or neo-Platonism

or some other philosophical system enables the poet to interpret his
experience to himself.
    In Irish literature every vision is what it seems at the moment to the
seer. Intuition does not penetrate to any deep of being. The alchemy of
the brooding mind distils no precious knowledge. In that literature too
every passion exists by itself. It is born and dies in the poet without any
of the consolations of philosophy. . . .

Thus the distinguishing characteristic of Irish literature, whether
written in Gaelic in the seventh century or Anglo-Irish in the late
nineteenth, is the immediacy and intensity of its emotionality, an
emotionality which, once it has flared into poetry, leaves only the
ashes of despair because its exhaustion has not been anticipated
by philosophy. The distinguishing characteristic of European
literature is the consolation provided by philosophy, which
enters the poem even as the emotion that has inspired it begins
to consume itself in its expression.

'I would like to speculate', Russell concludes, 'on the offspring of a marriage of [the] cultures, the Irish with the European, which cannot be kept apart for ever. There are intimations in the later poetry and prose of Yeats what an exciting literature might be born from that union.'[4]

Beynd this provocative remark, Russell does not venture. This paper will examine some of the presuppositions that he has used to launch his speculations, and it will develop some of those speculations further in an attempt to describe and locate the Europeanism of Yeats.

The distinction that Russell draws between the Irish imagination and the European imagination can be effectively illustrated by using a poem Yeats first wrote in 1890 and then revised in 1925. Towards the end of 1890, Russell and John Hughes were walking on Two Rock Mountain when they encountered an old peasant. As Russell was to record in his unpublished autobiography, *The Sunset of Fantasy*:

[The old peasant] was hugging his body as if there were none other in the world but himself that would hold it with familiar hands and he was talking to himself, and his grief seemed so great he must speak . . . He stepped before me [and said]: 'Over those hills I wandered forty years ago. Nobody but myself knows what happened under the thorn tree forty years ago. The fret is on me. The fret is on me. God speaking out of his darkness says I have and I have not. I possess the heavens. I do not possess the world. Abroad if you meet an Irishman he will give you the bit and the sup. But if you come back to your own country after being away forty years it is not the potato and bit of salt you get[,] but only "Who's that ould fella?" The fret is on me. The fret is on me!'[5]

On his return to Dublin, Russell recounted the old peasant's outburst to Yeats, who promptly used it for a poem.[6] He called it 'The Old Pensioner' and submitted it to *The Scots Observer*, where it was published on 15 November 1890.

> I had a chair at every hearth,
> When no-one turned to see
> With 'Look at that old fellow there;
> And who may he be?'
> And therefore do I wander on,
> And the fret is on me.

> The roadside trees keep murmuring —
> Ah, wherefore murmer ye
> As in the old days long gone by,
> Green oak and poplar tree!
> The well-known faces are all gone,
> And the fret is on me.[7]

Yeats admitted in a note that his poem was 'little more than a translation into verse of the very words of an old Wicklow peasant'.[8] His choice of the simple ballad form of alternating tetrameters and trimeters and his use of reported speech evidence his desire to capture the actuality of the experience. But he has achieved only partial success. The last line of each verse, though it closely echoes the old peasant's cry, lacks most of its dramatic intensity. The second verse is perhaps more effective. The pathetic fallacy of the first line, the vagueness and menace evoked by the onomatopoeia of 'murmuring' and 'murmur', and the contorted structure ending with the archaic 'ye' (an echo of Coleridge's archaism perhaps) realistically convey a sense of the old man's distraction. The poem, to employ Russell's distinction, is quintessentially Irish in that Yeats has simply given expression to the intensity and immediacy of an emotion which is left to exist by itself. The emotion is only what it seems at that moment to the poet. And it exhausts itself in despair because there is nothing to arrest its decline.

Yeats rewrote the poem in 1925 for *Early Poems and Stories* and changed the title to 'The Lamentation of the Old Pensioner'. His revisions, to continue to employ Russell's distinction, disclose his Europeanism:

> Although I shelter from the rain
> Under a broken tree
> My chair was nearest to the fire
> In every company
> That talked of love or politics,
> Ere Time transfigured me.
>
> Though lads are making pikes again
> For some conspiracy,
> And crazy rascals rage their fill
> At human tyranny,
> My contemplations are of Time
> That has transfigured me.

> There's not a woman turns her face
> Upon a broken tree,
> And yet the beauties that I loved
> Are in my memory;
> I spit into the face of Time
> That has transfigured me.[9]

The Europeanism of the poet is immediately evident both in the introduction and in the treatment of the theme of *tempus edax*. Though the original rhyme scheme has been retained, the iambic metre has been considerably strengthened to bring out the old man's contempt for the timid passions of the present. What was simply a lament about the past, when he had been welcome at every hearth, has been transformed into a jeremiad against the despotic fact that he can no longer command the love of women. And what was the greatest weakness of the original ballad, the old peasant's repeated passive complaint that he is doomed ('The fret is on me!'), becomes, because it is rendered philosophically, one of the greatest strengths of the revised version. The intensity and immediacy of the peasant's emotions have been set against the ravages of 'Time', which he alleges have *transfigured* him, and the cycles of political protest, which he claims enmesh his fellow-countrymen in the immediate but release him to contemplate 'Time'. The poem ends not in despair but in defiance, as for Yeats the fading energy of the emotion that seeks expression is countered by the rising force of a philosophical framework for that emotion. Thus, as Russell points out, one of the characteristics that enables us to distinguish between the Irish and the European is the degree to which the intensity of emotionality has been countered by the consolations of philosophy.

The second distinction that Russell draws between the Irish and the European grows out of the first. It is particularly helpful in assessing Yeats's early poetry. Russell draws the distinction in *The Sunset of Fantasy*. The title and the main argument of the autobiography, which was never completed, derive from a lecture he prepared in the summer of 1930 for his second lecture tour of America, which he undertook between September 1930 and May 1931.[10]

The evolution of both the title and the main argument can be traced through his correspondence with James Pond, the owner and manager of the American bureau that was organizing the tour. Pond initially proposed that Russell should prepare three lectures: an anecdotal but informative account of his literary

contemporaries, a survey of the relationship between Irish
literature and Irish legend, and a 'more or less serious lecture on
a philosophical theme'.[11] Russell found all of the suggestions
appealing, though he particularly liked the challenge of a serious
lecture. 'I have a lot of ideas about dreams which are my own,
unusual, and which I think might interest intelligent audiences',
he replied.[12] But the more he considered these ideas the more
difficult he found it to bring his 'subtleties to a clearness which
would make them intelligible'. 'So I am thinking of another
lecture', he informed Pond, 'which might be called "The Last of
the Fantastics".'[13] Eight days later, however, he wrote again with
a new title which he hoped would enable him to distinguish
between the anecdotal lecture about his literary contemporaries
and 'the more or less serious lecture on a philosophical theme', 'I
think a better title would be *The Sunset of Fantasy*', he advised
Pond:

I can make it as interesting & amusing as the lecture on 'Some Characters
in the Irish Literary Renaissance'. It will deal with the end of the romantic
Irish culture which lasted for two thousand years, its sunset and the way
it affected poets and peasants.[14]

It was in part the success of this American lecture tour that
prompted Macmillan to approach Russell in May 1934 to write his
autobiography. Their proposal excited his interest. 'I have started
on the book of reminiscences you suggested', he informed his
publisher on 30 June 1934:

I think I have got one or two root ideas to hang all memories together. I
am going to call it *The Sunset of Fantasy*, that is the period in which I lived
when the fantasy in the Irish mind began to darken. In that sunset Yeats,
O'Grady, Stephens, Shaw, Joyce, Lady Gregory, Synge, Moore, and many
others were lit up like figures in the last rays of the sun. The new
generation is grey in comparison. I hope to make it an interesting book.[15]

Between the end of June and the beginning of October 1934
Russell roughed out the first ten thousand words. Though he was
confident of his main argument, he realized that he would have
to revise his draft several times to improve the style. So when
Seumas O'Sullivan asked him for part of it for *The Dublin
Magazine*, he reworked the first two chapters to the point that it
was possible to publish them posthumously.[16]

Russell begins *The Sunset of Fantasy* by defining himself in
terms of nationality. He rehearses the distinction he had drawn

in his foreword to *The Wild Bird's Nest,* and then offers another characteristic that distinguishes the Irish from the European mind:

I will try to conjure up a vivid image of what I remember, but in this I will select as all artists must do out of their own character and out of that part of me which is Irish and therefore fantastic. We of the Anglo-Irish have a dual character partly quickened by the aged thought of the world and partly inherited from an Irish ancestry. Ireland was never part of the ancient Roman Empire, and the imagination of the people had never been disciplined by philosophy or dialectic or science as other European peoples had been in whose minds something of the thought [of] Plato or Aristotle had incarnated. Our Irish ancestors continued for long centuries to live by imagination[,] which was I think the culture of the world before the Grecian mind became dominant. I think imagination has its own truth, a relation of image, myth or symbol to deep inner being, the truth which is in religion or poetry[,] or the relations the drama of dream may have to our waking desires or to being in the world beyond dream. When imagination does not fly so high as the spirit it indulges in fantasy. [No] literature is fuller of imagination or fantasy undisciplined by philosophy than the Irish. [The] peasant in Ireland had for culture the folk tales[,] the shrivelled remains of once mighty religions or epical narrative.[17]

There are two juxtapositions in this passage that should engage our attention: the juxtaposition of imagination and fantasy, and the juxtaposition of literature and peasant Irish literature, Russell suggests, can be distinguished from European by the degree or extent of its fantasticality, a fantasticality preserved by the peasantry and periodically recovered by the poets.

The distinction is a bold one. It is easy to caricature fantasticality, to denigrate it as a flight from the real, as an engaging whimsicality that is endearing, momentarily entertaining, but essentially irresponsible. Furthermore, the weight of English disapproval, from Shakespeare through Coleridge to the present day, is sufficient to make any of the colonized pause before claiming it as a distinguishing characteristic.

The fantasticality, and thus the essential Irishness, of Yeats's early poetry has been too little remarked, even though the poet himself described his imagination as 'excited, passionate, fantastical'. It met with English disapproval very early. On 7 November 1886 Gerard Manley Hopkins, who had recently been presented with some of Yeats's poems, confided to Coventry Patmore that his intense dislike for one of the dramatic poems, *Mosada,* had forced him to praise a poem called 'The Two Titans', 'a strained

and unworkable allegory', 'but still containing fine lines and
vivid imagery', 'about a young man and a sphinx on a rock in the
sea'. 'How', he asked belatedly in his letter, 'did they get there?
what did they eat? and so on: people think such criticisms very
prosaic; but commonsense is never out of place anywhere . . .'[18]
His fellow countryman agreed. 'You have Coleridge's authority
for requiring good-sense in every kind of poetry', Patmore
replied. ' "A palace", he says, "should at least be a house".'[19]

Hopkins's unease comes from his inability to accept 'The Two
Titans' on its own terms. It is neither imaginative, as defined by
Coleridge, nor allegorical. It is mythical and fantastical, and so
the criterion of 'commonsense' does not apply. As rereading
Coleridge would have reminded Hopkins: 'the fancy is indeed
no other than a mode of memory emancipated from the order of
time and space'; and 'equally with the ordinary memory [the
fancy] must receive all its materials ready made from the law of
association'.[20] Though these materials are provided by the primary
imagination, and though the fancy functions in a way analogous
to the secondary imagination, it is confined to the phenomenal.
It does not have access to the noumenal. That Russell would agree
with Coleridge is indicated by his assertion that 'when imagination does not fly so high as the spirit it indulges in fantasy'.
The fancy, Coleridge argues, possesses 'the power more or less
capriciously to manipulate its materials, but not to modify,
reshape, and unify them'.[21]

The definition that Coleridge offers, and Russell appears to
endorse, can be clearly illustrated by a snippet of peasant speech
that the Irish poet often quoted when he was talking about the
atavism of the English of the Irish speaking districts. In the early
days of the Co-operative movement, when he was cycling through
the west of Ireland organizing credit banks and helping farmers
to improve their production and increase their markets, Russell
stopped by a cottage where he heard the woman of the house
welcome one of her friends with the greeting: 'Come in. Ah sure
your shadow is only a light at the door.'[22] The greeting is fantastical.
It is confined to the phenomenal. It has 'received its materials
ready made from the law of associations'. And it has been constructed by manipulating the contrast between light and dark in
such a way as to surprise and delight. Finally, the energy of the
expression derives from the capricious reordering of the listener's
expectations. Fantasticality is self-generative and self-referential.

Russell seems to have been the only contemporary critic fully
to appreciate the fantasticality of Yeats's early poetry. In his first

piece of literary criticism, a review of the 1895 *Poems* published by
T. Fisher Unwin, he wrote of *The Wanderings of Oisin*:

For the first time in our island since the days of the mystic De Danaan
races and their coeval bards there has been heard the cry of a Royal
Imagination. King of dreamers, most enraptured seer of the magic land,
his beautiful fantasies have a more authentic life, a more convincing
reality of their kind, than anything I know. He has lived in his phantasmal
world until he knows every emotion haunting the wanderer amid its
wizard twilights. Here is a misty picture:

The wood was so spacious above them that He who has stars for His flocks
    Could fondle the leaves with His fingers, nor go from His
                                        dew-cumbered skies;
So long were they sleeping, the owls had builded their nests in their locks,
    Filling the fibrous dimness with long generations of eyes.

And over the limbs and the valley the slow owls wandered and came,
    Now in a place of star-fire, and now in a shadow-place wide:
And the chief of the huge white creatures, his knees in the soft star-flame,
    Lay loose in a place of shadow — we drew the reins by his side.[23]

The passage, which Russell rightly identifies as fantastical, is
from the description of the 'monstrous slumbering folk' that Oisin
and Niamh encounter shortly after arriving at the last of the three
islands, the Island of Forgetfulness. The image of the owls living
in the sleepers' locks echoes part of a poem entitled 'Jealousy',
and subsequently called 'Anashuya and Vijaya', that Yeats had
published two years before. Anashuya wants her lover to

            Swear by the parents of the gods,
    Dread oath, who dwell on sacred Himalay,
    On the far Golden Peak; enormous shapes,
    Who still were old when the great sea was young;
    On their vast faces mystery and dreams;
    Their hair along the mountains rolled and filled
    From year to year by the unnumbered nests
    Of aweless birds . . . [24]

Richard Ellmann claims that this description was inspired by
some poorly executed portraits of 'Koot-Hoomi' and 'Morya', the
two Tibetan adepts who were supposed to have initiated Madame
Blavatsky into the occult mysteries of the secret *Book of Dyzan*.
Yeats, he says, was moved to celebrate them in verse after he had
visited the prophetess of Theosophy in London.[25] The association

with Madame Blavatsky is supported by Russell, though he claims Yeats was moved to write the lines after reading *The Occult World*, a defence of her supernatural powers written by one of her disciples and read by the young poets some time late in 1884 or early in 1885. Yeats, he recalled,

had a marvellous collection of tales about Madame Blavatsky, whose Masters, he said, lived in the Himalayas amid the snows meditating through long centuries, and their beards grew and grew, and lay upon the mountain sides, and the birds built their nests in their beards.[26]

The image itself, however, as Yeats reveals in his essay on Shakespeare entitled 'At Stratford-on-Avon' is derived from folklore. In the course of arguing for greater harmony between the plays and the way they are staged, he says: 'In [Shakespeare's] art, as in all the older art of the world, there was much make-believe, and our scenery, too, should remember the time when, as my nurse used to tell me, herons built their nests in old men's beards!'[27]

Thus, Yeats's use of the image in both 'Anashuya and Vijaya' and *The Wanderings of Oisin* illustrates the symbiotic relationship between poetry and peasantry that Russell posits in *The Sunset of Fantasy*; while the image itself discloses the fantasticality, and thus the Irishness, of the early poetry. It confirms Coleridge's assertion that 'fancy is indeed no other than a mode of memory emancipated from the order of time and space'. It also illustrates the way that the fantastical is confined to the phenomenal. The image is purely visual. And, finally, the substitution of 'owls' for 'aweless birds' for 'herons' affirms Coleridge's contention that the fancy possesses 'the power more or less capriciously to manipulate its materials, but not to modify, reshape, and unify them'. Neither the shape nor the unity of the image is affected by the substitutions.

The Wanderings of Oisin is richly embroidered with the fantastical. An early example is Oisin's description of the first island:

> But now a wandering land breeze came
> And a far sound of feathery quires;
> It seemed to blow from the dying flame,
> They seemed to sing in the smouldering fires.
> The horse towards the music raced,
> Neighing along the lifeless waste;
> Like sooty fingers, many a tree
> Rose ever out of the warm sea;
> And they were trembling ceaselessly,

> As though they all were beating time,
> Upon the centre of the sun,
> To that low laughing woodland rhyme.
> And, now our wandering hours were done,
> We cantered to the shore, and knew
> The reason of the trembling trees:
> Round every branch the song-birds flew,
> Or clung thereon like swarming bees;
> While round the shore a million stood
> Like drops of frozen rainbow light,
> And pondered in a soft vain mood
> Upon their shadows in the tide,
> And told the purple deeps their pride,
> And murmured snatches of delight . . . [28]

The description is both self-generative and self-referential. It is built up by accretion, each fresh image for the most part being introduced either by a conjunction or a preposition. Most of the constructions are coordinate, and most of the momentum for the coordination is generated by the metre, a steady iambic tetrameter that propels the poem forward. Skilful variations in rhyme, however, prevent the persistence of the rhythm from becoming relentless. Though there are some aural images, most are visual, and all are confined to the phenomenal. The imagery also exhibits that capricious manipulation of vehicle and tenor that is characteristic of fantasticality. The trees are said to be like 'sooty fingers', while their ceaseless trembling is compared with 'beating time, upon the centre of the sun'. Yet the song-birds, whose constant flight creates the illusion that the trees are trembling, are said to be 'like drops of frozen rainbow light'. The incongruity of birds which look like drops of frozen rainbow light but whose flight resembles the pulsations of the sun is evidence that in this passage Yeats's imagination is operating at the level of the fantastic. The entire description has been constructed by the capricious manipulation of a group of related images: 'flame', 'fire', 'sooty', 'the centre of the sun', 'rainbow' and 'light'.

The extent of the fantasticality, and thus the essential Irishness of *The Wanderings of Oisin*, should give pause to those critics who have tried to appropriate the poem for Romanticism, and thereby claim Yeats as a European. Of these, Harold Bloom's *Yeats* (1970), has been the most clamorous and the most influential, though he has principally attempted to claim Yeats only for English Romanticism. He begins chapter six of his book on Yeats, 'Anglo-Irish Poetry and *The Wanderings of Oisin*', by observing that:

The Anglo-Irish poetic tradition is not easily defined or described, but seems nevertheless an authentic one. Its inventors would appear to be Moore, in only one aspect of his work, and J. J. Callanan, like Moore a Romantic disciple of Byron. Callanan's original lyrics are mostly derived from Byron and Moore, but his versions from the Gaelic introduce a different kind of effect into English poetry.

Bloom does not say what this 'different kind of effect' is; we would need to turn to Thomas MacDonagh's *Literature in Ireland* (1916) for an illuminating, if hesitant, analysis of the Irish mode in English poetry; but Bloom does say that 'it' is 'not without its hazards', the chief seeming to be 'a certain unrestrained exuberance of rhetoric'. But instead of examining the sources of this rhetoric, and the way it functions in the poetry, Bloom simply invokes a passage from the 'mature' Yeats and sends the nineteenth century packing. 'Yeats's problem as an Anglo-Irish poet', he continues, 'was therefore in part having to commence *ab ovo*, but as though an actual achievement lay behind him.' Having transformed Yeats into an anxious progenitor of ghosts, Bloom passes to *The Wanderings of Oisin*, which, he claims, was the poet's 'principal overt attempt at Anglo-Irish mythological poetry'.

The matter of *Oisin* is Irish, based largely upon an eighteenth-century poem by Michael Comyn that Yeats found translated in the *Transactions of the Ossianic Society*. At a later time, Yeats perhaps received his material a bit more directly from the folk, through Lady Gregory, if we are to believe him in this regard. But, with *Oisin*, the reader must begin by remembering how far the poet actually is from his supposed sources; he sits in the British Museum, himself knowing no Gaelic (he never bothered to learn any) and he reads a version of a version. He is so far from mythology, and indeed in every sense so far from Ireland, that we need not be surprised to discover that his poem, despite its Celtic colorings, is in the center of the English Romantic tradition, and indeed in one particular current of that tradition, which I have called the internalization of quest-romance.[29]

The final sentence is as inaccurate as it is mischievous. Bloom's anxiety to appropriate Yeats for English Romanticism has led him into a number of misconceptions. Not only is the matter of the poem Irish, but so is its theme. As Russell has pointed out:

There are in Irish literature many voyages to heaven world or faery. But there was not as in Europe any rationalizing by philosophy of these heavenly adventures. Philosophy might have been the net to catch and sustain the spirit in its descent to earth and keep it from despair at its fall. But the Irish never seem to have made any attempt to rationalise their vision.

The closing lines of *The Wanderings of Oisin* reveal a characteristically Irish treatment of a traditional Irish theme:

Oisin.   Ah me! to be shaken with coughing and broken with old age
                    and pain,
              Without laughter, a show unto children, alone with
                    remembrance and fear;
              All emptied of purple hours as a beggar's cloak in the rain,
              As a hay-cock out on the flood, or a wolf sucked under a weir.

              It were sad to gaze on the blessed and no man I loved of old
                    there;
              I throw down the chain of small stones! when life in my body
                    has ceased,
              I will go to Caoilte, and Conan, and Bran, Sceolan, Lomair,
              And dwell in the house of the Fenians, be they in flames or at
                    feast.[30]

Confronted with St Patrick's Christian philosophy, Oisin can only despair. Thematically, *The Wanderings of Oisin* is not an internalized quest-romance; it is an Irish poem, derived from two Gaelic sources, *Oisin i dTir na nOg* and *Agallamh na Senorach*, about a voyage to the heaven world.[31] Neither does Oisin as a central figure derive from the figure of the solitary in Wordsworth's *Excursion*, as Bloom claims, or from the heroes of *Alastor, Endymion* and *Childe Harold III*, or Browning's *Pauline, Paracelsus* and *Sordello*, or for that matter, the heroes 'throughout early Tennyson' as he further claims.[32] The essential difference between *The Wanderings of Oisin* and all these is that Yeats's poem is not underpinned or framed by a philosophy, whether it is the 'egotistical sublime', pantheism, Platonism or neo-Platonism. That Yeats himself seems to have felt anxious about the inability of his poem to incite the reader to engage more than its surface is evident from his defence of it to Katharine Tynan:

In the second part of *Oisin* under disguise of symbolism I have said severel [sic] things, to which I only have the key. The romance is for my readers, they must not even know there is a symbol anywhere. They will not find out. If they did it would spoil the art.[33]

The critic who tries to encode or decode these symbols faces the same problem as an archaeologist who mounts a dig on a mosaic. Once he has removed the surface he has gone beyond the subject he wants to study. As John Unterecker has shrewdly observed: 'To ask what the symbols mean is a lure that can lead [the reader] spectacularly astray.' The pertinent question is to ask what the symbols do, for the poem is, in essence, 'a tissue of interlocked images'.[34] This lack of philosophical framework is characteristically Irish, for as Russell reminds us, 'In Irish literature every vision is what it seems at that moment to the seer. Intuition does not penetrate to any deep of being'.

Finally, *pace* Bloom, *The Wanderings of Oisin* was not written in the British Museum. Yeats began the poem in Dublin in October 1886. Between April and August 1887, when he was living in London, he worked mainly in the Art Library at the South Kensington Museum. To get to the British Museum he had to take a bus, and in those days he could rarely afford the fare. But a significant portion of the poem was written between 11 August and 18 November 1887 while he was staying with his uncle, George Pollexfen, in the west of Ireland.[35] The egregious folk images of a beggar's cloak, hay-cocks and drowned wolves in the penultimate stanza should have directed Bloom to the poet's letters to check the facts. None of these images belong to the iconography of the 'internalized quest-romance'.

To employ Russell's distinctions to recover the early poetry for Ireland and to reveal an Irish Yeats whose imagination was as yet untinctured by Europeanism is, however, only part of the task. Two further questions remain. When did Yeats's imagination begin to display those characteristics which Russell describes as European? And how did that development take place?

That Yeats developed a European imagination has already been implied by our analysis of the two versions of 'The Old Pensioner'. It is an analysis that could be repeated by comparing the descriptions of 'the parents of the gods' from 'Anashuya and Vijaya' and 'the monstrous slumbering folk' from *The Wanderings of Oisin* with the 'Hermits' of 'Meru'. In 'Meru' the fantastic imagery associated with the adepts is framed by a vivid analysis of the recurrent turmoil of the world and a terse account of the extent of the hermit's occult knowledge:

> Civilization is hooped together, brought
> Under a rule, under the semblance of peace
> By manifold illusion; but man's life is thought,
> And he, despite his terror, cannot cease
> Ravening through century after century,
> Ravening, raging, and uprooting that he may come
> Into the desolation of reality:
> Egypt and Greece, good-bye, and good-bye Rome!

> Hermits upon Mount Meru or Everest,
> Caverned in night under the drifted snow,
> Or where that snow in winter's dreadful blast
> Beat down upon their naked bodies, know
> That day brings round the night, that before dawn
> His glory and his monuments are gone.[36]

In dealing 'with ultimate reality, or with the most general causes and principles of things and ideas and human perception and knowledge of them'[37] the poem is indisputably philosophical, and in a European rather than a British way. It has more affinities with Nietzsche than with Locke. The poem also displays that type of the historical imagination that one usually associates with Europeanism.

The fantasticality of Yeats's early poetry becomes less and less exuberant as one passes from 'Crossways' to 'The Wind Among the Reeds'. This is evident if one compares 'The Indian to His Love' with 'The Rose of Peace' with 'He Wishes for the Cloths of Heaven'. Again, it is Russell who has skilfully located and described the change that he senses has just taken place in his friend's poetry. 'I sigh sometimes', he said in his 1903 essay, 'The Poet of Shadows',

thinking on the light dominion dreams have over the heart. We cannot hold a dream for long, and that early joy of the poet . . . in Ildathach . . . has passed. It has seemed to him too luxuriant. He seeks for something more, and has tried to make its tropical tangle orthodox, and the glimmering waters and winds are no longer beautiful natural presences, but have become symbolic voices and preach obscurely some doctrine of their power to quench the light in the soul or to fan it into a brighter flame. I like their old voiceless motion and their natural wandering best. . . . Sometimes I wonder whether that insatiable desire of the mind for something more than it has yet attained, which blows the perfume from every flower, and plucks the flower from every tree, and hews down every tree in the valley until it goes forth gnawing itself into a last hunger, does not threaten all the cloudy turrets of the poet's soul. But whatever end or transformation or unveiling may happen, that which creates beauty must have beauty in its essence, and the soul must cast off many vestures before it comes to itself. We, all of us, poets, artists, and musicians, who work in shadows, must sometime begin to work in substance, and why should we grieve if one labour ends and another begins.[38]

Whether Yeats cast off his 'coat' because it had become the distinctive dress of 'fools', or whether the 'insatiable desire of the mind' drove him into 'the desolation of reality', the Europeanism of the poetry derives from this need to exchange shadow for substance, to move beyond the self-referential and self-generative fantasticality of the early poetry.

Yeats attempted to meet this need in a number of ways, all of which are instructive for understanding the Europeanism of his poetry. By way of conclusion, we will briefly consider four of them.

The least satisfactory was his study of the occult, which was as various as it was consuming. His enquiries took him from the semi-respectable Kensington parlour of that old Russian emigré, Madame Blavatsky, to the Latin Quarter to take hashish with some followers of the eighteenth-century mystic, Saint-Martin.[39] It was a search for both a personal apotheosis and a system of philosophy that would enable him to unify the increasingly disparate images of poetry. He conducted numerous occult experiments with symbols in an attempt to establish networks of correspondence, only to find that 'image called up image in an endless procession'.[40] Most of his enquiries and almost all of his research was undertaken for his Irish mystical order, 'The Castle of Heroes'. 'I had an unshakeable conviction', he was to write later in the *Autobiographies*,

arising how or whence I cannot tell, that invisible gates would open as they opened for Blake, as they opened for Swedenborg, as they opened for Boehme, and that this philosophy would find its manuals of devotion in all imaginative literature, and set before Irishmen for special manual an Irish literature which, though made by many minds, would seem the work of a single mind, and in turn our places of beauty or legendary association into holy symbols.[41]

But his attempts to repeat the triumphs of visionary synthesis of the great European mystics failed. Stories like *Rosa Alchemica*, *The Adoration of the Magi* and *The Tables of the Law*, and his unfinished novel, *The Speckled Bird*, dramatize the causes for and extent of that failure.[42] In the end, the Europeanism of Yeats's poetry owes more to the network of correspondences set up within his own work than it does to his study of the occult.

More satisfactory was his work for the theatre. From the beginning, Yeats asserted the Irishness of his theatre by invoking European parallels. Through the Irish National Theatre Society, he announced, he would do for Ireland what Ibsen had done for Norway, Calderon for Spain.[43] None other than Victor Hugo, he would repeat, had affirmed that 'in the theatre the mob become a people'.[44] The Antient Concert Rooms and the Molesworth Hall were not local venues; they were the Dublin equivalents of Le Théâtre Libre and Le Théâtre Independent managed by a poet who had attended Parisian productions ranging from Villiers de l'Isle-Adam's *Axel* to Alfred Jarry's *Ubu Roi*.[45] And when some of the 'unmannerly' Dubliners insinuated that a theatre, like a silk bow-tie, was simply part of the trappings necessary to be a great poet, Yeats replied with articles on Goethe and Maeterlinck.

But the means which most enabled Yeats to exchange the shadows for substances, to develop those imaginative qualities that Russell has distinguished as European, were reading and literary criticism. His discovery of Nietzsche, Balzac and Castiglione are crucial, as recent criticism has shown. Some attention has also been paid to the function of his literary criticism, though no attempt has been made to explain the way it worked in terms of Yeats's own imagination. A passage in the *Autobiographies* is illuminating. Yeats reveals that O'Leary had once said to him that 'neither England nor Ireland knows the good from the bad in any art, but Ireland unlike England does not hate the good when it is pointed out to them'. Accepting this as a truism, and observing that his fellow countrymen had turned from politics to literature after the fall of Parnell, Yeats says that he began 'to plot and scheme how one might seal with the right image the soft wax before it began to harden'. The right image, he decided, could come from 'a national literature that made Ireland beautiful in memory, and yet had been freed from provincialism by an exacting criticism, a European pose'.[46] The final two words are the most significant. As with his work in the theatre and his reading, Yeats, as a critic, assumed a European pose. It is necessary to remember that, particularly in his early days, this pose was not always well-informed. On 2 December 1898, at the height of the *Express* controversy about nationality and cosmopolitanism in Irish literature, Russell wrote with some urgency to Lady Gregory:

I wish Willie would leave the Decadents alone and apply his fine sentences properly. His theory is right enough but he sweeps in illustrations in the most reckless way, men whom he has not read, like Mallarmé. . . . Would you believe it! He only knew two of Mallarmé's lyrics. Willie Magee, who reads French like a native, wonders at Yeats's application of mysticism to such men.[47]

Though this letter should not be taken as an index of the poet's knowledge of European literature, it should be read as a cautionary tale about that knowledge. The issue for Yeats, an issue which

Russell could not understand, was not the extent of his knowledge of Mallarmé but that he should range himself alongside the French poet.

Two images are instructive for understanding the way this 'European pose' affected Yeats's imagination. There is Auden's metaphor of the dyer's hand.[48] Yeats's imagination slowly but perceptibly took its colour from his reading of European literature. The tincture of Europeanism that is evident in the poetry from the early nineteen-hundreds gives way to deeper dyes as one progresses from 'The Wind Among the Reeds' to 'In the Seven Woods' and beyond. The second image is contained in a sentence from Goethe's *Wilhelm Meister*, which Yeats declared was one of his great books, and from which he loved to quote: 'The Poor are; the rich are enabled so to seem.'[49] By assuming a European pose, to some extent in the theatre, but more so through his reading and his literary criticism, Yeats, as a poet, was enabled so to seem European.

Though this Europeanism distinguishes many of the great poems of the mature Yeats, the fantastic begins to reassert itself in the late poetry through figures like Crazy Jane and Tom the Lunatic. It is as if, having won Ireland for Europe, Yeats can revert to reclaiming Ireland for himself. So confident is he of the power of his poetry that he can again delight in the fantastic.[50]

YEATS THE EUROPEAN

C. K. STEAD

I suppose everyone preparing a paper for this conference must have given a long thought to the word 'European'. Or perhaps not. A European (whatever that might be) — a resident of Europe — might give less thought to it than an American; and I think an American might give it less thought than a New Zealander.

Am I a European? Am I more or less European than W. B. Yeats? What is Europe? What are its boundaries? Is it a racial category, or a geographical one? Or again, is it cultural?

I was born and brought up in New Zealand. Racially I am European, and I suppose culturally — though geographical removal begins to have a bearing on culture, and the official (and therefore not entirely truthful) description of New Zealand is that it is a bi-cultural society. Neither of my parents ever crossed the equator into the Northern Hemisphere; and although I have crossed it many times it has always been with the intention of crossing back again after a given period.

On the other hand one of my great-uncles was killed in France in the 1914-18 war and must be buried there; and an uncle was wounded and captured in Crete in the 1939-45 war and spent a number of years in a German prisoner-of-war camp. Does New Zealand's eager participation in Britain's recent wars make it more European than Ireland? Or could one turn the argument around and say that Ireland, a Catholic country, retained links with continental Europe which Protestant England severed? But how would that argument affect Yeats, who was of Protestant stock?

Here is another (slightly contentious) way of looking at the subject: In 1922, when Catholic Ireland finally succeeded in severing its ties with Britain — or, if you prefer, succeeded in throwing off the British yoke — Irish people became aliens in Britain. But Northern Ireland remained part of the United Kingdom. Workers from the Republic continued to be allowed free access to find employment in Britain. Tourism and trade continued; and the

119

English appetite for dairy products was as important to Ireland as to New Zealand. The BBC was listened to, and more recently watched, in Ireland. And now that Ireland has joined the European Community the two are part of a larger political bonding. One could argue that in some degree Ireland has never ceased to be part of the United Kingdom; that its freedom, when it came, was more symbolic than real. The dominant language was English, not Irish, and remains so. If Yeats is a great European poet he is great in the English language; and if the language were Irish, the sense of 'Europeanness' would be less, if only because it would be inaccessible.

I have introduced these random and perhaps rather idiosyncratic questions and comments in order to subvert as far as I can what might seem to be the purpose or hope underlying the title given this conference: Yeats the European. It suggests an invitation for us all to nod wisely and agree that though Yeats was a great poet, and Irish, he was not just a great Irish poet; he was also a great European. There's a sense in which this is true. How could it be otherwise? But the truism seems to me so obvious, it must be more interesting to challenge it than to affirm it.

With these general remarks in mind I'm going to discuss now the poem Yeats called 'Nineteen Hundred and Nineteen'. I may have to do a wide circle around the subject of the 'Europeanness' of Yeats, but by the end, or before the end, we will have come back to it.

Thomas Whitaker, in his reading of the poem,[1] tells us that 'the title of "Nineteen Hundred and Nineteen", reminds us of the Black-and-Tan terrorizing of the Irish countryside'. I'm not sure who is indicated by Whitaker's 'us'. Yeats scholars, I suppose — we who learn, and mislearn, Irish history by studying Yeats. And I have no precise knowledge of what, if anything, that date would immediately signify to most Irish readers. It does seem however that Yeats wanted to use the Black and Tan brutalities as his example of the breakdown of an old order. We know that the stanza about the mother murdered by 'drunken soldiery' describes a Black and Tan atrocity;[2] and that it is mentioned also in Lady Gregory's journal. But we don't know that from the poem; and whether we can agree with Whitaker that it is somehow indicated by the date appears doubtful. This is something I will come back to.

Let's look first at the overall movement of the poem; because it is not primarily *about* its occasion. Another instance of violence might have been chosen. The poem is about impermanence. It is, for most of its length, an anguished acknowledgement that nothing endures — not even art. And the anguish comes from the recognition by the poet that he has pursued an illusion of permanence — that in some degree he is still pursuing it. His activity and achievements have been in the sphere of time, and because of that, time will do its work on them.

The Tower as a collection is remarkable for the way it sustains and extends certain Yeatsian truisms and dogmas; and more remarkable for the way in moments of stress it throws them overboard. Yeats can be seen hanging on to his romantic devotion to Maud Gonne; but part II of the poem he called 'The Tower' can be read as a bitter rejection of that devotion — as if it had been a waste of youth and of life. In 'Sailing to Byzantium' he bids farewell to the world of 'dying generations' in favour of the undying world of art. But then, in the last stanza of 'Among School Children', that very Yeatsian proposition is suddenly reversed. Art is rejected in favour of nature, eternity in favour of time. The notion of an eternal beauty, represented in 'Sailing to Byzantium' by the image of the golden bird of art, becomes another of those 'self-born mockers of man's enterprise', while the images of perfection — dancer and tree — are taken from the mutable world, the region of mortality.

Finally there is Yeats's valuation of politics as something time-bound and inferior compared to art which partakes of eternity. This has been throughout his career surely the most consistently sustained dogma of the Yeatsian value system; and perhaps its consistency explains why no one seems to have noticed the extraordinary reversal that occurs in 'Nineteen Hundred and Nineteen'. It is not that politics is suddenly valued. It is that art is put on a level with it. After a life of insisting that art is superior to the political mode he suddenly stands back and sees them both as temporal — equally subject to time — equally illusory.

So we begin with the great works of the ancient world which are gone. They seemed 'sheer miracle' — protected against time and change — but that was an illusion. And from art in stanza 1 we move to politics in stanzas 2 and 3. The great artifact of 19th century Europe was not artistic but political and social — peace, stability, law, and with them a belief in Progress. All that has gone. Violence has broken out again. If we can face the reality (the poet tells us) it is that nothing — neither the work of great artist nor that of great statesman — has power to endure:

> no work can stand
> . . .
> No honour leave its mighty monument.

The despair which this induces in the poem is odd, and distinctly subjective. It comes not so much from the pity that nothing is stable and enduring, as from the fact that the poet is identifying with those whose great work will not last:

> no work can stand
> Whether health, wealth or peace of mind were spent
> On master work of intellect or hand.

Not too well hidden there inside the public eloquence is a private and familiar Yeatsian lament against the nature of things. *He* has spent health, wealth and peace of mind; he has worked to make these wonderful poems and now, late in life, he faces the thought that if time destroyed the work of the great Athenians it will certainly destroy his. 'Man is in love and loves what vanishes.' The only comfort is that

> all triumph would
> But break upon his ghostly solitude

— and we need to wait to section III of the poem to be quite sure what that means.

But now in section II there is a reconciling image — a very beautiful and important one. The nights of terror in section I are 'dragon-ridden' — the dragon represents the return of violence; or as Yeats says in a letter, 'the return of evil'.[3] In section II Yeats remembers Loie Fuller's Chinese dancers in Paris floating a ribbon of cloth so that it seemed a dragon. That is likened to the 'Platonic year' — the astrological cycle bringing change, destruction and renewal. In the aspect of eternity — *sub specie aeternitatus* — there is order in all things:

> All men are dancers and their tread
> Goes to the barbarous clangour of a gong.

The clangour is barbarous. Things are destroyed. But there is an order, a dance. Individual works are destroyed, but they come and go within the greater work of eternity. To create individual works is to try to stand out against the flow. One is not fortunate to have any success in this attempt, because ultimately it must fail; and also, more importantly, because it distracts the soul from its true work, which is to be absorbed into the larger order of things:

> A man in his own secret meditation
> Is lost amid the labyrinth that he has made
> In art or politics.

There again art and politics are surprisingly put together, and of no use in soul-making — because (as we learn from the lines that follow) after death the soul tends to cling to its bad earthly habits, artistic or political. The more we succeed in the world the more ill-prepared we are for what is to follow. Success develops the ego and the ego won't readily give up the ghost. It won't go out gracefully. Like other poems that would be collected in *The Tower* volume, this one is partly about man's preparation for death.

Whether the poem requires us to accept that the soul persists after death is unclear, as it often is in Yeats, I suppose because he believed and disbelieved at different levels of mind. In the opening of stanza 3 the soul's *life* is described as a 'brief gleam' —

> Before that brief gleam of its life be gone.

And in the last stanza the soul as swan leaps into a heaven which is 'desolate' —

> The swan has leaped into the desolate heaven:
> That image can bring wildness, bring a rage
> To end all things, to end
> What my laborious life imagined, even
> The half-imagined, the half-written page;
> O but we dreamed to mend
> Whatever mischief seemed
> To afflict mankind, but now
> That winds of winter blow
> Learn that we were crack-pated when we dreamed.

Is the despair total here? Does it come from the feeling that the soul too must die — that it has nowhere to go — that 'heaven' is 'desolate'? Or does it come only from the recognition that the world must be left and that time will destroy our achievements? Whichever way Yeats meant it — if it was clear to himself what he meant — there's no doubt that he is suffering once again that recurring sense of having wasted a life in literary labour — 'this sedentary trade' as he calls it elsewhere — rather than having lived it to the full in action. The phrase 'my laborious life' harks back to that line about spending 'health, wealth and peace of mind' on master works which time will treat with the same indifference it has shown to the sculptures of Phidias. Now politician and poet merge into one. Both had the same good intentions, though the means were different:

> O but we dreamed to mend
> Whatever mischief seemed
> To afflict mankind.

Death approaches, the winds of winter are blowing, and he knows that dream was 'crack-pated'. Everything moves in its due cycle, despite our efforts and our naive notions that we can promote 'Progress'. The latest turn of the wheel is bringing new violence and horror into the world. Honour and truth have become empty words:

> We, who seven years ago
> Talked of honour and of truth,
> Shriek with pleasure if we show
> The weasel's twist, the weasel's tooth.

So what is left but mockery? Section V mocks in turn the great, the wise, the good, and finally turns on itself, mocking the poet who has nothing left to offer but mockery. In the nihilism of the poem's concluding sections we come clear of questioning and into a direct expression of the poet's current mood of despair. As Harold Bloom says, 'self-mockery in Yeats is always a sure gate to poetic splendour'.[4]

And so the poem concludes as 'The Tower' does also, with visionary lines representing the destruction of old order. Out of the 'tumult of images' and the 'labyrinth of the wind' lurches the 'insolent fiend' Robert Artisson, 'his great eyes without thought/ Under the shadow of stupid straw-pale locks' — a figure at once mindless, sexual and anarchic. Both in the section on mockery, and in this final vision of destruction, there is a kind of exaltation, as if Yeats is glad at last to have freed himself both of optimism and of analytical discourse. If Samson has to die he's glad he has at least the power to go out in the grand manner. And because there is a kind of joy in the contemplation of destruction, the conclusion renders section II of the poem, with its image of the dragon of cloth and the universal dance, more than ever central.

In its general sweep, then, this was not — and is not — specifically an Irish poem. In fact Yeats first called it 'Thoughts Upon the Present State of the World'. It was published with that title in the *Dial* in September 1921 and again in the *London Mercury* in

November. It retained that title when it appeared in a little collection called *Seven Poems and a Fragment* in 1922, and didn't receive the title 'Nineteen Hundred and Nineteen' until it appeared in *The Tower* in 1928. In that collection it received not only its present title, but also the date 1919 at the end of the text — and it is on this authority, I suppose, that Professor Jeffares and others date it as having been written in that year. But it was not written in 1919, and could not have been. As Jeffares tells us, the lines about the Black and Tan murder derive from an incident also described in Lady Gregory's journal; and that journal entry shows that the event occurred in November 1920.[5] Further, in letters written in April 1921 Yeats mentions that he is writing the poem. On April 9 he writes to Olivia Shakespear that he has written two sections; a day later to Lady Gregory that he is writing the third.[6] But there is an odd discrepancy. In the letter to Olivia Shakespear he tells her:

I am writing a series of poems ('thoughts on the present state of the world' or some such name). I have written two and there may be many more. They are not philosophical but simple and passionate, a lamentation over lost peace and lost hope.

To Lady Gregory a day later he writes:

I am writing a series of poems about the present state of things in Ireland and am now in the middle of the third.

To Mrs Shakespear in London, poems about the present state of the world; to Lady Gregory poems on the state of things in Ireland. Is the difference of the description significant? I think it is. I think it represents Yeats's curiously ambiguous position as between England and Ireland. But if the text is to sanction one of these descriptions then clearly the one to Mrs Shakespear — which became the title until he changed it in 1928 — is much more accurate. This is not a poem *about* Ireland. It is a poem about the state of the world — the European world — as Yeats saw it at that time.

So I come to the question of his changing the title and altering the date. Why did he not only rename the poem 'Nineteen Hundred and Nineteen', but give it that date at the end of the text when in fact it was written in 1921?

Before I noticed this discrepancy I thought the poem — one I've always admired — had one curious weakness. Stanzas 2 and 3 of section I so clearly describe, from a distinctly British point of

view, the great peace and stability of the latter half of the 19th
century. The event which destroyed that tranquil order was the
Great War of 1914-18. But Yeats doesn't write about that war in the
poem — and that seems to leave a curious hiatus. We leap from
those sweeping images summing up a whole era — the optimism,
the faith in Progress, the durable peace, the dependable law and
stable order — not to a European war but to a parochial incident,
the shooting of an Irish mother at her door by drunken soldiers.
I don't mean to minimise the horror. Such a killing is awful
wherever and however it occurs. But incidents of that kind had
happened at intervals everywhere in the Empire, and sometimes
in Europe, throughout the great peace which the previous stanzas
describe. In fact massacres occurred, and wars which, though
short, were nasty and brutish. (There was one in New Zealand in
the 1860s.) If an era had come to an end the Great War was the
event that marked its conclusion. Why does Yeats not say so?

It is, I think, because he has no satisfactory perspective on that
war — or at least can't allow himself one publicly. What he wished
said about it publicly he had put into the mouth of Major Robert
Gregory:

> Those that I fight I do not hate,
> Those that I guard I do not love;
> My country is Kiltartan Cross,
> My countrymen Kiltartan's poor,
> No likely end could bring them loss
> Or leave them happier than before.
> Nor law, nor duty bade me fight,
> Nor public men, nor cheering crowds,
> A lonely impulse of delight
> Drove to this tumult in the clouds.

'An Irish Airman Foresees his Death' is among the most perfectly
turned of Yeats's short poems but it is doubtful whether it represents what Gregory's feelings would have been about the war
he died in; and I'm sure it doesn't truly represent Yeats's either.
He was not indifferent to the outcome. Certainly he didn't want
to see Britain defeated by Germany. But the complexities of
internal politics in Ireland did not permit him to say so.[7] There
could be no acknowledgement anywhere in his poetry that he
favoured the British as against the German cause; and no
acknowledgement that war was an event whose magnitude and
consequences dwarfed everything happening in Ireland. To
admit that would among other things have seemed to offer an

excuse to the British for the severity with which they had dealt with the 1916 uprising.

Yet Yeats knew perfectly well the relative scale of things as it must appear to European eyes. In preparing a speech for the opening of the Tailteann Games in 1924 he wrote:

A fortnight before the great war a friend of mine was standing beside an English member of Parliament watching a Review in one of the London Parks. My friend said as the troops marched past 'It is a fine sight.' And the Member of Parliament answered 'It is a fine sight, but it is nothing else, there will never be another war.' There will never be another war, that was our opium dream.[8]

That is the same thought we find in the poem — but here it's clear, as it's not in the poem, that it was the 1914-1918 war which brought an end to the era of peace and order. In the same 1924 speech Yeats seems to welcome the onset of a new era of violence and violently imposed order. And, remembering that his audience will be international, he writes the acknowledgement that is lacking in the poem:

I see about me the representatives of nations which have suffered incomparably more than we have, more than we may ever suffer. Our few months of war and civil war must seem in their eyes but a light burden.[9]

I repeat, seen close to, the killing of the woman in 'Nineteen Hundred and Nineteen' is a horrendous event. But seen as an event in the kind of panoramic spectacle that precedes it, it is relatively insignificant. The switch from a European perspective to a parochial Irish one creates what I've suggested is the poem's one serious fault — that hiatus between stanzas 3 and 4 of section I. And the same problem is reflected in the two descriptions of the poem — to Mrs. Shakespear in London, a poem about the state of the world; to Lady Gregory in Ireland, a poem about the present state of Ireland.

So it appeared in England and America first, in periodicals, as 'Thoughts upon the Present State of the World'; and in *Seven Poems and a Fragment*. But when Yeats came to put together his 1928 collection he altered the title, and, as if to emphasize it, dated the text 1919.

I don't pretend to be able to answer with certainty why the date 1919 was chosen; but I do reject one suggestion put to me after this paper was first delivered, that it was simply a matter of

forgetfulness. A date at the foot of a text might well be wrong
simply through carelessness; but a date as *title* means that the
year chosen signifies something particular.

Many commentaries[10] take the year as simply signifying the
Black and Tan terror, and that was my own first assumption. I'm
assured however[11] that no Black and Tan troops were deployed
until the early months of 1920; and certainly 1920 was the year
when the particular killing described in section I occurred. On
the other hand 1919 is the year when the post-war Irish troubles,
leading finally to independence, began.

But Yeats's view of history at this time, and in this poem, is not
just Irish. It is European. By 1919 the fear for some, excitement
for others, of the 1917 Bolshevik revolution was extending its
influence through Europe. A Communist International was
founded in that year; and Yeats was nervous that the Nationalist
struggle in Ireland might begin to take the form of a socialist
revolution. 1919 was also the year of the Versailles treaty which it
had been vainly hoped might include some consideration of
Ireland's claim for self-determination.

For Yeats personally 1919 was significant because it was the
year in which he became at last a father, and his excitement mixed
with apprehension can be felt in 'A Prayer for my Daughter' and
'The Second Coming', both written in that year. And all of this,
for him, was given a 'philosophical' context by his thinking
towards *A Vision*. 1919 (if I understand these matters correctly)
saw the world, in Phase 22, beginning to move back from 'antithetical' (aristocratic) towards the primary (democratic) darkness
in which the cycle began, and out of which the new cycle of history
would be violently born.

One can see that 'Thoughts upon the Present State of the World'
was an unsatisfactory title for the 1928 volume unless the text was
dated. He was not, after all, writing about the state of the world
in 1928. But why was not the original title kept and the true date,
1921, put at the foot of the text? If that had been done there would
not have been the problem which now occurs in section IV:

> We who seven years ago
> Talked of honour and of truth,
> Shriek with pleasure if we show
> The weasel's twist, the weasel's tooth.

Seven years ago in 1921, when the poem was written, takes us
back to 1914 and the outbreak of the European war, which was no

doubt what he meant when he wrote it. Seven years back from 1919 takes us to 1912 and nothing in particular.[12]

I offer speculation at this point, not confident assertion; and it seems more important to have raised the question of the dating and title than to pretend to answer it finally. But I have in mind that some essential conflict is represented here between Irish Yeats and Yeats the European. In a letter written to George Russell in the crucial year, 1919, Yeats speaks of Ireland's 'lunatic faculty of going against everything it believes England to affirm'. And he adds in a postscript:

Do you remember a European question on which Ireland did not at once take the opposite side to England? — well, that kills all thought and encourages the most miserable form of mob rhetoric.[13]

What is monumentally missing from 'Nineteen Hundred and Nineteen', though it also lurks there shadowy and undeclared, is the Great War — just as the most notable gap in Yeats's *Oxford Book of Modern Verse* is the result of his refusal to include the English poets of that war. For Yeats and the Irish Republicans it was England's war, not Ireland's; and if Robert Gregory fought and died in it that was his business and had nothing to do with England, Germany, politics, or morality. 'A lonely impulse of delight, Drove to this tumult . . . ' Gregory's nobility as an aristocrat and artist were displayed there; while the English war poets, making mirrors of their minds, consumed with pity for the men under their command ('the poetry is in the pity', Owen had said), lacked 'tragic joy' and turned the war into something philosophically meaningless: 'some blunderer has driven his car on to the wrong side of the road — that is all.'[14]

Here, as elsewhere in Yeats, one feels the short Irish view to be at odds with the long European one. On the one hand 'Nineteen Hundred and Nineteen' is saying 'We Irish were promised Home Rule when the war was concluded and got instead the Black and Tans'; on the other it is saying 'Europe thought it had order, peace, law and progress for all time but now the new phase of history brings violence and terror back into the world'. Those are two orders of discourse, one political, the other historical-philosophical, and it is not easy to reconcile them within a single poem. It is this problem, I suspect, which leads to Yeats's fiddling with title and date. My suggestion is, then, that Yeats is sometimes, inevitably, guilty of the Irish 'lunatic faculty' he describes in his letter to George Russell. His Irish fix on, or fixation with,

England, distorts the wider European focus. It is in this sense that he can sometimes seem *parochial* Irish, causing his greatness as a European to waver.

THE PRESENCE OF THE POET: OR WHAT SAT DOWN AT THE BREAKFAST TABLE?

MICHAEL SIDNELL

In his *Nobel Lecture*, Czeslaw Milosz speaks of the 'insoluble contradiction . . . giving no peace of mind either day or night . . . the contradiction between being and action . . . between art and solidarity with one's "fellow men" '.[1] For him, political circumstances made solidarity imperative and largely defined the poet's role as that of the insistent preserver of language, historical memory and values against a totalitarianism that threatened their obliteration. Under such conditions the poet's social role — his involvement and presence — becomes clear, not only to himself but to the audience for whom poetry is a means of survival. But part of the terrible price for this necessary solidarity, says Milosz, is the exclusion of that poetic contemplation of life in its given and permanent character for which a poet 'free from the snares of history'[2] may have leisure and room.

If the necessity for poetry is never so clear as when the governors think it worth their while to silence or censor it, then the defence of poets that Socrates invited may well start from that point. Henry Gifford did so in his 1985 Clark lectures at Cambridge, which were founded on the conviction 'that poetry will be called upon to play everywhere the part it has taken in Russia and generally in Eastern Europe'.[3] Whatever truth may lie in that grim prophecy, such a resolution of the Milosz 'contradiction' has seldom been forced on poets in this century in the West, though a number of the poets of the Great War and some Irish ones might be cited as exceptions. On the contrary the role of poet has become ever more indefinite and, in comparison with artists (or mere hacks) using other media of expression, persuasion and cultural self-definition, the poet would seem to be of the smallest consequence.

More often than not, modern poets have had some other role in life that implies 'solidarity' and may inform their words and actions for, though the idea of the poet as an accomplished

amateur whose real business in life is something else has been
discountenanced in our culture for close on two centuries, it
became and remains quite conventional in the twentieth century
for professional poets to hold a job, neither assuming nor being
granted a privileged position of observation. Thus they seem to
appease both Mammon and Socrates — the Socrates who would
have banished the mimics of all trades and masters of none.

Scorning Mammon and rejecting the Socratic idea of imitation
as applied to poetry, Yeats, though he engaged in many activities,
was by a self-definition, constantly reasserted, a mere poet. When
he wrote essays, letters, memoirs, plays and even (with more
mixed ambition) when he wrote stories he did so as poet. More
extraordinarily, in his public and political activities he claimed
the authority of poet, or allowed that role to qualify his words and
actions. In the late nineteen-thirties, writing the songs for the
Blueshirts, he assumed a rather frenzied, irresponsible, instinctive
poetic stance. Earlier — in *Poems Written in Discouragement*, for
instance — the poet is, by virtue of his poetic understanding,
social critic and moralist. But the most important aspect of Yeats's
role is that, while hankering after traditional, but unviable, roles,
he found himself having to fabricate it for his own place, time
and person. Pursuing this vocation so exclusively and with such
distinction and for so long, Yeats was and remains pre-eminent
and, in certain ways, an alarming example of what it has meant
and might mean to be a poet in the modern world.

In describing his poetic development, Yeats represented his
poetry as some kind of compensation for, or consequence of, the
absence of religious belief and lost love, strongly modified by the
particular circumstances of family, nation, and his own personality.
He insisted on the peculiar affinities of Ireland and poetry and
even his bitterest criticisms of his country — perhaps especially
them — implied that, for it, poetry was vital to its formation. He
made strenuous efforts to reawaken and to preserve the national
memory and, on emergent occasions, he made the poet's role that
of memorialist. And he used autobiographical narrative to order
his poetry and to link poet and country to each other and both to
a large scheme of history. But he remained deeply preoccupied
with the role of the poet, in itself, and ultimately committed
himself to a poetics of alienation that recognizes an extraordinary
sense of detachment of the poetry from the social and personal
substance of which it seemed to be made. This detachment is
associated with a great confidence in the permanence of the
poetry in the future to which it belongs — a characteristic of great

poetry perhaps — marked by the anticipations of responses to it in the 'coming times'[4]; and also by a profound sense of personal deprivation of an authentic existence for the poet in his own time, rather on the lines of the 'first till last alchemist' of *Finnegans Wake*, who

> wrote over every square inch of the only foolscap available, his own body, till by its corrosive sublimation one continuous integument slowly unfolded all marryvoising moodmoulded cyclewheeling history (thereby, he said, reflecting from his own individual person life unlivable, trans-accidentated through the slow fibres of consciousness into a dividual chaos, perilous, potent, common to allflesh, human only, mortal) but with each word that would not pass away the squid-self which he had squirtscreened from the crystalline world waned chagreenold and doriangrayer in its dudhud. (p.185-86)

Yeats's career was marked by what he and others perceived as radical transformations of himself as poet and this process was internalized as a major theme of his poetry and prose. A signal of one such transformation was given in 1902 in what may be the first reference to himself by name in a fictive context. It appears in the expanded edition of *The Celtic Twilight*, at the end of a story of lost love, told by an old man to the narrator's friend and now being re-told by the narrator, who identifies himself as Yeats and, even in this prose work, as a poet.

When the old man had finished the story, he said, 'Tell that to Mr. Yeats, he will make a poem about it, perhaps.' But the daughter said, 'O no, father. Nobody could make a poem about a woman like that.' Alas! I never made the poem, perhaps because my own heart, which has loved Helen and all the lovely and fickle women of the world, would be too sore. There are things it is well not to ponder over too much, things that bare words are best suited for.[5]

It would seem that the 'bare words' are those of this prose anecdote and that 'Mr. Yeats's' fears were borne out in 'The Old Age of Queen Maeve', a poem written at about this time, in which the poet's own story is represented as forcibly interrupting his attempt to tell the old one.[6] But, in retrospect, the allusion to Mr Yeats in the story and the 'interruptions' in the poem are the entrance into a kind of dramatization of the self that began in some poems of *In the Seven Woods* and continued through *The Green Helmet*, and *Responsibilities*: 'self portraiture', as Yeats described it, in 'a speech so natural and dramatic that the hearer would feel the presence of a man thinking and feeling'.

Significant features of this self-portraiture are the causal relation between the frustration of the man to the production of poetry and a questioning of the poetry so produced. In the poem 'Words', for example, Yeats tells how he has tried to make his 'darling' understand what he has done and tried to do 'In this blind bitter land' (p. 255) and how, despite his achievement at successive stages of an increasing mastery over words, a mastery that *should* have enabled him to make her understand, he has always failed to do so. The poem ends:

> That had she done so who can say
> What would have shaken from the sieve?
> I might have thrown poor words away
> And been content to live. (p. 256)

Whether being 'content to live' be a paradisal state or merely a complacent one hardly matters, since it is purely hypothetical; and the antithesis of this hypothetical state and poetic labour does not locate the real source of the frustration, which is inherent in the use of words as a mode of action. The poet has learned to make words obedient to his call and, he says, 'the best that I have done/Was done to make it plain'. What he has done is verbal and what he is left with is words; and whatever it may be, being 'content to live' is not acquiring a mastery of words in an attempt to explain what the exercise of mastery of words is. If neither his 'darling' nor his country seems worthy of the verbal effort, there is also something intrinsically self-defeating in such an *écriture*, whatever its motive.

In 'Upon a House Shaken by Land Agitation', by contrast, words are represented as richly satisfying. Here, Yeats asserts a continuity between aristocratic breeding and 'gradual Time's last gift, a written speech/Wrought of high laughter, loveliness and ease . . .'. (p. 264) But the relation between his own lineage and his writings is troubled by a fear of the betrayal of blood by words. In 'Pardon Old Fathers', he confesses that he has 'no child . . . nothing but a book . . . to prove your blood and mine'. (p. 270) In a much later poem, in which he addresses his ancestors on the same theme, the issue remains in doubt:

> Have I, that put it into words,
> Spoilt what old loins have sent?
> Eyes spiritualized by death can judge,
> I cannot, but I am not content. (p. 604)

Shakespeare made himself a gentleman-born, retroactively, by securing a coat of arms for his father: Yeats sometimes appears to be making a similar effort to prove his gentility through his poetry. But the problematic relation between poetry and breeding at the personal and historical level was subsumed by the more fundamental and positive concern which appeared, eventually, in such forms as his ordinance to his artistic successors to 'Bring the soul of man to God,/Make him fill the cradles right'. (p. 638)

This mission implies the resolution of the oppositions of life and work, poet and natural self, that were so emphatically present in the middle poetry. This resolution Yeats had achieved, in theory, in the discovery that informs some poems in *The Wild Swans at Coole* and the whole of 'Per Amica Silentia Lunae' — the discovery that he had not, after all, been attempting to portray an existing self:

> As I look backward upon my own writing, I take pleasure alone in those verses where it seems to me I have found something hard and cold, some articulation of the Image which is the opposite of all that I am in my daily life, and all that my country is . . . [7]

The creation of this opposing image makes the frustration of the natural self a mode of transcendence, not through a knowledge revealed to, and passively borne by, the poet, as in the very early and symbolist work, but through the deliberate transformation of nature into image or, to use his own – later – word, 'emblem'; it being the inescapable and determining function of the poet to effect this transformation; and to effect it first of all, in his own being.

In his account of this process in 'A General Introduction for My Work' Yeats uses the one word 'poet' for the writer and the written, and he makes it impossible to substitute for his single word some such pair as 'poet' and *'persona'*. The grammar of the passage harshly disallows such a straightforward distinction. 'A poet', Yeats wrote,

> writes always of his personal life, in his finest work out of its tragedy, whatever it be, remorse, lost love, or mere loneliness; he never speaks directly as to someone at the breakfast table, there is always a phantasmagoria. . . . even when the poet seems most himself . . . he is never the bundle of accident and incoherence that sits down to breakfast; he has been reborn as an idea, something intended, complete. A novelist might describe his accidence, his incoherence, he must not; he is more type than man, more passion than type. He is Lear, Romeo, Oedipus, Tiresias; he has stepped out of a play . . . [8]

If the reader should ask who sits down to breakfast the stony answer is that it is never the poet. And if the reader assumes that 'the bundle of accident' is the poet when he is off-duty, as it were, that is the reader's assumption. Grammatically, the bundle could be the next-door neighbour. And if the opening statement affirms that the poet does indeed have a personal life, even a tragedy, of which he writes, the reader is shortly reminded that, in the writing, the poet 'has been reborn as an idea'. Having 'stepped out of a play' he may be said to have a personal life in the sense that Lear has one. In theory the poet has displaced whatever exists of a personal self that is not mere type, passion or idea. That part, as in itself it is, was, or might have been, is no longer present to be expressed.

For a certain time, in the 'nineties and later, Yeats was troubled, he said, by a kind of poetry – invariably inartistic – inspired by common emotions associated with the Irish struggle for independence. One of his anecdotes on this theme tells how,

> some old Irish member of Parliament . . . recited with great emotion a ballad of his own composition in the manner of Young Ireland, repeating over his sacred names, Wolfe Tone, Emmet, and Owen Roe, and mourning that new poets and new movements should have taken something of their sacredness away. The ballad had no literary merit, but I went home with a troubled conscience; and for a dozen years perhaps, till I began to see the result of our work in a deepened perception of all those things that strengthen race, that trouble remained. I had in mind that old politician as I wrote but the other day —

Our part
To murmur name upon name
As a mother names her child.[9]

The image, in 'Easter 1916', of a natural love is, indeed, followed by a recital of names but the named men are also said to be 'transformed utterly' from the natural images of them presented earlier in the poem. (pp. 391-94) In a later poem this transformation is given more specificity when the poet asks 'What stalked through the Post Office?' (p. 611) and makes Pearse summon to his side not the historical persons but Cuchulain.

What Yeats meant by 'a deepened perception of all those things that strengthen race' would seem to be some phenomenal effect of the creation of poetic images. And this would be consistent with his assertion that the creation of an opposing image was not only a poetic discipline but a moral one, by which we 'imagine ourselves as different from what we are and assume that second self', and that 'Active virtue . . . is theatrical, consciously dramatic, the wearing of a mask'.[10]

This practical application of the poetics had political implications and it complicated the poetics. Insofar as the theatrical discipline – the wearing of the mask – was effective, the opposing image approximated an unaccommodated self, rooted, to use Synge's phrase, in the 'clay and worms'.[11] And, indeed, in the later poetry such images are sought. But, as images, they are inescapably simulacra of nature, seeming not being, and there is a deep pathos in the acknowledgement of this necessity; as we hear in 'A Prayer for Old Age':

> O what am I that I should not seem
> For the song's sake a fool?
>
> I pray — for fashions's word is out
> And prayer comes round again —
> That I may seem, though I die old,
> A foolish, passionate man. (p. 553)

This image, of the passionate old man, figuring in a number of the late poems, converges, it appears, on Yeats's recollection of his grandfather Pollexfen, whom Yeats recalled as both Lear-like and also as given to using very few words.[12] The figure deeply impressed T. S. Eliot, who cited an example of it as an illustration of the later Yeats's achievement of a form of impersonality together with 'that sense of a unique personality which makes one sit up in excitement and eagerness to learn more about the author's mind and feelings . . .'.[13] The fusion of the personal and the impersonal was enabled, in Eliot's view, by the excellence of 'the character of the poet' – by his will power, by his devotion to poetry, and by the completeness of his confession – and by the fact of his being 'a man who was essentially the same as most other men', which similitude Eliot sought to demonstrate with a reading of 'The Spur':

> You think it horrible that lust and rage
> Should dance attendance upon my old age;
> They were not such a plague when I was young:
> What else have I to spur me into song? (p. 591)

'The tragedy', says Eliot, 'is all in the last line', and since his ideal reader, at this point, is designated 'an honest man' and one who

is 'old enough', it would appear that the tragedy has to do with
the desperation of ageing and failing powers.

Not to dispute this, the last line also utters an old Yeatsian complaint which is specific to a poet. Here, it turns on the transaction
between the first persons nominative and accusative. The 'I' has to
put up with the 'lust and rage' in order to spur the poetic 'me' into
song. But for the necessity of song, the unpleasant emotions need
not be entertained or – to consider the matter more desolately –
worked up. The use of the third person in 'You think it horrible
. . .' dramatizes the situation and whether 'you' be taken as some
unspecified but particular person, as the reader in all generality
or as an inner voice, 'you' is, in any case, another consciousness
of the self. Together, the 'I' who is plagued, the 'me' who may be
made to sing and the observing 'you' constitute something like
Nietzsche's figure for the 'genius in the act of creation . . . the
weird image . . . which can turn its eyes at will and behold itself
. . . is at once subject and object, at once poet, actor and spectator'.[14]

The self that the weird image beholds, at the moment of the
poem, is, however, contemplating the stated emotions, not
experiencing them. Moreover, Yeats's metaphor represents them
as unauthentic, subordinate and feeble. Lust and rage 'dance
attendance' on old age, like lackeys, not it on them. Lust and rage
do not demand expression: they are used to stimulate it. The
pathos of the statement lies more in the want of these emotions
than in their horrible effects.

The most precisely and fully developed image, in Yeats's work,
of lust and rage as poetic spurs is the occasion of the composition
of the song 'The Twisting of the Rope' in the story of that name,
written when Yeats was twenty-seven, in which Hanrahan is
represented as making out with the daughter of the house and
being tricked out of doors, left disconsolate but with the poetic
frenzy on him on the sea-shore. When he reappropriated the
image, some forty years later, in 'The Spur', Yeats made the act of
contemplating it part of the poem, and fused narrator and subject.
Hanrahan, in the story, is the poet who suffers lust and rage and,
consequently, sings: the speaker in 'The Spur', understanding
this process, seeks to apply it.

Shirley Neuman has remarked that 'Hanrahan projects into the
world the persona that was Yeats's ideal for himself and anticipates
his final achievement of that ideal by many years'.[15] But what
does she mean by 'achievement'? The pattern of Hanrahan's life
in the set of stories is similar to that presented autobiographically
in the poems, but the unconsciousness of the Hanrahan *persona*,

spurred by wretched experience into poetry, is entirely inconsistent with the self-image of Yeats, the poet without illusions, who has 'discovered the law of his own being'.[16] Even in Yeats's earliest poetry, such spontaneous involvement as Hanrahan's in an experience of life that is 'unforeknown' (p. 413)[17] is presented as an image of an unattainable desire; as it is, also, in the explicit comparison of Hanrahan and Yeats in 'The Tower'.

One of the similarities in the portrayal of the lives of Yeats and Hanrahan is the vigorous cursing of old age attributed to both. But, even before he created Hanrahan, this was an established theme in Yeats, who claimed, accurately, to have made his 'first denunciation of old age . . . before I was twenty'.[18] Considering this, and the early appearance and recurrence of all the thematic elements in 'The Spur', the narrative of the self, supposedly here unfolding, resolves into paradigm. And this, I believe, is an overall effect of the reiterations and re-appropriations that are so essential to the structure of Yeats's work. In it, the autobiographical ordonnance and the emphasis on history sustain, *pro tempore*, the illusion of a reality from which poetry derives its language and images, but that supposed reality is challenged and undone with an increasing power and also pathos.

Mastery of the poetic image proclaims and demonstrates its remoteness from any supposed object and because it is enacted in the words the achievement is irreducible and terrible. The process is summarized and the meanings of the achievement are intimated in 'The Circus Animals' Desertion'.

The central part of the poem tells how certain poetic images and themes germinated in the poet's emotional responses to experience – in 'the embittered heart'. These themes and images assumed an emblematic form, that is to say they became figures of an assigned – not intrinsic or symbolic – meaning. These emblems, in their turn, generated dreams, which took possession of the poet's thought and became the objects (displacing the original ones) of his love. This crucial statement that, in the course of the poetic process, love is re-directed from the 'things' of experience to the contents of dreams, is repeated.

The last stanza celebrates the past production of poetic images and re-enacts the process:

> Those masterful images because complete
> Grew in pure mind, but out of what began?
> A mound of refuse, or the sweepings of the street,
> Old kettles, old bottles, and a broken can,

> Old iron, old bones, old rags, that raving slut
> Who keeps the till. Now that my ladder's gone,
> I must lie down where all the ladders start,
> In the foul rag-and-bone shop of the heart. (p. 630)

Of this poetic statement, Geoffrey Hill has asked: 'How is it possible . . . to revoke "masterful images" in images that are themselves masterful? Can one renounce "completion" with epithets and rhyme patterns that in themselves retain a certain repleteness?'[19] Pursuing the point further, the supplementary set of images – emblems of the heart's filthy commerce with the detritus of life: its use and re-use of the used, of the old, the worn-out, and disgusting – is newly wrought, by contrast with images from the early poetry that have just been cited. The immediate demonstration of the capacity to create masterful images is, paradoxically, in the context of a lament for the loss of this very ability and by means of what is said to be mere raw material for such images. So if the final lines of the poem sound exultant, there is reason for this in the rhetorical evidence that poetic failure has somehow been averted, notwithstanding what has been said. But the bravura of the last stanza and the eerie accomplishment of the transformation of the rubbish also presents us with a poet who not only does not fail but who cannot – not yet. He has lost his ladder but, like some unreconstructed Prospero, he is not ready to abjure his magic, not ready to relax the pose and not ready to sink down into the heart. The ambivalence is concentrated in the poem's last word, which is both the delayed identification of a masterful image and a reversion to the source of all images, to what, as itself, cannot be expressed: 'the embittered heart'.

What Coleridge called the secondary imagination – the faculty of idealizing and unifying, as in the making of poetry – became, in Yeats's poetics (with Nietzsche's help), the primary one. He proposed willed acts of imagination as instruments of temporal power by which the man, or the nation, might be remade in conformity with idea or image, the word to be made flesh. Ireland's obdurate resistance to Yeats's image of unity provided him with matter for much impassioned and bitter writing and even led him, at times, to look for a political adjunct to his poetics: 'No art can conquer the people alone – the people are conquered by an ideal of life upheld by authority.'[20]

The self he had at his disposal was more tractable, but his immensely powerful attempts to recreate it, in the poetry at least, as image or idea, something written and complete, were accompanied, and perhaps redeemed, by a desolate acknowledgement of, and longing for, something inevitable and, perhaps, tragically absent from this image and irrecoverable, something that a naive, linguistically innocent, poetry of 'no literary merit', based on illusion, perhaps, but expressing 'solidarity' and wholly involved with its subject could express. The problem of the relation of image and experience, language and thing, that Yeats engaged with characteristic rigour would seem to be a not unimportant one at the present time.

YEATS, TITIAN AND THE NEW FRENCH PAINTING

RONALD SCHUCHARD

Édouard Manet's death in 1883 went unnoticed by W. B. Yeats, who at eighteen was not only indifferent to Manet's battles with the Salons but already enraptured by his first master, Tiziano Vecelli. Nourished on the spiritual art of the Quattrocento, Yeats's delicate sensibility was now steeped in myth and symbol and shaped by Renaissance canons of subject, form and style. 'In my heart', he wrote, 'I thought that only beautiful things should be painted, and that only ancient things and the stuff of dreams were beautiful.'[1] Entranced by the dreaming eye of Titian's 'Ariosto'[2], which he loved above all paintings, his few modern excursions were to Titian's apostle and apostate, William Blake, and to the mythical figures of Rossetti and the Pre-Raphaelites. But in the following year, when Yeats enrolled in the Metropolitan School of Art, the spectre of Manet arose to violate the sanctity of Yeats's Renaissance reverie. From that bitter moment, Titian and Manet, embodying as they did the disparate visions of ancient and modern art, became the primary antagonists in Yeats's mind, the crucial contraries for the progression of his artistic vision. Again and again Manet would reappear to confuse and disrupt the formulation of his symbolist aesthetic, and repeatedly Yeats would oppose him with Titian's art, using it as model and corrective, turning to it for example and liberation. In the full historical context of this neglected conflict, we see Yeats emerge as the last Renaissance symbolist in Europe, as the true citizen of European art in Ireland.

Yeats's introduction to the new French painting came mainly from more venturesome students who returned from Paris parading theory and rhetoric. They urged him to admire Whistler and Degas, Bastien-Lepage and Carolus Duran, whose indifference to subject and whose devotion to externalities put Yeats in a rage. He particularly hated Lepage's 'Les Foins' for its depiction of a 'clownish peasant staring with vacant eyes at her great boots'

'Portrait of a Man', also known as 'Ariosto', by Titian.
Courtesy the Trustees of the National Gallery, London.

Above: 'Les Foins' by J. Bastien Lepage. Courtesy La Réunion des Musées Nationaux, Paris.

Left: 'Les Bockeuses' by Edouard Manet. Courtesy the Burrell Collection, Glasgow Museums and Art Galleries.

Above: 'Olympia' by Edouard Manet. Courtesy the Trustees of the National Gallery, London. Below: 'The Venus of Urbino' by Titian. Courtesy the Uffizi Gallery, Florence.

'Bacchus and Ariadne' by Titian. Courtesy the Trustees of the National Gallery, London.

'Eva Gonzales' by Edouard Manet. Courtesy the Trustees of the
National Gallery, London.

'Angelica saved by Ruggiero' by Jean-Auguste-Dominique Ingres.
Courtesy the Trustees of the National Gallery, London.

'Ta Matete' by Paul Gauguin. Courtesy Öffentliche Kunstsammlung Basel, Kunstmuseum.

'Portrait of William Morris' by George Frederick Watts.
Courtesy the National Portrait Gallery, London.

(*Aut* p. 125), and he was repelled by faces 'contorted with extravagance or curiosity, or dulled with some protecting stupidity' (*Aut* p. 170). His reaction to the realists was unequivocal, fierce and fixed, and in the *Autobiographies* he would forever harness Lepage and Duran with Huxley and Tyndall as a quadriga of scientific realism. But the most indelible offence to his romantic notions of art took place at the Royal Hibernian Academy when he saw exhibited there the antithesis of all he held sacred — Manet's canvas of yellow-faced *cocottes*, the pastel entitled 'Les Bockeuses'.[3] 'I was miserable for days', he wrote. 'I found no desirable place, no man I could have wished to be, no woman I could have loved, no Golden age, no lure for secret hope, no adventure with myself for theme out of that endless tale I told myself all day long' (*E & I* p. 242). His misery over this gross sacrilege gave way to hostility toward those who exalted it. 'All that I had thought beautiful, lofty, serene was attacked, not so much [by] the picture — that I could pass by — but by the enthusiasm of my father and other artists.' (*IR* p. 84) In the general adulation of Manet among his friends Yeats felt *la trahison des clercs*, and in their midst he longed for Titian's symbolic pattern, for Pre-Raphaelitism, 'for an art allied to poetry' (*Aut* p. 81). But wherever he turned for comfort, to early mentors like W. E. Henley, he found an opponent of Pre-Raphaelitism. Henley not only 'despised' Rossetti, but 'praised Impressionist painting that still meant nothing to me'.[4] In his insensitive scorn, Henley was perhaps chief among those who made Yeats feel ashamed and secretive in his taste. 'I have always loved those pictures where I meet persons associated with the poems or the religious ideas that have most moved me; but never since my boyhood have I had it without shame, without the certainty that I would hear the cock crow presently.' (*E & I* p. 347) In retreat, Yeats took refuge from Impressionism in the Cabbala with Macgregor Mathers and in the prophetic works of William Blake.

After shifting his medium from paint to poetry, Yeats was of course swept into all the intellectual cross-currents of the French *avant-garde*, rebuffing with rage or befriending with prophecy this painter, that poet, this dramatist. He heard eagerly from Arthur Symons of the symbolist poet Verlaine, but he dissociated himself from *la musique avant tout chose* as quickly as he did from *vers libre*, complaining in the papers, before he ever went to Paris, of 'the narrow devotion to mere verbal beauty of the newest generation of literary men in France and England'.[5] His enthusiastic discovery of Villiers de l'Isle Adam's *Axël* on his first visit in 1894 heightened his hopes that the symbolist tide in France would sweep away the Realist and Impressionist schools, a hope that was sharply dashed on his second visit in 1896 by the *première* of Alfred Jarry's *Ubu Roi*. 'I was in despair', he wrote, 'at the new breath of comedy that had begun to wither the beauty that I loved, just when that beauty seemed to have united itself to mystery' (*Aut* p. 333). He found more of the mysterious and Gothic in the symbolist paintings of Gustave Moreau, but that new exuberance was dramatically deflated in the Luxembourg Gallery, where he was suddenly arrested by the 'Olympia' of Manet.

Yeats disliked the painting instinctively, but his intemperate attitude toward Manet's beer-drinkers had abated and he was now deeply puzzled by this shameless courtesan. He observed it, as he said, 'without hostility indeed, but as I might some incomparable talker whose precision of gesture gave me pleasure, though I did not understand his language. I returned to it again and again at intervals of years, saying to myself, "Some day I will understand".' (*E & I* p. 242) By 1896 Yeats was trying overmuch to look at French painting with a more mature, appreciative eye, and he could see that Manet was a first-rate innovator with paint. He perhaps allowed himself to take some pleasure in the technique and 'vitality' — a gallery word for which he would later express contempt — but the painting was nonetheless troubling, the more so for its striking contrast to Titian's 'Venus of Urbino' in the Louvre. He would not have known, would he, that Manet had been a devoted student of Titian and had indeed faithfully copied Titian's 'Venus of Urbino' and his 'Venus del Pardo'? Nor would he have sensed, even subconsciously, that beneath the surface of Manet's *fille publique* there lay, as X-radiographs show us, a *fille honnête*, a voluptuous Titian woman?[6] No, but he did perceive that the 'Olympia' was Manet's leap into modernity, and Yeats found the impulse behind that leap both disquieting and intriguing. 'I shall some day like that athletic spirit', he said, 'and feel when I share its contemplation that I live for a moment another's stronger life.' (*IR* p. 84) Yeats was uneasy with the 'Olympia' because she had solicited from him a latent modernist urge. Whenever Manet found Yeats off-guard he would elicit that urge again.

Yeats's counter-urge was to bring order and hierarchy to the symbolist fold. Not only had he surrounded himself with a variety of symbolist types; for several years he had willingly surrendered himself to Blake's eccentric system, and to find needed distance from it he had to confront Blake's damnation of Titian. The pressure of Manet, too, may certainly be felt behind the writing of 'William Blake and his Illustrations to the *Divine Comedy*' (1896), for one purpose of that essay is to establish Titian firmly at the head of what Yeats termed, after Blake, 'the processional order' of visionary poets and painters (*E & I* p. 191). To Blake, Titian was that 'spectrous fiend' whose spirit dominated the Venetians and whose demonic blots and blurs obscured the lineaments of divine beauty. For twenty years, until he discovered the engraved, bounding line of the Florentines, Blake felt that his visionary imagination had gradually dimmed under the tutelage of Titian and his blurring demons.[7] To Yeats, the limitation of Blake's idiosyncratic view of Titian 'was from the very intensity of his vision; he was a too literal realist of imagination' (*E & I* p. 119). Blake's too severe association of divine beauty with the bounding line blinded him to the power of symbolic 'pattern' in painting. Titian was indisputably a great visionary, and it was unfortunate that Blake could not accept the technique of that vision. 'What matter', Yeats asked, 'if in his visionary realism . . . he refused to admit that he who wraps the vision in lights and shadows, in iridescent or glowing colour, until form be half lost in pattern, may, as did Titian in his 'Bacchus and Ariadne', create a talisman as powerfully charged with intellectual virtue as though it were a jewel-studded door of the city seen on Patmos?' (*E & I* p. 121). As he would state in 'Symbolism in Painting' (1898), where he brought magical analogues to symbolic art, 'All art that is not mere story telling . . . is symbolic, and has the purpose of those symbolic talismans which mediaeval magicians made with complex colours and forms, and bade their patients ponder over daily, and guard with holy secrecy; for it entangles, in complex colours and forms, a part of the Divine Essence' (*E & I* p. 148). Indeed, Titian's stature as painter and humanist in Yeats's imagination grew enormously with his study of the Cabbala. He saw Titian as the supreme inheritor of the hermetic, talismanic tradition of vision and symbol, integrating it successfully with the Christian tradition. In the 'Bacchus and Ariadne', quite apart from Christian asceticism, Titian commingled sexual desire and intellectual *virtu*. In rediscovering joyous movement, pagan abundance and the voluptuous body, he readmitted passion and desire to the chariot of vision. Thus it was Titian, not Blake, who emerged as the leader of Yeats's procession, the larger humanist spirit behind his symbolist writing.

The poem that illuminates this new ordering is 'The Two Trees' (1892), and while Titian may have painted joyously in both, to

Yeats the only joy for the modern artist is to be found in the 'holy branches' of the Cabbalistic Tree of Life, the branches of the Christian Tree of the Knowledge of Good and Evil having become inhabited by 'The ravens of unresting thought'. One by one Yeats had seen his friends, drawn inexorably toward Catholicism in the nineties, become prey to those ravens. Dowson, Johnson, Beardsley and others, unable to integrate their passions and desires into their ascetic spiritual quests, became lost in the morbid reaches of the self, members of a 'doomed generation'.[8] But Yeats was under the illusion that symbolists languishing in France had wisely bolted to the Tree of Life. Indeed, in 'The Autumn of the Body' (1898) he stands as apologist for their spiritual weariness, characterizing it as temporary exhaustion after a successful battle with reason and science. He saw his fellow symbolists on the Continent as weary adepts, and though their paintings and stories might portray 'frail and tremulous bodies unfitted for the labour of life' (*E & I* p. 190), he betokened not only an anti-Impressionist change in French painting but the advent in Europe of a supersensual apprehension of reality: 'We are', he wrote, 'at a crowning crisis of the world, at the moment when man is about to ascend . . . the stairway he has been descending from the first days.' (*E & I* p. 192)[9] Determined to turn away altogether from the 'bitter glass' of the Christian Tree, he soon announced publicly the Cabbalistic presuppositions of his mind and art in a new manifesto, 'Magic' (1901). He would later discover that most of his would-be adepts on the Continent were to remain aesthetes or to become communicants, but it would be years before Yeats could remove them from the processional order.

Such prophecies and manifestos were quickly lost on the Irish Literary Theatre, where from the outset Yeats's theories of symbolic drama met the mockery of George Moore and the realism of Edward Martyn, both Ibsenites. Seceding actors and nationalist societies took their impatient toll on Yeats's idealism, and so when he prepared the Abbey Theatre for its debut in December 1904 it was more coincidental than ironic that Hugh Lane brought the French Impressionists to town for an exhibition that would dramatically upstage the Abbey in the minds of most Dubliners. The apparent irony lay in Yeats's enthusiastic reception of the exhibition, and yet for all his sardonic exclusion of 'men like Degas' (*UP2* p. 134) from his personal vision of art, in his artistic politics he gave them the most non-partisan welcome to his vision of Dublin's cultural future. As early as September 1898, when AE called for the first Loan Exhibition of modern French art in Dublin, Yeats had responded with a public letter of support. 'I can well remember the excitement', he wrote, 'that the few good contemporary pictures exhibited in Dublin awoke among us . . . Every epoch has certain emotions peculiar to itself, and the student can only learn to express these emotions, and himself, from good contemporary pictures.'[10] Yeats now threw himself wholeheartedly into Lane's project of establishing a Municipal Gallery of Modern Art. Working tirelessly on the subscription committee, he even persuaded the Irish National Theatre Society to support the purchase of an Impressionist painting. When it seemed that the exhibition would be cut short because the Royal Hibernian Academy had booked its exhibition rooms to the 'paper-hangers' of the Decorators' Guild, Yeats wrote to the papers in protest and proclaimed the importance of the exhibit to Dublin. 'I myself am for the first time beginning to feel that I understand French Art a little', he added. 'I go almost every day to the Exhibition' (*UP2* p. 331). What he did not say was that the rooms of the RHA had become his trysting place, for what drew him back day after day was the 'Eva Gonzales' of Manet.

To heighten public interest in the exhibition Lane arranged for George Moore, J. B. Yeats and Sir Walter Armstrong to give a series of public lectures on the paintings. On 8 December, George Moore, *L'Anglais de Montmartre* as they had called him in Paris, gave his famous lecture on 'Reminiscences of the Impressionist Painters'.[11] To the disbelief of all who knew them, Yeats was on the platform with Moore, who was there not only to pay homage to the pantheon of Impressionist painters he had known at the café Nouvelle Athènes, but to glorify Manet as the god-like genius of the school. The 'Eva Gonzales', said Moore, 'is an article of faith. It says: "Be not ashamed of anything but to be ashamed." . . . he who admires that picture is already half free — the shackles are broken, and will fall presently.' (*RIP* pp. 19-20) Yeats patiently endured Moore's excruciating gospel of modernism, hearing him tell Dubliners that 'we moderns no longer feel and see like the ancient masters' (*RIP* p. 22) and assert unabashedly that 'the joy we get from the gift of painting like Manet's is a joy that lasts for ever' (*RIP* p. 28). But when the lecture was over Yeats stood up to give the vote of thanks with an earnestness that moved one observer to write to the *Irish Times* of how 'Mr. W. B. Yeats pleaded with us on Thursday night, with an earnestness that surely will not soon fade from the memories of those who heard it, to serve the generations yet to be in this matter, even it may be, at some

present sacrifice'.[12] Yeats reserved his personal response to
Moore's dogmatic reflections for the discussion following his
father's speech on 'The Art Instinct', in which J. B. Yeats defended
Millet against Moore's charges of sentimentality. Joining the
defence, Yeats suggested that the modern painter take for motto
' "Who wants to know the truth" (loud laughter)'. 'Do you mean
by the absence of truth deception?' asked the chairman. 'I mean
too great a respect for outer appearance', Yeats replied, 'and a
greater respect for internal reality.' [13]

It was this respect for internal reality that Yeats brought to his
third rendezvous with a portrait by Manet. In the 'Eva Gonzales'
Yeats experienced no Moore-inspired conversion to Manet, nor
felt any marvel for pose or paint. (Indeed, the only complete
pleasure Yeats ever found in Manet was his caricature of George
Moore at the Nouvelle Athènes, 'a man carved out of a turnip,
looking out of astonished eyes' [*Aut* p. 405].) But Yeats suddenly
isolated from that large canvas precisely what he disliked in
Manet — the displacement of 'personality' by 'character'.[14] 'How
perfectly that woman is realised,' he said to himself, 'as distinct
from all other women that have lived or shall live.' (*E & I* p. 242)
In the wholesome figure of Mademoiselle Gonzales he now
understood Manet's whole chronicle of Parisiennes, from *les
bockeuses* to *les cocottes* to *l'étudiant* — understood at last his former
half-pleasure in the 'Olympia', behind whose unashamed eyes
he saw no passion, no active reverie. Standing before the 'Eva
Gonzales' he comprehended the nature of his long quarrel with
Manet: 'I was carrying on in my own mind that quarrel between
a tragedian and a comedian which the Devil on Two Sticks in Le
Sage showed to the young man who had climbed through the
window' (*E & I* p. 242). Reimagining Le Sage's exemplum in
Le Diable boiteaux (1707), Yeats saw himself as a Don Cleophas
watching not the tragedian Giblet and the comedian Calidas, but
himself and Manet, each tearing the other by the throat in the
belief that his own art required more genius and skill. In Le Sage's
clashing characters Yeats found a fresh set of contraries for his
criticism, and in Manet he found a worthy antagonist, a comedian
for the diabolical fray in which he would fight for the superiority
of his tragic art. He should have heeded Le Sage's caveat, but
Yeats's father knew what prepossession drove him into tedious
combat: 'You are haunted by the Goethe idea . . . that a man can be
a complete man. It is a chimera — a man can only be a specialist.' [15]

The 'Eva Gonzales' brought Yeats a great release of spirit, freedom from the last vestiges of intellectual intimidation by Manet,

or so it seemed. Nowhere is his newfound certainty of mind more evident than in the series of philosophical 'discoveries' begun in his diary in 1906, its entries unified by his belief that great art must contain the 'personality' of the whole man, 'blood, imagination, intellect, running together' (*E & I* p. 266), and by his desire to show the effect on modern art of an absence of personality. Here, with a new exuberance of style, he began to infuse his Cabbalistic precepts directly into his prose, playing off the magical Tree of Life, with its full integration of human passion in the visionary process, against the Christian Tree of Knowledge, with its exclusion of passion from vision. But since the Cabbalistic context of his critical language remained undefined, the terms that characterize 'personality' in his artistic world — desire, passion, energy, reverie, dream, exaltation, ecstasy — would remain confusing to readers outside his magical coteries, especially when he used them interchangeably with their modern meanings.

Returning to his Italian masters in the National Gallery, London, Yeats stopped before Tintoretto's 'Origin of the Milky Way', afterwards writing in his diary: 'nearly all the great men of the Renaissance, looked at the world with eyes like his. Their minds were never quiescent, never, as it were, in a mood for scientific observations, always in exaltation, never — to use known words — founded upon an elimination of the personal factor; and their attention and the attention of those they worked for dwelt constantly with what is present to the mind in exaltation' (*E & I* p. 279). Unlike the saint, who must renounce the great passions of the world to find his eternity, the artist must devote himself to those passions permanent in the soul of the world to create eternal art. In direct criticism of the Impressionists, Yeats wrote that if an artist dwells on what is impermanent, so 'will his mind losing rhythm grow critical, as distinguished from creative, and his emotions wither. He will think less of what he sees and more of his own attitude towards it, and will express this attitude by an essentially critical selection and emphasis'. And, he added, 'we all feel the critic in Whistler and Degas, . . . in much great art that is not the greatest of all' (*E & I* pp. 286-7). Whistler, Degas, Manet, the Impressionists generally — all are to Yeats fine painters, but they do not belong to the processional order, do not partake of the ancient revelation, would not understand Yeats's newest definition of art: 'The end of art is the ecstasy awakened by the presence before an ever-changing mind of what is permanent in the world' (*E & I* p. 287).[16]

In the midst of these discoveries came a momentous invitation to join Robert and Lady Gregory in Venice for a tour of Northern

Italy. His mind was already there, engrossed in the sixteenth century through Edmund Gardner's books on Ariosto and the Dukes of Ferrara.[17] Late in April 1907, in full retreat from the *Playboy* controversy, he set out to relive the Italian Renaissance, to visit the Casa di Lodovico Ariosto, to walk with the poet in 'the green shadow of Ferrara wall',[18] to encounter him in a vision as he walked alone across the Apennines to Urbino, to find Titian and other painters in the 'sacred company' (*VP* p. 386) of Veronese. From town to town he reaped pictoral images from galleries, cathedrals, and tombs on a vicarious journey through a lost world of personality and great passions. Here he discovered anew his favourite images: the hollow-cheeked faces of the Quattrocento, the 'ghostly astonishment'[19] on Francesca's faces, the dreaming eyes of Titian, the symbolic pattern of colour and line spurned by Blake in the Venetian painters. But everywhere, too, his eye was alert for the first signs of restlessness, ambition, revolt, of 'an unstable equilibrium of the whole European mind' that he first saw evident in Shakespeare's mental journeys to Italy (*E & I* p. 297).

In Florence, inspired by paintings in the Uffizi Gallery, he resumed work on a discovery, 'The Holy Places'.

When all art was struck out of personality, . . . there was little separation between holy and common things . . . A man of that unbroken day could have all the subtlety of Shelley, and yet use no image unknown among the common people, and speak no thought that was not a deduction from the common thought. (*E & I* pp. 295-6)

His reflections on the gradual separation of art from common life by the close of the nineteenth century led him to cast off his earliest symbolist ally: 'And at last we have Villiers de l'Isle Adam, crying in the ecstasy of a supreme culture, of a supreme refusal: "As for living, our servants will do that for us"' (*E & I* p. 296). While he had Villiers on view, Yeats desanctified the once-sacred *Axël*, disavowing his interest in 'strange and far-away places' for the scenery of art, and declaring that he could no longer believe 'in the reality of imaginations that are not inset with the minute life of long familiar things and symbols and places' (*E & I* p. 296).[20]

In the discoveries that circumscribed the trip to Italy, Yeats had begun to excise the impurities that had encrusted his symbolist aesthetic since the 1890s, for his theory of the mask, based upon a Cabbalistic visionary technique — the externalization of the internal man — was rapidly forming in his mind.[21] Already he had described his sudden realization that, after years of trying to put his self into poetry, 'the more did I follow the opposite of myself' (*E & I* p. 271). And in his vision of an aged Ariosto in a medieval tower in the Apennines he knew that what he saw was the mask, the whole man: 'Certainly as he stood there he knew from behind that laborious mood, that pose, that genius, no flower of himself but all to himself, looked out as from behind a mask that other Who . . . ' (*E & I* p. 291).

By summer's end Lady Gregory had read out to him at Coole Castiglione's *The Book of the Courtier*, and as she read he heard in a single line the crystallization of his Italian discoveries, a description of beauty as 'the spoil and monument of the victory of the soul' (*IR* p. 88).[22] It came too late to effect the shape of his diary entries, collected and sent off to his sister's press as *Discoveries* in September. But Castiglione had set his mind running afresh on the relation of personality, beauty and tragedy, and all that had welled up from the Dublin Loan Exhibition and the Italian trip could not be contained in a slender volume.

It was in this abounding state of mind that Yeats attended the formal opening of Hugh Lane's Municipal Gallery of Modern Art on 18 January 1908, just as the Fays were leaving the Abbey Theatre. In the past three years the collection had grown to 300 paintings and drawings, and Yeats, who visited it daily, reported proudly to John Quinn that the gallery 'is a wonderful thing. Everybody seems agreed that it contains a finer selection of modern French paintings of the Impressionist school especially, than even the Luxembourg, certainly than any gallery in England. It seems popular too, for it is crowded all day'.[23] Pleased that his publisher, A. H. Bullen, had honoured his request to advertize his forthcoming *Collected Works* in the catalogue, Yeats wrote to him that, though he was terribly busy with the theatre, 'if all goes well, I shall write another set of Discoveries to fill your eighth volume . . . '[24] Yeats also had the scenario of a tragedy in mind, *The Player Queen*, which he began to think of as his first modern play, for in the presence of Manet and the Impressionists he felt again an old urge to find a modern face for his ancient art.

Before beginning to write the play he wanted first to return to the Paris galleries, for he had become absorbed in the history of European painting since his visit to Italy. When Maud Gonne kept putting him off, he fell into an affair with Mabel Dickinson. Meanwhile, as will be seen, something unforeseen had happened between Yeats and Manet at Lane's gallery. During the winter and spring his diary shows a sharp turn from the ebullient immersion in personality to an increasingly morose interest in the superfices

of the Impressionist mind. When Maud Gonne finally called him
to Paris early in June he was overly preoccupied with the centrality
of character in modern art. It would become a near-obsession that
would disrupt the articulation of his theory of the mask.

Yeats wrote to Quinn from Paris that he had 'come over here
partly to see Maud Gonne and partly to look at pictures',[25] but he
reserved for Mabel Dickinson a description of his movements. 'I
have spent my days at the Louvre for the most part', he wrote on
20 June. 'I find the things that delight me this year at the Louvre
are the big classic pictures by David & by some of the men of the
seventeenth century for the moment I am tired of modern mystery
and romance, & can only take pleasure in clear light, strong bodies
bodies having all the measure of manhood.'[26] The Davids — 'The
Consecration of Napoleon', 'The Sabine Women', 'The Oath of the
Horatii' and others — do indeed display the muscularity of
manhood, and Yeats's delight in them reflects his ongoing disin-
heritance of those faint souls adopted in the nineties, passive
mystics swept from the processional order like so many George
Russells. The major disavowal, however, was of Gustave Moreau,
whom he discovered through AE's early admiration. 'I was to
Gustave Moreau's pictures', he told Miss Dickinson, 'kept in the
house where he lived. I used to delight in him . . . Ten years ago
when I was last in Paris I loved all that was mysterious and gothic
& hated all that was classic & severe.' He then confided archly to
Miss Dickinson, 'I doubt if I should have liked you then — I
wanted a twilight of religious mystery in everybodies eyes'. But in
his diary he knew that he must record the serious transformation
of attitude towards Moreau, the final separation of disciplined
magical from vague mystical experience:

I could not sink myself to the dreams of kings and queens, witches and
unicorns, and strange jewels . . . of good and evil luck . . . A few years ago
I would have gone day after day . . . All those pictures would have been
to me as mystic gates that would make me long for [an] instant in the
shadow of a Pyramid, that I might pause there and meet the gods and
speak to them face to face. (*IR* p. 85)

Back in the Louvre, Yeats displaced his thoughts of Moreau with
his fascination for the more energetic Ingres, whose 'Perseus', he
reported to Miss Dickinson, 'is all classic romance — the poetry
of running feet & clear far sighted eyes — of a world where you
would be perfectly happy and have innumerable pupils'.[27]

However much this letter was tilted by romance, Yeats's primary
interest in Paris was historical — the movement and degeneration

of the Renaissance canon between Titian and Manet. 'Here and there', he wrote in his diary, 'even in modern times it has produced some masterpiece that does not any longer rouse to enthusiasm, "The Source" of Ingres, or the like, and many painters of power give it a half-acceptance — even the romantics that I have loved were not all academic — but at last', he continued, pointing to the Impressionists, 'a school has arisen which insists on the vision of the eyes and that alone' (*IR* p. 86). Yeats had now traced first-hand the European fall into disunity. In his dismay over the popularity and influence of the Impressionists, he must have found it particularly unsettling to discover that Manet's 'Olympia' had been transferred from the Luxembourg to the Louvre.

Yeats hurried back to Dublin, where he spent a week going 'again and again' (*IR* p. 85) to the Municipal Gallery, looking with experienced eyes upon familiar Impressionist paintings. Saturated with images, he made his way to Coole and then to Lady Gregory's summer house in Burren, Co. Clare, where he immediately began to dictate the scenario of *The Player Queen*. He wrote to Miss Dickinson that it was 'the only modern play' he had ever written — 'wild gay & extravagant, full of the sound of trumpets', meant to be a play of energy and passion.[28] On 17 July he wrote to his father that he was writing a second set of 'Discoveries' — his latest thoughts on Impressionist pictures, Lane's gallery, Castiglione's *Courtier* and pictures that surrounded him at Coole (*L* p. 532-3).[29] Mulling the changing canons of form in his diary, he wrote in recollection of the shock and anger that Manet's painting had brought twenty-four years earlier and of his subsequent reaction to the 'Olympia'. 'I now set out', he wrote candidly, 'to understand all these doubtings, shrinkings, hatreds, reconciliations . . . I wish to find out if I am a romantic of some kind, or only an ignorant man, puzzled at the middle of a revolution that has changed all about him' (*IR* p. 84).

Yeats was, of course, incorrigibly romantic. He refused to relinquish the canons of his magical world and believed it his role as poet-critic to defend and renew them. Sitting with his astrological charts on his knees, an 'old thought' came back to him:

We are completing in this age a work begun in the Renaissance; we are reuniting the mind and soul and body of man to the living world outside us . . . What the painters and poets who rediscovered landscape, joyous movement, the voluptuous body began, the astrologer . . . the spiritist and the student of Eastern contemplation are carrying into the very depths of the soul. (*IR* pp. 82-3)

His room at Coole was a sanctum of Quattrocento paintings by Gozzoli, Botticelli, Giorgione, Mantegna and others.[30] 'Here everywhere is the expression of desire', he wrote in his diary, and even the saints and martyrs who have renounced passion and desire 'must show the capacity for all they have renounced' (*Aut* p. 502). 'The men that Titian painted', he wrote in a later image of contained passion, 'seemed at moments like great hawks at rest' (*Aut* p. 292).

On the other hand, Yeats was uncompromisingly realistic in his admission that he was surrounded by an Impressionist revolution that had altered the vision of modern poets, who 'are proud only of the discovery of new material and of an impression of modern-ness. We are discovering always in our work what makes us different from all other men . . . For the first time the arts have become a drama of character, and of that alone, in subject and in style' (*IR* pp. 86-7).[31] Everywhere he looked he saw evidence of it; he needed only to step outside his room at Coole to confront the etchings of Augustus John, who worked 'without even a memory of those traditional forms imagined by artists, who were half men of science, out of a dream of bodily perfection' (*IR* p. 87).

Yeats had become increasingly possessed by the ubiquitous drama of character ever since attending the opening of Lane's gallery in January 1908. At the very moment that he had begun to desire 'a more modern, a more aggressive art — an art of my own day' (*IR* p. 84), he recognized that modern art was merely an art of character, that he could not take on its trappings because, as he wrote, he must be able to see 'precisely how each poem or play goes to build up an image of myself, of my likes and dislikes, as a man alive today' (*IR* p. 84). Yeats believed that if he was to prepare a way for his own art he had not only to re-educate his audience but to dismantle and discredit the art of character before their eyes. This overwhelming task, more than the theatre, was the sapping 'fascination of what's difficult' (*VP* p. 260).[32]

In December 1908 Yeats returned to Paris to work on *The Player Queen*, but it would not come, and as that play vacillated between tragedy and comedy it led him into a period of paper-tearing sterility. Gordon Craig asked him to write on the tragic theatre for his new journal, *The Mask*, but Yeats could not bring his new discoveries to rounded coherence for Craig or the *Collected Works*. Through 1909 his diary entries continued to record his paralysed preoccupation with passion and character, tragedy and comedy: 'Tragedy is passion alone, and rejecting character, it gets form from motives, from the wandering of passion; while comedy is the clash of character' (*Aut* p. 470). In their diabolical quarrel, Manet the comedian clearly had him by the throat. Only once in the year, under the pressure of his parallel reading of Balzac,[33] did the neglected theory of the mask force its way into script: 'I think that all happiness depends on the energy to assume the mask of some other self; that all joyous or creative life is a rebirth as something not oneself' (*Aut* p. 503).

Shortly after Synge's death in March 1909 Yeats went to dine and grieve with Charles Ricketts, his primary instructor in art for the past decade. Inevitably they talked 'of the disordered and broken lives of modern men of genius and the so different lives of the Italian painters' (*Aut* p. 518). Ricketts was deep into his study of Titian, who must have become one of the antipodes of their conversation. When Ricketts' book, *Titian*, appeared in April 1910, Yeats thumbed and re-thumbed the plates as he wrote the preface to Synge's *Deirdre of the Sorrows*. Yeats had rescued Synge from the ravens of morbidity after the deaths of Dowson and Johnson, and he had seen joy come into Synge's work. Now the elements of reverie and passion in Synge's last play gave Yeats an entry to the essay he owed Craig. Thus in July 1910 he gathered the fragmented thoughts of his diaries into 'The Tragic Theatre'.

What is startling and confusing about this brief essay is that it is not about the tragic theatre at all. It is about the haunting, irreconcilable conflict of Manet's art and Titian's art in Yeats's mind. Yet again Yeats catalogues his encounters with Manet's paintings, and yet again he counters them with Titian's symbolic art, with the 'Ariosto' and the 'Bacchus and Ariadne'. Superior to Manet's art of character, which is understood aesthetically by 'a delicate discrimination of the senses' (*E & I* p. 243), is Titian's tragic art, which breaks the distinctions of character that separate man from man and 'moves us by setting us to reverie, by alluring us almost to the intensity of trance' (*E & I* p. 245). Titian's passionate art is 'an art of the flood' — the flood of images perceived by the artist in the visionary ascent from reverie to ecstasy, the flood of images that enrich the imagination of the adept-observer of symbolic art. If we are painters, says Yeats, using his interpretation of Titian's art to define the principles of his own, 'we shall express personal emotion through ideal form, a symbolism handled by the generations, a mask from whose eyes the disembodied looks, a style that remembers many masters that it may escape contemporary suggestion' (*E & I* p. 243).

Whatever the readers of Craig's new journal made of this essay, it sharply reflects the frustration of mind behind Yeats's failed effort to elucidate his magical art, the Cabbalist drama of the soul. For his conclusion, he had at hand the interlocking images that reveal the cause of frustration: 'Certainly we have here the Tree of Life and that of the Knowledge of Good and Evil which is rooted in our interests, and if we have forgotten their differing virtues it is because we have taken delight in a confusion of crossing branches' (*E & I* p. 245). Yeats knew that his entanglement with modern poets and painters and the cross-purpose language of his criticism stemmed from those mixed branches. Thinking of his own gods, Yeats was the forlorn Arnoldian figure, 'Wandering between two worlds, one dead,/The other powerless to be born'.[34]

In November 1910, a month after Yeats's essay appeared, Roger Fry opened his famous exhibition in London, 'Manet and the Post-Impressionists'. When a portion of the exhibition was transferred to Dublin late in January 1911, Yeats immersed himself in it compulsively. On 1 February he wrote to Lady Gregory: 'I find seeing them as I do more constantly they grow on me greatly. I am buying some larger photographs . . .'[35] The primitivism of the paintings put Yeats back into a familiar prophetic mood, and after visiting the Tate Gallery in 1913 he wrote in 'Art and Ideas' that 'In the visual arts, indeed, "the fall of man into his own circumference" seems at an end, and when I look at the photograph of a picture by Gauguin, which hangs over my breakfast-table, the spectacle of tranquil Polynesian girls crowned with lilies gives me, I do not know why, religious ideas' (*E & I* pp. 354-5).[36] The subtle motive of this new essay, however, was to excise from Pre-Raphaelitism its elements of aestheticism, for he had come to associate the 'delicacy of sensation' with the Impressionist perception of reality. Once this dissociation was made, Yeats ceased his struggle with the many facets of Impressionism, pointing to the price that the imaginative arts had paid under its aegis: 'in our poems an absorption in fragmentary sensuous beauty or detachable ideas had deprived us of the power to mould vast material into a single image' (*E & I* pp. 353-4). In concluding the essay, he called for nothing less than a reintegration of the modern mind and a rediscovery of Titian's Renaissance consciousness, 'our more profound Pre-Raphaelitism, the old abounding, non-chalant reverie' (*E & I* p. 355).

The encounter through reverie of that single image — the anti-self, or mask — is at last the subject of Yeats's poem of liberation, 'Ego Dominus Tuus' ('I am thy master'). The poem is organized as Yeats's last dialogue with 'blasphemous men', and the Latin anonymity of *Hic* is a role for Manet and the moderns to assume.

When *Hic* questions *Ille's* pursuit of 'the unconquerable delusion /Magical shapes', he must suffer *Ille's* reply that the 'modern hope' of finding the self is the greater delusion, that 'by its light/ We have lit upon the gentle, sensitive mind/And lost the old non-chalance of the hand;/Whether we have chosen chisel, pen or brush,/We are but critics, or but half create' (*VP* p. 368). That said in verse, the quarrel with Manet was over.

It remained only for Yeats to cast off those French poets whom he read anew with Iseult Gonne in the summer of 1916 — Claudel, Jammes, Péguy. To Yeats, these poets, who had once affirmed that they, too, 'saw the world with the eyes of vine-dressers and charcoal-burners' (*Myth* p. 368), had surrendered the ancient vision. 'It was no longer the soul, self-moving and self-teaching — the magical soul — but Mother France and Mother Church.' 'Have not my thoughts run through a like round', he asked, 'though I have not found my tradition in the Catholic Church . . . but where the tradition is, as I believe, more universal and more ancient?' (*Myth* pp. 368-9).

Now, after thirty-two years, he was free of the French habitation of his mind. *A Vision* was upon him, and Titian was a central figure as man and artist. Yeats asked his spiritist communicators:

How are the images [of] the life after death state affected by the creations of genius. The ideal forms of Titians art let us say. The genius has received an element of ideal form from the past after death state & adds to this an element from its own experiences. What is the effect upon the images in the corresponding after death state in the future?[37]

There was no reply, but Yeats, who clearly believed that he was a distant inheritor of Titian's images of ideal form, continued to move Titian around in his mind. As a man, Yeats saw him as 'so markedly of the 14th Phase',[38] but as an artist he was placed in the 18th with Goethe and Watts, one phase away from Yeats himself (the 17th), both phases where minds are capable of Unity of Being. Watts's portrait of William Morris now hung over Yeats's mantle, because its 'grave wide-open eyes, like the eyes of some dreaming beast, remind me of the open eyes of Titian's 'Ariosto', while the broad vigorous body suggests a mind that has no need of the intellect to remain sane, though it give itself to every fantasy; the dreamer of the Middle Ages' (*Aut* p. 141). In *The Trembling of the Veil* (1922) that Titian-eyed portrait of Morris was held up unashamedly by Yeats as a rare modern reflection of Titian's 'resolute European image', one that has 'no trait in common with the wavering, lean image of hungry speculation' (*Aut* p. 142).

When Yeats and his wife George began to map out *A Vision* in 1917, Yeats and Lady Gregory had already begun to chart a decade of failed strategies to recover for Dublin the Lane pictures, which had gone to the National Gallery in London by a legal error in Lane's will after he went down on the *Lusitania* in 1915. As *A Vision* was communicated, Yeats was in relative peace, dreaming with Castiglione (and writing into the text) that beauty is 'the spoil or monument of the victory of the soul' (*AV-B* p. 293). But Yeats was never to be long at peace with the modern imagination, and when the new generation of post-war poets emerged his mind would record the after-shock of *The Waste Land*. Recalling the impact in *The Oxford Book of Modern Verse* (1936), where he dismissed dozens of poets from Owen to Eliot for their passive suffering, he focused on the monotony of accent in lines from 'The Fire Sermon':

> When lovely woman stoops to folly and
> Paces about her room, again, alone,
> She smooths her hair with automatic hand,
> And puts a record on the gramophone.

'I was affected,' he wrote, 'as I am by these lines, when I saw for the first time a painting by Manet. I longed for the vivid colour and light of Rousseau and Courbet, I could not endure the grey middle-tint — and even to-day Manet gives me an incomplete pleasure; he had left the procession.' (*OBMV* pp. xxi-xxii)

This excommunication, in a breath, of Eliot and Manet from Titian's train was, ironically, followed by the apotheosis of those French painters who inhabited the Municipal Gallery. 'The next time I go', he wrote in *A Speech and Two Poems* (1937), as he began his leave-takings,

I shall stand once more in veneration before the work of the great Frenchmen. It is said that an Indian ascetic, when he has taken a certain initiation on a mountain in Tibet, is visited by all the Gods. In those rooms of the Municipal Gallery I saw Ireland in spiritual freedom, and the Corots, the Rodins, the Rousseaus, were the visiting gods. (*VP* p. 840)

Yeats was ever the European citizen, true to the lifeline of art between Ireland and the Continent, selflessly loyal to the enrichment of his country's imaginative life. And if in other ways that citizen's impatience with the 'filthy modern tide' became more volatile in *On the Boiler* (1939), we are reminded there of another time and place, of Titian 'painting great figures of the old, simple generations'.[39] We recall then, in *Last Poems*, the flood of images that summons Titian's world with death-bed peace and fury, images of measurement and ideal form, images of 'Gardens where a soul's at ease' (*VP* p. 639), images of Ireland's eventual recovery of an ancient, plundered, European birthright:

> We Irish, born into that ancient sect
> But thrown upon this filthy modern tide
> And by its formless spawning fury wrecked,
> Climb to our proper dark, that we may trace
> The lineaments of a plummet-measured face. (*VP* p. 611)

Thus we must begin to see Yeats as a great Renaissance humanist, as the lonely, out-of-phase custodian of the ancient processional order, of that symbolist drama of the soul that the modern Europeans, fallen into the circle of themselves, had abandoned for the drama of character.

CAELUM NON ANIMUM MUTANT . . .

JOHN KELLY

'Caelum non animum mutant qui trans mare currunt' — those who change their skies do not change their souls, as Horace pointed out to his friend Bullatius as long ago as 20 BC. It is arguable whether Yeats ever changed his soul, either at home or abroad. In late life he said that 'our intellects at the age of twenty contain all the truths we shall ever find',[1] an observation which, however debatable in its general application, was certainly true for him. His whole intellectual and artistic development may be seen as one of working and re-working the compelling intuitions of his youth. His poetic enterprise starts from the *a priori*, and whether he ran over the seas, to Sligo, Paris, London, Florence, Coole or back to Dublin, his quest was, as Paul de Man felicitously puts it, 'Quixotic rather than Faustian'.[2] But a paradoxical Quixote: a Quixote not because he blindly follows an unfashionable code but because he is goaded by the very knowledge that it is unfashionable. A self-reflecting Quixote, perpetually interrogating the tradition he is desperate to revive and sustain.

This is where Europe was important to him: certainly not in orginating any of his ideas, but in helping, at certain crucial points in his career, that process of refinement and sophistication which constituted his artistic progress. We look in vain in Yeats for those cross-cultural creative shocks that made Eliot's reading of Laforgue, Carlyle's of Goethe, Baudelaire's of Poe, or Hölderlin's of Rousseau, so rich in their repercussions. What Yeats sought was not confrontation with the new but confirmation of the old, and he was especially delighted when that confirmation expressed itself in unexpected ways or foreign guises.

We are speaking here of a double process. Normally he took pleasure in those European writers who most corroborated his own thinking and who most gave him confidence to pursue his own aesthetic more vigorously — the discovery of the French symbolists, of Balzac, of Nietzsche, of Castiglione, and of Spengler fall into this category. At first sight the excitement and intensity

of these encounters suggest the jolt of something completely
new, but on closer inspection the shock turns out to be of
recognition rather than revelation. Balzac is commended because
he 'makes me understand, as I think, Irish life of 60 years ago';[3]
Nietzsche, although for a time 'that strong enchanter', is valued
not as an originator, but because he 'completes Blake';[4] and
Spengler's theory of history matches that of *A Vision's* instructors.
But on a few occasions Europe was able to give him experiences
that had a catalytic effect on his thinking and work. As 'catalytic'
will suggest, the elements that underwent the sudden recombi-
nation were already present in his gathering experience. But an
alien location, distancing him from the familiarity of Ireland and
London, forced him to start back and recognize as a culmination
or new direction what had been implicit but not hitherto explicit
in the process of his thought. It is this kind of experience that I
wish to discuss, picking out in particular three visits to Paris
which suddenly crystallized elements of his thinking that until
then had been held only in a fluid solution. These three occasions
— his presence at the first night of Villiers de L'Isle Adam's
symbolist play *Axël* in February 1894, his attendance, again at the
first night, of Alfred Jarry's *Ubu Roi* in December 1896, and his
discovery of the paintings of Ingres and David in the Parisian
galleries in 1908 — constitute three nodal points in his journey
from late Romanticism to early modernism. In these visits, Europe
acted not merely as a touchstone, but also as a whetstone for his
developing ideas.

It is no surprise that each of these events was visual rather than
literary, and if we distinguish two movements in Yeats's experience of the Continent, corroboration and shock of recognition,
we can, I think, make a further discrimination: corroboration
tended to be literary, shock visual — whether in art gallery or
theatre. There were compelling reasons for this: Yeats was a
notoriously bad linguist. Indeed, he was never able to master any
English (or Hibernian) ideolect other than his own, and foreign
languages were for ever beyond him. He made gallant attempts at
French, starting with lessons at William Morris's where, as he
unpromisingly reported, 'every one tries to talk French whether
they know any or not'.[5] His sister recorded his fellow-pupils'
amusement at 'Willie's dramatic intence way of saying his french
with his voice raised to telling disctinctness & every pronouncia-
tion wrong as usual . . . Willie of course divided it up into any
amount of full stops where there were not any so Madame said
"Mr. Yagtes you dont read poetry like that do you". "Yes he does

Yes he does" volunteered Mr Sparling & in truth he was rather like his natural way of reading.'⁶ This mildly amusing scene is not without its symbolic significance: in the very process of engaging with a new tongue, Yeats is characteristically appropriating it and adapting it to his already practised strategies of articulation.

No less emblematic is the way in which his linguistic deficiences rendered farcical one of the greatest non-meetings of the late nineteenth century. Yeats went to Paris in March 1894 armed with introductions to Mallarmé and Verlaine. Mallarmé, however, was in London but since neither his wife nor daughter spoke English, it was difficult to explain this to the 'espèce d'Anglais, qui est arrivé hier après-midi, voulant te voir et ne sachant pas un mot de français'. As Genvieve reported to her father, 'Maman a mimé ton voyage et il a enfin saisi, puis s'est retire'.⁷ This bizarre scene in the rue de Rome, although more appropriately Laforguean than Mallarmean, no doubt illustrated the Master's distinction between the representation of mime and the gesture dance, for thus — such is the hazard of the dice — was the eager questor-poet of the Celtic twilight cheated of his goal by the supreme artist of Absence.

Had he met Mallarmé, who taught English and could have conversed with him, what would have been the consequences? By 1894 not perhaps many. Mallarmé had moved beyond the dramatic interests of his early life to a more rarefied concern with gesture and the expressive (im)possibilities of language and typography. Symons later read out translations of his poems at Fountain Court, and Yeats was to suggest that they 'may have given elaborate form to my verses of those years, to the later poems of *The Wind Among the Reeds*, to *The Shadowy Waters* . . .'⁸ But Symons's versions were of the earlier Mallarmé, and he regarded the period after *L'Après-midi d'un Faune* as 'that fatal "last period" which comes to most artists who have thought too curiously or dreamed too remote dreams, or followed a too wandering beauty'.⁹ Yeats was later to tell Ernest Boyd that his symbolism derived from Blake, Boehme and Swedenborg (the last two, surely, the earliest and most significant of all his European mentors), and that he had 'never had any detailed or accurate knowledge' of the French symbolists.¹⁰ He has not contradicted himself: in *Autobiographies* he owns a debt of 'elaborate forms', not of symbolic texture. About the authenticity of his symbols Yeats rarely entertained doubts: they were inherited or had been vouchsafed; what occupied him in the nineties was how they might be sited and disposed to their full effect. And in this the Mallarmé of *Un coup de dés* could not help him so much as the dramatically richer Mallarmé of *Hérodiade*.

The one French symbolist Yeats did manage to meet on this trip, Verlaine, more than made up for missing the austere Mallarmé. Here, it seemed, was the authentic, almost more than authentic, left-bank Bohemian, living in a garret with an ageing mistress, crippled by diseases contracted in a misspent youth, gossiping with sometimes malicious intimacy about his fellow poets in an aura of easy-going adultery. As so often in Yeats, it is the vivid theatrical promise of the personality that engages him, the spectacle rather than the doctrine, and, certainly, on this occasion discussion of poetry seems to have been restricted to a series of one-line well-rehearsed judgements by Verlaine on his contemporaries. Yeats's memorial article recalling the meeting falls, however, into two parts as an anecdotal beginning swells abruptly into a vision of his ideal poet. Verlaine, we are assured, 'was a great temperament, the servant of a great daimon'[11] — portentious enough observations on a man he met only once over a cup of coffee, especially since Verlaine is the one major French poet from Baudelaire to Valéry to whom these terms conspicuously do not apply. Yeats seems to be foisting an image onto Verlaine with the purpose of alerting his Irish and British audiences to the differences between poetic and quotidian morality; he was to permit himself a more authentic comment at the Shorters four years later, when he 'spoke of P. Verlaine as looking like a Socrates who had been on the booze through the Christian era'.[12]

*   *   *

Despite some similarities, Mallarmé's poetic concerns were too intricately his own for Yeats to have been able to learn much from him. Where Mallarmé sought *l'infini* in *le Neant*, Yeats sought it in conflict; where Mallarmé resigned himself to the random chances of the dice, Yeats spent his life trying to call the odds and calculate the dice's fall. Nor were Verlaine's temperamental oscillations and musical plangencies sympathetic to his poetic personality or within his linguistic grasp. But drama was different, and in the winter of 1893-4 drama was much on Yeats's mind. He had already published *The Countess Cathleen* (which had, unknown to him, a French source) and the just-finished *Land of Heart's Desire* was in rehearsal — the first of his plays to be given a public performance. He was eager to establish a poetic drama on the British and Irish stage but troubled by the persistence of what he termed the 'commercial' theatre, and by the growing influence of Ibsenite realism. Exhausted after his efforts with *The Land of Heart's Desire*, he went to Paris for rest and recuperation, 'a quiet dream with the holy Kabala for bible & naught else, for I am tired — tired'.[13] He had, however, received a commission from *The Bookman* to review a posthumous production of *Axël* by the symbolist poet Philippe-Auguste Villiers de l'Isle-Adam, and this not merely prolonged his visit (the opening was postponed three times) but galvanized it. Even after thirty years he recalled the performance vividly, writing that Villiers' symbols 'became part of me, and for years to come dominated my imagination . . I was in the midst of one of those artistic movements that have the intensity of religious revivals in Wales and are such a temptation to the artist in his solitude'.[14] Here, then, is first-hand witness to that catalytic shock of which we have been speaking. Yet it is important to assess what elements combined and which did not, since where Yeats is concerned all reactions tend to be more complex than appears at first sight.

The works of Yeats most generally supposed to have been influenced by *Axël* are his play, *The Shadowy Waters* and his prose writings in the late 'nineties, particularly those in *The Secret Rose*. Before testing that supposition, let us recall the plot of this play which so fascinated him. In an article written soon after its performance he himself provided a reasonably accurate synopsis:

Sara, a woman of . . . strange Medusa-like type, comes to the castle of a Count Axel, who lives in the Black Forest studying magic with Janus, a wizard ascetic of the Rosy Cross. When she arrives he has already refused first the life of the world, typified by the advice of a certain 'commander' his cousin, the life of the spiritual intellect labouring in the world but not of it, as symbolized by the teaching and practice of the adept Janus; and she herself has refused the religious life as symbolized by the veil of the nun. In the last great scene they meet in a vault full of treasure — the glory of the world — and avow their mutual love. He first tries to kill her because the knowledge that she is in the world will never let him rest. She throws herself upon his neck . . . The marvellous scene prolongs itself from wonder to wonder till in the height of his joyous love Axel remembers that this dream must die in the light of the common world, and pronounces the condemnation of all life, of all pleasure, of all hope. The lovers resolve to die. They drink poison, and so complete the fourfold renunciation — of the cloister, of the active life of the world, of the labouring life of the intellect, of the passionate life of love. The infinite is alone worth attaining, and the infinite is the possession of the dead. Such appears to be the moral.[15]

From this and the tenor of the rest of the review it appears that Yeats was particularly impressed by five aspects of the play: by its occult trappings, by its symbols, by its ritualistic unfolding, by its heroine's self-presentation, and by its 'moral'. Yet of all these only the last two were to exert any palpable influence on him, and even they were overshadowed by the event itself. For, finally, the impact of the play was less a matter of the symbols it articulated than of the articulation of itself as a symbol — as an unfashionable but (he trusted) proleptic cultural manifestation, situated in its historical moment.

It is worth stressing this. Some critics have suggested that Yeats's exposure to Villiers' occultism, and later to the Sâr Péladan and the Saint Martinists, focused and deepened his occult concerns.[16] This is not so. In so far as *Axël* has any coherent philosophy it resides in half-assimilated notions trawled from Hegel, and an occultism heavily dependent upon Eliphas Levi; both of which sit uncomfortably with Villiers' new-found Catholic piety. Villiers dabbled with ideas Yeats took seriously and pursued more earnestly. Even by 1894 Yeats had learned more of, and thought harder about, occultism than Villiers had in his whole life.

This deeper concern manifests itself in the different quality of Yeats's and Villiers' symbolism. Although Yeats was to claim that *Axël's* symbols 'became part of me', those he lists — 'the forest castle, the treasure, the lamp that had burned before Solomon' — were evidently not sufficiently assimilated to become part of his creative work, and in fact he makes little use of them. It is true that Forgael's sailors find treasure in the later versions of *The Shadowy Waters*, but this has a quite different symbolic role from the hoard discovered in Villiers' play. Just as Yeats took occultism more seriously than Villiers, so (and for the same reason) he took the potential of symbolism more seriously. This was partly because he was more urgent — more 'Quixotic' even — in his desire for some larger sanction for his beliefs, but it is also because he not only believed that he had something to convey, but that he could call upon a potential audience to whom it could be conveyed. The failure of *La Révolte* in 1869 had turned Villiers' already vigorous antipathy for the theatre-going public into sullen contempt, and *Axël* was conceived more as a private work than one for open performance. While Yeats also disparaged bourgeois audiences, he cherished a more robust hope that he could find a public for symbolic drama, especially if its symbols were rooted in the imagination of the people by association with

myth and folklore. In all his revisions of *The Shadowy Waters* up
until the final one, his struggle is to order and control the
symbolic and legendary elements. For Villiers, who remained in
many respects closer to the Parnassians than to the Symbolists,
the struggle is with language not with symbols. Like Mallarmé,
Villiers distinguished firmly between poetic and quotidian language, and in *Axël* holds various discourses and rhetorics up to
scrutiny. Indeed, it seems almost as if the Commander is killed
more for the glibness of his small-talk than for any other mis-
demeanour. 'Tout verbe, dans le cercle de son action, crée ce qu'il
exprime', we learn. 'Mesure donc ce que tu accorda de volunté
aux fictions du ton esprit.'[17] For Villiers, it seems, words are more
than certain good. Compared with the artistic weight he placed
on language, his symbols perform a decorative rather than instru-
mental function: the rose that Sara plucks as she flees from her
convent, the Rosicrucian dagger with which she tries to kill Axël,
are stage props rather than integrated symbols. Moreover, in
organizing his language Villiers inclines to music rather than
symbol, and his most telling effects are achieved by the subtlety
of his prose rhythms, which require long paragraphs and set
declamations to work their spell. His inspiration is Wagnerian
and he needs the Master's length and amplitude to work his effects
towards a static ecstasy. Such ecstasy could only be attained, he
believed, through a carefully contrived poetic language, a language
which self-consciously distanced itself from the discourses and
registers of the everyday world and word. Ultimately Villiers'
lexicon and its effects are based on rigorous exclusion. Yeats, on
the other hand, even in his poetry of the nineties, was consciously
seeking to accommodate a transcendental metaphysic within a
wider linguistic reach, and symbolism was a crucial agent of
reconciliation.

Nor was Yeats's inspiration Wagnerian. He is a dramatist
because conflict is fundamental to his nature and to his
apprehension of the world. For this reason, even at his most
symbolic, his genius seeks embodiment; deed as well as speech.
The weight of *The Shadowy Waters* is carried by the action and the
symbolism. His effects are not accumulative as in the case of
Wagner and Villiers: he strives instead for a drama of climax —
'Tragedy wrought to its uttermost' — and to achieve this dis-
penses with prologue and exposition in favour of a more econom-
ical configuration of symbol and action, or, more often, symbol in
action. Such configurations owe more to ritual than conventional
dramaturgy and it was this aspect of *Axël*, that he found so

arresting: it 'did not move me because I thought it a great masterpiece, but because it seemed part of a religious rite, the ceremony
perhaps of some secret Order wherein my generation has been
initiated'.[18] Once again Yeats's views seem to coincide with those
of Villiers, but, once again, on closer inspection they are found to
be divergent. If Villiers draws inspiration from Baudelaire, Hegel
and Wagner, Yeats discovers his sources, among others, in the
anthropological writings of Sir John Rhys, Alfred Nutt, Andrew
Lang, and Sir James Frazer. The result is more *outré*, more
grotesque, more elemental than Villiers would have thought
proper. Yeats's imagination was more radical than Villiers' and as
such was quite capable of astonishing even his friends — Lady
Gregory, at an early meeting, was 'rather startled' to hear that in
The Shadowy Waters 'about half the characters have eagle faces'.[19]
His rituals reach further back into primitive thought than those
of Villiers, and one of his difficulties in writing *The Shadowy Waters*
was to incorporate a late Romantic hero into such a legendary
setting, while at the same time playing out through the masks of
drama the emotional problems that were troubling his private
life. In the end Villiers could not help him here, and he had to
seek deliverance from the unwieldy mythological clutter of his
play from George Moore, the quondam naturalist.

A fourth aspect of *Axël* which particularly impressed Yeats, and
one that did perhaps influence him directly, was the portrayal of
Sara, the last in a line of Villiers' 'cold women' that had begun
with Tullia Fabriana in *Isis*. Yet, even here we should beware of
ascribing to Villiers too central a significance. Sara takes her place
in a long line of precursors: Cythna in Shelley's *The Revolt of Islam*,
Keats's belle dame sans merci, and Rossetti's and Swinburne's
heroines. Nevertheless, Villiers had brought the archetype forth
in a new and compelling guise, making her a manifestation of that
'cold passion' which was to become a touchstone of true intensity
for Yeats. When Axël makes to kill her, because knowledge of her
existence will never let him rest, she exclaims, and Yeats quotes
her with rapture:

I am unforgettable . . . All the favour of other women were not worth my
cruelties. I am the most mournful of virgins. . . . I know the secrets of
infinite joys, of delicious cries, of pleasures beyond all hope . . . Oh, to
veil you with my hair, where you will breathe the spirit of dead roses.[20]

This was just the kind of woman to fascinate a sex-starved young
gnostic, and Yeats was to be similarly taken with Symons's version

of Mallarmé's Hérodiade, going to the trouble of quoting in
Autobiographies a passage for which (although he did not know it)
Mallarmé is heavily indebted to Villiers' Tullia Fabriana:

> The horror of my virginity
> Delights me, and I would envelop me
> In the terror of my tresses, that, by night,
> Inviolate reptile, I might feel the white
> And glimmering radiance of thy frozen fire,
> Thou that art chaste and diest of desire,
> White night of ice and of the cruel snow! [21]

Sara, like Hérodiade, contributes to one of the Yeatsian presenta-
tions of woman. Her tent of hair has been anticipated in Browning's
Pauline and in Rossetti's poetry, but takes a new inflection in
Yeats's work after *Axël* and becomes a reiterated motif in *The Wind
Among the Reeds*. He had long been obsessed with the Woman as
Sorceress, but in his early poetry his enchantresses owe more to
'The Witch of Atlas': Vivien, Mosada, Niamh, and the Enchantress
in *The Island of Shadows* are all more victim than vamp. After *Axël*,
for a brief period, a more disturbing and more predatory woman
makes her appearance in his work, inspired in part by Sara. But
these figures are only one of a number of Yeatsian versions of the
Ewigweibliche, for, whereas Villiers produced an identifiable
'type' from Tulla though Elën to Sara, Yeats is more interested in
the varieties and enigmas of the female psyche. In its most
extreme form, his *belle dame* is a muse figure, deriving as much
from Keats's Moneta and the Gaelic Leanhaun Shee as from Sara,
and issuing in his portrayal of the White Woman of numberless
dreams, and the Queen of the Great Clock-Tower. In none of her
manifestations does Dectora take on this role; rather her role is of
a second-order Shekinah in Forgael's divine fantasy. For the rest,
Yeats never lost sight of the fact that 'substance can be composite',
and that if there was one type of woman to be found in Swinburne
and Rossetti, there was another, antithetical type in Morris. [22] If
he dramatizes Grania as one kind of Gaelic heroine, he turns
shortly afterwards to her opposite, Deirdre.

Villiers' portrayal of Sara is essential to the theme of his play, a
theme that Yeats was happy to interpret for his readers:

The infinite alone is worth attaining, and the infinite is the possession
of the dead. Such appears to be the moral. Seldom has utmost pessimism
found a more magnificent expression. [23]

Yeats is at once fascinated and repelled by Villiers' pessimism, a reaction that pessimism was to provoke in him throughout life. Again, we are involved with a fundamental Yeatsian binary: the antithetical quest with its promise of self-transcendence, fulfilment and completion, that might after all turn out to be delusively Faustian or perhaps Quixotic, is opposed to a primary involvement with action and public good. Before he saw *Axël* Yeats's heroes tended to divide into those who opt for the world (for example the Countess Cathleen and Oisin who returns at last to Ireland and resumes life through lending a helping hand to a fellow-mortal), and unsatisfied questors such as Goll, Fergus, and the Man Who Dreamed of Fairyland. After *Axël* Yeats begins to brood more deeply on the possibility of fulfilment through the ecstasy and terror of transcendence. The quest becomes more energetic and the destination more apocalyptic.

This shift was gradual and always qualified, as becomes clear if we compare *Axël* with a story from *The Secret Rose* and with the version of *The Shadowy Waters* on which he was currently working. At first sight the story 'Out of the Rose', in which a last questor of a Rosicrucian Chivalric order meets his ultimate and fatal challenge, might seem imbued with the influence of *Axël* both in decoration and theme: the Knight bears a 'Rose of Rubies' on his helmet, 'the symbol of my life and hope', and his life has been one of ascetic dedication.[24] As it turns out, the tale was published a year before Yeats saw Villiers' play, but it is not merely chronology that disproves any influence: the spirit of the story is also quite different. Where Villiers praises ecstatic renunciation, Yeats's concern is impassioned conflict. Indeed, Yeats's thought and emotion are closer to Janus than to Axël: like the Mage he wished to explore 'the spiritual intellect labouring in the world but not of it' — the quest that Axël renounces — and much of his work is inspired by the conflicts that this ambition generates. Thus in 'Out of the Rose' the Knight and his Rosicrucian comrades are expressly ordered by their leader to turn aside from Axël's choice:

At first we thought to die more readily by fasting to death in honour of some saint; but this he told us was evil, for we did it for the sake of death . . .[25]

Instead, they are instructed to fight for good against evil, and the knight loses his life in a scuffle over those most ignoble of creatures, pigs. Villiers' hero yields triumphantly to a transcendental solipsism: Blakean Yeats was always seeking a way out of self-enclosure, and his conviction that art at its highest is communal and teleological was one of his exits. As the dying Knight tells the uncomprehending idiot boy, he and his fellows were under instruction to 'choose our service for its excellence'. And what was excellent was service to others — even if that meant fighting for pigs. Such a choice involves sympathy and compassion — qualities that are felt in the versions of *The Shadowy Waters* that Yeats was grappling with at the time he saw *Axël*, but which are far from evident in Villiers.

Although it went through numerous changes, the basic theme of *The Shadowy Waters* remained the same: a man driven by desire for the absolute sails with a woman to find it. In the version Yeats began writing after he saw *Axël*, Forgael, the piratical instrument of the dark Fomorian gods has grown weary of self-enclosure, of a world which seems but his own emanation, and is consequently in danger of being killed by his allies for ingratitude. He is saved by the approach and capture of a galley, crewed by the followers of the bright Danaan Gods, and in particular by a poet Aleel and his beloved Dectora. Forgael slays Aleel, woos Dectora by means of a magic harp, and wins her. In this early draft of the play, however, he realizes that she, too, is merely an emanation of his own mind, and so agrees to deliver her up to the Fomorians, only to relent at the last moment and sacrifice himself instead. After death his spirit resolves itself into a white Fomorian who announces that Forgael 'knows now the true love which is woven of/love for immortality & compassion for mortality'.[26] In other words, the experience of seeing and attempting to read *Axël* has not altered the theme which informed 'Out of the Rose'. If Axël's cry was 'As for living our servants will do that for us', Yeats's might have been 'As for dying we will do that for our servants'. Nor was this to change. If Villiers' ecstasy was to be recuperated for Yeats in the Nietszchean concept of 'tragic joy', it was always off-set by the Castiglionean precept of *noblesse oblige*. Where Villiers' characters are single-minded, Yeats's vision is teased into competing possibilities by his more richly complex imagination.

If the influence of Villiers' play was of limited importance to the texture and themes of Yeats's creative work, it certainly had a practical influence on him. It was the excitement of seeing it that persuaded him to take up once again his own abandoned manuscript of *The Shadowy Waters*, which he had started nine years before. The very fact of the production convinced him that the time was right for such an enterprise, since it allowed him to put a reassuringly optimistic complexion on recent theatrical history,

which he now saw in dialectical terms: the old commercial theatre
had been swept away by 'scientific' Ibsenite drama, which had
thus cleared the stage for symbolism and poetry, 'the imaginative
method of the great dramatists'. In announcing this, his enthusiasm
soared quickly to revolutionary — albeit conservative revolutionary
— fervour, for where France had led the way, others must follow:

The barracades are up, and we have no thought for anything but our
weapons — at least here in England. In France they had their Independent
Theatre before we had ours, and the movement which must follow the
destructive period . . . has come to them already. Those of the younger
generation whose temperament fits them to receive first the new current,
the new force, have grown tired of the photographing of life, and have
returned by the path of symbolism to imagination and poetry, the only
things which are ever permanent.[27]

The drama which had elicited this enthusiam lasted 'from two
o'clock until ten minutes to seven' (the precision with which he
noted the time of the final curtain suggests that even he may have
been reduced to clock-watching by the end) but the knowledge
that many in the audience found the play too wearying merely
increased his conviction that its performance was the first battle
in a victorious campaign:

It is nothing to the point that the general public have since shown that
they will have none of 'Axel', and that the critics have denounced it in
almost the same words as those in which they denounce in this country
the work of Dr. Ibsen.[28]

His immediate concern on his return to London at the end of February was the production of *The Land of Heart's Desire* by Florence
Farr. But his imagination, inflamed by the Parisian experience,
was already racing ahead, and he informed John O'Leary that she
was 'desirous of doing my next play as it is a wild mystical thing
carefully arranged to be an insult to the regular theatre goer who
is hated by both of us. All the plays she is arranging for are studied
insults'.[29] His brush with the left bank had given him a defiant
bravura that was to stand him in good stead, for, if he was spoiling
for a fight, his play, and *The Comedy of Sighs* by John Todhunter
that accompanied it, seemed to provoke one. 'For two hours and
a half', he recalled of the first night, 'pit and gallery drowned the
voices of the players with boos and jeers.' 'The whole venture has
had to face the most amazing denunciations from the old type of
critics' he complained to O'Leary, but added that it 'will be history

any way for it is the first contest between the old commercial school of theatrical folk & the new artistic school'.[30] This was to inflate a managerial mischance into an ideological occasion since, as D. J. O'Donoghue later pointed out, the disturbances at the Avenue Theatre were due not so much to 'outraged convention' as to the fact that it usually played pantomime and that its regular customers were deceived by the fey titles of the plays into supposing that this is what they would be getting.[31] They order these disorders better in France, as Yorick might have put it; but Yeats was bucked up by his London contretemps, and determined to believe that he was fighting on the Thames the same glorious battle as that being waged by the symbolists on the Seine. The prospect inspired him: by June he was announcing that *The Shadowy Waters* would be put on in Dublin that autumn; autumn however finds him delaying it until November; and by the year's end he is confessing forlornly to his publisher that he 'may have the play ready for you in a month but may not be ready for you quite so soon'.[32]

Nor was it ready. Despite the impetus of *Axël*, and despite all Yeats's strenuous efforts over the winter of 1894-5, *The Shadowy Waters* was not to be produced until nine years later, and the final version did not appear until 1906: a delay which greatly qualifies the influence Villiers might be thought to have exerted on its genesis. For, although a number of critics have been at pains to draw parallels between the two plays and one, Harry Goldgar, has even claimed to find verbal echoes, we should be as alert to the dissimilarities as to the likenesses. The first point to be made is that although in the months following *Axël* Yeats made an energetic new start on his play, the version that emerged shows, as we have seen, no trace of Villiers' influence. Curiously enough, Goldgar makes his major claims for that influence in the very last version of the play, the one that Yeats wrote in the summer of 1905 after watching a very unsatisfactory performance by the Theosophical Society. That Yeats should have waited eleven years before recalling a play that had been so immediately vivid to him should warn us that although *Axël* had been an incitement it could not be a model, and was certainly incapable of solving the artistic problems that *The Shadowy Waters* raised. Yeats found his play intractable because it tried to dramatize conflicting and often contradictory imaginative drives — drives that were further complicated by the emotional oscillations in his relationship with Maud Gonne — but failed to anchor these in any consistent mythological or symbolic framework. As in all his best work he is exploring the depths of his mind, but (perhaps because he is trawling even deeper here) the play not only cannot resolve the antinomies he discovers there, but finds it difficult to articulate them coherently. It is tempting to reach for Eliot's phrase and declare that Yeats could find no 'objective correlative' for his emotions in writing the play, or, rather, that it is encumbered by oppositional correlatives in such profusion that they fail to objectify themselves. The crux of the matter is that he can never decide whether to go on endorsing Forgael, the idealized youthful portrait of himself as Manfred, or, as maturity brings a change of view, whether the Danaan world of love and creativity is to prevail. If in its early versions the play is thematically rich, it is with an embarrassment of riches.

The very unsatisfactoriness of the Theosophist production brought home to the middle-aged Yeats the inadequacies, as he now regarded them, of his less mature vision. His ire spent itself upon Robert Farquharson, the actor who played Forgael, and he wrote in anger to Synge:

I think the most despicable object I ever set eyes on — effeminate, constantly emphatic, never getting an emphasis in the right place, vulgar in voice and ridiculous with a kind of feeble feminine beauty. The very sign and image of everything I have grown to despise in modern English character, and on the English stage. He is fitted for nothing but playing the heroine in Stephen Philips plays, a sort of wild excited earthworm of a man, turning and twisting out of sheer weakness of character.[33]

Farquharson was clearly far from ideal as the brooding Forgael, but underlying Yeats's invective is an acute discontent with his own play, with a style which he had now outgrown. He immediately retired to Coole to begin a thorough rewriting, and after a few weeks he was able to tell Florence Farr:

I am making Forgael's part perfectly clear and straightforward. The play is now upon one single idea — which is in these new lines —

> When the world ends
> The mind is made unchanging for it finds
> Miracle, ecstasy, the impossible joy
> The flagstone under all, the fire of fires,
> The root of the world.

There are no symbols except Aengus and Aedane and the birds — and I have into the bargain heightened all the moments of dramatic crisis — sharpening every knife edge. The play as it was, came into existence after years of strained emotion, of living upon tip-toe, and it is only right in its highest moments — the logic and circumstances are all wrong.[34]

Such revisions were not without cost, and some critics have regretted that dramatic power is gained through an over-rigorous simplification. It is in this process of simplification that the influence of Villiers has been most clearly detected: like Axël and Sara, Forgael and Dectora give up the world for a transcendent moment of pure passion; in their rejection of the world they even, we are told, echo Villiers' very words.[35] The matter is not quite so simple. As far as language is concerned, Yeats is in fact veering further away from Villiers in an attempt to gain directness through salty colloquialisms. He proudly introduces phrases about 'liquorice roots' and squeaking shoes, while a sailor announces that he is so randy he would even bed 'Red Biddy with the squint'. All this is as far from the careful exclusivity of Villiers' sonorities as it is from Yeats's early style: Red Biddy is out of Synge's Red Dan's Sally's ditch rather than the Count of Auersperg's mausoleum.

Nor is the mood of this late version close to *Axël*, even if the theme appears to be. Axël and Sara die in an ecstatic Wagnerian consummation; Forgael and Dectora do not die but drift off towards a promised but still undetermined fate, and their wooing is so asexual that they do not even touch, let alone embrace. Nor can their *lieberstod*, if and when it occurs, be unmixed ecstasy, since, in taking Dectora, Forgael thinks he is taking second best. He wanted an immortal passion: the gods have fobbed him off with a mortal love.[36] Hobson's choice no matter how loftily symbolic is still Hobson's choice. In this, *The Shadowy Waters* is some distance from *Axël*, and Harold Bloom argues convincingly that the play is unresolved because Yeats is trying to reconcile the spirit of *Alastor* with that of 'Epipsychidion'.[37] There is an even closer parallel with Keats. Forgael is like a disgruntled Endymion: somehow Cynthia and the Indian Maid have failed to coalesce in Dectora.

In his later poetry Yeats was to make extensive use of sexual coupling as an image of reconciled antinomies, but here he cannot put sufficient flesh on figures which were conceived in so symbolic a mode. He was aware of this, and even in its final form *The Shadowy Waters* is already anachronistic in Yeats's canon. The workmanlike way he set about putting Forgael right suggests a man with unfinished business, but business so long delayed that it no longer really engages him. Down-to-earth side-kick Aibric was beginning to sound more convincing than the unsatisfied questing hero: it was time to finish the thing.

* * *

One of the reasons Yeats took so long to finish *The Shadowy Waters* was that in the nineties he was constantly reappraising his aesthetic, a process greatly complicated by his second trip to Paris in December 1896. At first the mood of the city seemed to corroborate his own, for he had gone there 'to study some local things & people for a novel which . . . is to be among other things my final study of the Irish Faery Kingdom & the mystical faiths of this time'.[38] To this end he took hashish with the Saint-Martinists, met a Jewish Persian scholar who showed him an alchemical ring, and was introduced to Strindberg who was looking for the Philosophers' Stone. But the detonating and wholly unforeseen event was the performance of Alfred Jarry's *Ubu Roi*, the most tumultuous evening in the French theatre since the first performance of Hugo's *Hernani* in 1830. He was totally unprepared for this. Although he confided to John O'Leary that after finishing his novel he intended to 'return to more earthly things',[39] Jarry's play brought him down to earth with a far more resounding bump than he could have anticipated.

Alfred Jarry, the son of an unsuccessful bourgeois father, and a mother with social pretensions, was to live for a while in Saint-Brieuc, quondam home of Villiers de l'Isle Adam, before moving to the lycée at Rennes where he encountered the unhappy Félix Hébert, a well-meaning but hopelessly incompetent physics master. Jarry and his friends, the Morin brothers, composed plays and extravagant stories about him, one of which, *Les Polonais*, they staged in an attic. Jarry carried the text of the plays with him when, at the age of seventeen, he went to Paris to study at Lycée Henri IV. From school he became a man of letters, associated with *Le Mercure de France*, and counted himself among the symbolists.

Encouraged by Gustav Kahn and Paul Fort, Jarry began to rework the Père Hébert sketches and now called him by the infantile name 'Ubu'. Becoming secretary to the Théâtre de l'Oeuvre, which under Lugné-Poë's management had gained a reputation for both symbolism and anarchism, he insinuated his own play into the programme. Like Yeats, he wanted to challenge the commercial and realist dogmas of the contemporary theatre, and his play, no less than *The Shadowy Waters*, was among other things 'carefully arranged to be an insult to the regular theatre goer'. The care he took in such an arranging is evident from a letter he wrote to Lugné Poe setting out a six-point plan for its staging:

1. A mask for the main character, Ubu . . .
2. A cardboard horse's head, which would hang at his neck, as in the old English theatre, for the only two equestrian scenes . . .
3. Adoption of a single set, or better, of a single backdrop, dispensing with raising and lowering the curtain during the act. A person dressed correctly would come in, as in puppet shows, to hang up placards indicating where the scene was set . . .
4. Doing away with crowds, which are often bad on the stage and clutter understanding, thus, a single soldier in the parade scene, and only one in the scuffle when Ubu says: 'What a mob, what a rush, etc'.
5. Adoption of an 'accent' or better still a special 'voice' for the main character.
6. Costumes with as little local colour or historical accuracy as possible (which better conveys the idea of something eternal) . . . [40]

In the production the acting was even more stylized than this suggests, since Jarry took up the advice of his friend, Mme Rachilde, that he should emphasize as much as possible the puppet element in the play, although her idea that the actors should be attached to the theatre by strings 'since they are even bigger puppets than the others', was not in the end adopted.

It is striking how closely some of these instructions resemble a number of Yeats's own later theories on dramatic representation — the use of masks, the single non-representational set, the non-specific costumes — and yet what different aesthetic and philosophical ends they are intended to serve. They could not fail to make a powerful if disconcerting impression on him, and something of that impact is captured by Arthur Symons, the 'Rhymer' who accompanied him to the performance:

. . . the scenery was painted to represent, by a child's conventions, indoors and out of doors, and even the torrid, temperate, and arctic zones at once. Opposite to you, at the back of the stage, you saw apple trees in bloom, under a blue sky, and against the sky a small closed window and a fireplace . . . through the very midst of which . . . trooped in and out the clamorous and sanguinary persons of the drama. On the left was painted a bed, and at the foot of the bed a bare tree and snow falling. On the right were palm trees, about one of which coiled a boa-constrictor; a door opened against the sky, and beside the door a skeleton dangled from a gallows. A venerable gentleman in evening dress . . . trotted across the stage on the points of his toes between every scene and hung the new placard on its nail.[41]

The effect was completed by an accompaniment of fairground music composed by Terrasse. As instructed by Jarry and Mme

Rachilde, the actors imitated the stiffness of puppets and Symons described them as playing 'the part of marionettes, hiding their faces behind cardboard masks . . . and mimicking the rigid inflexibility and spasmodic life of puppets by a hopping and reeling gait'.[42] All literary Paris was primed for the opening night on 11 December 1896. The first word 'Merdre' brought the house down; pandemonium reigned for 15 minutes, and order was never fully restored. Immediately after the production, the critic of *L'Évènement* rushed home to take a shower: 'Malgré l'heure tardive, je viens de prendre une douche. Mesure préventive indispensable quand on sort d'un pareil spectacle.'[43] Dryer, perhaps grubbier, but certainly sadder, Yeats ruminated in his hotel room on the implications of what he had just seen:

> The audience shake their fists at one another, and [Symons] whispers to me, 'There are often duels after these performances', and he explains to me what is happening on the stage. The players are supposed to be dolls, toys, marionettes, and now they are all hopping like wooden frogs, and I can see for myself that the chief personage, who is some kind of King, carries for sceptre a brush of the kind that we use to clean a closet. Feeling bound to support the most spirited party, we have shouted for the play, but that night at the Hotel Corneille I am very sad, for comedy, objectively, has displayed its growing power once more. I say, 'After Stephane Mallarmé, after Paul Verlaine, after Gustave Moreau, after Puvis de Chavannes, after our own verse, after all our subtle colour and nervous rhythm, after the faint mixed tints of Conder, what more is possible? After us the Savage God.'[44]

It is an index of how far Yeats was from the spirit of symbolism, or at least late symbolism, that Mallarmé, named here as one at odds with the spirit of Jarry's play, wrote to congratulate the author in terms which are perhaps without irony:

> Vous avez mis debout, avec une glaise rare et durable aux doigts, un personnage prodigieux et les siens, cela, mon cher ami, en sobre et sûr sculpteur dramatique. Il entre dans le répertoire de haut goût et ma hante; merci.[45]

and Laurent Tailhade went so far as to describe the performance as 'une date qui fit époque dans l'histoire du symbolisme'.[46] With hindsight we may say that it marked not so much a milestone in the history of symbolism, as that point when a certain thrust of symbolism transformed itself into a certain kind of modernism. If Mallarmé gave it his blessing, Artaud and the surrealists were to reap its astringent harvest. As André Breton later reflected, 'beginning with Jarry far more than with Wilde, the differentiation long considered necessary between art and life has been challenged, to wind up annihilated as a principle'.[47]

Yeats instinctively recognized this. The Savage God was to slouch more and more into modern consciousness, and to take many aspects. For Yeats one of its more potent forms was as a levelling laughter. Implicit in *Ubu Roi* and explicit elsewhere in Jarry's writing, is the recognition that all hierarchies are pretensions because they rest on values of correctness imposed upon society, language, and meaning from without. Thus, as a compound distorted image of several tragic heroes, notably Macbeth and Julius Caesar, Ubu parodies cultural and aesthetic notions of the heroic that were dear to Yeats. He can also, recalling the categories de Man applies to Yeats, be seen as a gross Faust, or even as a materialistic Quixote. But the parody is not mock-heroic, for this would imply a prior scale of genuine values; rather it is an aggressive onslaught on the very concept of 'value'. As Apollinaire noted, Jarry's satire 'in its operations upon reality surpasses its object so totally that it completely destroys it'.[48] Yeats scorned the world but hoped to bring it to a sense of its own potential: Jarry takes it as axiomatic that the world is unsavable.

Yet Jarry's roots were in symbolism, and his concerns insist on reflecting Yeats's as in a crazily twisted mirror. More doggedly (if not more intensely) than Rimbaud he was preoccupied with abolishing the separation traditionally supposed to exist between sleeping and waking, between 'reality' and hallucination. Yeats believed that dream or trance might vouchsafe contact with a higher and more intense reality. Jarry's view was altogether more promiscuous: he refused to predicate a higher and lower reality: all life was a single entity, a sustained hallucination. He was to develop this view into a theory of 'Pataphysics' a kind 'of reasonable unreason similar to the workings of our dreaming minds'. Again, there is an apparent affinity with Yeats in a shared fascination with, and suspicion of, science: but whereas Yeats was to attempt to use the language and procedures of science to 'prove' his mystical and spiritualistic intuitions and experiences, Jarry was interested in the assumptions of science only as a method of subverting science. Yeats tries to build; Jarry to destroy.

But perhaps what Yeats found most frightening and insidious in the Savage God's laughter was the echo of his own subversive self-doubts. Looking back on the nineties, he recalled that as his literary and cultural plans 'became quickly or slowly everything

I despised, one part of me looked on, mischievous and mocking, and the other part spoke words which were more and more unreal, as the attitude of mind became more strained and difficult'.[49] As we have seen, he later realized that *The Shadowy Waters* was flawed precisely because it was the product of this unreality, having grown, as he confided to Florence Farr, out of 'years of strained emotion, of living on tip-toe'. Yet his temperament was not of the sort that was willing to succumb for long to its own disabling laughter and now, as later, he tried to save himself from the possibility of futility by reconstructing history. In the years immediately following *Ubu Roi* he therefore insisted, with ever more extravagance as conviction waned, that the symbolist aesthetic was alive and well. The author of *Axël* might be dead, but it was possible to believe that Maeterlinck had taken up 'the red bonnet from the hands of Villiers de Lisle Adam', and become the inspired leader of a movement which would dominate Europe in the coming century.[50] In a paragraph later omitted from 'Rosa Alchemica', he traced the history of

> that mood which Edgar Poe found in a wine-cup, and how it passed into France and took possession of Baudelaire, and from Baudelaire passed to England and the Pre-Raphaelites, and then again returned to France, and still wanders the world enlarging its power as it goes, awaiting the time when it shall be, perhaps, alone, or, with other moods, master over a great new religion, and an awakener of the fanatical wars that hovered in the gray surges, and forget the wine-cup where it was born.[51]

Under all lay a deep unease. Even in the review of July 1897 which announced Maeterlinck's apostolic succession there is an undertow of discontent. Maeterlinck has a 'beautiful pathos and tenderness' but his 'book lacks the definiteness of the great mystics';[52] already Yeats is half aware that 'this curious pathetic beauty' is too pathetic, too lacking in will, to bridle a Savage God. Maeterlinck's bonnet indeed turned out to be less red than a pallid pink, decorated with ineffectual bluebirds, and if such an art was no match for the fierce energies that Jarry had unleashed, nor could it contain or fully express Yeats's own unruly imagination — as his struggle with *The Shadowy Waters* illustrates. Still less could it bear witness to his increasingly harsh apprehension of the world. As early as 1894 he had told Alice Milligan that his 'experience of Ireland over the last three years has changed my views very greatly' and that 'Ireland is greatly demoralized in all things — in her scholarship, in her criticism, in her politics, in her social life'.[53] His sense of artistic isolation was deepened after he

experienced the political in-fighting on the '98 Centennial
Commission of which he was a Chairman. His increasing consciousness of the gap between the audience he sought and the
aesthetic he had embraced enpurpled his prose, and nowhere
more so than in a newspaper dispute of 1898 over the future
direction of the arts. In an article he entitled 'The Autumn of the
Body' he once more and even more magniloquently declaimed
the inevitable march of cultural history. The realism of Flaubert
has given way to *Axël*, 'the first great dramatic invention' of the
new Romantic movement, for

Count Villiers de l'Isle-Adam swept together by what seemed a sudden
energy, words behind which glimmered a spiritual and passionate
mood, as a flame glimmers behind the dusky blue and red glass in an
eastern lamp; and created persons from whom has fallen all even of
personal characteristic except a thirst for that hour when all things shall
pass away like a cloud, and a pride like that of the Magi following their
star over many mountains . . . [54]

This movement, he argues, is also manifest in French painting —
clearly he is thinking of Puvis de Chavannes and Moreau — and
sees

indeed, in the arts of every country those faint lights and faint colours
and faint outlines and faint energies which many call 'the decadence',
and which I, because I believe that the arts lie dreaming of things to
come, prefer to call the autumn of the body . . . We are, it may be, at a
crowning crisis of the world, at the moment when man is about to ascend,
with the wealth he has been so long gathering upon his shoulders, the
stairway he has been descending from the first days.[55]

But in the two years the new century was born, and looking back
in later years, he announced that in 1900 everyone got off his
stilts. Jarry, not Villiers, was the prevailing voice of modernism in
this aspect, as Yeats had unwillingly reflected on that December
night in the Hotel Corneille.

*   *   *

In 1908 Yeats was in Paris once again, staying for over a month
while he tried to finish *The Player Queen*. As this may suggest, he
was still absorbing the repercussions of his last visit, for it is not
too fanciful to see in this new play (which gave him as much
trouble to finish as *The Shadowy Waters*) an attempt to accommodate

the disturbing impact of *Ubu Roi* within a wholly Yeatsean framework. Jarry's influence was not direct, nor could it be since Yeats's thought and temperament were opposed to his, but Jarry, in offering a view of life and art that was more radical than that of the symbolists with whom Yeats sympathized, represented a challenge that had to be recognized. As in *Ubu Roi*, the central theme of *The Player Queen* is usurpation of royalty, and the use and abuses of masks. But the function of Yeats's masks is far from merely reducing humanity to its grotesque common denominator as in Jarry; they explore the possibility of escaping that reduction by questioning the relationship of character to personality, choice to chance, and self to self-transcendence. His protagonists are creatively bohemian not appetitively bourgeois, and his comedy far less savage and relentless. He had already tried to articulate the challenge of subversive laughter in *Where There is Nothing*, where Tolstoian assertion is opposed to Jarrian levelling, and in which the protagonist, Paul Routledge, is obsessed with an image goaded into life by Jarry's corrosive laughter: 'a very terrible wild beast with iron teeth and brazen claws that can root up spires and towers . . . My wild beast is Laughter, the mightiest of the enemies of God.'[56] This image haunts Yeats's imagination hereafter. In 'The Second Coming' it slouches towards Bethlehem to be born. Multiplied, it appears as the brazen hawks in the phantasmagorical conclusion of 'Meditation in Time of Civil War'.

> grip of claw, and the eye's complacency,
> The innumerable clanging wings that have put out the moon[57]

where the moon stands for that symbolist inspiration of Villiers and Moreau — still, as represented by the ladies on unicorns, seductively beautiful, but also insidiously and ineffectually narcissistic:

> their minds are but a pool
> Where even longing drowns under its own excess.[58]

It was not only the spirit of Jarry's play which invaded Yeats's view of the world; there is also evidence that he was receptive to the décor and staging of *Ubu Roi*. The 'old man with a red dressing-gown, red slippers and red nightcap, holding a brass candlestick with a guttering candle in it' who was to have acted as the Prologue of *The King's Threshold* in 1903,[59] may have been in part inspired by Jarry's 'venerable gentleman in evening dress' who

'trotted across the stage on the points of his toes between every
scene and hung the new placard on its nail'. Symons had described
Ubu Roi as 'a symbolic farce', an apparent contradiction in terms,
so far does farce seem from the ritualistic mysteries of symbolism.
In 1911, when he was more accustomed to the Savage God, Yeats
was to describe *The Green Helmet* no less oxymoronically as an
'heroic farce'. A few years after this he wrote an open letter to Lady
Gregory, 'A People's Theatre', where he confessed that objectivity
and comedy had come to dominate even the Abbey Theatre's
stage, and contrasted them with his own symbolic art. The letter
sets in opposition two modes of art, two states of soul, which had
been exemplified for him by *Axël* and *Ubu Roi* among others,
and he goes on to wonder whether mankind is 'approaching a
supreme moment of self-consciousness, the two halves of the
soul separate and face to face?'[60] Significantly, he symbolizes the
objective half as puppets, moving with the awkward artificiality
of Jarry's actors:

> Constrained, arraigned, baffled, bent, and unbent
> By these wire-jointed jaws and limbs of wood,
> Themselves obedient,
> Knowing not evil and good.[61]

The other half of the soul he represents as a dancing girl, another
version of Mallarmé's Hérodiade, and Villiers' 'cold woman':

> I knew that I had seen, had seen at last
> That girl my unremembering nights hold fast.[62]

This confrontation of Yeatsean symbolism with elements of the
Jarrian manner is seen at its most daring in the later works. In his
letter to Lugné-Poë, Jarry had compared his method to guignol, to
primitive drama. As an old man Yeats began to see his productions
in this light: the circus rather than the stage becomes his
metaphor. The play which owes most to this strange combination
is *The Herne's Egg*. The priestess Attracta is a parody of Hérodiade
and the ex-nun, Sara:

> Women thrown into despair
> By the winter of their virginity
> Take its abominable snow,
> As boys take common snow, and make
> An image of god or bird or beast
> To feed their sensuality . . .[63]

while Corney's Donkey, 'a donkey on wheels like a child's toy, but life-size'[64] was perhaps inspired by a recollection of Père Ubu's strikingly life-sized *cheval à phynance*, which had cost 100 francs to make and helped to plunge the Théâtre de l'Oeuvre into debt. The stylized battles between the Connacht and Tara soldiers with table legs and candlesticks also seem to owe something to the skirmishes in Jarry's play, as do Attracta's entranced movements: 'Her limbs grow rigid, she seems / A doll upon a wire. . . . You mean that when she looks so / She is but a puppet?'[65]

To argue that the influence of Villiers or Jarry upon late Yeats was extensive would, of course, be absurd. Rather, aspects of their influence combined with many others to help to articulate in new forms and under new conditions 'all the truths' he would ever find and which he thought his intellect 'at the age of twenty' contained. Neither *Axël* nor *Ubu Roi* altered Yeats's fundamental ideas or aesthetic, but both helped to crystallize attitudes to art and life that were latent but not yet explicit in his thought. Over the years following their catalytic effect he worked out their implications at greater length.

His 1908 trip to Paris, like the earlier visits, also gave him an opportunity to stand back and take stock of himself. Once again, he tried to learn the language, and he took regular lessons which, as he informed Lady Gregory, continued after his return to Dublin: 'At 5.30 a young French woman comes & takes me in French conversation for an hour. . . . I really begin to think I shall learn French. It will be a new world & very good for me.'[66] But once more he failed and that world remained linguistically closed to him. And yet Paris as she divulged herself in visual terms could still astonish, and he wrote in some wonder to a new mistress of the changes that he perceived in himself:

I find the things that delight me this year at the Louvre are the big classic pictures by David & by some of the men of the seventeenth century for the moment I am tired of modern mystery & romance, & can only take pleasure in clear light, strong bodies, bodies having all the measure of manhood. I am in the mood of the eighteenth century — it will not last long. I was at Gustave Moreau's pictures — kept together in the house where he lived. I used to delight in him, but now I am all for David & above all Ingres whose Perseus is all classic romance — the poetry of running feet & clear far sighted eyes . . . Ten years ago when I was last in Paris I loved all that was mysterious and gothic & hated all that was classic & severe. I doubt if I should have liked you then — I wanted a twilight of religious mystery in every bodies eyes.[67]

For Wallace Stevens a change of style was a change of subject; for Yeats a change of style involved, it seems, a change of girl friends. Axel's Sara and his own Dectora have given way to Mabel Dickinson, who was reputedly of Junoesque proportions and had trained both as masseuse and as what was then known as a 'medical gymnast'. There was, evidently, little of the autumn about her body. His perceptions in the Louvre during this trip were, as Professor Schuchard shows elsewhere in this volume, the culmination of long thought about the plastic arts. They also mark a reappraisal of his literary ideas. He has rejected the disembodiment of high symbolism in favour of embodiment, and the wavering, incantatory rhythms praised in his essay on 'The Symbolism of Poetry'[68] for the 'running feet' of a more vigorous mode: in a Yeatsean coinage that would be an aesthetic contradiction for anyone else, he now delights in 'classic romance'. Such an aesthetic could encompass, with many other influences, the energies of Jarry, without yielding to their undiscriminating subversions, and the Romantic gestures that had attracted him to Villiers and the symbolists, while escaping their radical solipsism.

Yeats had undergone such a transformation that to many readers his old poetic personality must have seemed dead. It was not dead — merely transformed and transforming — but the notion seems to have penetrated to the University of Paris. At Maud Gonne's house he met a young man who was writing a thesis on his poetry. 'He is to do an elaborate essay', Yeats reported, '& another guest a friend of Oscar Wilde says that the Sorbonne must have thought me to be dead or they would never have let him choose me.'[69] He had learned from Paris; now, it seemed, Paris was to learn of him.

LILY YEATS, WILLIAM BUTLER YEATS, AND FRANCE

WILLIAM M. MURPHY

One of the oldest jokes in academia is of the student who composes a paper on the Holy Roman Empire by looking up the entries for each word in the Oxford Dictionary and expanding upon the definitions. For the past several years I have been working on the writings of Lily Yeats, who once visited France, and on her relationship with her brother William Butler Yeats, who died there. Possessing, I hope, as much ingenuity as the fictional student, I have put the three elements together to make a brief memorandum of three parts with little theme and less message but, I trust, some interest. It will require twenty minutes of your time and none of your intelligence.

Within the Yeats family were, as in every family, divisions and tensions. Lily and Jack were the sociable, likeable children who in many ways resembled their father in temperament. Willie and Lollie tended to be more crusty and difficult, though he had the advantage of universal recognition and acknowledged accomplishment. Lollie yearned for personal recognition but never received it, was highly excitable to the point of neurosis, and constituted an unsettling force wherever she went. Naturally she and her older brother did not get along at all. WBY, who didn't suffer fools gladly, was constantly irritated by Lollie, with whom he was forced to have dealings all their adult lives in her role as publisher of the Dun Emer and, later, Cuala Presses. Lily and he, on the other hand, got along beautifully. 'I am very much attached to my sister Lily', he once told a friend.[1] With her he shared confidences which she was careful to keep; he and his wife George often invited her to tea at their Dublin home while not letting Lollie know what was going on. And with her he shared his interest in the occult, for Lily herself had prophetic visions of extraordinary accuracy. There was a difference in the nature of their relationship to the otherworldly. Lily sat quietly, and visions came to her. Her brother actively sought messages from higher places. Her record for accuracy was higher than his, though neither was able to repeat the Laws of Chance.[2]

In the early summer of 1895 Lily was resting at the family home on Blenheim Road in Bedford Park contemplating her coming visit to Sligo. Lollie was away visiting her cousins the Orrs and wrote to Lily complaining that she found the place 'dull and lonely'. Lily commented drily in her diary that there were '9 persons in the house'.[3] On August 23rd Lily reports that Willy told her fortune. There would be a 'sudden message of communication which will lead to considerable success', he told her. After a time she would 'lose interest in the particular form of it'; it would 'lead to a quiet contentment' but involve 'a certain amount of rather unprofitable work to do'. Lily would enjoy a 'very considerable increase of money' and would 'take up something that falls outside [her] own control'. In apparent contradiction to what he had just predicted he added that there would be a 'loss of money' (a difficult achievement for anyone in the Yeats family, as there was so little money to lose) and a 'narrowing' of her life.[4]

One month later Lily was in Sligo enjoying the beauties of what she called 'our Paradise'.[5] She marvelled in one entry at the 'lovely dazzling day, the cottages so white and the sea so blue and sparkling',[6] and on another spoke of 'the bright sunshine and, behind, everything blotted out by mist and rain and the end of a rainbow in a mist over Lissadell'.[7] Then suddenly came the letter that was to change her life: an offer to go to Hyères in southern France as a governess to take charge of three children.[8] Everyone in her family and many of her friends urged her to accept, and so on the 15th of October she left Victoria Station for the long journey to Hyères. From Paris she took the train to Lyon, stayed overnight, and set out for Hyères next morning, changing at Marseilles, 'which smelt of garlic, and Toulon, which smelt like Barrack St., Sligo'.[9] Lily was delighted with the big house in Hyères where she was to serve as governess, and she wrote of the sights and sounds and smells of southern France with almost as much enthusiasm as she had of Sligo.

Then, not long after she began her work, she came down with a debilitating illness which proved to be typhoid fever. Lily had been physically weak all her life, always, as she put it often, low in energy. She felt psychologically enthusiastic all the time, but her body failed to respond. The typhoid took away whatever little energy she had, and after a year of convalescence in France, Italy, and Switzerland, she was forced to return home. What she didn't know then and didn't learn until 1929 was that her thyroid gland was larger than it should have been, and had sent out branches throughout her chest causing difficulties in breathing and other respiratory problems that mimicked tuberculosis. The attack of typhoid had a far worse effect on her than it would have had on others.

Still, her trip was in many ways a success. She was liked by her employers, she met people who became lifelong friends, she expanded her own knowledge of a distant world. Her brother's predictions proved remarkably accurate, the 'quiet contentment', the 'certain amount of unprofitable work', the development of 'decision and strength', the taking up of 'something that falls outside my own control', all fit the details well. The only difficulty with Willie's success as an oracle is that he superseded the first fortune, told in August, with another told in September just before Lily left for France. In this one he told her she would 'go a journey' and 'come back better health and more energy'. In the year to follow, 1896, although the forces governing her would be 'out of [her] control', she would have 'very much better health', would 'begin to make money and have some hopes', would have 'a good deal more power and skill and considerable success'. Like many fortune-tellers, WBY was hedging his bets, for the second set of predictions stood at variance with the first. Willie should have quit while he was ahead. Contemplating the later of the two fortunes, Lily wrote simply: 'Devil a word of truth in it.'[10]

Now entertain conjecture of a time twenty years later when Lily was in Ireland and her brother in France. WBY was spending a vacation with Maud Gonne in Colleville, in Calvados, while Uncle Alfred Pollexfen lay dying in Bray, where he had been taken from the Elpis nursing home in Dublin. Lily informed her brother of developments regularly, for they were both fond of the man whom WBY called 'the stout and humorous uncle',[11] the man who was like one who, in Lily's words, 'has lived all his life in [a] little walled-in place with a concrete floor and walls so tall he got neither sun nor air, but yet was happy'.[12] When he died she wrote WBY a letter containing her own observations about Alfred, and he wrote a poem which was, in his own words, simply 'an expansion of the end of your letter'.[13] One example of the closeness in wording between the letter and the poem can be found in the following comparison. WBY wrote of Alfred:

> Now that his fiftieth year had come
> He had found it best to journey home
> And 'Mr. Alfred' be again

On the lips of common men
Who had still in memory
His childhood and his family.[14]

Lily had written:

. . . the last six years have been a sort of harvest. He had money and was
no longer one of a great army of no-bodies in Liverpool but had become
again 'Mr. Alfred' in places where he was known and which had known
and respected his people before him.[15]

So the poem, called first 'In Memory' and later 'In Memory of
Alfred Pollexfen', written in France by Yeats the European, was
directly attributable to the thoughts of the poet's favourite sister.

Twenty years or so later WBY was again in France, this time ill
in Cap Martin. In the intervening years the relationship between
him and his sister Lollie grew more and more acrimonious. If he
had not been involved as editor of the Cuala Press and therefore
of necessity inextricably tied to her daily affairs he probably
would have had nothing to do with her. If Lily had had the money
to set up her own home she too would have separated herself
from Lollie without hesitation, but her impecuniousness forced
her to live in uneasy companionship with her flighty, excitable,
and thoroughly annoying sister. Exasperation with Lollie became
indeed another of the links binding Willie and Lily together.
Not until 1938 was he able to arrange things so that Lollie was
essentially stripped of her power at the Press. A new Board of
Directors was established, in which Lollie could be outvoted by
the other three, Willie, his wife George, and F. R. Higgins. Frank
O'Connor came aboard as Advisor. As 1938 moved toward a close
Lollie became increasingly frustrated by her inability to have the
other members of the Board listen to her. The shift in power was
supposed to send a message to Lollie, but Lollie was not the kind
of person who got messages, continuing to believe that she was
running the show. In January 1939, when Yeats the European lay
ill at the Hotel Idéal Séjour in Cap Martin, the two sisters showed
again the differences in their way of doing things. Both knew
their brother was not only ill, but seriously so. Lily wrote a letter
on January 14th, a cheerful note reminding Willie that only two
months hence, on March 16th, would fall the 100th birthday of
their father, John Butler Yeats. She suggested it would be nice if
they could mark it in some way, and her very suggestion implied
a faith that he would still be alive to celebrate it.

Lollie wrote a quite different kind of letter. Dated January 25th,
it would have arrived the day before her brother died and could

quite possibly have caused his death from apoplexy if his weakened heart had not already done its work. In it she said nothing about his health but addressed only the subject of Cuala. It is full of the underlinings that mark all her letters. She had been trying to get something done at Cuala, she complained, but was prevented at every turn by the refusal to act of both F. R. Higgins and Frank O'Connor. 'Neither of these gentlemen have kept any of the promises I myself heard them make to you at the meeting held here in October.' She had received no balance sheet, the Press was idle, she got constant queries about *On the Boiler* and did not know how to respond. Would Willie please write to these two men and rouse them to action? 'This is merely a business letter', she concluded. 'I am very worried. Result, I got that violent pain again twice this week.'[16] The fact that her brother lay dying did not deflect her from the single-minded pursuit of her own interests.

A few days later the news about WBY came to Dublin. Jack telephoned the sisters about 2pm Sunday to say their brother was 'seriously ill', but this was only his way of breaking the news gently, for WBY had died twenty-four hours earlier. Jack came later in the day to tell them the truth. Daughter Anne was at Lennox Robinson's, Michael at St Columba's School. Lily, who sternly disapproved of drinking, wrote to her cousin Ruth that Lennox 'was in a state of shock and possibly something else as well', that he 'had done a mad thing and taken Michael out by air to France', angering George, who wanted her son to remain in Ireland. Lennox, with his young charge, beat a hasty retreat back to Dublin without ever reaching the south of France.

During the last week of his life WBY had been remarkably cheerful. Among his visitors were Mr and Mrs Dermot O'Brien. Mrs O'Brien wrote Lily a long account of their experiences and Lily summarized it in a letter to Ruth Pollexfen Lane-Poole:

They had been to call the Sunday before Willy's death. George was out, but Willy saw them and they were some time with him. He was in bed but not at all an invalid. He told them he was 'very happy writing lots of poetry.' Then on Saturday Dermot was called to the telephone to be told that it was all over. They went to George, who asked them to get a clergyman. They went and got a Canon Carey, who came and read prayers in 'the quiet little room while all knelt'. Willy she says looked beautiful and dignified.

Dermot we hear wrote to Miss Purser and said he had always thought Willy handsome, but when he looked at him lying dead he saw that he was beautiful. He wanted to make a sketch of him and went back during the night, but a change had come, so he did not.

On Wednesday night, February 1st, George phoned Lily from London 'to say she wished to hold a family council and then make an announcement to the papers'. Nothing was to be done or said till after the family had met. Care had to be taken that no one make commitments. 'The Dean of St Patrick's had rung up at once offering a place in the cathedral by Swift's grave.' George telephoned Con Curran and gave him a message for the press. 'Next night she and Anne and Jack met us here, and she gave us a poem of Willy's in which he had stated his wish to be buried in Drumcliffe Sligo.' Olive Jackson, a Pollexfen cousin, had written to say that 'Sligo is very proud that he should wish to be buried there at the foot of Ben Bulben. Well, Sligo was our Paradise'.[17]

Lily believed there was more to the universe than met the five senses and was convinced that things that seemed to be coincidences were in fact determined by mysterious forces. William Butler Yeats had not had the opportunity to respond to Lily's last letter, but when the English admirers of Yeats's poetry decided to hold a memorial service of their own at St Martin's in the Field in London, the date they chose, quite without consultation with any member of the Yeats family — as Lily put it, 'by chance, if there is such a thing as chance' — was March 16th, the centenary of John Butler Yeats's birth. It was an event which neither Willie, for all his occult powers, nor Lily, for all the accuracy of her visions, could have foretold. 'I thought we ought to mark it in some way,' she told Ruth. 'Well, it is to be marked in a way I could not have foreseen.'[18]

GEORGE HYDE LEES: MORE THAN A POET'S WIFE

ANN SADDLEMYER

This is a report of work in progress, bearing all the marks and deficiencies of that genre: certainties linked by suppositions, theories occasionally buttressed with facts, names and dates seeking a context. The search for Bertha Georgie Hyde Lees (a fact — the name on her birth certificate) is made more difficult still by the discretion and reticence of that remarkable woman the poet celebrated, George Yeats. Yet in order to come to terms with what is one of the most extraordinary and creative partnerships in the literary world (another certainty), we must first brave her own embargo which politely and firmly deflected all (or most) direct questions with the unvarying formula: 'That's too personal.'

How 'personal' becomes increasingly obvious with the publication of the admirable and persevering work by George Harper and his colleagues on *A Vision* and related papers.[1] The Automatic Script deals with every aspect of their personal life. What also can no longer be denied is the extent to which George (or Georgie — the names are interchangeable during the first year of their marriage) collaborated with her husband. Surely it is time to take seriously what Yeats had been saying all his life and an embarrassed world of scholarship has frequently tried to ignore or even deny: an exploration of the world of the supranatural was as important to him as his poetry; indeed the two must be considered together. And with that certainty another equally significant: his most essential partner in this continuing study was his wife. The concept of partnership is central, extending out from the collaborative dramatized 'apprehension of the truth' discovered through their occult studies[2] into every aspect of their lives.

What becomes increasingly clear in their letters, especially those to each other, is the frankness, equality, and frequent joy in shared decision-making on literary, artistic, critical, visionary, and domestic fronts (assertion supported by facts). George Yeats

191

was far more than a poet's wife, although clearly for her the making of poetry was primary. In fact occasionally it became her responsibility to express a salutary reminder in the midst of her mate's various enthusiasms. One lengthy quotation from a letter must suffice as an example here of the directness, good humour, and objectivity with which she could invoke her own and her husband's permanent role within a contemporary context. The letter, to one of her closest confidantes, Tom McGreevy, is written on the last day of 1925:

I have been trying to get Willy to leave the Senate after the Education Bill is through — he is always full of verse that never gets time to be written . . . There is really nothing more he can do, and he hasnt been well again for some time . . . He talked to Lady G[regory] about it and she said she thought he ought to remain in 'to keep a worse man out'. That's how your enlightened country looks on poets . . . He becomes more and more wrapped up in matters that are purely Irish and therefore insular, and provincial. I have been reading nothing but poetry just lately *not his!!* and it has made me realise how damnably national he is becoming. Nationality throws out personality and there's nothing in his verse worth preserving but the personal. All the pseudo-mystico-intellecto-nationalistico stuff of the last fifteen years isnt worth a trouser button, or rather as a trouser-button is a most necessary article one might say a pillowcase button! As long as there was any gesture in it, as long as there was a war on and so on and so on, it was worth it, but really now to spend hours listening to rubbish in and out of the Senate and going to commit-tees and being visited by fishermen's associations . . . and nincompoops and miaows and bow-wows of all sorts mostly mongrel is a bit too much.[3]

Who was this forthright, witty, thoughtful and dedicated young woman who courageously took on William Butler Yeats in that action-crammed autumn of 1917? (Another fact to correct what she referred to as 'Joe Hone's allergy to dates'[4]: the marriage certificate, witnessed by Georgie's mother and her good friend Ezra Pound, is dated 20th, not 21st, October. Her memory of the unpleasantness of Registry Office ceremonies is recalled fourteen years later in advice given as Dolly Travers Smith prepared to marry another of her closest friends, Lennox Robinson.) What was her background? From what has so far been discovered it is clear that she came from 'good family': on her father's side, a long line of county squires, JPs, Eton and Oxford educated yet independent of thought and manners; while her mother's family traced their lineage through younger sons of the law, clergy and military, again formed by Eton and Oxbridge, to Baron Lord

Erskine the Earl of Buchan (whose family mottos were 'Je pense plus' and 'Trial by Jury'). Her paternal grandfather Charles James (or Henry) Hyde, still remains a mystery; but her father was adopted by his uncle Harold Lees, J.P., of Pickwick Hall, near Wrexham, Denbighshire — hence the surname Hyde Lees and, presumably, some if not all of the family money.

Much more is known about her maternal grandparents: her mother was the eldest daughter of Montagu Woodmass, a Barrister of the Inner Temple, J.P. for County of Chester, and — according to Georgie's mother's marriage certificate — a manufacturer of objects unknown (the only reference I have found to 'trade'). Again there are indications of strong will and independence of spirit: Georgie's mother appears to have quarrelled with *her* mother shortly after marriage and so her own children may never have visited the family home in 7 Southwell Gardens. Mrs Woodmass, whose husband predeceased her, lived on until 1927; she appears to have relented towards her daughter, who received an annuity in her will, and George was awarded a settlement nine years later. I have encountered no references to her in any of the Yeats family correspondence.

Nelly, as Georgie's mother Edith Ellen was known, was small, attractive, and musically inclined; she may, like her younger sister, have studied music at a finishing school in Dresden. She was also headstrong, generous, and opinionated, fond of creating whirlpools of excitement; in later years her daughter carefully avoided announcing too many of her plans before the fact. William Gilbert Hyde Lees, Georgie's father, was attractive, reckless, witty, and also musical; he was given to pranks, such as shocking his clergyman brother-in-law by singing offcolour words to hymnal accompaniment, and seems to have resigned his commission in the militia (Manchester Regiment, 4th Battalion) once he came into his uncle's inheritance. He is listed on Georgie's marriage certificate as 'barrister-at-law', but there is no other suggestion of a legal profession. The marriage (which took place on 18 December 1889) did not last, indeed may have been over by the time Georgie was born on 17 October 1892, for her birthplace (Hartley Wintney near Odiham, Hampshire — not Wales as John Butler Yeats erroneously reported) is not one of the addresses listed in *Walford's County Families*. William Gilbert died under apparently sordid circumstances in 1909 at the age of forty-four and the only recorded reference to him by his daughter is again reported by John Butler Yeats, that both her father and her grandfather died of drink.[5] But she was very close to her mother, visiting her regularly until Nelly too, died, in February 1942. Perhaps because of that inclination to intervene, her own children Michael and Anne were kept at a distance from their grandmother; George had very strong ideas about independence, for herself and her family, and probably Willy's innumerable relations were quite enough.

Georgie's only brother Harold, two years her senior, seems to have spent most of his early years with his father until he too went to Eton and Wadham College. Perhaps because he attended his father's deathbed, in an Ibsenite reversal he became an Anglican clergyman with rigid moral standards and a less than joyous existence, his only artistic indulgence a fine collection of drawings and etchings. He married Gwynne Younghughes, a classmate of his cousin Grace at St Hugh's College, Oxford, and a promising poet; they had no children. But although she saw little of her brother except for school holidays, and far less after her marriage (family rumour has it that Harold's extensive list of disapprovals included Irishmen and poets), George was very fond of Harold and deeply mourned his death in 1963.

Dobbs, the family name for Georgie which Willy adopted, seems to have had the usual kind of education for young ladies of Knightsbridge. She once told her daughter that she had been 'kicked out of seven schools'. I have only been able to trace three so far — St Stephen's High School, Clewe; St James's School for Girls, West Malvern; and Miss Amabel Douglas' School in Queens Gate, London. There were also several art schools, both in London and on the south coast — identification as yet unknown. But I have found no record of misdemeanours, and suspect the frequent changes of venue were the result of her mother's way of living more than any theory of education. Like her parents, Georgie was highly musical, played the piano, and seems to have had a well-trained ear; she was also an accomplished linguist with her own theories of how languages should be learned (what we would now call the 'immersion' method). Despite the interrupted schooling, she had a good grounding in the classics and an excellent memory — could quote freely from German, Italian, French, certainly knew Latin and seems to have had a reading knowledge of Spanish also. Obviously she was an avid reader, judging from her list of philosophical texts that Yeats turned to after the publication of *A Vision* in 1925, and those books still in the Dalkey library which can be identified as hers.[6]

Did she travel? Her cousin Grace Jaffe thinks that as a young girl she did, extensively, with her mother; such absences would explain her frequent change of schools and also why Harold spent so many school holidays with the Spurways (Grace's parents, Nelly's sister and brother-in-law) in the Old Rectory at Baldock north of Letchworth, in Hertfordshire. Certainly she was knowledgeable about (and sensitive to) European culture and travel long before she married, and her familiarity with languages suggests more than rote learning. Then, in 1909, the record becomes much clearer. For by that time Nelly had met Harry Tucker, beloved brother to her Kensington neighbour Olivia Shakespear, and Georgie, in turn, had met Olivia's daughter Dorothy.

Dorothy Shakespear had also attended St James's School, although she and Georgie do not seem to have coincided there. (On one of their frequent country sketching tours they later visited Malvern and gained entrance privileges into the famous school gardens.) Despite six years difference in age, the two cemented a close friendship which lasted throughout their lives. Georgie signed her letters 'your Step-pest'; Dorothy described her as having a square face (this symbol frequently took the place of her name in letters) but also 'very handsome . . . awfully intelligent . . . alarmingly intuitive at 18'.[7] Together they took art classes, visited museums and attended concerts and lectures, helped each other escape from the confining restrictions of Victorian respectability, suffered through the innumerable and constant country house rentals to which their parents were addicted, joined the same sedate ladies' club, and twice travelled to Italy. When Nelly and Harry Tucker were married on 1 February 1911, they (with Georgie) moved even closer to the Shakespears. All attended the gatherings of which Olivia was centre, and to which Nelly in her turn brought newly-discovered musicians and young writers. The names Walter Rummel, Jelly d'Aranyi, Frederic Manning, Eva Fowler, crop up again and again — as do those of Ezra Pound and Olivia's old friend and former lover, W. B. Yeats. Thanks to the recent edition of letters between Dorothy and Ezra during the years from 1909 until their marriage on 20 April 1914, we can follow Georgie's itinerary as she moves with Nelly, and often Dorothy, to Margate, Suffolk, Norfolk, Devon, Sussex (the Tuckers were partial to Lynton and Coleman's Hatch), and through the artistic circles of London.

George wrote to Allan Wade that she 'knew EP quite well from 1910' but did not meet WBY until May 1911. Virginia Moore, who offers the date 1910, describes that momentous first meeting: 'One morning when her mother thought she was at art school, she went to the British Museum, where she saw Yeats rush past her like a meteor; and that very afternoon, taking tea with her mother at Olivia Shakespear's was formally introduced.'[8] Later Olivia took Willy to Brighton to visit the Tuckers; soon his letters to Lady Gregory and others record one or two-week visits (but without Olivia), to Margate, Lynton, and especially 'The Prelude' (a cottage in Ashdown Forest the Tuckers frequently rented). Meanwhile Georgie, who had always been known in the family as being psychic (poltergeists especially found her attractive), was attending G. R. S. Mead's lectures on the paranormal in London with Dorothy, studying astrology, and delving more deeply into philosophy (she read Hegel, for example, before Yeats did). By 1914 she had joined Rudolf Steiner's Anthroposophical Society and been sponsored by Yeats as a member of the Stella Matutina section of the Golden Dawn. The following year, while Yeats was enthusiastically studying Bessie Radcliffe's automatic writing, she was contributing her own research, attending seances with him, and on another front, reading plays to him. By then also Dorothy and Ezra were married and spending the winters with Willy in Stone Cottage, just down the road from 'The Prelude' in Sussex. Did Georgie visit now that there were appropriate chaperones? Probably not. Nelly, as Olivia had with Dorothy (who did not marry until she was twenty-seven), would have seen that the proprieties were strictly observed.

Nor did this burgeoning relationship elude her concerned mother, who later admitted to Lady Gregory that she had feared a proposal as early as November 1915; that may well be when Georgie visited her young cousin Grace at Cheltenham and swore her to secrecy about her plans to marry WBY.[9] But then three events intervened: the war, which led Georgie into a number of hospital service jobs; the Easter 1916 rebellion, which turned Yeats's mind and sentiments back to Ireland; and most significantly his increasing obsession with Iseult Gonne. Then early in 1917 after a hiatus in the country visits, 'feeling a little unkind at [her] long neglect of him', Nelly invited Yeats to come and see her. By then Georgie may well have been through with her more menial patriotic duties (as hospital cook, then a nursing assistant); there were, Nelly hinted to Lady Gregory, prospects of a more suitable job in the Foreign Office in the autumn. Certainly contact was re-established before Yeats made his final journey to Maud Gonne's retreat in Normandy. Georgie Hyde Lees was not quite so obviously an afterthought as received biographies imply.

Nor was she the simple naive rebound. Willy was always indiscreet, a trait she would have to chastise him for — and rescue him from — many times during their marriage. Family propinquity would pretty well ensure her knowledge of the origins of his friendship with Olivia. It would be impossible for her not to know about his long-term passion for Maud, probably equally so not to be aware of his plans for his Galway castle and the longings for home and family, and — given the frequency with which his personal affairs seem to have been discussed during seances — difficult not to have observed his increased interest in French literature, a knowledge of which Georgie shared with Iseult. In addition, during those heady days of August and early September 1917, Willy himself was all too aware of his conflicting emotions, complex rationalizations, and consistent desire to do the right thing by everyone. It is likely that in his effort to be honest — but not too frank, and sincere — but not too revealing, he let slip more than he meant to about his proposals to first Maud and then Iseult. Hence Nelly's urgent appeal to Lady Gregory for help in preventing what she felt to be an unsuitable match, Willy's flight to Coole for persuasion and reinforcement, and Georgie's return to London (*without* her mother) for the publishing of the banns on October 1st. Hence also, Georgie's realization four days into their honeymoon as Yeats became more and more distressed, that something dramatic would have to be done to save her marriage.[10] Neither she nor Yeats could have foreseen the impact that incursion into automatic writing would have. For instead of providing a harmless and temporary distraction, Georgie was herself seized by a power beyond her control — we have no reason to doubt that rare admission, especially from a woman so committed both to honesty and reticence. The psychological, feminist, and philosophical implications of these two 'confessions' — and their juxtaposition — have yet to be explored, as do the manuscript materials and Yeats's commentary for the second edition of *Vision*. Thus encouraged by the Instructors of the Automatic Script, theirs was to become a marriage of deep and lasting affection, absolute frankness, and complete trust.

That the marriage immediately ceased to resemble the unnaturally prosaic solution mocked by the Gonnes must have become obvious even to Iseult when within weeks of the start of the Automatic Script Georgie, confident in her husband's affection and loyalty, took responsibility for Iseult's domestic arrangements. At her suggestion Willy took 'Maurice' (as Iseult continued to be referred to in their letters) to Nelly for advice and kindness, and invited her to spend Christmas with them in Stone Cottage, the site of their honeymoon. George was even prepared to entertain

Maud, and supported her husband's various escapades over the next few years in trying to extricate Iseult from hers. Yeats's praise of his bride's 'nobility of character' was not empty words.

The decision to settle in Oxford followed on Yeats's oft-repeated desire to live and write in the country, away from the distractions of life in Woburn Buildings. The previous three winters spent with Ezra in Stone Cottage had been successful experiments; George herself was not averse to getting out of London; and Oxford — with summers in Thoor Ballylee — seemed a sensible compromise. Oxford in its turn palled, Cork was briefly considered, but Dublin won out. Now, added to theatre and Cuala business was the seduction of Senate affairs, an increasing worry to George: poetry was what counted, 'personal' poetry. Ballylee was pleasant for the gardening, the fishing, and the children, but even there Coole was close by with its constant reminders of the Abbey Theatre, the Lane pictures, the needs of that 'fool-driven land'. Nor was the Irish climate suitable for Willy's lung or Michael's health. Europe beckoned even more persuasively than it had during the early Oxford years, and with it George's opportunity to provide her children with the freedom and independence she was determined they should achieve. Like herself, Anne and Michael would become citizens of both their father's nation and the world.

*   *   *

Georgie Hyde Lees married the fifty-two year old poet three days after her 25th birthday. She was not yet 47 when she became a widow, and a little less than two months short of her 76th birthday when she died in Dublin on 23 August 1968. The early years of her marriage were perhaps the most public ones of all. Despite the responsibilities of a young family and the demands of house-keeping (though she loved Ballylee, living there must have caused her considerable hardship), she accompanied her already famous husband on a lengthy and successful lecture tour to America; she went with him to receive honours and awards culminating with the Nobel Prize, on official Senatorial visits (her private report of the Waterford school and kindly nuns is an earthy contrast to the philosophical musing of 'Among School Children'), and eventually on the travels abroad they both longed for. Everywhere there were people — relations, old friends and new acquaintances, poets and musicians, reporters and scholars. And always there were financial worries, for despite the rumours of WBY having bagged 'a rich wife', her private income was only moderate and primarily devoted to her children's needs. This middle third of her life is in one sense better documented, in another far less so even than the earlier years. For what we know is seen through the eyes of what she dubbed (and to a great extent created) 'the industry', and even before her husband's death she controlled much of what was made public. After 1939 her stewardship was complete, but those years are still too close to those who knew her to be readily evaluated. Also, she protected herself. Far easier not to comment, to brush aside any suggestion of influence or responsibility, to let obliging and sympathetic scholars close (often unconsciously) the gaps between the paragraphs of Yeats's public life.

Still, there are hints of the paths yet to be explored. How many friends from Olivia's and her mother's circles continued to remain in contact? Ezra and Dorothy Pound of course, not only during the later winters in Rapallo but Dorothy's annual summer visits to Sidmouth where the Tuckers had retired. The musicians, certainly: Walter Rummel was to compose incidental music for *The Dreaming of the Bones* and visited them in Dublin, as did the violinist Jelly d'Aranyi who was to remain one of George's special friends (and in 1933 made her own excursion into the supranatural with Schumann's message concerning his 'lost' Concerto). Richard Aldington appeared on the fringes of the Riviera, but what of Ezra's H.D., whose concept of the 'Overmind' bears some resemblance to the Anima Mundi? H.D. did not rate inclusion in *The Oxford Book of Modern Verse* ('our anthology' George calls it in one of her letters).[11] But before that project — and perhaps after — George was far more familiar with contemporary poetry than her husband, and much more conversant with other literary forms.

Her important role in the creation and maintenance of the Dublin Drama League has been largely overlooked. Many of the plays selected were of her choosing, and as Treasurer of the League and close chum to Lennox Robinson, she played a significant role in production also. Not only was she sensitive to musical effects in verse and drama, but as would be expected from her training she had a keen eye for setting and costume (frequently was in fact responsible for selecting the dresses for her husband's productions). Her literary standards were high — she was without doubt her husband's severest and most helpful critic, and seems regularly to have reviewed for AE's *Irish Statesman*. There is evidence that she herself wrote at least two plays and one novel, but vowed to publish under a pseudonym if she published at all. On the other hand, Grace Jaffe's statement that George burned the memoirs she had begun probably refers to her contemplation, then rejection, of Frank O'Connor's request to write a small book on her late husband for Cuala.

Her work with the Cuala Press proved her ability as editor and critic long before that controversial responsibility for Yeats's posthumous publications. It was she who edited AE's letters for the series and after Yeats's death made all editorial decisions for the Press. She also proved herself a decisive and tactful business woman, on the death of F. R. Higgins inviting Frank O'Connor and Sean O'Faolain to join the Board of Directors. Had it not been for production difficulties caused by the war, the Press might well have continued in new directions. (Her contribution to the Industry run by her sisters-in-law extended elsewhere: for some time the Cuala letterhead advertized her name alongside Lily's in the Embroidery division.)

But the clearest indication so far of her literary ability, critical astuteness, forthright judgment and, above all, her sense of humour, can be found in her correspondence. 'Your letters are the best I have ever received they are so gay and vivid', Willy wrote to her from Coole during the long 1931-32 winter. Those alone — and I devoutly hope more will turn up — are positive evidence of the character of the young woman of whom Yeats wrote to Lady Gregory, 'Georgie is a good friend and an always pleasant companion & seems to be entirely unselfish as good a wife as a man could have — indeed a very perfect character'.

SAVANTS AND ARTISTS: POUND AND YEATS

MICHAEL ALEXANDER

As a pseudo-mediaevalist I begin with a genuine trope of modesty. The comparison between Pound and Yeats as Europeans, primarily as manifested not in their prose, letters or lives but in their poetry, is one I can conduct principally from Pound's side, not only because I know Pound's poetry better, but because, on the basis of their poems, we can know more of Pound's view of Europe: he tells us more, it meant more to him, he lived most of his life here, whereas Yeats who 'had many pretty toys when young', was able to take Europe for granted.

To begin with, what their views have most obviously in common: Europe as the place where the cultural, artistic and literary tradition of what we now call the West developed. Europe, physically speaking, meant France and, more especially, Italy. Both had this conventional and commonplace starting point, a romantic view of classical ground, gleaned from books and pictures, and books of pictures: the glory that was Greece and the loveliness of Italy, especially the poems of Shelley, Keats and Byron and the pictures of the Italian renaissance.

Physically, their Europe did not then include Sweden, however bountiful, nor Greece — it was too far and not civilized. I exclude Pound's Provence and his Paris and Spain, and his reluctant visits north of the Alps. But the physical side of Europe looms large in these remarks. I asked Pound in 1966 if he had been to Greece, which he mentions in his work more than Yeats does. No, he replied, he wouldn't get there now. I suggested that he might fly there. 'I have been in an aeroplane only once in my life', he replied shortly. This was, of course, in a plane taking him back to the United States to face trial in 1945. When released in 1958 he naturally crossed the Atlantic in a liner, as he first had in the nineteenth century and had twice before the First World War and once before the Second. He did fly to Greece eventually, to see Delphi. I don't think Yeats ever sailed to Byzantium, though I presume he had been to Innisfree.

So Europe was the home of culture, a German word in Pound's embarrassed spelling, but a thing which lived in Latin Europe, *wo die Zitronen blühn*. Yeats uses the more gentlemanly word 'civilization', and mentions especially those of Greece and Rome and Italy. Pound's 'coherent idea' around which, he said towards the end, 'his muddles accumulated' was that 'European culture ought to survive'. Europe was a country or continent of the mind for both Pound and Yeats, but Pound went to live, explore and prospect in his dream, and renders it physically present in a thousand details of his work, whereas for Yeats Europe remained a source for presences and images — Urbino, Michaelangelo, Athena's image, Helen, the Homeric pantheon, Oedipus, Plato's ghost, Byzantium. There is nothing as specific as the grey eighteenth century houses of Dublin, the swans on the lake at Coole Park or Thoor Ballylee's moorhens. The European images are part of the theatre of W. B. Yeats's mind. Europe in his verse is not a place. Pound celebrated Europe for its nature, Yeats for its culture.

In his prose or letters Yeats can describe Urbino or Rapallo well enough, but his view in the poems is loftier, purged of detail. 'Urbino's windy hill' (in 'To a Wealthy Man who promised a second Subscription to the Dublin Municipal Gallery if it were proved the People wanted Pictures') confines description to the grand typifying adjective. The dependence of Yeats's rhetoric upon adjectives and on proper names has been remarked. It includes the classically established use of the single epithet, an isolating gesture, useful in the theatre or in the senate, a gesture implying (as Homer, Virgil and Dante do) that we all know, or will know, Urbino and how windy its hill is. Yeats's *A Packet for Ezra Pound* begins with a cameo of Rapallo. The paragraph concludes with this non-sentence: 'The little town described in the Ode on a Grecian Urn'. In what precedes this there are reflections of 'Baiae's bay' as described in Shelley's 'Ode to the West Wind'. The bronze lamp of Callimachus mentioned in 'Lapis Lazuli' is one described in Pausanias but not extant: so with 'Phidias' famous ivories' and 'the ancient image made of olive wood' and the statue of Athena, all described by Pausanias as standing in the Parthenon, but now gone, as we are told in the first stanza of 'Nineteen Hundred and Nineteen'. But let us return to Rapallo, 'The little town described in the Ode on a Grecian Urn'. What little town? It is not on the Grecian urn, nor is it described in the 'Ode on a Grecian Urn', but a Mediterranean archetype imagined, implied, alluded to by Keats.

> What little town by river or sea-shore
> Or mountain-built with peaceful citadel
> Is emptied of its folk, this pious morn?

It might just as well be an evocation (for it is not a description) of Monte Carlo, which Yeats once described more mundanely and specifically in a letter to Lady Gregory as 'A wondrous land of the rich with no side-walks upon the roads which are intended only for murderous motor-cars'. This would not do in a poem.

Ezra Pound knew Languedoc and Italy well; I spent much time in 1962-3 retracing his steps in Languedoc, but confine myself here to Italian things, to make the comparison with Yeats. Ezra Pound visited Venice for the first time as a boy and went there several times for long stays on his own in his early twenties, notably in 1908. In 1907 Yeats (who was twenty years Pound's senior) visited Italy for the first time in the company of Lady Gregory and Robert Gregory.

Italy was Pound's spiritual home, whereas, although it is not clear that Yeats had or even sought a spiritual home in this world, he made a serious effort in his earlier work to domesticate his yearnings in Ireland. Italy at first appears as an incidental in his involvement with Lady Gregory and Hugh Lane as patrons of the arts. 'To a Wealthy Man' draws on Castiglione's idealized memoir of the court of Guidobaldo at Urbino:

> What cared Duke Ercole, that bid
> His mummers to the market-place,
> What th' onion-sellers thought or did
> So that his Plautus set the pace
> For the Italian comedies?
> And Guidobaldo, when he made
> That grammar school of courtesies
> Where wit and beauty learned their trade
> Upon Urbino's windy hill,
> Had sent no runners to and fro
> That he might learn the shepherds' will.
> And when they drove out Cosimo,
> Indifferent how the rancour ran,
> He gave the hours they had set free
> To Michelozzo's latest plan
> For the San Marco Library,
> Whence turbulent Italy should draw
> Delight in Art whose end is peace,
> In logic and in natural law
> By sucking at the dugs of Greece.

Cardinal Bembo said that he wished to be a shepherd on the
Apennines that he might look down every day on Urbino. Yeats
improves on Castiglione's scorn for the onion-sellers by reversing
Bembo's wish. Yeats wishes to be Urbino himself to look down
upon the shepherds. The moral of the poem is that Lane should
have emulated the munificence and love of art of Ercole, Guidobaldo and Cosimo in giving the 'hours' to the artist: my leisure
the basis of your culture.

To Yeats, then, it seems to be the thought of Urbino, rather than
the experience or sight of it, which provokes him into passionate
meditation on art, patronage and social values, a means of pre-
cipitating an utterance at a critical point in his life-history. 'To A
Wealthy Man' is a meditation upon patronage, an allusion to
Castiglione, in which Urbino is only the locus. For such a mind
it was not necessary to go to see the Parthenon or Byzantium; for
Pound Byzantium was a place where craft was preserved by just
interest rates and laws; only in his use of China does Pound
approach Yeats's visionariness.

For Yeats Europe was not a place he had to go to to believe in,
but the more positivistic American needed empirical experience
to bring his poetry alive with radiant particulars. Yeats's use of
Michaelangelo as a grand example is characteristically conventional in method and original in application. He refers to Veronese
and Mantegna and refers to images from famous paintings by
Poussin and Botticelli, but the only artist of Italy he deals with
more than incidentally in his poetry is Michaelangelo, whose
'hand moves to and fro' in 'Long-Legged Fly',

> That civilisation may not sink,
> Its great battle lost,

so

> That girls at puberty may find
> The first Adam in their thought

and (in 'Under Ben Bulben IV') that man (or God) may 'fill the
cradles right'. Michaelangelo creates 'profane perfection of mankind', and is (along with 'the geometric arts of Greece' from which
he derived) the exemplar for W. B. Yeats of absolute art which
arouses jet-setting madams and challenges man to live at his
most intense, a cloud-piercing art which emulates eternity and
divine prototypes. Even if it perishes 'into the desolation of reality'
it has called men and women to live in a noble and godlike way.

European artists, then, in the late Yeats not only keep the vagueness of many-headed Asia at bay, but are indirectly responsible for the conception of children and the filling up of heaven with souls. Art is the pump in the systematic cycle of spirit and matter and the artist is the genie of the pump, or (to mix my metaphors this pious morn) a non-Platonic pimp for eternity. Pound, folding his blankets in Pisan meadows, lifts up his eyes not to the Sistine Chapel roof but to the mountains and lowers them to the grass and the insects. For Pound man-the-artist, like the Capaneus of *Mauberley*, is chidden by nature to 'pull down thy vanity' and 'learn of the green world what can be thy place'.

Pound's respectful, affectionate attitude to Yeats in the *Cantos* is consistently that he is a dreamer; not that this is an unusual view. Pound's own early poems are dreamy; he arrived in England in 1908 admiring Yeats as the greatest of living English poets; and, as his selection in *From Confucius to Cummings* indicates, he continued to prefer Yeats's early work, the Yeats of the Celtic Twilight. Pound rapidly became Yeats's acquaintance, literary collaborator and friend, seeing him daily for weeks and months at a time, as one can see from the letters between Pound and Dorothy, the daughter of Olivia Shakespear. Pound married the daughter of Yeats's former mistress and lifelong friend in 1914. Yeats married Dorothy's closest friend, Georgie Hyde-Lees, in 1917, and Ezra was his best man. Yeats and Pound collaborated in translating the Japanese Noh plays (and in much else) in the winters of 1913, '14 and '15 at Stone Cottage, Sussex. Pound was, as he dismissively says of himself in his own epitaph in *Hugh Selwyn Mauberley*, 'born in a half-savage country, / Out of date'. This made him Yeats's contemporary, in that they shared an admiration for the Pre-Raphaelites, the arts-and-crafts movement, and the aesthetes, especially Lionel Johnson, to whom both men became related by their marriages. Pound's early poems are deeply influenced by the early poems of Yeats; he paid final tribute to this phase in his parody, 'The Lake Isle' in *Lustra* (1912). But he continued to share with Yeats an admiration for beauty and heroism, and some spiritual beliefs. Pound believed that time is an illusion, and that permanent 'divine' archetypes (usually Hellenic) remain in nature and in human nature. Pound's poetry is full of goddesses, heroes and (less willingly acknowledged than by W. B. Yeats) demons.

Pound was himself a different kind of dreamer, as we see in Canto 83. Earlier in the *Pisan Cantos* Pound remembers in his roll call of 'companions' (with Ford and Joyce) William 'who dreamed of nobility'. In Canto 102 of *Thrones* he wrote in the mid-fifties:

But the lot of 'em, Yeats, Possum, Old Wyndham

had no ground to stand on
Black shawls still worn for Demeter
in Venice,
in my time,
my young time.

And in the last *Cantos* he thrice recalls Yeats saying, or rather murmuring, 'when the mist came to Tigullio' (the gulf on which Rapallo sits) 'Sligo in heaven': an affectionate recognition that it was right for Yeats to see things through an Irish mist. Heaven is the theme of the final Cantos, and also enters into Canto 83: 'le paradis n'est pas artificiel'. 'Old Ez, folding his blankets in Pisan meadows' begins Canto 83 with water, and the part it plays in the natural cycle.

ὕδωρ
HUDOR et Pax
Gemisto stemmed all from Neptune
hence the Rimini bas reliefs
Sd Mr Yeats (W.B.) 'Nothing affects these people
Except our conversation'.

Gemisto is Gemistus Plethon, the Neo-Platonic Greek philosopher who attended the ecumenical Council of Florence in 1438. Pound has much earlier presented him in conversation with Sigismundo Malatesta of Rimini, encouraging a syncretic revival of ancient Greek religion and of the mythopoeic imagination registered in the fine bas-reliefs Sigismundo commissioned in his Tempio. The conversation of savants thus creates the culture of the future.

The Canto proceeds in its reverie upon natural and cultural cycles, and returns after 16 lines to Yeats:

Le Paradis n'est pas artificiel
and Uncle William dawdling around Notre Dame
in search of whatever
paused to admire the symbol
with Notre Dame standing inside it
Whereas in St Etienne
or why not Dei Miracoli:
mermaids, that carving.

Paradise was for Pound not in the next or another world but in this one (see his early 'Blandula, Tenulla, Vagula'), to be arrived at naturally and not by the drugs of Baudelaire and the decadents.

The churches of St Etienne in Poitiers and of Santa Maria dei
Miracoli in Venice (where the mermaids are carved) actually
contain and show us paradise in their particulars. For Pound the
form is inside the object, for Yeats the object is inside its symbolic
halo, and exists (Pound suggests) as a peg for the significance
Yeats puts upon it.
Now 'in the drenched tent there is quiet' but, Pound reflects,

> the sage
> delighteth in water
> the humane man has amity with the hills

> as the grass grows by the weirs
> thought Uncle William *consiros*

The common denominator between '*consiros*' and 'Down By the
Salley Gardens' is youthful folly. In Dante's *Purgatorio* (26, 143)
the troubadour Arnaut Daniel says in Provençal 'consiros vei la
passada folor' ('troubled I behold my past folly'). Old Ez reflects
that he himself has not heeded the advice given him by his love
in youth 'to take life easy / As the leaf grows on the tree' because
then he was young and foolish and now is full of tears.
    Much later in this Canto of the consolations nature brings the
poet, he writes:

> Plura diafana
>   Heliads lift the mist from the young willows
> there is no base seen under Taishan
>   but the brightness of *'udor*   ὕδωρ
> the poplar tips float in brightness
> only the stockade posts stand

> And now the ants seem to stagger
>   as the dawn sun has trapped their shadows.

Throughout Pound mythologizes the Pisan landscape, populating
it here with diaphanous sun-spirits who lift the water vapour
from the willows in front of the mountain he calls by the Chinese
name for a heavenly mountain. From dawn the sight of the work
of ants, the appearance of a baby wasp, and the growth of grass
console him:

> When the mind swings by a grass-blade
> an ant's forefoot shall save you

But

> There is fatigue deep as the grave.
> The Kakemono grows in flat land out of mist
>   sun rises lop-sided over the mountain
>   so that I recalled the noise in the chimney
> as it were the wind in the chimney
>   but was in reality Uncle William
> downstairs composing
> that had made a great Peeeeacock
>   in the proide ov his oiye
>   had made a great peeeeeeecock in the . . .
> made a great peacock
>   in the proide of his oyyee
>
> proide ov his oy-ee
> as indeed he had, and perdurable
>
> a great peacock aere perennius
>   or as in the advice to the young man to
> breed and get married (or not)
>   as you choose to regard it
>
> at Stone Cottage in Sussex by the waste moor
> (or whatever) and the holly bush
>   who would not eat ham for dinner
> because peasants eat ham for dinner
>   despite the excellent quality
> and the pleasure of having it hot
>
> well those days are gone forever
>   and the traveling rug with the coon-skin tabs
> and his hearing nearly all Wordsworth
>   for the sake of his conscience but
> preferring Ennemosor on Witches
>
> did we ever get to the end of Doughty:
>   The Dawn in Britain?
>   perhaps not
>   (Summons withdrawn, sir.)
> (bein' aliens in prohibited area)

It may be the 'mist' in the second line of this passage which leads
to the 'so that' in the fourth, or perhaps Pound recalls waking one
dawn in Sussex in 1915 and hearing Yeats composing what became
'The Peacock' of *Responsibilities*, a poem beginning:

> What's riches to him
> That has made a great peacock
> With the pride of his eye?

Pound recalls the perdurability of Horace's *aere perennius* and Shakespeare's Sonnets. Pound admired Yeats's endless patience as a craftsman, which he had much opportunity to observe as they worked together on the Noh plays (where the Kakemono appears). The final line is a jocular excuse for not finishing Wordsworth or Doughty: since neither Pound nor Yeats was English, they were trespassers in the dawn in wartime Britain. The Canto returns to Yeats's remark about 'our conversation' and ends with a reflection on cultural transmission and standards, perhaps thinking in 1945 of the triumph of democracy over fascism. Yeats was a senator and Pound's grandfather was a congressman.

> and in my mother's time it was respectable,
> it was social, apparently,
>   to sit in the Senate gallery
> or even in that of the House
>   to hear the fire-works of the senators
> (and possibly representatives
> as was still done in Westminster in my time
> and a very poor show from the once I saw it)
>
> but if Senator Edwards cd/ speak
> and have his tropes stay in the memory 40 years, 60 years?
> in short/ the descent
> has not been of advantage either
>   to the Senate or to 'society'
>   or to the people.

Pound's mother and father were both still alive and in Italy when he wrote this, but Yeats was dead, and Pound, who concludes the Canto by referring to himself as 'an old man' who needs rest, had no reason to suppose his own life would last for another 27 years.

Pound and Yeats are both poets of allusion, often to European culture, to which they were both in some sense 'aliens'. Pound allows things to speak for themselves ('the natural object is the only and adequate symbol'), whereas Yeats dramatizes and sometimes overstates. In his search for fullness of form and coincidence of syntax and stanza, and his use of rhetorical syntax, Yeats takes standard *exempla* from the classical repertoire, usually familiar names, to maximise impact and not lose attention: 'character isolated by a deed / To engross the present and dominate memory.'

The instances are often used in the service of unconventional
ideas, but the technique is not so different from that of the
dramatic Shelley or even the rhetorical Byron. Pound nearly
always uses counter-conventional examples, usually of things
and places seen, known, felt, experienced, or discovered by
himself: Pound uses history as a detective story and a quarry to
be puzzled over and picked at; Yeats uses history, with conscious
sprezzatura, as a repertoire. Urbino's windy hill is crowned for
Pound with a palace built by Federigo Duke of Urbino, 'Nick-nose'
as Pound names him, 'that s.o.b.'. Federigo, the patron of Piero
della Francesca, and an ally of Pope Pius II (an ideal Renaissance
patron in Burckhardt's book), was the enemy of Sigismundo
Malatesta, the *condottiere* builder of the Tempio at Rimini, and
also a patron of Piero. Pound once refers to Sigismundo, in an
access of stage Irish, as 'Siggy me darlint'. Pound would have
found the court of *Il Cortegiano* insufferably haughty and artificial,
preferring real birds, even peacocks, to golden nightingales. For
Pound, Michaelangelo belongs to the decadence that set in with
Titian. Although he too believed in 'changeless metal', he prefers
and communicates the perennially renewed life and beauty of
nature, and spring to summer or autumn; as in the instances of
the grass and the wasp and the dryad. But his allusions are too
idiosyncratic in substance and manner always to communicate
fully, as could easily be illustrated from Canto 45. Yeats's European
allusions work well enough for the educated, but his ideas are at
least as strange as Pound's. Pound was himself a dreamer, for all
his empiricism and his mistrust of yearnings for false ideals. His
American Quattrocento earthly paradise is beautiful enough. Yet
he had to admit that his ideal society in the *Pisan Cantos* and after
was 'a dream in mind indestructible' (Canto 74), an aesthetic,
pastoral, American, Confucian dream; politically impossible, to
say the least, but one to which every guest here subscribes if only
by his or her presence. For, as Pound wrote in Canto 13, translating
maxims from Confucius via French:

> When the prince has gathered about him
> All the savants and artists, his riches will be fully employed.

*   *   *

In postscript I would like to challenge the impression, which
has been offered in conversation here, that the *Cantos* do not
cohere, and that Pound admitted as much. On the penultimate
page of the *Cantos* proper, it is true, appear the words

I cannot make it cohere.

This news was grasped at by drowning specialists almost as if these were the last written or spoken words of Conrad's Mr Kurtz; or even as a repentance. To have to accord the author's word full authority as to the coherence of his work, on the 796th page of that work, would pose an interesting theoretical problem. But we are rescued from this difficulty by some of the following lines.

      but about that terzo
                third heaven,
                      that Venere,
      again is all 'paradiso'
          a nice quiet paradise
                      over the shambles,
      and some climbing
                before the take-off,
      to 'see again,'
      the verb is 'see,' not 'walk on'
      i.e. it coheres all right
                even if my notes do not cohere.
      Many errors,
                a little rightness,
      to excuse his hell
                and my paradiso.
      And as to why they go wrong,
                thinking of rightness
      And as to who will copy this palimpsest?
          al poco giorno
                    ed al gran cerchio d'ombra
      But to affirm the gold thread in the pattern
                      (Torcello)
      al Vicolo d'oro
                (Tigullio).
      To confess wrong without losing rightness:
      Charity I have had sometimes,
                I cannot make it flow thru.
      A little light, like a rushlight
                to lead back to splendour.

'I cannot make it cohere' is a trope of modesty, of a kind which accompanies Pound's every reflection on his work during the *Cantos*, in each of which a *recul* is followed by a *meilleur saut*. The 'it' which coheres is life, the universe, and the effort to follow the way: 'What you depart from is not the way' is another maxim of the *Pisan Cantos*. On earth all we can hope for is to see the stars, as Pound says in allusion to the final words of Dante's *Inferno*, not walk upon them. This attribution of final authority to life rather than to letters, which can themselves only '*lead* to splendour', makes an interesting contrast with the achieved splendour proudly proclaimed in 'Under Ben Bulben'. In conclusion I feel that Pound's last published words on T. S. Eliot could be applied to Pound himself: 'READ HIM'.

LADY GREGORY: COOLE AND CA' CAPPELLO LAYARD

BERNARD HICKEY

When Sir William Gregory married Isabella Augusta Persse in 1880 he opened new worlds to her: the treasure trove of Coole itself, the possibilities for extensive foreign travel, and an introduction to cultivated London society, where she could be hostess in her own residence. All these flowered in the remarkable achievement of the Irish Literary Theatre. Much has been written on these points, yet there still remains much to be done on the significance of the other aspects of their union:

Sir William himself, who was aged sixty-three when he married his twenty-eight-year-old bride, was by then in many ways quite different from the parliamentary representative of the Landlord class of the 1850s; the *bon viveur* with an undisciplined passion for the turf. By this time he had demonstrated his *sagesse* as Governor of Ceylon in many ways. Among them were: his courageous awareness of the impracticability of justifying Anglicanism as an Established church, a sore point in his native Ireland; his ability to see from his Australian trip that participatory democracy could produce satisfactory results, another point with relevance to Ireland; again, he respected and preserved Singhalese texts. As Brian Jenkins writes:

The preservation of Ceylon's 'national monuments and literature' Gregory had every reason to believe, was an important legacy of his rule.[1]

His attitude to 'reliques' can have a bearing on Lady Gregory's later researches into Gaelic lore and language, something to be added to Mary Sheridan's role in her childhood formation in this sphere.

Ever his sensitive self, Sir William chose to spend much of his honeymoon journey with his old friends Sir Henry Layard and his wife, Enid, at the Ambassadorial residence in Constantinople.

213

From then on they visited each other, as couples, a custom which continued when the wives became widows, in London or above all at Ca' Cappello Layard on the Grand Canal in Venice. Lady Gregory wrote to Yeats in 1909:

> I am in my old state room, at the corner of the water floor, looking through four ivy-trellised windows at the sunlight on the water, and only hearing the splash of oars and the gondolier singing. The room is full of beautiful furniture, and when I came in last night, at midnight, from the long dusty journey and found the Italian housemaid who has welcomed me for twenty-five years, on the steps to kiss my hand, and other servants bringing chianti in a flask and soup in a silver bowl, it felt like fairyland.[2]

Except for matters concerning Irish/English relations (including Kitchener) the two women had much in common. They were two energetic women married to husbands in public life, who were much older than themselves; they were both fully involved in the manifold tasks undertaken in the spirit of *noblesse oblige*; both chatelaines of great houses renowned for their hospitality and their collections. As Elizabeth Coxhead writes on their relationship:

> for Enid Layard, her ideal as a hostess and a great lady, she [Lady Gregory] felt a hero-worship which developed into the closest intimacy she ever had with another woman.[3]

Lady Layard found expression for her talents through her home in Venice. Her qualities were threefold: firstly, the organizing and maintaining of her husband's prodigious collection during his lifetime and after his death; secondly, continuing the enterprise of her mother, Lady Charlotte Guest (the translator of the *Mabinogion*), whose collections, when she became Lady Charlotte Schreiber, were legendary in her own lifetime; thirdly, as an acknowledged moving spirit of a group of persons (Kitchener included), themselves concerned with building up their own 'great house'. Lady Gregory — and Coole — were fortunate in having such examples as Lady Layard and Ca' Cappello Layard.

Lady Gregory acknowledges her affectionate gratitude when recalling Lady Layard (and the practical gift of a typewriter) when writing *Our Irish Theatre*:

> She who had given it to me has gone. She gave me also the great gift of her friendship for more than half my lifetime, Enid, Lady Layard,

Ambassadress at Constantinople and Madrid, helper of the miserable and the wounded in the Turkish-Russian War; helper of the sick in the hospital she founded in Venice; friend and hostess and guest of Queens in England and Germany and Rome. She was her husband's good helpmate while she lived — is not that Cyprus Treaty set down in that clear handwriting I shall never see coming here again? And widowed, she kept his name in honour, living after him fifteen years, and herself leaving a noble memory in all places where she had stayed, and in Venice where her home was and where she died.[4]

W. B. YEATS AND OTHER EUROPEANS

ANDREW PARKIN

'I have no theories about her. She is simply a note of interrogation. "Olcott is much honester than I am," she said to me one day, "he explains things. I am an old Russian savage," that is the deepest I ever got into her riddle.'[1] Thus Yeats described Mme Blavatsky to his more influential mentor, John O'Leary. Yeats's first contact with her was in London in 1887. His attitude at the time was, it seems, a mixture of fascination, amusement and gentle irony; in commending her to O'Leary he wrote, 'she is the most human person alive, is like an old peasant woman, and is wholly devoted, all her life is but sitting in a great chair with a pen in her hand. For years she has written twelve hours a day'.[2] In 1891 she was dead. But through her Yeats perhaps made his first contact with Russia. From her, he would have absorbed a great deal of wayward personality and Russian 'soul'. In 1888 he was reading Tolstoy in translation and preferring Turgenev.[3] Yeats, though, makes little mention of Russian literature, French being a far greater influence on him. Although his library contained two books by Chekhov, his interest in Russia seems to have been more in its ideas and its politics. O'Shea's *Descriptive Catalog of W. B. Yeats's Library* reveals that he had a copy of Harold Laski's *Communism* (1927) and owned Lenin's *Materialism and Empirio-Criticism* (1927), Minsky's *Lenin* (1931) and Stalin's *The October Revolution* (1934).[4] The Russian Revolution, together with the collapse of the Chinese empire and the mass slaughter of the First World War, must have convinced him that this was the turmoil which always accompanied the arrival of a new phase of history.

Great and irreversible changes in European society could not help but be anticipated by artists and at the same time drive them to seek new modes of expression. This was no less true of Yeats than it was of others. Drama has always been a form responsive to social change. In founding the Irish Literary Theatre, the National Dramatic Company, the Irish National Theatre Society, and the Abbey Theatre, Yeats and his colleagues were responding to Yeats's own need for dramatic expression, Ireland's need for a living drama, and a current of European theatre experimentation we now know as the little theatre movement. The Abbey, under the influence of Yeats, Synge, and Lady Gregory, takes its place as part of that European reform of the theatre we find in the work of the Saxe-Meiningen players, the Théâtre de l'Oeuvre, the Théâtre Libre, the Independent Theatre, the Stage Society, and the Moscow Art Theatre. As Hugh Hunt reminds us in *The Abbey, Ireland's National Theatre 1904-1979*, 'Yeats had always intended that the Abbey should include plays by continental dramatists in its repertoire'.[5] This repertoire, however, was made up entirely of Irish plays until the Abbey's 1907 production of Maeterlinck's *Interior*. Lady Gregory's translations (of Sudermann and Molière) do not begin to appear until 1908. It is not until 1913 that we find the Abbey producing Gerhardt Hauptmann's *Hannele* and Strindberg's *There are Crimes and Crimes* and *The Stronger*.

The reason for the neglect of European drama in the Abbey's repertoire is not hard to find: the Irish National Theatre had to encourage new Irish dramatists. It needed Irish plays. But such needs have to be balanced against others to avoid parochialism. From one point of view the Abbey was a plucky National theatre creating from scratch a modern Irish drama; from another it was a rather backward provincial theatre on the edge of Europe. The realism which avant-garde English and continental artists had already rebelled against in the little theatres had become at the Abbey the dominant kind of drama. Audiences which had been receptive to verse were now largely ignoring the fact that Ireland had in Yeats the only interesting verse dramatist in the entire English-speaking world. Little did they know or care that Yeats had from the beginning of his career in the theatre not only learned his craft but contributed through theory and practice to the revolution in the modern European theatre. When Yeats and Lennox Robinson founded the Dublin Drama League in 1918 to bring largely continental European works to the Irish stage, they had to justify what would be accepted as a matter of course in London. Lennox Robinson explained the situation bluntly in *Curtain Up*:

Here in Ireland we are isolated, cut off from the thought of the world, except the English world, and from England we get little in drama, except fourth-rate. I ask you, for the young writer's sake, to open up the door and let us out of our prison. Seeing foreign plays will not divorce our minds from Ireland . . . but being brought into touch with other minds who have different values of life, suddenly we shall discover the rich material that lies to our hand in Ireland.[6]

These words are interesting for another reason: they reveal very clearly the philistinism that Irish artists sometimes try to quieten by blatantly patriotic statements or anti-English salvoes to reassure listeners.

Katharine Worth has explored very thoroughly Yeatsian drama considered in the context of developments in the modernist theatre of Western Europe.[7] Picking up on the similarities rather than the differences between Yeats, Synge, O'Casey, and Beckett, she has argued persuasively for the existence of an Irish drama of the interior stemming from the plays of Maeterlinck and not just exerting a strong influence on modernist European drama but, through Beckett himself, becoming central to it and providing precedents for playwrights as powerful as Pinter in the English theatre.

To see Yeats as a European dramatist has always been necessary in view of the influence on him of Maeterlinck's plays, French *symboliste* writing, and the work of Edward Gordon Craig. What was less obvious, until the appearance of Katharine Worth's astute book, was the *centrality* of Yeats to European modernist theatre. And there is a paradox involved: Yeats spent much of his time on the outer edge of Europe where the Abbey theatre was an obscure semi-amateur affair, before its writers and its acting style made it internationally famous. Yet, right at the other end of Europe, remarkable things were happening in the theatre.

Another aspect of this enormous subject, and one which has been little considered, is the remarkable similarity between Yeats's idea of an avant-garde theatre and that developed in Russia by Vsevolod Meyerhold. The interest of this unexpected link is not a matter of the influence of Yeats on Meyerhold, or vice-versa. There were, of course, links between Yeats and Russian theatre: there were productions at the Abbey of Nikolai Evreinov's *A Merry Death* in 1921 and Chekhov's *The Proposal* in 1925. Ninette de Valois, trained by Diaghilev, formed the Abbey School of Ballet in 1927. As Ann Saddlemyer has commented, Signora Esposito (formerly Nathalia Petrovna Klebnikoff) 'was a staunch supporter of the early society and Holloway recalls her serving as wardrobe mistress during rehearsals in December 1904'.[9] She translated Synge's *Riders to the Sea* into French and Russian. The most direct link between Yeats and Russian theatre, however, was no less influential a person than Edward Gordon Craig. That Craig and

Yeats had ideas in common, and that Craig influenced Yeats's thinking and theatre practice is well-known. That he could have told Yeats about developments in Russia on his return from working there on his famous *Hamlet* in collaboration with Stanislavsky is likely, though not certain. That Yeats was well aware of the 'new decorative method' in the theatre, and the work of the Russian Ballet in that respect, is clear. Yeats was anxious that his essays on theatre together with designs by Edward Gordon Craig and Robert Gregory should be published in a new issue of his *Collected Works*. He knew that his own theatre work had clear affinities with developments in avant-garde European theatre and wanted the publication to be a timely reminder of that. The new issue, however, did not appear.[10] But here I am more interested in the fact that Yeats and the young Meyerhold had worked totally independently of one another to formulate very similar ideas about theatre. What makes this significant for the student of Yeats the dramatist is that Meyerhold is firmly and widely acknowledged to be a director of genius. Indeed, he is arguably the greatest stage director of this century.

That Meyerhold knew little of Irish drama is fairly certain. Although Shaw's plays have been produced in Russian and many of O'Casey's have been translated,[11] Meyerhold's only ventures with Irish drama were confined to Shaw, a minor production of *You Never Can Tell* on 15 July, 1912 (at Teryoki, near Petersburg) which Meyerhold omitted from his list of the works he directed, and a production of *Pygmalion* on 30 September, 1915 at the Alexandrinsky Theatre.[12] Furthermore, Meyerhold always maintained that his experiments in theatre were independent of Craig. Craig's work was confirmation rather than inspiration.

Remarkably, Craig, Yeats and Meyerhold searched for an anti-realistic theatre each in his own fashion, each at first failing to gain widespread recognition and public acclaim, and each contributing profoundly to the revolution in theatre of our century and the development of recent production methods. Though it will be necessary to mention Craig's work in passing, the concern here is with the similarities between the work of Yeats and Meyerhold.

In his 1901 *Samhain* essay, a stocktaking after a decade of apprenticeship to drama, Yeats made it clear that the Irish Literary Theatre was a public trial of Irish national feeling that 'would show whether the country desired to take up the project, and make it a part of the national life'; Yeats judged the experiment successful enough to declare 'that a dramatic movement which will not die has been started'.[13] The first task was no less an undertaking than to express in dramatic terms the Irish people's imagination. But Yeats's involvement in first, writing plays and second, producing them turned out in the case of the first activity to be a major part of his life's work; in the case of the second, theatre business and *mise-en-scène* occupied him far more than the mere three years he had hoped for at the start of the venture. Theatrical management (a large part of which was what we now call directing) he considered not to be part of his 'proper work'.[14] Like playwriting, however, it turned out to be one of his many talents. Over the next eighteen years Yeats had worked out his own symbolist drama inspired by Ireland and Europe and had also created in his dance plays, a startlingly beautiful modernist verse drama.[15] It was over roughly the same period that Meyerhold, at the other fringe of Europe, carried out his own experiments in symbolist, non-realistic theatre which led to his revolutionary modern style of *mise-en-scène*.

At the outset of his career in the theatre Yeats saw that the dominant influence of the English commercial theatre had to be resisted in favour of a more eclectic, largely European influence, though, as we have seen, this proved more a pious hope than an actuality in the Abbey's early repertoire. It was an influence very much alive, though, in the minds of Irish dramatists such as Yeats, Synge, and Lady Gregory. Yeats urged his colleagues to go beyond Shakespeare (too much English influence) for, he insisted, 'It is of the first importance that those among us who want to write for the stage should study the dramatic masterpieces of the world . . . if Irish drama is to mean anything to Irish intellect'.[15] In his stocktaking, Yeats noted that the conventions of English poetic drama were 'worn-out', that Ibsen was 'the one great master the modern stage had produced' and that the Irish writers need 'the severe discipline of French and Scandinavian drama' rather than 'Shakespeare's luxuriance'.[17] Yeats saw that Irish writers faced a choice between upper-class exploitation of Ireland and what he called 'the intellectual movement which has raised the cry that was heard in Russia in the 'seventies, the cry, "To the people" '.[18] Interestingly, Yeats in 1901 was looking to another European culture rich in peasant life and folklore for analogous experience.

The following year in *Samhain: 1902*, Yeats describes the kind of acting and staging he thought was best suited to poetic drama. He had imagined such acting, and at last found it in the National Dramatic company, whose actors, being mainly amateur and so uncorrupted by the fussy mannerisms of the professionals in the commercial English plays, 'kept still enough to give poetical writing its full effect upon the stage'. To this stillness, Yeats acutely added the 'rhythmic progression' he closely observed in Sarah Bernhardt's and de Max's acting in *Phèdre*. Yeats admired in this production the statuesque white-robed figures of the chorus. Such 'blocking' gave the stage picture incredible beauty, and an 'extraordinary reality and intensity'.[19] A member of an Irish audience at the Antient Concert Rooms, watching the Irish players, and the simplicity and stylized quality of their acting, exclaimed 'They have got rid of all the nonsense'. Yeats approved. He wanted a poetic symbolist drama that would use a simplified stage décor and costuming not only because it was less costly but also less realistic than the norm in the commercial theatres. He argued that 'poetical drama, which tries to keep at a distance from daily life that it may keep its emotion untroubled', should be 'staged with but two or three colours'. Scenery would be austerely unrealistic 'with perhaps a few shadowy forms to suggest wood or mountain'.[20] The images of the poetic text must be allowed to suggest the scene to the imaginative viewer by staging that avoided the solidity of clutter which, in the box set realistically furnished, distracted the mind, forcing it to take in a museum display of household objects or the archaeological restoration of the past rather than to focus on the play. This stylized theatre needed its own kind of speech instead of realistic colloquial delivery. Hence Yeats's concern about the musical qualities of stage diction and his experiments with Florence Farr's 'cantillation' over which many of his contemporaries made merry. By contrast, we should not forget that Yeats was striving for a common speech, expressive of personality, not a dead, literary, idiom. He wanted 'the breath of men's mouths' or the spoken word 'even though we have to speak our lyrics to the psaltery or the harp' to create a speech that rejects 'the base idioms of the newspapers'.[21] His authorities for this view of style were the European writers Sainte-Beuve and Zola. Born a Victorian, Yeats quickly learned to avoid the excesses of Victorian poetic diction by turning to folk idiom, the common speech of the country people: 'our movement', he declared, 'is a return to the people, like the Russian movement of the early 'seventies.'[22] That his actual productions were not always successful is a matter of record. But this does not invalidate his basic principles. The resources of the Irish players were limited. Yeats's principles, however, grew from the perceptions of an artist of genius rethinking theatre practice to accommodate a modern non-realistic drama during the heyday of stage realism. He was well aware that drawing-room realism belonged to the cities and the smart audiences and the realistic acting so brilliantly achieved in the English theatre. His artistic needs were different, and he saw a chance for Ireland to create a different but distinguished tradition based on the life of its countryside that could 'ennoble the man of the roads'.[23] In Russia, Meyerhold similarly rejected the realistic method he had learned from Stanislavsky and the Moscow Art Theatre. The confrontation of realistic method with non-realistic and symbolic method in the theatre was dramatized by Chekhov and enacted prophetically on the evening of 17 December 1898, by Meyerhold and Stanislavsky playing respectively the aspiring symbolist playwright, Treplyov and the established commercial dramatist, Trigorin. It was the opening night of Chekhov's *The Seagull* at the Moscow Art Theatre. Treplyov wants '. . . new art forms. New forms are wanted'. When Nina objects that his play has 'no real living characters in it' his answer is true to the symbolist idea of a theatre of dream: 'Living characters! We don't have to depict life as it is, or as it ought to be, but as we see it in our dreams.'[24] Yeats, always more concerned with real life than was Chekhov's Treplyov who, of course, commits suicide, could nevertheless have replied in similar vein to such criticisms of *The Countless Cathleen* or *The Shadowy Waters*. The confrontation of two theatrical modes offers a choice, and as Paul Schmidt remarks, it is a choice that 'must still be made today: in distinctions between the work of Stanislavsky and the work of Meyerhold is the definition of a modern theatre to be found'.[25] Stanislavsky's triumph and vast influence seems now clearly the great culmination of the nineteenth century realism in the theatre. The paths followed by Meyerhold and Yeats are the recapturing of an older tradition anterior to realism and capable of sustaining a characteristic twentieth century search for modern expression.

In *Samhain: 1903* Yeats recalled and systematized his well-considered objections to the theatre as he found it at the time: the plays, speaking, acting and décor were all wrong. The remedy is to write plays full of intellectual excitement, as in the great periods of drama in Greece, England, France, and Scandinavia. Such plays demand vital, beautiful, unique speech: the 'sovereignty' of words. They also require strong structure to 'arrange much complicated life into a single action' able to 'hold the attention or linger in the memory'. It follows that words must be made 'even more important than gesture on the stage'.[26] Hand in glove with this goes the third demand: 'We must simplify acting, concentrating on voice and grave, infrequent gesture.' This entails simplified scenery and colour, thought out 'as if it were the background of a portrait, and this is especially necessary on a small stage'.[27] His objections to modern realism make it clear that Yeats looks to the future with Meyerhold, turning his back on a nineteenth century art brought to its apogee by Stanislavsky: 'But an art which smothers these things with bad painting, with innumerable garish colours, with continual restless mimicries of the surface of life, is an art of fading humanity, a decaying art.'[28] Yeats's basic principles remained much the same, except that he added under the influence partly of Craig and partly of Japanese Noh drama, the use of masks, on-stage music and musicians to serve also as a chorus, and the potent figure of the dancer whose movements become the more significant because set against stillness. The principles all serve what Yeats found in drama as in all great art: 'a moment of intense life'.[29]

Konstantin Rudnitsky characterized the duality in Russian theatre in the period just before the First World War by describing the differing styles of Stanislavsky and Meyerhold in their respective studios:

Refined naturalism and attempts to mobilize the actors' subconscious in the First Studio were diametrically opposed to the refined cult of acting, the physical, bodily virtuosity practiced in Meyerhold's Studio. In each case we have one-sidedness carried to an extreme. The extreme polarization of these experiments by Stanislavsky and Meyerhold was a crude and declarative indication of the duality in the art of the pre-war years.[30]

A major distinction between these two great theatre artists was that where Stanislavsky developed his 'method' by working on internal techniques for the actor, Meyerhold worked on external techniques of acrobatic movement, gesture, and dance, believing that talented, as opposed to mediocre artists always felt the role emotionally, whatever else they were accomplishing.

Meyerhold was trained at the drama school of the Moscow Philharmonic Society and emerged as one of two A+ students, the other in his year being Olga Knipper, later to become Chekhov's wife. Both were awarded the Society's silver medal for acting. In the same year, 1898, Stanislavsky and Vladimir Nemirovich-Danchenko founded the Moscow Popular Art Theatre and invited Meyerhold to join its company. For the next four years Meyerhold served an 'apprenticeship' in theatre by playing eighteen roles, character parts and juvenile leads. He also worked as an assistant director. While Yeats was learning his craft as a playwright and formulating his theory of non-realistic theatre in *Samhain*, Meyerhold and his colleague, Alexander Kosheverov, hired the municipal theatre at Kherson in the Ukraine for the 1902-03 season, and there played with the company they founded[31] a repertoire based on that of the Moscow Art Theatre. As Meyerhold later pointed out, he 'began as a director by slavishly imitating Stanislavsky'.[32] But even at this early stage he was questioning in theory what he could not yet abandon in practice. Meyerhold's dissatisfaction with materialism in the theatre may have been sparked off by Chekhov at a rehearsal of *The Seagull* on 11 September, 1898. When an actor told him about the planned sound effects of croaking frogs, humming dragon flies and barking dogs, Chekhov asked the reason:

'Because it's realistic' — replied the actor. 'Realistic!' — repeated Chekhov with a laugh. Then after a short pause he said: 'The stage is art. There's a genre painting by Kramskoy in which the faces are portrayed superbly. What would happen if you cut the nose out of one of the paintings and substituted a real one? The nose would be "realistic" but the picture would be ruined.'[33]

Chekhov's theatre of mood certainly taught Meyerhold that the limits of realism were already questioned within the Chekhovian canon. In addition, Meyerhold was trying to find a method for staging the new drama that was emerging from the symbolist movement. At Sevastopol, his group performed Maeterlinck's *Intruder* and Schnitzler's *The Last Masks* in 'an evening of new art' as they billed it.[34] The notion of a new art of the theatre appealed to Meyerhold so much that he changed the name of his company to 'The Fellowship of the New Drama' for its second season in Kherson.[35] Now Meyerhold was sole director and as Konstantin Rudnitsky puts it, 'From distant Kherson he was throwing down the gauntlet to Moscow and the Art Theatre'.[36]

It was his production of *Acrobats* by Franze von Schonthan in 1903 which shows Meyerhold clearly in transition from the style of the Art Theatre. The set, behind the scenes at a circus, with glimpses of a live audience seated at the back of the stage watching the circus, was realized as meticulously as possible in the Moscow manner. Meyerhold wore a real clown costume to play Landovsky, the hero. Landovsky is an ageing clown in decline, and his great moment occurs in Act III when he comes on from the circus ring to stand facing the real audience in the theatre silent, motionless, and waiting his applause from the on-stage audience. Instead, after a long wait, there is applause for another performer. The tormented jester Rigoletto has been given a modern life. The clown obsessed Meyerhold as it did other modern artists, such as Picasso. This role prepared him for Alexander Blok's play *The Puppet Show*. Similarly, Yeats was using his version of the image at the other end of Europe. The Black Jester, projected but abandoned, the Fool of *The Hour Glass*, the Fools in *On Baile's Strand* and in *The Herne's Egg*: all attest to Yeats's subtle and distinctive use of the image. The clown, the Fool, Pierrot — indeed the Commedia dell'Arte as a whole — interest both Yeats and Meyerhold because they arise from an ancient imagination, they suggest the irrational element in life, and they embody the disruptive forces that cannot be contained within ordinary materialistic notions of reality.

Meyerhold's attempts to find a symbolist method of performance for the new drama lagged behind those of Yeats, for the latter had the advantage of having already seen Gordon Craig's productions. Meyerhold's close friend and play adviser in the Kherson company, Aleksei Remizov had, like Yeats's friend, Arthur Symons, assimilated the symbolist ideas and attitudes. In a remarkably Yeatsian description of a symbolist idea of theatre he asserted, 'The theatre is not a copy of human mediocrity. Rather it is a cult, a Mass in whose mysteries perhaps Atonement is concealed . . . The New Drama dreams of such a theatre'.[37] Meyerhold was quick to see Maeterlinckian strains in *The Cherry Orchard*. In a letter to Chekhov he recognized that Chekhov's drama of modern life had Maeterlinck's horror mixed with its comedy. 'There is something of Maeterlinck, something terrifying in this act', he wrote, and added, 'When one reads foreign writers, one is aware of your unique originality. The West is going to have to learn drama from you.'[38] The linking of Chekhov and Maeterlinck now seems less justified, but Meyerhold produced both *The Intruder* and *Monna Vanna* in Kherson. Although his production there of *The Cherry Orchard* was Stanislavsky without a trace of Maeterlinck, Meyerhold developed his hunches and new ideas rapidly. He was eager to leave Kherson where he had deviated little from his training;[39] taking the company to the more cultivated environment of Tbilisi in 1904. There he tried out some innovative ideas in his production of Stanislaw Przybuszewski's *The Snow*. Each of its three acts began in darkness. But the play was not as significant a vehicle for symbolism and the new acting as Meyerhold had thought. The production failed, going down amid the hisses of a noisy young audience. Meyerhold, however, was more successful with his production of Schonthan's *Acrobats*.

Ready for more experiment, Meyerhold responded with great relief when, the season over, he was free to join Stanislavsky in a new project. Stanislavsky, too, had realized the need for fresh approaches, agreeing with Nemirovich-Danchenko that symbolism could lead the Art Theatre out of a dead end. In attempting to account for the allure of symbolism for Russian artists of the period, Konstantin Rudnitsky suggests that the ambiguity of symbols accords with the uncertainty and ambiguity of Russia itself, part European, part Asiatic. This could, perhaps, be applied slightly differently to part Irish, part European Anglo-Irish artists and to Yeats himself. Be that as it may, Rudnitsky's analysis of symbolist drama and its fascination for Meyerhold can be illuminating too when considering Yeats:

> Symbolist drama was unavoidably and consistently characterized by paradox: negation in a symbolist play was equivalent to disbelief, protest emotionally close to despair, *a longing for wholeness of soul was accompanied by a sense of dichotomy* . . . And the most consistent Russian producer of symbolist plays, Meyerhold, grappled with this very paradox and in the end gave in.[40] [my italics]

One of the things Yeats discovered in his search for a symbolist theatre was the lesson that spirit and flesh need each other, need 'desecration and the lover's night': symbol and reality need each other; and so Yeats found a form in which he could use a realistic enough situation and dialogue to balance the dancer from the depths of the mind while still preserving a decorous balance that achieved artistic unity in a non-realistic form. Stanislavsky failed to find such a balance when he staged in 1904 three Maeterlinck plays, *The Sightless*, *The Intruder*, and *Interior*. Tired of realistic crowds, he tried statuesque, posed stillness instead, but the plays were not a success. Stanislavsky the realist decided that he needed to send for Meyerhold, if he was to revitalize the Art Theatre. They probably met in March 1905 to discuss a studio which later became the Studio on Povarskaya Street changed 'into a laboratory of formalist experiments'.[41] Meyerhold and Stanislavsky were agreed that they would create, through the Povarskaya Street experiments, a symbolist theatre. Inevitably, the repertoire included Maeterlinck. Meyerhold saw symbolism as a powerful force for socialist change in Russian society. In a speech he drafted for his production of *The Death of Tantagiles* in Tbilisi he suggested that the audience should share Ygraine's indignation not against death, but against its cause, and you will see not just a symbolist play . . . Then the island on which the action takes place becomes our life. The queen's castle represents our prisons and Tintagiles the youth of mankind, trusting, admirable, ideally pure. And someone ruthlessly puts these young people to death . . . On our island thousands of Tintagileses suffer in prisons.[42]

While Yeats used symbolism to put his audience in touch with a magical revolution in feeling and an aesthetic rebellion against materialist thinking, the social conditions in Russia led Maeterlinck to a very different kind of symbolist rebellion. This fundamental difference in social thinking in turn led Meyerhold to develop a stagecraft in the end very different from that of Yeats. But in the years before the Bolshevik revolution, the two were remarkably close in method: like Yeats, Meyerhold arranged figures on stage as if they were in bas-reliefs and frescos. He observed the 'bewilderment' of audiences faced by realistic productions of Maeterlinck plays, and concluded that the playwright's objection that his plays were produced in 'too complex a fashion' was sound. Meyerhold was convinced that Maeterlinck's plays needed simple, stylized productions, with subtle acting capable of immobility and silence to create effects 'almost to the point of resembling puppet plays'. Like Yeats, he concluded 'The need is for a static theatre'. And like Yeats, he turned to the great precedent of Greek tragedy. Like Yeats again he realized that the new dialogue demanded a new delivery, for

every dramatic work contains two levels of dialogue: one is the 'external', necessary dialogue, made up of words which accompany and explain the action; the other is the 'inner dialogue' which the spectator should overhear, not as words but as pauses, not as cries but as silences, not as soliloquies but as the music of plastic movement.[43]

In his work at the Theatre-Studio, as it became known, Meyerhold worked out with his designers and actors ways of escape from Meiningen and Art Theatre naturalism by means of stylization. As Valery Bryusov described it, 'In movement there was plasticity rather than impersonation of reality', while scenery suggested by a few significant details the milieu, rather than attempting to rebuild reality on the stage, and 'dialogue was spoken throughout against a background of music'.[44] There was a problem, however, similar to that facing Yeats at the Abbey. Most of the actors, trained in the realistic mode of Stanislavsky, found it difficult to act in the new way. Both Yeats and Meyerhold, though, realized that the key to a new style was rhythm; and some of the Art Theatre actors were able to capture the rhythm of Chekhov's *The Seagull*. This rhythm of dialogue was the basis of Chekhov's theatre of mood, and for Meyerhold it was a step away from naturalism in the direction of stylization. At the Theatre-Studio Meyerhold in his own opinion 'came very near to achieving ideal stylized drama with its first production, *The Death of Tantagiles*'.[45] In this same essay of 1907, Meyerhold speculated on two approaches to production, the triangular and linear. In the triangular, 'The spectator comprehends the creation of the author and actor through the creation of the director', in the linear approach, 'The actor reveals his soul freely to the spectator, having assimilated the creation of the director, who, in his turn, has assimilated the creation of the author'.[46] Meyerhold favours the linear approach which follows from the premise that *'Above all, drama is the art of the actor'*.[47]

It follows that the reform of the theatre entails the reform of the actor. Meyerhold applied that logic, and so did Yeats. Yeats did it through the mask, music and the dance. A new kind of actor (who is really an old kind of actor) is required. By the time he had written *Deirdre*, Yeats had realized a drama in which the musicians on the stage were not merely a chorus, but actors inspired to commemorate by their art of song the tragic story enacted on stage by a heroine who is following some fore-ordained scenario. In *The Words Upon the Window-Pane* the script Mrs Henderson might have had in mind is rewritten by the ghosts. In *A Full Moon in March* the chorus has been asked to improvise by an unseen director. The play seems one generation's improvisation of an ancient scenario. In *The Death of Cuchulain* the director comes on stage as prologue, and establishes the idea of performance, metatheatre, one style of drama as opposed to another; and within the play itself the morrigu appears as an on-stage choreographer drawing attention to the anti-realistic style of the play. Yeats developed his elegant and sophisticated form of anti-illusionist ritual theatre and its staging from his own sensibility and imagination, his need to find his own way out of the late Victorian theatre, from seeing the work of Gordon Craig and the Parisian avant-garde theatre of the 1890s, and from assimilating what he needed of Japanese Noh. Nor must we leave out his reading of Maeterlinck.

Meyerhold found it at first difficult to go beyond his Stanislavskyan training. He did so eventually partly because he needed artistically to establish his own directorial style, and partly because as a practical man of the theatre preparing productions, he had to find a style to suit the new drama. It was his reading, his assimilation and his production of Maeterlinck which led him into the anti-illusionist theatre and the radical experimentation that made him so famous, and so influential, and so dangerous for his Soviet masters. From his work on Maeterlinck, Meyerhold learned the art of grave diction, musically phrased, and 'Tragedy with a smile on the lips'.[48] He tells us that he could not fully see why this was necessary, however, until he read the remarks of Savonarola:

Do not assume that Mary cried out at the death of her son and roamed the streets, tearing her hair and acting like a mad woman. She followed Him with great humility. Certainly she shed tears, but her appearance revealed not so much sheer grief as a combination of *grief and joy*. Even at the foot of the Cross she stood in grief and joy, engrossed in the mystery of God's great mercy.[49]

Tragedy with a smile on the lips was discovered too by the Yeats of 'Lapis Lazuli'. Meyerhold also saw the need for plasticity of gesture and movement so that the actor, against a stark, perhaps monochrome background would have the stylized quality of an icon; he urges that 'The actor must study *the plasticity of the statue*'.[50] But in pursuing plasticity and the three dimensional in the theatre Meyerhold began to part company with Yeats. He now rejected the decorative panel in favour of architectural approaches to setting, and this later, in my view, led to the constructivist set. But the emphasis on the actor's body is very Yeatsian, for the actor becomes a dancer. In liberating 'the actor from all scenery creating a three-dimensional area in which he can employ natural, sculptural plasticity'[51] Meyerhold also removed the footlights and broke out beyond the proscenium arch. The transaction of spectator and actor became more intimate. Yeats's dance plays also abolished the proscenium arch theatre, theatre lighting and created at once distance and intimacy. Both Yeats and Meyerhold created a theatre in which 'the spectator should not forget for a moment that an actor is *performing* before him . . .'.[52]

This comparative study has uncovered no direct influence of one artist upon another; rather it has shown that both artists, living on the edge of Europe, one to the West, the other to the East, found independently their own similar paths away from realism and the established commercial theatre. Both were crucial to the building of a strong National theatre in their respective countries. Both belonged firmly to Europe, yet were not totally part of it. And for this reason, perhaps, as Borges points out in comparing the Argentines and Jews, 'they are outstanding in Western [European] culture because they act within that culture and, at the same time, do not feel tied to it by any special devotion'.[53] Borges is following here a theory of Thorstein Veblen. Borges goes on to apply the same idea to the Irish in English culture. We can with a certain measure of confidence say as much for the Russians in European culture.

I have indicated at certain points that Meyerhold of course developed in other than Maeterlinckian directions, as did Yeats. Yeats resisted fiercely those who tried to force the theatre in Ireland to abandon truth and beauty for mere propaganda. Meyerhold, a convinced Bolshevik before the party took power, used his considerable genius as a director in order to help create the new Soviet drama. Tragically for Soviet theatre and for the Meyerholds themselves, Stalin's favoured socialist realism during the thirties turned the 'culture bosses' against Meyerhold's experimental productions. From 1936 attacks on 'Meyerholdism' appeared in the press, including *Pravda*. The humiliation of genius continued. On 7 January, 1938 the Committee on the Arts 'resolved to liquidate the Meyerhold State Theatre'[54] because of Meyerhold's 'thoroughly bourgeois formalistic positions alien to Soviet art'.[55] On 8 April 1936, Yeats posted a letter to Ethel Mannin in which he explained his refusal to react as she desired politically. He wrote, 'as my sense of reality deepens . . . my horror at the cruelty of governments grows greater . . . Communist, fascist, nationalist, clerical, anti-clerical, are all responsible according to the number of their victims.'[56] He reminded her that he was the author of the prophetic 'The Second Coming'. He was so alert to Europe and its new political nightmare that he confessed 'every nerve trembles with horror at what is happening in Europe, "the ceremony of innocence is drowned" '.[57] It was not for nothing that Yeats depicted in *Purgatory* an old man knifing his own son, nor a blind man cutting the throat of a hero in *The Death of Cuchulain*, his last play left unrevised at the time of his death in January 1939. Meyerhold was arrested that June and executed in prison on 2 February, 1940. In mid July, 1939, Meyerhold's wife, the actress Zinaida Raikh, famed for the beauty of her expressive eyes, was taken into custody by the secret police with no explanation. On 17 July she was found 'in her apartment with eleven knife wounds in her body, her eyes put out and her throat cut, she was rushed to a hospital, but died four hours later'.[58]

The end of Meyerhold's theatre is very Russian, very European, very Yeatsian. Everyone knew the theatre had been officially 'liquidated'. Meyerhold had not yet received the documentation. He therefore went ahead with the matinée performance of Gogol's *The Inspector General*. Here is Mixhail Sadovskij's account.

The Inspector General began, and each scene as it was played disappeared forever. The play concludes with the well-known dumb scene; Meyerhold had replaced the actors in this final scene by life-size dummies. Each dummy was costumed and made up to resemble the character it replaced. The dummies were put in place in darkness. The sound of a gong. The lights went up. And those dead dolls, which Meyerhold had conceived of as a final image of deadness and petrification, were especially terrifying . . . in that last performance of *The Inspector General*. The sound of the gong again. Darkness. End of scene. End of theatre.[59]

FOUR PLAYS FOR DANCERS: JAPANESE AESTHETICS AND A EUROPEAN MIND

MASARU SEKINE

When theatrical realism was fashionable, Yeats went against the current, writing and inspiring the writing of poetic plays. The new literary movement in Ireland was an antidote to the work of the Scandinavian dramatists Strindberg and Ibsen; it centred on Yeats's formation of the Irish Literary Theatre in 1901, which developed into the Abbey Theatre in 1904. Yeats's ingrained respect for the poetic tradition, his burgeoning talent, and his personal ambition to create an Irish theatre put him in a position to practise what he preached.

His verse play, *Deirdre*, first performed at the Abbey Theatre in November 1906 by the National Theatre Society (it was first published in 1907), is, in essence, very close to a Noh play, though Yeats wrote it before he came to know the Noble plays of Japan. He adopted a sort of story-telling structure by using a chorus and then letting the play proper develop. This play is based on the well known Irish legend, the love and tragedy of Deirdre and Naoise. Yeats brought the lovers back to life on stage, and made his audience experience their tragic love in the most aesthetic poetic form. This use of chorus, legend and poetry combine in a way that is very similar to the usage of the Noh.

Yeats came across the manuscript of Fenollosa's translation of Noh plays through Ezra Pound, who edited them in 1913. (This was when Yeats was renting Stone Cottage in Sussex and Pound was acting as his secretary.) Yeats was fascinated by this encounter with aristocratic Japanese drama. He thought he had found an ideal form which he could adopt for his own poetic theatre, and consequently began to experiment. He wrote four plays for dancers, based on the structure of Noh plays. They are *At the Hawk's Well* (first performed in April 1916; first published in 1917), *The Only Jealousy of Emer* (first performed in 1922; first published in 1919), *The Dreaming of the Bones* (first performed in 1931; first published in 1919) and *Calvary* (first published in 1921).

Yeats's sources of information were limited. Apart from Fenollosa's translation, he found almost nothing to read about the Noh,
as it was still unknown in the West. But the vagueness of his
knowledge of the Noh was actually a great advantage for him
since he was, after all, a European who wanted to adopt the form
of the Noh for his own plays without changing his ultimate
beliefs, ideas, and ideals. If he had known the Noh theatre in
depth, Yeats might have found it more difficult to use its form to
achieve his own goal. Later he met Michio Ito, who performed
the role of the Guardian of the Well in *At the Hawk's Well* at its first
production in Lady Cunard's drawing room in London in April
1916. Yeats also met a couple of amateur Japanese Noh singers.
But Ito was in Europe to learn European dancing and was not
interested in the Noh, nor trained in this theatre. So Yeats did not
get much out of him. As for the two amateur singers, there is a
tremendous gap between professionals and amateurs in the Noh,
and they could not have been much use to Yeats either, particularly
as he was tone deaf.

Spiritually alert, and curious, Yeats ignored the conventional
Buddhist framework underlying all Noh plays. He kept free, for
example, from the reincarnational and similar conventions of the
Noh. The Noh is a purely religious drama, an enactment of basic
Buddhist tenets — similar to the Miracle plays which deal with
the saints, and the cycles of Mystery plays which dealt with Biblical
themes from the Creation to the Ascension. Yeats, however,
certainly did not in any way become a conventional believer in
Buddhism, and this is very obvious in his four plays.

At the Hawk's Well is not religious, though it includes a supernatural character, the Guardian of the Well, and there are mystical
war cries at the conclusion, which allure the youthful warrior
Cuchulain away from the well, where once he sought a few drops
of immortal water. Yeats threw mystical elements into this play
without the slightest hesitation: after all, the Noh was mysterious
to him, so why not?

The source of this play could well have been *Yoro*, a Noh play
included in Fenollosa's translations. The central theme is the
same, a search for immortality. But the way the theme is developed
in each case is very different. In the first part of the Noh play, a
courtier is ordered by the Emperor Yuryaku to search for the
rumoured site of life-giving water in the northern mountains.
When he arrives at this site, he is met by a father and his son, who
consequently relate their unexpected discovery of the miraculous
water. In the second part, the courtier hears heavenly music, and

meets the god of mercy, Yoro Kannon Bosatsu: through the grace of this god the hard-working son had discovered the immortal water, so that he could have fresh energy while his aged parents gained longevity. The god of mercy concludes the play by praising the emperor for a successful reign marked by peace and prosperity. As a theme, this may not be very convincing to contemporary playgoers for its obvious propaganda and acceptance of the emperor as a deity. But we have to be aware that the most of the Noh plays were written in the fourteenth century when people did still believe that the emperor was a living god. The time gap between the existing material and the period when this play was written was roughly three to four hundred years, while Yeats's case is altogether different. He took his material from the Cuchulain legend which dates back, in written form, to around the eighth century, but he wrote it in 1915/1916. So the time gap was roughly three times longer between him and his material. And, while Yeats's spiritual values were heartfelt and idealistic, they were personal to him and not part and parcel of the accepted views of his contemporaries. He was trying to achieve a very different goal from that of the Noh when attempting to adapt the mythical theatre of aristocratic Japan in order to revive one of Ireland's heroes as a national symbol.

Aoino-Ue (Lady Hollyhock), also included in Fenollosa's translations, may have provided another source of inspiration, for *The Only Jealousy of Emer*. Both plays deal with wives' jealousy of young mistresses. The Noh Play records how a princess vents her anger on a young mistress, Aoino-Ue. The princess Rokujo suffers intensely, enacting bitterness and rejection, as she concentrates on projecting her venom onto her rival. Aoino-Ue has stolen her husband's love, and made a public mockery of her — deliberately crashing her carriage into that of the princess and breaking it. This impertinence enrages Rokujo, whose strong desire for vengeance begins to undermine her rival's health. Aoino-Ue's illness becomes so critical that a priestess is sent for. She discovers the emotional background to Aoino-Ue's collapse, but the priestess's prayers cannot subdue the feelings of intense hatred which are attacking Aoino-Ue. A saint is then sent for, and his devotion to his faith enables him to enact a cure, pacifying her spiteful rival.

Yeats, in his version, showed in Emer a woman who could forgive all earthy rivals, such as Eithne Inguba, her husband Cuchulain's mistress, because she clings to the hope of being re-united with him in his old age. It is a fairy woman's designs on her husband, however, which finally cause Emer to become jealous. Thus Yeats included scientifically unproven realities — supernatural beings represented by the fairyfolk, the woman of Sidhe and Bricriu, as well as the ghost of Cuchulain. But while various supernatural forces such as demons are all finally quelled by a higher spiritual authority in Noh plays, Yeats provided no such hierarchy. Here the Sidhe seem to exist more or less on their own. Fairies practise trickery — the Woman of the Sidhe, boasting of her immortality, deviously tries to gain Cuchulain for herself by making Emer, his wife, promise not to hope for his love if he is returned from the dead — and then she, in turn, is tricked by Bricriu. Their meddling seems effectively disruptive (though they hasten to bear tales of each other's wrongdoing to the fairy king). Having sacrificed her hope of regaining Cuchulain in order to save his life, Emer loses him to her earthly rival, Eithne, as his ghost awakens. Thus, while this is an odd adaptation of a Noh dream play, a curious experiment in different interwoven realities, the ending smacks of worldly ironies rather than divine justice.

The Dreaming of the Bones, definitely the most successful of the four plays for dancers, is closest to the conventions of the Noh theatre. As in *The Only Jealousy of Emer*, Yeats included two main characters as ghosts, in the tradition of Noh dream plays (though strictly speaking neither of Yeats's plays are dream plays, as the second halves of the play never occur in the dream of the supporting characters). The leads are Dervorgilla and Dermot, while the supporting role is taken by a young man who fled from the General Post Office in Dublin after the Irish rising against the British in 1916. This youth is, therefore, a representative of the contemporary Irish people. Like the supporting role in a Noh play (a *waki*), he helps the self-revelation of the dead couple, Dervorgilla and Dermot, who had betrayed and sold their country to the British seven hundred years earlier, and now appeal to him for salvation. He is given the power by the ghosts to pardon their suffering spirits, again, like a monk in the Noh, though this kind of power is not at all religious by any orthodox standards. He is given this authority when the ghost of Dervorgilla says, ' . . . and yet they are not wholly miserable and accursed if some one of their race at last would say: "I forgive them", and if some one of their race forgave them at last lip will be pressed on lip'. Guilty conscience has kept the lovers' spirits apart, but a word of forgiveness would dissolve their anguish. But the Young Man refuses to forgive them, and consequently these ghosts remain earth-bound, bound together in guilt and bound up with events enacted seven hundred years earlier. As Yeats wrote his play almost immediately after the 1916 rising, it seems natural that he could not write the line 'I forgive you', to expiate past errors. The Young Man, before leaving the scene, says, 'I had almost yielded and forgiven them it all — this is indeed a place of terrible temptation'. This may express Yeats's own ambivalent attitude to history. Immediately after the 1916 rising, the general feelings of Irish people were much harsher toward the legendary lovers, whom Yeats explored as an aesthetic example of tragic love. *The Dreaming of the Bones* was, therefore, a potentially powerful piece of propaganda, and so was not produced until later, in 1931.

Here *Nishikigi* was the Noh play inspiring Yeats, though it has no political elements whatsoever in it. *Nishikigi's* theme is one of tragic love where love is not reciprocated. In *Nishikigi*, the theme is not one of guilty conscience, but, more simply, the rejection of a man by the woman he loves. This play is based on an old custom of the Japanese Ainu race. If a man fell in love with a woman, he would bring an ornate branch, a *nishikigi*, to her house. If she took this love token into her house, it was a sign that she had accepted his wooing. If she did not, the man was supposed to keep bringing such love tokens to her house, even a thousand times, until she accepted him. But in *Nishikigi*, the woman refused the lover even after he had brought the *nishikigi* to her door for a thousand nights. He died despairingly, and she, exhausted by his attentions, died immediately afterwards. His obsessive desire for her, and her obsessive rejection of him linked their souls, which, according to Buddhist teaching, were held back from heavenly peace. The spiritual intercession of a stranger monk, who felt for them, released them from the grip of their negative emotions and earthly bondage.

Calvary, the last of this series of four plays, shows a definite departure from the Noh. Although its characters are central figures from the Bible, Jesus, Lazarus and Judas, the play itself hardly corresponds to any Christian doctrine. Lazarus, called back from death by Jesus, shows his contempt, and seeks isolation. Judas challenges Jesus: '. . . knowing that a man betrays a God, he is the stronger of the two . . . You cannot even save me'. The two challenges are followed by Roman soldiers, behaving disrespectfully, both conversationally and with a dice-throwing dance to determine who is to have Jesus's cloak after his death. Tellingly, the drama does not include the Resurrection.

Yeats, dealing with these personalities from the Bible, deliberately chose negative ideas. Miraculous, ritualistic renewals, belief in divinity allowing for the growth of inner vitality — such themes are avoided. So, although interested in aesthetic and artistic aspects of the Noh arts practised five hundred years previously, he omitted the Noh's concluding, and vital, features. In all Noh pieces guilt and suffering are set, finally, against forgiveness and time-transcending harmony. The Noh plays emphasise the positive side of the wheel of consciousness. Noh dramatists believed that, in seeing a soul or souls tormented, and in consequently witnessing how prayer brings peace, an audience is brought into a shared understanding of forgiveness and grace: a blessing is evoked.

YEATS, IBSEN AND THE 'NEW WOMAN'

GEORGE WATSON

So heavily is Yeats the dramatist associated with the creation of an Irish theatre, and later with the Japanese Noh, that one of the most useful functions of a context such as this is to remind us of the influence of, and his considerable interest in, European drama. The impact on the young Yeats of the music drama of Richard Wagner, and of the symbolist plays of Villiers de l'Isle-Adam and of Maeterlinck, is well documented,[1] and he may even have picked up some ideas from Strindberg whom he met briefly in Paris in 1894.[2] Much later, in 1930, he is praising Pirandello; and in 1935 speaks enthusiastically of his 'great sensation of recent weeks', the plays of Ernst Toller.[3]

It seems to me that we need to look again at Yeats's relationship to Henrik Ibsen, who, with Zola and Tolstoy, was one of the colossi dominating the literary firmament at the time of the young Yeats's starting out. Much of what follows is a twice-told tale, but the evidence is worth reviewing, and requires us, I would suggest, if not to draw a new map, at least to alter the contours in the one we are familiar with.

That Yeats did not like Ibsen's plays is firmly established in the critical orthodoxy, and the famous moments of critical confrontation are expressed with all of Yeats's authoritative and — in this context, damning — eloquence. Thus, in 1904, in pursuit of his argument that art delights in the exception, not the average, he recalls the first performance of *Ghosts*, some thirteen years earlier:

All the characters seemed to be less than life-size; the stage . . . seemed larger than I had ever seen it. Little whimpering puppets moved here and there in the middle of that great abyss. Why did they not speak out with louder voices or move with freer gestures?[4]

Two years later, in 1906, discussing the play of modern manners and its difficulties in the providing of passionate speech, he remarks cuttingly:

Ibsen understood the difficulty and made all his characters a little provincial that they might not put each other out of countenance, and made a leading-article sort of poetry — phrases about vine-leaves and harps in the air — it was possible to believe them using in their moments of excitement, and if the play needed more than that, they could always do something stupid. They could go out and hoist a flag as they do at the end of *Little Eyolf*.[5]

In 1922, he opens 'The Tragic Generation' with a sort of general retrospect on Ibsen — how he had hated *A Doll's House* more than thirty years previously — 'what was it but Carolus Duran, Bastien-Lepage, Huxley and Tyndall all over again?' — how he carried Archer's translations (which he did not admire) 'to and fro upon my journeys to Ireland and Sligo', how in *Rosmersholm* 'there is symbolism and a stale odour of spilt poetry'; and yet, as he admits, 'neither I nor my generation could escape him'.[6]
    It is no part of my project to pull a revisionist rabbit from the hat, and argue that Yeats, despite this, was a closet Ibsenite. Yeats was, after all, committed to poetic drama (though not as indifferent to realistic and even naturalistic canons as the familiar battle-lines suggest: he objects in 1903, for instance, to the unrealistic placing of a door in a Hyde play; and Lennox Robinson recalls Yeats's searching interest in the details of stage-managing realist plays, and Yeats complaining that 'I had hung the pictures too high, the farmer's daughters were too clean — ("Smear cow-dung on their faces!" I remember him exclaiming)'.[7]
    The very intensity of recoil embodied in the remarks already quoted might, however, suggest that Ibsen was necessary to Yeats, if we accept the general proposition of Joseph Hassett's recent study,[8] that Yeats's were 'the poetics of hate': that Yeats's detestation of, for example, realist painters and Victorian science led him to desire to create an antithetical imaginative space for himself, the hated object rousing his 'will to full intensity' in proportion to the obstructive force in the hated object. Ibsen was a doughty antagonist. In short, 'Yeats transforms hatred into creativity', and — extrapolating freely from Hassett's ideas — *A Doll's House* becomes the major influence on *The Shadowy Waters*. While there is some connection between Hassett's overall thesis and the Yeats-Ibsen relationship, it is all too easy to end up in such a *reductio ad absurdum*.
    We do not need such Blooming dialectics to show a more positive and direct link between Ibsen and Yeats. You will have noticed that the remarks on *Ghosts*, *A Doll's House* and *Rosmersholm* are

retrospective, considerably after the event. In the 1890s, the years of his dramatic apprenticeship, Yeats spoke much more favourably of the Norwegian. He values Ibsen highly as a national and nationalist writer, who 'carried the little seaboard towns of Norway everywhere in his imagination',[9] and whose exploitation of ancient legends in works such as *Peer Gynt* and the *Vikings at Helgeland* provides a model for those who would found a National Drama, and gives the lie to those — such as John Eglinton — who argue that 'these subjects . . . obstinately refuse to be taken out of their old environment and be transplanted into the world of modern sympathies'. Yeats counters that Ibsen's *Peer Gynt* 'founded on "these subjects" is not only "national literature" . . . but the chief glory of the "national literature" of its country'.[10] His proselytizing for the Irish Literary Theatre, his dreams of the Ideal Theatre for Ireland, constantly invoke the example of Ibsen, whose assured European reputation guarantees his usefulness and potency as a theatrical referee in the argument with the doubters. He could not use Villiers de l'Isle Adam or Maeterlinck in the same way. And Ibsen even becomes, as late as 1901, a corrective model for Irish dramatists: 'If Irish dramatists had studied the romantic plays of Ibsen, the one great master the modern stage has produced, they would not have sent the Irish Literary Theatre imitations of Boucicault, who had no relation to literature.'[11]

Yeats himself had clearly studied the 'romantic plays of Ibsen'. He reviewed *Brand*, in a verse translation by F. E. Garrett, in *The Bookman*, October 1894; and perhaps the spectacular conclusion to Ibsen's 'beautiful Puritan opera' (as Gosse described it),[12] where Brand is swept away by the avalanche in the mountains, while the heavens open and the mysterious voice speaks, played its part in shaping Yeats's revision of *The Countess Cathleen* in 1895. In the first version the play ends *diminuendo*, in interior space, with room and oratory; the revision has thunder and lightning, darkness broken by visionary light, dim forms on the rocky slopes of a mountain, and the sound of far-off horns.[13] Yeats's reading of *Brand* shows considerable insight (much more than Shaw's), and his comments reveal that his imagination has been gripped:

Brand . . . seeks to rise into an absolute world where there is neither hunter, nor troll, nor merchant, nor prophet, but only God and his laws, and to transmute by the force of his unchanging ideal everything about him into imperishable gold, only to perish amid ice and snow with the cry in his ears, 'Die! the earth has no use for thee!' His mistake is not less disastrous, though immeasurably nobler, than the mistake of Peer Gynt, for the children of the earth can only live by compromise, by half-measures ... Poetry has ever loved those who are not 'piecemeal', and has made of them its Timons and its Lears, but Nature, which is all 'piecemeal', has ever cast them out.[14]

While *The Shadowy Waters* is generally agreed to have been influenced by *Axël*, which Yeats saw in 1894, some of the phrasing in his review of *Brand* suggests how congenial Ibsen's play was to an imagination grappling with the problem of dramatizing 'renunciation . . . for the call of the Infinite'. Forgael, like Brand, also seeks to 'rise into an absolute world' and 'to transmute by the force of his unchanging ideal everything about him into imperishable gold'.[15]

However paradoxical it may seem initially, it was probably the realist, problem-play, Ibsen who did even more than the romantic Ibsen to help make possible the kind of theatre Yeats wanted. The critical furore over Ibsen's plays in England, from the 1889 production of *A Doll's House*, through *Ghosts*, *Rosmersholm*, *Hedda Gabler* and *The Master Builder* in the four crucial years up to 1893, led to the formulation of certain principles and procedures without which it is difficult to imagine the Irish theatre, for all of its different emphases, coming into being. Though there were a number of differing lobbies, represented by the followers of naturalism, of poetic drama (and here we may recall Yeats's pleasure at the Bedford Park production of *A Sicilian Idyll*), and of symbolism and aestheticism on the stage, the greatest challenge to the values of the commercial theatre and the power of the actor-managers was unquestionably provided by Ibsen. As that shrewd contemporary observer, Holbrook Jackson, remarked:

what can be credited to the period [the eighteen-nineties] is the creation of an atmosphere in which a new drama might flourish at the appointed hour. This was done by the art of criticism, and chiefly by Bernard Shaw, William Archer and J. T. Grein, whose example and ideal was Ibsen.[16]

Ibsen was the proof of the rightness of insisting on the primacy of the dramatist, not the actor-manager or his theatre — as Shaw put it in *Our Theatre in the Nineties*, in summing up this aspect of Ibsen's influence, 'in all higher developments . . . the theatre will follow the dramatic poet, and not the dramatic poet the theatre'.[17] Secondly, the controversial nature of Ibsen's subject-matter gave powerful impetus to the establishment of the many little theatres and independent theatres which prepared the way for the Irish theatre. Yeats's friend Arthur Symons — who was to become one of Ibsen's more influential supporters in England — visited Paris in 1890 to see the production of *Ghosts* at André Antoine's Théâtre Libre, itself a classic example of the new phenomenon, an amateur company dedicated to presenting the plays of young French writers, as well as work by Ibsen, Strindberg and Tolstoy. Symons wrote of his experience in the *Pall Mall Gazette* in 1890:

We have not yet a Théâtre Libre and it is possible that the Lord Chamberlain might have but little desire to license a play which is not even an adaptation from the French. But a Théâtre Libre could be improvised for the occasion, and *Ghosts* in this way at least, performed — privately, if the guardians of our morality forbid the production of a play which contains so much that is 'properer for a sermon'.[18]

The symbolic moment, where the symbiosis of Ibsen and a new kind of theatre is manifested, is of course the opening of Grein's Independent Theatre on March 13, 1891, with its famous first production of *Ghosts*. Next day, in the magazine *Black and White*, Grein spells out the significance to the whole notion of a different kind of theatre of the choice of Ibsen:

The selection of *Ghosts* is in itself a manifesto — a demonstration of my plan of campaign. The question whether *Ghosts* is a moral play or not has nothing to do with the case. The point is, does this drama embody, in every sense, the purpose of the Independent Theatre? Is it, to express my policy in a few telling words, 'a play that has a literary and artistic, rather than a commercial value'? And to this question there can be but one, an affirmative reply.[19]

While Yeats would have approved, he did of course desiderate a different kind of drama from that of Ibsen. Nonetheless, even the more 'poetic' new theatres were indebted to Ibsen's trail-blazing. For example, Lugné-Poë's Théâtre de l'Oeuvre, founded in reaction against Antoine's more naturalistic principles in the Théâtre Libre, became known in Paris mainly for its productions of Ibsen — *Rosmersholm* in 1893, *An Enemy of the People* in 1893, *The Master Builder* (*Solness le Constructeur*) in 1894, *Little Eyolf* in 1895, *Brand* in the same year, *Pillars of Society* in 1896 and *Peer Gynt* in the same year, and *Borkman* in 1897. When Lugné-Poë brought his theatre to London in 1895, at Grein's invitation, he opened with *Rosmersholm* and *The Master-Builder*. It is as if Ibsen were the necessary authenticating seal on the commitment and integrity of the new theatre. Certainly, it is hard to imagine the proliferation of independent theatres in London and on the Continent, however different their aims may have been, without the example of the great Norwegian and the fierce controversy stirred by the staging of his plays. The Irish Literary Theatre itself, we may recall, needed Ibsenite drama to achieve its launch.

Two final points may be made about the significance to Yeats of what may be called 'the Ibsen years' in London's theatrical history. First, the rise of the new little theatres, itself connected with the impact of Ibsen, led to a new kind of acting, and both Shaw and Archer pay respectful attention 'to amateur and semi-professional companies devoted to non-commercial experimental forms of new drama'.[20] The Théâtre Libre was itself an amateur organization, and its example helped the development of such companies as The New Century Theatre, the Stage Society, The Pioneers and The Pioneer Players, The Play Actors' Society, The English Drama Society, and the New Stage Club. As George Moore put it, as early as 1888, in words which anticipate Yeats's own desire to find a different kind of actor, and his pleasure in the Fay brothers when he eventually encountered them:

Personally I believe that amateurs will prove of real service to those who would break with the soul-wearying conventionalities of the modern stage.[21]

Second, the Ibsen controversy in the 'nineties helped produce a new kind of theatre and drama critic, and a higher level of debate about the nature of drama and the future of the theatre — one need only mention the names of Shaw, Archer, Henry James — who wrote highly perceptive pieces on *Hedda Gabler* and *The Master Builder* — and A. B. Walkley. Of course, they were in the minority: the majority, in the words of Gosse, poured 'the wash-pot of journalism' over the poet's head.[22] The hostile majority, however, with its debased journalistic and populist standards, could only confirm Yeats's reluctant admiration of Ibsen. As he says in *Autobiographies*, 'though we and he had not the same friends, we had the same enemies'.[23]

While the impact of Ibsen on new critical standards, on ideas for a new kind of theatre and a new kind of acting, and on the primacy of the dramatist, may all have helped to give Yeats the budding theatre manager some direction, it may still be asked whether Ibsen had any impact on Yeats's dramaturgical art. Here the answer is conventionally a fairly resounding 'no'. However, it is not the case that Ibsen in the nineties was seen simply as a

naturalist, with whom Yeats could have no truck. Ibsen's symbolism
caused at least as much discussion as his realism, and not everyone was to see it as dismissively as Yeats did, thirty years later, as
spilt poetry. Despite his hesitations, in 1903 Yeats himself admits
Ibsen as among those dramatists who, unlike the French, creates
in at least some of his plays, 'emotion of multitude': 'Ibsen and
Maeterlinck have . . . created a new form, for they get multitude
from the wild duck in the attic, or from the crown at the bottom
of the fountain, vague symbols that set the mind wandering from
idea to idea, emotion to emotion.' [24] The tone of the discussion of
Rosmersholm, produced at the Vaudeville Theatre in 1891, with
Yeats's admired Florence Farr as Rebecca, suggests that the more
thoughtful saw that Ibsen meant more than votes for women or
sanitary reform, or clinical treatment of venereal diseases. The
anonymous reviewer in the *Sunday Times* of 1 March, 1891, for
instance, realises, however fumblingly, that Ibsen is not to be
explained in terms of Zolaesque naturalism:

if one regards Ibsen, like Mr. Whistler, as an idealist and impressionist —
in the true artistic sense of the term — which he really is, and not as a
'realist', which he is commonly called, but certainly is not, for all his
apparent delight in dissecting the morbidities of life, there will be found
a poetry in his point of view, which transcends the ordinary experience
of human nature . . . it is not according to the logic of actual life that
Ibsen's creations act; rather it is in accordance with an ideal that draws
them as a magnet towards an end that may be imagined, but would
scarcely occur in real life . . . in *Rosmersholm* Ibsen the poet is manifest,
and mystifying as some of the episodes may be, the poetry of this play
explains Ibsen the dramatist.[25]

The reference to impressionism is especially interesting. Wilde
had just published 'The True Function and Value of Criticism';
Walter Pater, one of Yeats's aesthetic gurus, lurked in the background. Two of the more intelligent critics of the time saw
Ibsen through impressionist spectacles, in ways that challenge
conventional assumptions, since they deny the received views of
Ibsen as didactic, and as formally orthodox. A. B. Walkley says:

The 'hard-shell' Ibsenites, who insist upon regarding Ibsen as a moralist
rather than as a dramatist, will be sore put to it to find the moral of *Hedda
Gabler* . . . The play is a bit of sheer 'impressionism'.[26]

And Henry James, in words that anticipate Yeats's own special
pleasures in the static quality of the first act of Synge's *Well of the
Saints*, remarks that *Hedda Gabler* is a triumphant success,

but it does not conceal from us — on the contrary — that his drama is essentially that supposedly undramatic thing, the picture not of an action but of a condition. It is the portrait of a nature, the story of what Paul Bourget would call an 'état d'âme' . . . [27]

The Master Builder and its reception reinforced the critical perception that Ibsen's drama could not be explained, or explained away, in realist or naturalist terms. For years, William Archer had been claiming that Ibsen was a poetic dramatist, and an artist rather than a didactic sociologist. Yeats might have been unimpressed, given his distaste for Archer's admittedly antimacassar and what-not translations of Ibsen; but he was interested in Maeterlinck's drama and in Maeterlinck's opinions, and reviewed very favourably the translation of his volume of essays, *The Treasure of the Humble*, in *The Bookman*, in 1897. Yeats sees Maeterlinck as one of the leaders of 'an insurrection against everything which assumes that the external and material are the only fixed things, the only standards of reality'.[28] In which case, he would have been interested to read Maeterlinck's words on *The Master Builder* in these essays:

Hilda and Solness are, I believe, the first characters in drama who feel, for an instant, that they are living in the atmosphere of the soul; and the discovery of this essential life that exists in them, beyond the life of everyday, comes fraught with terror. Hilda and Solness are two souls to whom a flash has revealed their situation in the true life.[29]

What Maeterlinck recognises is Ibsen's ability to create a drama in which the everyday humdrum banality is suddenly 'riddled with light', in which the characters are seized, in the midst of the bundle of accidents of breakfast, office, work, triviality, with a perception of the validity of a non-material world. They speak a language which moves between inner and outer experience; and however delayed the reaction is, I believe that Yeats responded to Ibsen's example. In those curiously angry, typically honest and (to a point) self-lacerating essays in *Discoveries* (1906), Yeats abjures his early obsession with pure essences for a more mixed art. We have found, he says, 'a new delight in essence, in states of mind, in pure imagination, in all that comes to us most easily in elaborate music'. The price, however, is too high: 'we have lost in personality, in our delight in the whole man — blood, imagination, intellect, running together.' The market carts, while not as entrancing as the flight of the bird, can no longer be ignored.

Without knowing it, I had come to care for nothing but impersonal beauty . . . Then one day I understood quite suddenly, as the way is, that I was seeking something unchanged and unmixed and always outside myself, a Stone or an Elixir that was always out of reach . . . To put it otherwise, we should ascend out of common interests, the thoughts of the newspapers, of the market-place, of men of science, but only so far as we can carry the normal, passionate, reasoning self, the personality as a whole.[30]

That Ibsen is in Yeats's mind here is surely guaranteed by the fact that Yeats called his *Bookman* review of 1894 of *Brand* 'The Stone and the Elixir'. In a lètter of February 1906 he writes to Florence Farr that 'I once cared only for images about whose necks I could cast various "chains of office" as it were. They were so many aldermen of the ideal, whom I wished to master the city of the soul'. Now, he says, he wants 'to lay hands upon some dynamic and substantializing force . . . a movement downwards upon life, not upwards out of life'.[31]

While the popular journals may still have seen Ibsen as the sanitary inspector of the late century then, the Ibsen more intelligently discussed from 1891 and the production of *Rosmersholm* onwards, was this Ibsen who negotiated between realism and symbolism, and was acknowledged as a poet by writers as different as Maeterlinck and James Joyce. Ibsen's refusal to kick free altogether from this sublunary world stood as an example to Yeats just at the point where he is becoming dissatisfied with the filmy ethereality of much of his writing in the nineties, and with the *symboliste* drama. Thus in 1898, he writes that Maeterlinck has 'set before us faint souls, naked and pathetic shadows already half vapour and sighing to one another upon the border of the last abyss'. Count Villiers de l'Isle-Adam invests his characters with more energy, yet while praising *Axël* in the same essay ('The Autumn of the Body'), Yeats seems to recognise the extremely specialized and perhaps unrepeatable achievement of this work, so much more a ritual than a play, in which Villiers has 'created persons from whom has fallen all even of personal characteristic except a thirst for that hour when all things shall pass away like a cloud . . .'.[32] Villiers and Maeterlinck are both in the end unsatisfactory dramatic models for Yeats, whose feelings and outlook undergo the crucial change discussed in the major letter of April 1904 to George Russell:

In my *Land of Heart's Desire*, and in some of my lyric verse of that time, there is an exaggeration of sentiment and sentimental beauty which I have come to think unmanly . . . but between this energy of the spirit and the energy of the will out of which epic and dramatic poetry comes there is a region of brooding emotions full of fleshly waters and vapours which kill the spirit and the will, ecstasy and joy equally . . . As so often happens with a thing one has been tempted by and is still a little tempted by, I am roused by it to a kind of frenzied hatred which is quite out of my control . . . We possess nothing but the will and must never let the children of vague desires breathe upon it nor the waters of sentiment rust the terrible mirror of its blade.[33]

What Maeterlinck and Villiers lack, and what Ibsen so signally possesses, can be seen from the perspective of this letter to be an interest in the will, and in the creation of characters with strong wills. Yeats's stress on will may be self-induced, or aroused in him by his 1902 reading of Nietzsche; *the* dramatist of the will, however, was Ibsen, whose œuvre might even be described as a study in will, from Brand through to Hedda Gabler and Solness, described by even the unsympathetic Clement Scott as 'a new order of man . . . possessed of astounding force of will'.[34] In short, Ibsen has what is lacking in the *symbolistes*, the tragic sense, the ability to create heroic figures committed to a tragic passion; and while Yeats and Ibsen sought to restore tragedy to the modern stage in very different ways, both are in agreement that 'will' and 'passion' are essential elements of the tragic character.

Ibsen's work also affected, if indirectly, the presentation and treatment of women in Yeats's art. Ibsen in the nineties was most controversial because of his treatment of the woman question: 'the slamming of the Helmers's front door re-echoed in the Victorian and Edwardian mind for nearly a quarter of a century.'[35] Ibsen's fame — or notoriety — was due in part to his treatment of hitherto unmentionable subject-matter, but also to his creation of what Shaw was to call the 'unwomanly woman',[36] or the New Woman, emancipated in outlook, bold and free in her statement of her desires, intelligent and strong. The objectors saw it differently, their passion and fright intensified as they start to perceive the New Woman on both sides of the footlights:

The unwomanly women, the unsexed females, and the whole army of unprepossessing cranks in petticoats who have no opportunities just now to discuss the Contagious Diseases Act in drawing-rooms, sit open-mouthed and without a blush on their faces whilst a Socialist orator reads aloud *Ghosts*, the most loathsome of all Ibsen's plays, that illustrates freely enough the baneful result of the abolition of the Contagious Diseases Act in Norway.[37]

What Ibsen also did was to create a succession of superb parts for actresses, 'a dazzling array' as Henry James calls it — Nora, Rebecca, Hedda, Hilda Wangel, Rita Allmers — and the distinguished and necessarily intelligent actresses who played these parts — Janet Achurch, Elizabeth Robins, Florence Farr and to a lesser extent Mrs Patrick Campbell — also in their own way helped the New Woman to step off the stage and into life. Nobody who had heard of Ibsen — and everybody had heard of him — could have been unaware that Ibsen had somehow shifted the image of women.

What brought all this close to Yeats was his relation to Florence Farr,[38] the beautiful actress with whom he was to become most intimate until her departure for Ceylon in 1912, and whom he memorializes movingly in 'All Souls' Night' in 1920. Mrs Yeats tells us:

The letters continually reveal how great an influence she had on the shaping and re-writing of the early plays, but they do not, I think, suggest the intimate friendship of those many years. WBY once said to me 'She was the only person to whom I could tell *everything*'.[39]

In one sense, Florence Farr was a Yeatsian woman: the best verse-speaker he had heard, the actress of *A Sicilian Idyll*, his chosen speaker to the psaltery; he wrote for her *The Land of Heart's Desire*, she played Aleel in the first production of *The Countess Cathleen* in 1899, and five years later he gave her *The Shadowy Waters* to play privately at a London Theosophical Convention. Yeats describes her in *Four Years: 1887-1891*:

She had three great gifts, a tranquil beauty like that of Demeter's image near the British Museum Reading-Room door, and an incomparable sense of rhythm and a beautiful voice, the seeming natural expression of the image.[40]

She even shared Yeats's occult interests, as Sapientia Sapienti Dono Data outranking him in the Order of the Golden Dawn.

And yet there was an antithetical side to Florence Farr, which fascinated Yeats even as it exasperated him. For if Florence was a Yeatsian woman, she was also very definitely an Ibsenite woman, a 'New Woman'. The year after she appeared in Todhunter's *Sicilian Idyll* and charmed Yeats with her 'poetical culture', she starred as Rebecca West in Ibsen's *Rosmersholm*. She divorced her actor husband, Edward Emery, in 1894. According to Shaw, even her father had impeccable Ibsenite credentials — a sanitary reformer; though Dr Kelly remarks more soberly that he was a statistician.[41]

Shaw, with whom she had a close relation in the early nineties, conveys the flavour of her personality very vividly:

As she was clever, good natured, and very good-looking, all her men friends fell in love with her. This had occurred so often that she had lost all patience with the hesitating preliminaries of her less practised adorers. Accordingly, when they clearly longed to kiss her, and she did not dislike them sufficiently to make their gratification too great a strain on her excessive good nature, she would seize the stammering suitor firmly by the wrists, bring him into her arms by a smart pull and saying 'Let's get it over' allow the startled gentleman to have his kiss, and then proceed to converse with him at her ease on subjects of more general interest.[42]

According to Shaw, 'she set no bounds to her relations with men whom she liked, and already had [when he met her] a sort of Leporello list of a dozen adventures . . .':

She was in violent reaction against Victorian morals, especially sexual and domestic morals; and when the impact of Ibsen was felt in this country, and when I wrote somewhere that 'home is the girl's prison and the woman's workhouse' I became *persona grata* with her . . .[43]

Her unconventionality was remarked on by all who knew her: for York Powell, she was a 'gypsy'; Dorothy Shakespear wrote to Ezra Pound of Farr's emigrating to Ceylon: 'she is going to dress in blue bath towelling made loose — mercy! how odd! really odd!', to which Ezra replied; 'She always did dress in towling [*sic*] made loose — chez elle, that is — or in remnants of stage properties and improprieties'; and Mabel Beardsley remarked when she heard that Farr was to teach in Ceylon, 'How fine of her, but a girls' school! why she used to make even me blush!'[44]

Florence Farr's own writing confirms these impressions of a liberated 'new woman'. In 1907, in the *New Age*, she published a series of articles on Ibsen's women, in which, for example, Rebecca West is described as possessing 'all the freedom of the hopeless vagabond' and as being 'relentless as a young bird of prey', and where she states that Rita Allmers's mission, 'the noblest that a woman could undertake, is to disclose the real nature of the fetish of home'. She sees *A Doll's House* and *The Wild Duck* as complementary parables on the impossibility of ideal or absolute states; and everywhere there is evidence of a penetrating mind and an enjoyment of the complexities of human personality, as in her shrewd analysis of Hedda Gabler, that 'real lady of the suburbs', undersexed, morbidly curious rather than passionate, a 'great type of transitional womanhood'.[45] The spirit — in every sense —

of the essays contained in her 1910 publication, *Modern Woman:
Her Intentions* may be conveyed by some quotation: 'I must suggest
that the stigma might be removed from those who are not capable
of lifelong fidelity . . . This chapter deals with the subject of
prostitution from the point of view of public health, so that the
nervous reader had better skip it . . . most women are capable of
several love-affairs . . . I have often thought "It is not so much that
men must work and women must weep, but that men may laugh
and women must look shocked"'; and of women of intelligence
who do not wish to marry, she remarks 'passion served up with
cold sauce as in the Shaw-Barker school of sex revolts them'.[46]

Rather piquantly, Florence Farr's book bears as epigraph some
lines from W. B. Yeats's *The Shadowy Waters*.[47] Though it is unlikely
that they began an affair before 1903, her impact on Yeats was
always considerable; and it may be argued that, even more than
Maud Gonne or Olivia Shakespear, Florence Farr, the quintessen-
tial New Woman, helped to change Yeats's view of women and his
artistic representation of them. Yeats's early work is dominated
by the Pre-Raphaelite woman — pallid and weary of face, long of
neck, flat of breast, with sorrowful eyes and long, thin, nervous
hands, and heavily endowed with hair and lips.[48] This woman is
generally suffering and passive; and, as Yeats says, 'I was a
romantic, my head full of the mysterious women of Rossetti and
those hesitating faces in the art of Burne-Jones'.[49] Despite his
physical relationship with Olivia Shakespear, she is clearly, in
Yeats's eyes, too close to the ideal of his soul to make a satisfactory
lover — 'her beauty, dark and still, had the nobility of defeated
things, and how could it help but wring my heart?' . . . 'she was
like the mild heroines of my plays. She seemed a part of myself'
. . . 'she was too near my soul, too salutary and wholesome to
my inmost being'.[50] As for Maud Gonne, while the warrior in
her is duly reflected in Yeats's more aggressive queens, she —
unfortunately from Yeats's point of view — remained relatively
uninterested in love. Maud in Yeats's poetry is legendary, statuesque, Helen-like, and has the simplicity of a monolithic force:

> What could have made her peaceful with a mind
> That nobleness made simple as a fire,
> With beauty like a tightened bow, a kind
> That is not natural in an age like this,
> Being high and solitary and most stern?

She was also a fairly conventional woman — it is significant that
while Maud was outraged by Synge's *Shadow of the Glen* where an

Irish Nora in a sense imitates her famous Scandinavian cousin, Florence Farr wanted to act the part and was only hindered by Synge's last illness and death.[51] Richard Ellmann many years ago noted the new sensuality in Yeats's writings after about 1903:[52] it is most likely that the immediate source was Florence Farr, capricious, dynamic, confident, sexy (the horrible modern word may be forgiven for its appropriateness to this New Woman), imposing, vital. Her presence may be detected in *Diarmuid and Grania*, the play on which Yeats collaborated with Moore. Not an overall success as play, Grania is nevertheless an especially well-drawn character. Her wilfulness and lust are portrayed frankly and boldly, 'probably because Yeats and Moore were united, for once, in a mutual fascination with passionate women'.[53] There are new sensual notes in the language of *On Baile's Strand* and even in *The King's Threshold*, as Seanchan addresses the girls:

> Go to the young men.
> Are not the ruddy flesh and the thin flanks
> And the broad shoulders worthy of desire?

Deirdre, for all her dignity, pressed lips and breast on Naoise's to seduce; the musicians sing of the 'tumult of the limbs/That dies out before 'tis day'; there is a growing sense of women's complexity, and Deirdre's lines describe rather well Ibsen's unwomanly woman at least in one of her aspects:

> Although we are so delicately made,
> There's something brutal in us . . .

Cuchulain in the 1903 version of *On Baile's Strand* rejects the notion of the angel of the house, or of the mead hall;

> I think that a fierce woman's better, a woman
> That breaks away when you have thought her won;
> For I'd be fed and hungry at one time.
> I think that all deep passion is but a kiss
> In the mid battle . . .
> A brief forgiveness between opposites . . . [54]

And as well as the energetically squabbling women of *The Green Helmet*, there are poems which reflect and combine potent notions which occupy much of the rest of Yeats's creative life: his stress on the physicality of love, the devil between the thighs, and the fascination of the mask. (I am thinking of poems such as 'The

Three Beggars', 'Beggar to Beggar Cried', 'A Song from The Player Queen', 'The Witch', 'On Women' and 'The Mask'.)

Maud Gonne has been for so long — and rightly — the pre-eminent woman in Yeats's discussion that it may seem tendentious to advance the claims of Florence Farr as having done more to shape his artistic treatment of women. Perhaps it might be more judicious to say that she greatly widened Yeats's appreciation of the dramatic possibilities in different kinds of women. I think, however, that the influence of Florence Farr on *The Player Queen* is incontestable. He first mentions that he is working on the scenario of that infinitely troublesome play in a letter to Florence in September 1908;[55] and although Mrs Patrick Campbell came into his mind later, it is clear that Yeats thought Mrs Pat belonged to a school of actresses whose day was past. By contrast, Florence Farr had the essential variety and complexity, able to be both scullion and queen, who would have been perfectly cast as Decima, Yeats's 'study of a fantastical woman', in that play which is an articulation of many of the doctrines of the Mask. And Florence Farr owes her distinction in part to her training in 'intellectual drama', which includes Ibsen. Yeats writes to his father on 21 July 1906:

I feel that a change is taking place in the nature of acting; Mrs Campbell and her generation were trained in plays like *Mrs Tanqueray*, where everything is done by a kind of magnificent hysteria (one understands that when one hears her hunting her monkey and her servant with an impartial fury about the house). This school reduces everything to an emotional least common denominator. It finds the scullion in the queen, because there are scullions in the audience but no queens . . . A new school of acting is now growing up under the influence of the various attempts to create an intellectual drama, and of changes deeper than that. The new school seizes upon what is distinguished, solitary, proud even. One always got a little of this in Mrs Emery [Florence Farr] when she was good . . . [56]

It is right to end with reference to *The Player Queen*, itself so associated with 'the thought I have set forth in *Per Amica Silentia Lunae*', which, Yeats says, was coming into his head as early as 1907, and of which he found examples everywhere.[57] The contrasts between the important women in his life — Lady Gregory, Maud Gonne, Olivia Shakespear and Florence Farr — must have proved fertile ground. Florence Farr, in particular was to stimulate the poet's thinking, at an early stage, on the antithetical self, on the mask and on the vagaries of personality which makes Yeats's *Autobiographies* such fascinating reading. For surely it is a piquant contrast — the beautiful verse speaker with the Greek looks, the speaker to the psaltery, actress in *Sicilian Idyll* and *The Countess Cathleen*, is simultaneously the Ibsenite New Woman, 'the woman with the big nose' as George Moore described her,[58] the gypsy, the champion of women's rights and sexual liberation, who will even write against poetic plays.[59] The element of wilfulness in Farr's dismissal of what Yeats saw as her supreme gifts of beauty and voice may have exasperated Yeats in real life,[60] but it fascinated him artistically. How, as it were, is the woman from Ibsen's world going to fare in the Celtic Twilight; or rather, how is the Celtic Twilight going to cope with the new woman? Is it going too far to see in Florence Farr the lineaments not only of Decima but of Crazy Jane? At any rate what Farr embodied for Yeats was fruitful contradiction and variety; and if Peter Ure is right to lament Yeats's 'unwritten Cleopatra',[61] at least it can be said that Florence Farr came near to providing him with the model.

YEATSIAN STUDIES IN ITALY TODAY

TONI CERUTTI

The major Italian contribution to Yeatsian studies is Giorgio Melchiori's book *The Whole Mystery of Art: Pattern into Poetry in the Work of W. B. Yeats*, published in Britain in 1960. It is significant, as Professor De Logu has pointed out, that together with the other relevant study by an Italian, Corinna Salvadori, *Yeats and Castiglione: Poet and Courtier*, 1965, it should be written in English and printed outside Italy.[1] Yeats's popularity in a country which can boast of an active school of English studies has lagged behind that of some equally famous Anglo-Irish writers — Wilde, Shaw and Joyce. Before the end of the second world war not much had been written in spite of the Nobel prize which had gained him international renown. In 1937 Mario Praz wrote that he was not only the greatest of Irish poets, but also a writer of European standard. He was the unique case of an artist who over a period of fifty years had moved with the times and produced a faithful portrait of his age. Praz's view began to bear fruit in the fifties, when one can find signs of a growing interest among intellectuals.[2] When Yeats died, obituary essays still stressed the decadent elegance of his early poetry and the fascinating Irishness of his dramas. Melchiori's book marked the beginning of a new era and yet no standard work has so far been written in Italian. The major bulk of our scholarship has gone into preparing Italian editions of his works. Although there is no editorial enterprise comparable to the one in progress in Germany, new versions have become more and more frequent. While the nineteen fifties and the sixties concentrated on his poetry, his prose writings have more recently attracted attention. *Quaranta Poesie* published by Giorgio Melchiori in 1965 offers the best example of a literary translation of some of his major poems; an ample selection, *Poesie*, by Roberto Sanesi had already come out in 1961. After a lapse of some years, Anthony Johnson, an Englishman who works in Italy, wrote an introduction and notes to *The Tower* translated into Italian by Ariodante Marianni and published in 1984. Both volumes, which have

English and Italian text face to face, supply an interlinear translation for people with a reasonable knowledge of English but fail to
recapture the rarefied elegance of Yeats's diction. The prose works
which appeared first in Italian and which proved highly successful
were *A Vision* translated by Adriana Motti in 1973, and *Rosa
Alchemica*, which also contains *The Tables of the Law* and *The Adoration
of the Magi*, translated by Renato Oliva in 1975. It was not by
chance that both are among his esoteric writings. Occultism had
by then become very fashionable in Italy and is still the rage. 'Per
Amica Silentia Lunae', translated by Gino Scatasta, was brought
out last year. An anthropological interest in folklore, fostered by
the popularity of Propp's theories and Tolkien's fairyland, prom-
oted the publication of *Irish Fairy Tales, (Fiabe Irlandesi)* in 1982,
admirably translated by Maria Giovanna Andreolli and Melita
Cataldi. They were immediately so popular that a shorter selection was reprinted the following year in a volume elegantly illustrated by Carla Guidetti Serra Spriano, *Le dodici oche selvatiche (The
Twelve Wild Geese)*. Judging from first reviews in the papers, equal
success seems to be in store for *The Celtic Twilight*, recently translated by Rosita Caprioli. Yeats has no doubt benefited from current cultural trends. A more genuine interest in Yeats's art lies in
the editions by De Logu of *John Sherman and Dhoya* (in a volume
of 1982, translated by Dario Calimani), and of *The Speckled Bird*,
now in the press.

Yeats's dramas which were first to receive attention from Italian
quarters — the earliest translations date from 1914 — have been
neglected in recent years. The last major publication dates from
1966, *W. B. Yeats: Drammi celtici*, translated by Francesco Vizioli
with a foreword by Sanesi. There are, however, some signs of a
reawakened interest: Giovanni Serpillo is preparing an edition of
The Pot of Broth and is planning its staging by a students' company
in the University of Sassari; *Cuchulain's Cycle*, translated by Melita
Cataldi, is also about to be published. In 1969 an Italian publishing
firm of old, influential standing, UTET, printed a reader, *Opere di
W. B. Yeats*, the best so far available to a general Italian audience,
edited by Salvatore Rosati in the Nobel prize series, which includes
an ample spectrum from his poetry and drama, assembling earlier
translations, and adding some extracts from *The Secret Rose* and
The Stories of Red Hanrahan.[3]

Critical contributions of an academic standard began to appear
very slowly from the fifties, starting from Agostino Lombardo's
brilliant and penetrating pages in *La poesia inglese dall'estetismo al
simbolismo*, 1950. In 1954 Nemi D'Agostino wrote on poetry of the

middle period and in 1955 Claudio Gorlier wrote on Yeats and
Spenser; in 1963 Glauco Cambon debated the theme of the hero
in *La Lotta con Proteo*; in 1968 Melchiori added another landmark
to the study of Yeatsian sources and influences in his essay on
Yeats and Dante and so did Marcello Cappuzzo in 1972 with his
philosophical analysis of 'Leda and the Swan' and 'The Second
Coming'. In the late seventies Anthony Johnson contributed
structuralist readings of some major poems, while in more recent
years Massimo Bacigalupo has worked on Yeats and Ezra Pound.[4]
Two full length studies, *Esoterismo e magia nelle poesie di W. B. Yeats*,
by Fernando Picchi and *L'alchemia del sogno e della rosa*, by Gabriella
Corradini Favati, both published in 1977, show a prevailing
interest respectively in Yeats's occultism and in his earlier poetry.
'L'Arcadia di W. B. Yeats', an extensive, well-documented essay on
a juvenile experiment with dramatic form, *The Island of Statues*,
opens De Logu's search for the edenic element in Yeats, which
continues in the prefatory study to *John Sherman*, where he draws
a portrait of the artist as a young man, stressing the autobiography
in his early fiction.[5]

Some prefaces to the translations offer good general studies of
Yeats as a man and a writer — namely Rosati's, Oliva's and De
Logu's. In 1979 an introductory essay in *I contemporanei*, placed
him on a par with major British authors of the century.[6]

Of forthcoming Yeatsian studies in Italy one can mention
Renato Oliva's research on Yeats's art from a psychoanalytical
point of view, which should soon be published in book form,
and De Logu's analysis of *The Speckled Bird*, now due for
publication.

Though Yeats has not yet entered the realm of the European
tradition in the Italian literary imagination, his reputation is on
the rise. However uneven the quality of the translations and
however partial the choices from his texts are, Yeats is now
available in a wide and varied selection. Some areas are still to be
explored, such as his critical and autobiographical writings
which promise to be a fertile ground at a time when essay writing
is attracting large audiences. The metaphysical quality of his
diction, the cryptic allusions to occultism and his Irishness,
which fell outside the boundaries of Italian culture, did not fail to
attract the attention of two major poets, Eugenio Montale and
Giovanni Giudici. Their occasional translations from Yeats's
poems, together with the ones by Melchiori, show a keen perception of the original and make good reading for cultured Italians
who move outside the field of English studies. Evidence of his

penetrating under the skin of Italian intellectuals can be found in a forthcoming conference on the Sicilian poet Lucio Piccolo, who knew Yeats with whom he corresponded, and where his influence on Piccolo will be discussed.

YEATS IN GERMANY

HEINZ KOSOK

One aspect of the many-faceted subject 'Yeats the European' is the question of the reception of Yeats's work, the question whether Yeats created an audience for himself (a theatre audience, a reading public, and also a critical audience) in the various European countries, and whether he influenced any of the poets and playwrights working in other languages. It is in this respect only that the following brief remarks are to be seen. While the subject 'Yeats *and* Germany' would be a highly complicated one, involving such diverse names as Goethe, Wagner, Nietzsche, Hegel, Spengler and many others, the question of 'Yeats *in* Germany' is much more limited.

To judge from the available sources — translations, critical reactions, and references to Yeats by German writers — the reception of Yeats in Germany appears to have been surprisingly slow. This is confirmed by Patrick O'Neill's excellent study on Irish-German literary relations: 'Yeats is perhaps the most neglected in Germany of the world's great poets, or at any rate was until 1970.'[1] Among all the major writers from Ireland (it is debatable whether all of them can be called 'Irish writers') Yeats was the one who found the least response in Germany. Several among his contemporaries have always been regarded very highly in Germany. There are no less than four different translations of *The Playboy of the Western World* (one of them by Heinrich Böll), and Synge is regularly performed; Shaw for a long time was much more popular in Germany than he was in England; there is a veritable Joyce industry in Germany, and it has been joined, in recent years, by an equally extensive Beckett industry. Among nineteenth-century writers, Oscar Wilde was, for a long time, at the centre of quite a cult, and even minor figures such as Charles Lever and Tom Moore were, for a while, highly successful in Germany. As to the eighteenth century, Swift, Sterne and Goldsmith are accepted figures in the German canon of 'world literature'. Yeats, on the other hand, took a long time to arrive, and he has never exerted

258

the same impact as his fellow countrymen.

The lack of an enthusiastic response to Yeats may, in part, perhaps be accounted for by the contradictions and catastrophes of recent German history. Around the period of the First World War, naturally everything written in English met with a certain degree of mistrust because it was written in the language of the enemy, and where Yeats *was* appreciated he was seen as the representative of Ireland as opposed to England. The narrow view of Yeats as the poet of the Celtic Twilight persisted far into the second half of the century. The 1920s were a period of great political turmoil and social unrest in Germany. They were also perhaps the most exciting period in German literature with the one exception of the age of Goethe, and so much was happening all at once on the German literary scene that outside influences, unless they were trumpeted extremely loudly, did not stand very much of a chance. This period came to an abrupt end with the beginning of the dark age of Nazi Germany, from 1933 to 1945, when very little foreign literature was allowed into the country. After the War there began what was called, perhaps not too felicitously, Re-education; and Re-education brought American literature to Germany, Hemingway and Faulkner, O'Neill and Wilder, Eliot and Frost. Re-education did not primarily concern itself with a poet from a small country that had remained neutral during the War. It may be understandable therefore that, for political reasons, the German reception of Yeats's writings was delayed and was not so widespread as that of other writers from abroad.

There may be other and more purely literary reasons, too. The predominant and overwhelming influence on German drama during the past forty years has been that of Brecht, and it is perhaps difficult to imagine a playwright more different from Yeats than Brecht. On the other hand, the greatest single influence on German poetry was certainly the figure of Rilke, and Rilke, despite the obvious differences, may be said in many ways to be so similar to Yeats as to render unnecessary any influence from abroad. Also, the public role of poetry in Germany, as compared to other countries, has been relatively small. The dominant genre has been the novel; most of the major post-war German writers have been novelists, and novelists from abroad — Proust and Joyce, Hemingway and Camus, Orwell and Faulkner — have exerted a considerable and widespread influence on the German consciousness, while poetry has remained a minority interest. Finally, there is a very practical reason. A great deal of the attention given to Yeats's plays has been generated by the *amateur* theatre (or by

its most ambitious sector), in Ireland as well as in England and in
America. Germany has a highly developed professional theatre
system, but it has no amateur theatre comparable to that of the
English-speaking world. The professional theatre cannot produce a
Yeats play on its own, because the audience would consider it
had not received its money's worth, and it shies away from triple-
bills of short plays because audiences are not at all used to them.
Admittedly, such a brief and blunt enumeration of reasons cannot
do justice to the complexities and mysteries of international
literary relations, but it may at least account for some of the
effects.

To say all this, however, is not to suggest that Germany was
altogether unaware of Yeats. Not surprisingly perhaps in the
country of Herder and the Grimms, the first translation from
Yeats was his compilation of *Fairy and Folk Tales* which appeared
in Germany as early as 1894,[2] and it was followed by a trickle of
translations of individual poems and plays over the next twenty
years, usually published in small and short-lived literary
magazines.[3] *The Countess Cathleen*, for instance, was translated as
early as 1903 (in *Bühne und Welt*), but Yeats for a long time remained
a minority interest. One of those irrational and unpredictable
moves in the literary world that may influence the whole course
of a poet's reputation is reported by O'Neill:

The poet Henry von Heiseler, one of the first discoverers of Yeats in
Germany, had prepared translations of ten of Yeats's early plays while
serving (under constraint) in the Russian army during the First World
War; when Heiseler escaped from Russia in 1922 he brought with him as
his only possession the manuscript — only to find that the translation
rights had been sold elsewhere.[4]

The translation rights had, in fact, been acquired by Herbert E.
Herlitschka who retained them for several decades. He published
translations of individual poems, plays and prose pieces from
1927 and in 1958 eventually brought out what was then the only
collection of Yeats poems in book form.[5] His linguistic and stylistic
shortcomings as the authorized translator of Yeats were frequently
pointed out, and it cannot be ruled out that he is, at least in part,
responsible for the lack of German enthusiasm for Yeats's works.
It was due to his influence that Henry von Heiseler's translations
of the ten plays (which are considered to be much more faithful
to the originals, as well as aesthetically satisfying) could only be
printed in a private edition of 250 copies (1933).

There is little point in giving publication details of the translation of individual Yeats titles, but it may be worth remarking that, rather surprisingly, Yeats was awarded the *Goethe-Plakette* of the City of Frankfurt in 1934, *after* the beginning of the 'Third Reich', and on this occasion *The Countess Cathleen* was produced by the Frankfurter Schauspielhaus. It had been preceded by a production of *The Land of Heart's Desire* in 1919 by the same theatre, and it was followed by *Cathleen ni Houlihan* at the Giessener Stadttheater in 1939. As far as can be gathered from existing records, these were the only three Yeats productions before the War. There were, however, two Yeats productions on German stages during the War. As late as 1944, when the defeat of Germany was imminent, *The Land of Heart's Desire* was given an enthusiastic reception by the audiences of the Münchner Kammerspiele, due probably to the war-time situation more than to anything else. Four years earlier, *The Unicorn from the Stars* in the same theatre had caused a politically motivated riot, because its religious and pacifist overtones were unacceptable to part of the audience, and the producer (the great Otto Falckenberg) had apparently introduced certain elements that caused the play to be rejected even by those who were not naive supporters of Nazi ideology. Such politically sensitive concepts as that of the 'Führer' and the 'Volk' found a negative emphasis in the production, which had to be withdrawn after the première. Fifteen years later, the play had lost all such controversial energy, and the Köln production was classified as obscure and tedious. After the War, *The Unicorn from the Stars* (Kölner Kammerspiele in 1956, Landestheater Tübingen in 1959), *The Hour Glass* (Münchner Junges Theater in 1947, Bühnenstudio der Städtischen Bühnen Essen in 1959), *The Countess Cathleen* (Bühnen der Stadt Köln in 1962), *The Player Queen* (Büchner-Theater München in 1966) and a few amateur performances are the only productions on record. Werner Egk's opera *Irische Legende*, based on *The Countess Cathleen*, seems not to have gone beyond the first production (Salzburg 1955), because, it may be speculated, of the combined obscurity of Yeats's subject matter and Egk's orchestration.[6] Despite these occasional stage events, Yeats was still known to relatively few people, and even long after the War he was still seen as the poet of the Irish Renaissance of the late nineteenth century and little else.

Critical response (in the widest possible sense) to Yeats's works seems to have been equally slow in gathering momentum. As late as June 1965, on Yeats's hundredth birthday, the *Frankfurter Allgemeine Zeitung* could still use the headline 'Den Deutschen unbekannt' — unknown to the Germans, for Michael Haerdter's article. That this was not entirely true, can be gathered from what is probably the best known German contribution to Yeats Studies, Klaus Peter Jochum's massive bibliography of Yeats criticism, in many ways a model of bibliographical thoroughness, comprehensiveness and reliability,[7] continued by Jochum's contributions to *Yeats: An Annual of Critical and Textual Studies.* Jochum's work can serve as the basis for a brief survey of the critical reception of Yeats in Germany. The first detailed appreciation in Germany was probably that in Leon Kellner's voluminous history of Victorian literature (1909).[8] If one takes into account the date of publication, Kellner's judgements may be seen as less inappropriate than they might appear from a later point of view. Naturally, at this time (and Kellner had met him in 1899), Yeats appeared to him as an anti-materialist, a poet of the other-world, totally removed from the sordid realm of politics and the realities of social problems.

Throughout the nineteen-twenties and thirties, there was a trickle of articles and reviews in newspapers and small theatre magazines, most of them occasioned by the production of a Yeats play, but there was little continuity and little growth in appreciation and understanding. The award of the Nobel Prize to Yeats seems to have gone almost unnoticed; on the other hand, a number of newspapers and magazines, among them *Frankfurter Zeitung, Berliner Börsenzeitung, Münchener Neueste Nachrichten, Fränkischer Kurier* and *Deutsche Rundschau,* printed obituaries in early 1939, and the *Blätter der Städtischen Bühnen Frankfurt am Main* even published a separate memorial issue. The earliest dissertations, and the only ones before the fifties, were those by Elsbeth Schweisgut on 'Yeats's Feendichtung' (Giessen, 1927) and Gerta Hüttemann on 'Wesen der Dichtung und Aufgabe des Dichters bei William Butler Yeats' (Bonn, 1929).

The situation remained virtually unaltered until the mid-sixties, since when it has changed, not perhaps dramatically, but quite substantially. During the fifties, two scholarly articles in *Anglia* (on Yeats and Blake, and on Yeats and Chaucer, the latter not even by a German scholar), and two Ph.D. dissertations (on Christian elements in Yeats's symbolism, and on Yeats's relationship with French symbolism) could still be seen as exceptions to the general neglect.

With the beginning of the nineteen-sixties, the tide began to turn. From the mid-sixties onwards, German literary scholarship produced a flurry of collections of 'interpretations', detailed analyses of individual texts. The most popular among these volumes, Horst Oppel's *Das moderne englische Drama*, contained, among nineteen plays, no less than three analyses of Yeats's plays (Gerhard Stebner on *The Countess Cathleen*, Rudolf Stamm on *Deirdre* and Johannes Kleinstück on *At the Hawk's Well*), juxtaposing Yeats not only with Eliot and Fry but also with Osborne and Wesker and thus emphasizing the modernity of Yeats the playwright as opposed to the image of Yeats the neo-romantic. Dieter Mehl's two-volume collection *Das englische Drama* again discussed *The Countess Cathleen* (Heinz Bergner), while the present writer's *Das englische Drama im 18. und 19. Jahrhundert* added *The Land of Heart's Desire* (Klaus Peter Jochum). Oppel's companion volume *Die moderne englische Lyrik* emphasized Yeats's importance as (in Eliot's phrase) 'the greatest poet of our time' and underlined this by singling out Yeats as the only poet to be represented by three poems (Willi Erzgräber on 'Nineteen Hundred and Nineteen' and 'A Dialogue of Self and Soul', Arno Esch on 'Among School Children'). Karl Heinz Göller's two-volume collection *Die englische Lyrik* added 'Sailing to Byzantium' (Gisela Hoffmann) and 'The Wild Swans at Coole' (Gisela and Gerhard Hoffmann) to a slowly emerging canon of favourite Yeats poems in Germany. 'Sailing to Byzantium' was again interpreted in Horst Meller's *Zeitgenössische englische Dichtung* (Siegbert S. Prawer) and in Egon Werlich's *Poetry Analysis*; 'Among School Children' (Reinhold Schiffer) and 'The Wild Swans at Coole' (Peter H. Butter) were discussed in *Insight III: Analyses of English and American Poetry*, edited by Reinhold Schiffer and Herman J. Weiand.[9] The scholarly periodical *Die Neueren Sprachen* (also edited by Horst Oppel) which is written mainly for grammar-school teachers of English and French, added interpretations of 'The Second Coming' and 'Sailing to Byzantium' (Johannes Kleinstück) and 'Adam's Curse' (Erich Theumer) as well as the Cuchulain plays (Hans Jürgen Linke), thus indicating a new interest in Yeats in German schools.[10]

Encouraged, and sometimes perhaps also exasperated by these essays, graduate students in the sixties began to discover Yeats as a subject for Ph.D. theses. Since 1960 there have been more than a dozen Yeats dissertations, as compared to the four written between 1927, the year of the first Yeats dissertation, and 1960. Several of these were subsequently published in book form and have thus contributed not only to the German image of Yeats but also to the international world of learning. It is, of course, impossible to summarize these books in a brief survey, but it may

be interesting to list their subjects, which will give an idea of the
new variety of subject matter and approaches that is characteristic
of the more recent German attitude to Yeats. It will be advisable
also to include in this brief survey those few books that did *not*
originate from a dissertation.

The sixties saw an emphasis on Yeats's symbolism and imagery,
with a clear preference for the poetry, as exemplified by Johannes
Kleinstück's seminal book *W. B. Yeats oder der Dichter in der
modernen Welt*, as well as Theodor Klimek's study of symbol and
reality in Yeats, and Jeannette Lander's analysis of Yeats's
imagery, this last concentrating on the pervasive water imagery
that is an essential element in Yeats's symbolism.[11] Two 1971
publications included Yeats in a larger context: Hans-Joachim
Hahn discussed the 'crisis' (in the sense of 'decisive turning-
point') of modern poetry as exemplified in the work of Yeats and
Auden, and Lothar Hönnighausen in a sumptuously produced
book placed the early Yeats firmly in the context of late nineteenth-
century poetry.[12] The same year also saw the publication of Peter
Hühn's study of the relationship between man and woman in the
works of Yeats, indicating a new interest in themes with a certain
social relevance, as opposed to the image of Yeats as the poet of
poets. In addition, the early seventies produced the first book-
length study on Yeats's *Autobiographies*.[13] Perhaps even more
significantly, Yeats began to be appreciated as a playwright as
well as a poet. Already in 1969 Isolde von Bülow had published
her book on Yeats's use of the dance in drama, with the significant
sub-title *Untersuchungen zu W. B. Yeats' dramatischer Theorie und
Praxis*, indicating that Yeats was seen as a practical man of the
theatre as well as a theoretical thinker. This line was taken up and
extended by Klaus Peter Jochum's comprehensive analysis of all of
Yeats's plays, still a highly useful study both for the comprehensiveness of its approach and for many individual insights. Rudolf
Halbritter subsequently used the plays of Yeats as well as those of
Wilder and Pinter to demonstrate the specific features of the
short play as opposed to the full-length play and to distinguish
certain types of short plays, and he was particularly successful in
categorizing Yeats's plays as 'symbolist short plays'. Richard
Taylor's *Reader's Guide to the Plays of W. B. Yeats* may, by virtue of the
author's association with the University of Bayreuth, also be
listed among 'German' publications on Yeats.[14] Two other more
recent book publications are Eitel Friedrich Timm's detailed
analysis of Yeats's relationship to Nietzsche, a subject that had
already been touched upon in a number of German articles, and

Norbert K. Buchta's *Rezeption und ästhetische Verarbeitung romantischer Poetologie im lyrischen Werk William Butler Yeats.*[15] These book-length studies were supplemented by a number of articles in scholarly periodicals and *Festschriften*, such as comprehensive surveys by Kleinstück, Erzgräber and Manfred Pfister, comparative studies on Yeats and Mangan (Hans-Heinrich Freitag) and Yeats and Eliot (Hönnighausen), Ulrich Schneider's discussion of 'Yeats' Byzanz-Bild im Kontext seiner Zeit', Gerhard Hoffmann's analysis of the function of the songs in the plays, Jochum's discussion of Yeats's sonnets, and Joseph T. Swann's study of language and experience in the later poetry.[16] If one is painfully aware of the ineffectiveness of such a mere listing of titles in a brief survey, it may nevertheless become apparent that over the last twenty-five years Yeats studies in Germany have progressed considerably and have produced a body of work that, taken as a whole, is characterized by a great many original insights as well as by thoroughness of research, conclusiveness of argument and a wide variety of subjects and approaches.

Nevertheless, these various studies were clearly overshadowed by another publication, for the early seventies produced what may well turn out to be the major event in the German reception of Yeats, the publication of a six-volume edition of Yeats's works in German.[17] This is not, of course, a complete edition, but it is comprehensive enough to show, for the first time, what a multi-faceted body of work Yeats left behind. It was edited by Werner Vordtriede who also provided a lengthy general introduction, prefaces to the individual volumes, explanatory notes, and a biographical chronology. Translations are by some twenty contributors, including such well-known names as the novelist Stefan Andres, the poets Heinz Piontek and Georg von der Vring, the literary historian Wolfgang Kayser, and the first-rank translators Elisabeth Schnack and Susanne Schaup. Many of the translations had been published before but are here collected for the first time. This is to be welcomed, because (although in a few cases the German may appear slightly dated) it makes for a great deal of stylistic variety, and it prevents the 'German Yeats' from being imprisoned in the personal style of one individual translator. A brief survey of the contents of the individual volumes may indicate why this collection can serve as an excellent introduction to Yeats the poet, the playwright and the prose writer.

Vol. I, *Ausgewählte Gedichte*, contains some 190 poems, that is, approximately half the poetical work, by a dozen translators. The emphasis is on the later poems; from 'Crossways', only four poems are rendered here, while *Last Poems* is represented by no less than thirty. The volume is partly bi-lingual, giving the reader the welcome opportunity to check his own translation against the version printed here.

Vol. II, *Erzählungen*, contains narratives from *The Secret Rose, Stories of Red Hanrahan, Rosa Alchemica, The Tables of the Law, The Adoration of the Magi*, 'Per Amica Silentia Lunae'.

Vol. III and IV, *Dramen*, comprise eighteen plays. Of the twenty-six in the *Collected Plays*, only *The Pot of Broth, The King's Threshold, The Green Helmet, Calvary, The Resurrection, The Herne's Egg*, and the two Sophocles versions are not rendered here.

Vol. V, *Essays und Einführungen*, contains most of the essays from *Ideas of Good and Evil* and *The Cutting of an Agate*, and selections from the later two collections.

Vol. VI, *Autobiographien*, contains, with the exception of 'The Bounty of Sweden' and two shorter passages, the entire autobiographical writings.

The whole collection comprises some 1900 pages; the blue cloth-bound volumes, carefully printed and each embellished with a portrait of Yeats, are pleasing to the eye as well as invaluable in their contents. In the long run they will significantly change the German image of Yeats, and may even bring about some belated influence on German literature.

To say this is to admit that to date the influence of Yeats on German literature has been negligible. Even where one can detect obvious parallels of theme and technique, and similar views on the role of the poet in the modern world, it is next to impossible to establish any concrete points of contact; and where German writers actually mention the name of Yeats, these references remain isolated and do not seem to have resulted in any detailed interest in Yeats's writings.[18] There is nothing to indicate, for instance, that such poets and writers as Georg Heym, Else Lasker-Schüler, Ernst Stadler, Franz Werfel, Rudolf Borchardt or Franz Kafka were even remotely aware of the existence of Yeats.

The only reference to Yeats in the voluminous writings and correspondence of Rainer Maria Rilke comes in a letter of 18 September 1916, where he asks his publisher to send him (among other books) a copy of Yeats's *Erzählungen und Essays*, newly published by Insel Verlag in an edition by Friedrich Eckstein,[19] but Rilke's further writings yield no traces of Yeatsian influence, and it is not even known whether he read the book. Rilke's disregard of Yeats comes as a surprise, for two reasons: as has been pointed out repeatedly, 'Yeats was, of all contemporary poets employing the English language, the one who stood nearest to Rilke in his art and his outlook on existence . . .' Also, despite the 'haphazard manner in which Rilke was contented to let English books come his way, more anxious to keep them off than to attract them', he showed a decided interest in recent literature from Ireland, including George Moore, Wilde, Synge, Shaw and Joyce.[20] The most remarkable instance of an 'encounter' between these two great European poets who otherwise missed each other occurred, however, in *Ireland* when Yeats first sketched the lines of his epitaph (which eventually found their way into 'Under Ben Bulben') as an oblique and irritated reaction to Rilke's attitude to death.[21]

Rilke must have been aware of the name of Yeats through Rudolf Kassner's *Die Mystik, die Künstler und das Leben* (1900). The Austrian philosopher-poet was one of the first among German-language poets and literati to notice Yeats. In his early volume, subtitled *Über englische Dichter und Maler im 19. Jahrhundert*, he deals extensively with Blake, Shelley, Keats, Rossetti, Swinburne, Morris, Burne-Jones, Browning and others. However, he is aware of Yeats solely as the editor (together with Edwin John Ellis) of *The Works of William Blake: Poetic, Symbolic, and Critical* (1893), which he had bought during his sojourn in England in 1897/98. Kassner is full of praise for Yeats's and Ellis's editorial achievement, but even in the thoroughly revised version of his early book, published twenty years later (*Englische Dichter*, 1920), he still refers to Yeats only as the editor of Blake.[22] The only reference to Yeats in the works of Gottfried Benn comes in a letter to F. W. Oelze where he uses the name of Yeats, together with many others, to support his thesis that it is a 'bourgeois-romantic' prejudice to assume that poets are bound to die early — a mere indication that Benn was aware of the existence of Yeats.[23]

Very few German writers seem to have met Yeats personally. While it is highly unlikely that Stefan George met Yeats in Mallarmé's Paris house, as maintained by Wolfgang Kayser,[24] Max Dauthendey seems to have seen Yeats occasionally between 1894 and 1897 in occult circles in London and Paris; he is said to have fallen asleep during the première of *The Land of Heart's Desire*.[25] Stefan Zweig in his collection *Die Welt von Gestern* remembers his impressions of Yeats reading his own poetry (in 1904?).[26] Significantly, he registers his embarrassment at this act of priest-like 'celebration', a reaction that may have something to do with the German reluctance to take a deeper interest in Yeats. Conditioned by the existential (if not existentialist) seriousness of German poetry, and handicapped by their limited command of English, such writers as Zweig were not able to see behind Yeats's superficial poses, and tended to take the theatrical paraphernalia of his public appearances as the essence of his work.

At a slightly later stage, the poet, novelist, and playwright Henry von Heiseler and his son Bernt both took some interest in Yeats's writings. Henry von Heiseler, the unfortunate translator of Yeats's plays, comments on his translations in *Marginalien*. He stresses the (to him) exotic qualities of the plays, finding in them 'die Atmosphäre des irischen Mythos und Märchens, Sprache geworden in der Rede eines Dichters von hoher Kraft der Phantasie'. Heiseler's own verse plays may well have been influenced by his long-standing admiration for Yeats. His son published an equally enthusiastic, although factually incorrect appreciation of Yeats in his collected essays, without, however, indicating any influence on his own work.[27]

The greatest interest in Yeats before the Second World War, however, can be observed in the writings of Hugo von Hofmannsthal. The Austrian poet, playwright and essayist was such a voracious reader that not even Yeats escaped him. Michael Hamburger who made a study of Hofmannsthal's library discovered Hofmannsthal's copy of Yeats's *Erzählungen und Essays* (the same edition that Rilke asked for) and noticed Hofmannsthal's numerous notes, markings and underlinings, indicating, according to Hamburger, not only an unusually attentive reading process but also 'einen ausserordentlichen Grad von Übereinstimmungen zwischen den beiden Dichtern' — an extraordinary degree of common ground between the two poets.[28] Hamburger suspects that Hofmannsthal owned other works by Yeats as well, but the copies have been disposed of. Hamburger developed his findings on the relationship between Hofmannsthal and Yeats in his introductions to the English edition of Hofmannsthal's works.[29] He points to a number of similarities between Yeats and Hofmannsthal, without, however, postulating any outright influence. Such similarities, according to Hamburger, can be seen not so much in biographical parallels (although some of these are quite surprising), but in the two poets' general attitude to life and to the role that poetry has to play in it. Both were firmly rooted in the international symbolist tradition, depending in their early work on the medium of the dream, creating a poetry of pre-existence and contrasting the realm of symbolic poetry with the sordid world of mere factual existence. Both later tried to resolve the dualism of Life and Art through combining a philosophy of

literature that was esoteric in the extreme with an active participation in life — an ambivalence that resulted for them in
conflicts and crises. Both tried to go beyond lyric poetry by writing
verse plays, discovering in the short play a form that was far
enough removed from the atrocities of the commercial theatre.
Both experimented with combinations of mime, music, mask
and the spoken word, Yeats's plays for dancers corresponding in
many ways to Hofmannsthal's libretti for operas and scenarios for
ballets. Both developed the technique of the persona poem as
opposed to confessional poetry. Hamburger also sees direct
parallels between *Das Bergwerk zu Falun* and *The Shadowy Waters*,
describing both plays as turning-points where mature personal
experience and the intellectual climate of the age began to question the premises of the romantic-symbolist tradition. Again, he
compares the *Chandos* crisis in Hofmannsthal's work and the
experience expressed in 'The Circus Animals' Desertion'. Both
poets continued to the end to be fascinated by the stage-like
qualities of life which gave them the strength to struggle with the
irrelevancies of 'theatre business, management of men'. One
might also add that Hofmannsthal's attitude to his native Vienna
and to the Austrian-German relationship finds many parallels
in Yeats's stance toward Dublin and to the Irish-English confrontation.

Hofmannsthal quoted Yeats repeatedly, and with the assurance
based on relatively intimate knowledge of at least some of his
writings. In his first 'Vienna Letter' for *The Dial*, where he
attempts to describe the 'main current' of artistic life in Vienna,
the struggle to maintain its position as the cultural and intellectual
capital of South Eastern Europe, he quotes Yeats's 'Essay on
Theatre', contrasting the century-old tradition of popular theatre
in Vienna with the fight that Yeats, Lady Gregory and Synge had
to put up to establish something similar in Dublin. While he
congratulates the Austrian capital on its cultural heritage, he is
also full of admiration for Yeats's efforts.[30] In his *Buch der Freunde*
(1922), a collection of aphorisms, anecdotes and miscellaneous
quotations, Hofmannsthal inserts two Blake quotations that he
had gleaned from Yeats's essay on 'William Blake and his Illustrations to the Divine Comedy'.[31] In some of his sketches for *Die Frau
ohne Schatten* (ch. 6), Hofmannsthal refers to Yeats's essay on 'The
Philosophy of Shelley's Poetry' and quotes his views on the
importance of the symbol in overcoming the barrenness and
superficiality of a merely intellectual art.[32] Once the critical edition
of the works of Hofmannsthal is completed, it will be easier than

it is today to gauge the scope of Hofmannsthal's reactions to Yeats, and it is more than likely that this edition will produce quite a few additional references to the Irish poet. At the moment it appears that Hofmannsthal, like several other writers in German, found more to interest or stimulate him in Yeats's essays than in his poems or plays.

The neglect of Yeats by German-language authors continued after the Second World War. If Hofmannsthal is the exception before the War, Heinrich Böll is a similar exception among the post-War generation. His awareness of Yeats is not the great gesture from one Nobel Prize winner to another; it is deeply rooted in his personal experience of, and his spontaneous love for, Ireland. His early *Irisches Tagebuch* (1957) is a remarkable document of an author's growing understanding and appreciation of another country, its people and its culture, and his confrontation with Yeats in this book is briefly dramatized in his visit to Drumcliffe, where he takes Yeats's epitaph literally, returning to Sligo station rather than continuing to Innisfree.[33] Böll's personal contacts with Ireland, which encouraged him, together with his wife, to translate various Irish authors into German (Synge, Brendan Behan, Eilís Dillon, Flann O'Brien, Tomás O'Crohan among others), also led him to include references to Irish literature in many of his own works without any hesitation, and often with the ill-founded assumption that his readers would immediately understand them. Among Irish writers, Swift, Synge and O'Casey (about whom he wrote a number of articles) seem to have been his favourites, but one can also find a number of references to Yeats. In his novel *Gruppenbild mit Dame* (1971), for instance, he has his heroine sing 'A Coat' from *Responsibilities* (in a hitherto unpublished version by Böll that is superior to Vordtriede's translation in Yeats's *Werke*), and this leads the narrator to speculate whether Leni's literary understanding has not perhaps been underestimated 'because people found it difficult to pronounce the author's name'.[34] A few years earlier, Böll had ended his speech on Mauriac's eightieth birthday (11 October 1965) quite un-self-consciously with a Yeats quotation: 'Ich bin arm und habe nur meine Träume. Tritt sanft, du trittst auf meine Träume'.[35] There are several further references to Yeats in Böll's collected essays and speeches, especially where he deals with Synge and O'Casey,[36] and it is likely that one could discover hidden allusions in his novels, but the full extent of his awareness of, and perhaps even indebtedness to Yeats will not be known until the completion of the critical edition of Böll's collected works which is now under way.

In conclusion, the evidence of the preceding pages — the specific conditions and consequences of the reception of Yeats in Germany — may serve to underline the cultural diversity of Europe. If, from a British point of view, the terms 'Europe' or 'The Continent' are sometimes still today used to signify a homogeneous entity as opposed to the otherness of Britain, this bears no relationship to the realities of the cultural and literary situation. There is no 'European tradition' and no 'European style' just as there is no 'European food'; instead, there is a wide range of interlocking traditions and styles among which the English tradition or style may be identified as a highly specific one, but one that is not any more different from the rest than the Portuguese, the Swedish or the Hungarian.[37] The term 'Yeats the European' is useful to describe a man who was highly aware of a wide range of various literary developments, and whose reception, in its turn, has profited or suffered from that same cultural diversity.

THE CHAIRMAN'S CLOSING STATEMENT
(Extracts from a tape recording made on
25 May 1987)

If the mechanical, mathematical side of my brain is still function-
ing, I think that we have had twenty-four addresses. I won't work
out the wordage in these, because it would come to double the
length we hope to have in the book which will eventuate from the
seminar. I was very sorry there was not another address, a twenty-
fifth. So I will take those announcements just made by George
Sandulescu as an unofficial collective twenty-fifth contribution.
This immediately allows me, by numerology, that new academic
would-be science, to multiply by two (and being Irish I always
multiply everything by two anyway), and so I come to fifty.

This brings me to the point, fifty years ago, when I first spoke
to Yeats. I was a schoolboy at the High School in Dublin (an
Erasmus Smith foundation) and Editor of *The Erasmian*. I rang
Yeats up because I knew that the school I went to, which was the
one that he had gone to, would be happy to have a contribution
from its most famous schoolboy. When I rang him up, he said that
he was not writing poems at the time which were suitable for a
school magazine. God knows this was very true! But a little later
— he was very kind — he said: 'Well, there is one that might do',
and so I was to go out to Riversdale in Rathfarnham, just below
the Dublin Mountains, to collect it.

I went out to Riversdale, I may say, for other reasons of my own,
for I often visited a house there called Rosemount, further along
the road from Riversdale. It was a house where spiritualist seances
were held. (Indeed Yeats sometimes attended these.) But I used to
go out there to drive a friend's air-cooled Rover — rescued from
Cahill's scrapyard for five pounds — around garden paths and
fields since we were too young for driving licences and the open
road. Anyway, I went out to Riversdale to see the Yeatses, and was
given a poem which I find (with an obvious personal commitment
to it), one of the most charming and haunting that Yeats wrote:
'What Then'.

And that is when I first met George Yeats, in 1937. Time marched on, I was sucked away from my devouring interest in motorcars into reading classics at Trinity College Dublin. When I graduated I wondered what I should do next. Science came to the rescue in the person of David Webb, the botanist, who, one evening, when we had had quite a lot to drink, thrust one of Yeats's books at me and asked: 'What does that poem mean?' I hadn't a clue, so he said: 'Well, why don't you do a Ph.D. on Yeats? It's what you ought to be doing instead of more classics. There are enough people alive who knew him, who might know what that kind of poem means.' I thought it was a very exciting idea to move to something contemporary, away from a somewhat orthodox classical upbringing, and from my Greek Professor whom I liked but did not want as a supervisor. And H. O. White, the Professor of English, had known Yeats, knew a good deal about his work, and was ready to take me on to write a thesis on the sources and symbolism of Yeats's poetry. So, a lunch party, for me to discuss the possibilities with Mrs Yeats, was arranged by David's mother — that wonderful woman, one of the many wonderful women of Dublin, Doctor Ella Webb.

At this lunch party George Yeats and I renewed the acquaintanceship of 1937 and she said: 'Yes, you can come. The library is at your disposal, so am I. I'll try to answer anything you like to ask me and I am delighted you should do this. Let's see what you want to do!' It was a delightful reaction. And so I came to work on Yeats's papers and on the books in his library and to have the wonderful opportunity of learning so much about him and his work from his widow, whose information was, of course, invaluable.

Michael Yeats will understand that obviously I came by bicycle: he and I have in common one thing that was part of Dublin life in our youth: we bicycled everywhere — so I pedalled around to 46 Palmerston Park, and Mrs Yeats started me on my work. Well, I cannot say enough to convey what a marvellous person she was, how deeply learned, how discerningly, sharply critical she was. Like all interesting people she could be quirky, but she was superbly helpful and unselfish, and finely endowed with a sardonic yet tolerant sense of humour.

John Kelly quoted the hexameter 'Caelum non animum mutant qui trans mare currunt' and in the course of time I had myself to cross the seas quite often. Exile in Holland, exile in Edinburgh, but I used to go back to Dublin and would see George Yeats on these occasions. Then came a longer exile of seven years in

Australia. Academics in those days could not afford to fly, and the
seas seemed really long; 'currere' is hardly the *mot juste*; one did
not really run over them, one crawled over them. So I did not see
George for quite a long time.

Living in Australia was an extraordinary experience for me
because there was a time lag there: time seemed to have stood still,
for people still drove around in model T Fords, and stove bolt sixes,
those indestructible ancient Chevrolets. Why? Because, during
the war, the Repco Company had made spare parts for them. You
could keep a model T going when you could not keep a *modern*
British car going, or an American one. So I was transported back
to my own youth when the old Irish farmers cranked up their T
Fords, with one back wheel supported by a jack and then the cars
would lumber off their jacks in a cloud of dust, with their owners
cruising around till someone threw their jacks back into the cars.
Why do I mention this? Because Yeats knew about Fords. After
all, he was driven around in one supplied by Henry Ford on one
of his American tours. And he mentions the Ford cars that carried
the bodies of dead young soldiers in the West of Ireland, during
the Civil war; he travelled in Ford cars in Ireland and he thought
they might keep a Ford at Ballylee. He didn't, you see, have a
feeling for Morrises at all. The way he dismissed one William
Morris was brief: he was 'the man who made the motors'.

There in Australia I was back in my youth or well before my
youth — some of these cars were so wonderfully old; there was
even a vast local Gobron Brille — and it was all very simple: if a
T Ford didn't start, you took a great hammer and beat a box on the
running board and that would get it going. If that didn't work,
you took it to a blacksmith, and he would treat it to more violent
measures. Now, if I were to go back to Australia, I would find that
most people would probably have fashionable four-wheel drive
and nearwheel steering. They would have electronic ignition —
that bane of man and beast, they would have turbo-charging,
they would have intercoolers, they would have that other ghastly
thing — automatic transmission, and some would even have,
believe it or not, variable valve timing! This is complex stuff, and
this is like the Yeats industry today.

When I began work on Yeats, I can assure you it was virtually
in the pre-model T Ford age. No, that is a little rude, it was in the
Chevrolet stove bolt six age! There were really only two books on
Yeats to read, and I want to pay tribute to both of them. One was
Joseph Hone's biography. I have just been re-reading it. It is a
magnificent book, durable as a model T. Of course, it is full of

mistakes, but aren't we all full of them? If we think we are always right, we are often very wrong indeed — and I say that very firmly with many people in mind! The other book was, of course, Louis MacNeice's sometimes inaccurate, but provocatively stimulating book on the poetry, still a very good read, especially when the pioneering nature of its critical discussions of the later poetry is taken into account. These then were the two worthwhile books existing on Yeats.

What else was there? There was Dublin, pulsating with memories, most of them inaccurate, and so I went around to see the many people who had known Yeats and mythologized the experience. Mrs Yeats was, however, *always* accurate! I went to see Maud Gonne: a different experience. In one corner of Roebuck House was a spinning wheel and in the other a harp. The one was to show she was with the people. The other, the harp, had broken strings to represent the present state of partitioned Ireland. Old and grey, but still endowed with those great, luminous, mesmeric eyes, she motioned me to a seat by the fire, picked a book down from the bookcase, and said: 'I think Willie would have liked me to read this to you':

> . . . take down this book
> And slowly read, and dream of the soft look
> Your eyes had once . . .

She read all the rest of that poem 'When You Are Old', and then she began to play me what I indelicately call 'The Old 78', which was how she had always said to Willie: No, she would not marry him; but they should go on being such good friends; and he should go on writing her such lovely poems; and the world would thank her for not marrying him! Every time I saw her, she always told me this; it was as if it sorted things out for her, a kind of clearing of her throat, or, perhaps, in modern terms, of putting in the right tape.

In the course of time I went to see Iseult, who then lived in Laragh Castle in County Wicklow. And Iseult said to me: 'Who do you think will win the war?' And I tactfully said, 'Well, I don't know.' 'Ah', she said, somewhat to my surprise, in view of her reputed harbouring of a German agent parachuted into Ireland, 'I think I do not wish the Germans to win the war'. 'Why do you not?' I asked. 'Then my husband would be a diplomat, and I am not really made to be a diplomat's wife!' Anybody who knew Iseult would have realized that this was probably a very fair comment on her character . . .

Well, there was a lot of this kind of conversation with many people in the course of which one could build up biographical details and begin to understand some of the more arcane poems. Joseph Hone; I used to observe from a distance in the National Library of Ireland, in that extraordinary mustard-coloured coat he wore, with his vivid pale blue eyes. He was usually walking around the Library, while, in a corner, there sat Arland Ussher, that great thinking man, thinking his deep thoughts about Yeats and Shaw, and other Irish writers. There they both were, virtually pillars of the National Library. Joe and I used to talk to each other, until one day he discovered that I was working on Yeats, whereupon he distanced himself from me . . . He used to ask how my brother in Oxford was getting on, who was writing a book on Yeats, and I used to tell him how my brother was getting on. (By this time I had gone to Oxford to write a D.Phil there.) And George, on one occasion, sent me to get back something, because Joe often forgot about returning things, so I told Joe that the brother would very much like to see such and such a book, which I believed, or the brother believed, that he had. (Not George, but the brother . . . because George took a certain sardonic pleasure in this double game.) Joe said: 'Well, I can't give you that because, you see, your brother is in Oxford at present.' At least we had established that he had got the book. That was the first step . . .

Now I would like to throw in one unpublished anecdote about George, which I think may give Anne Yeats, and Michael and Grania, Michael Yeats's wife, pleasure. I was hunting around the shelves in Palmerston Road when I was working on the influence of Shelley on Yeats, a very obvious one. But there was no Shelley in the Library. That seemed very odd. Well, a lot of things were not in the Library, of course . . . I asked George about it and she said, 'It is most extraordinary, isn't it? There isn't a Shelley'. That was on Thursday. George rang me up at about 3 o'clock on Saturday afternoon and said: 'Get on your bicycle!' And so I got on my bicycle and came around. She handed me a rather popular edition, published by Routledge & Kegan Paul, of Shelley's poems inscribed, as far as I remember at this distance: 'To my dear friend, W. B. Yeats, with love and affection, Katherine Tynan'. And the interesting thing to me was that one or two of the things that I thought Yeats had got from Shelley were marked in the margins with pencil. And I said: 'George, where did you find it?' 'Ah', she replied, 'you may well ask that. It is worth asking. I went down town shopping and I missed my bus, so I walked up Camden Street, and I just happened to look at that old book stall there, and I bought it for sixpence.'

Well, some people have been lucky and have not had to give a paper at this seminar, but there is one of them I would like to praise for his great contribution to the work of other scholars. He is Stephen Parrish, whose concordance has been invaluable to Yeats scholars. You will find, by the way, in the collection of books here in the Princess Grace Irish Library, a thesis written for University College Dublin, which is just as valuable, a concordance to the essays of Yeats, a fine piece of work which I hope will be published, because, of course, we now want other concordances of other aspects of Yeats's prose. One of the things that has come out of this seminar again and yet again is the extraordinary richness of Yeats's allusion to the whole literary scene, something a concordance can convey so usefully and economically.

And Yeats never went to a University. He was able to function in a broad way, an eclectic way, without being an increasingly narrow specialist. He read widely, he read with enthusiasm, he read with feeling and found what he wanted, and he had a God-given flair for discovering it. He knew what to look for. Had he gone through a narrow University discipline, we would probably not have had our great poet, nor, as someone said, our essayist and our playwright.

What, then, has come out of our seminar? Well, I don't want to give a school-masterly summary of what everybody has said; it would be invidious because, quite frankly, I would want to dwell on some contributions more than others, not from any personal feeling one way or the other about their authors, but just because, obviously, certain things have interested me more than others. There were many hints about things all the way through our meetings that were fascinating, triggering off all sorts of reactions in one's mind. We did have, you see, a number of names mentioned but not dealt with in any detail, which was interesting, making one wish for more. What we did have, among other things, was the middle period of Yeats's life suddenly coming into a slightly sharper focus. There are dark places in it still to be explored, but there is, after all, a curious collective unconscious; people who are on the same intellectual wavelengths are working along the same lines. I always say to a student who happens to have a good idea: 'For goodness' sake, publish it!' There are always likely to be at least eight people in the world who have the same idea and the credit will depend on which of them gets it into print. There is often one new idea, which somebody (Erwin Schroedinger, I think) has described as being like the froth on the wave of thought; and if you're part of that froth, then you should do something

about it quickly, if you want to be known! So we have had all sorts
of new material, dealt with from very contrasting attitudes. We
have seen how Yeats treated Europe in different ways. One can
only record one's own personal interest. Let me give you an
example of the kind of thing that occurred to me. I was going to
say, at the beginning of my introduction, that Yeats, when he
wrote his local poetry, did so under the spur of reading William
Allingham, because Allingham grew up in the same kind of place
in the West of Ireland. The phrase he used about Allingham was
that he came from the same kind of seaport town. And then
George Watson reminded us that Ibsen came from the same kind
of seaport town, and here we all are in a seaport town, aware that
Yeats was born in a seaport town. And I begin to wonder about
it because this is a deeply-rooted idea I have: can you, if you have
been born and grown up by the sea, ever be fully happy inland?
I don't think you can and I think Yeats perhaps had this feeling.
Why did he like Rapallo? He was living by the sea there, he was
able to look out at the sea there, and perhaps no one really has
fully considered the effect of the sea on him. Yeats knew, by
instinct almost, the seabirds' cries before dawn, a good time to go
to the sea if you are still capable of fishing, but not perhaps if you
have been at a night club all night, or at the Casino . . . Here, in
this seaside air, our meetings have left stimulating suggestions
and ideas for future foam on the sea of thought.

I would like to conclude by saying what a great pleasure it is to
me that Michael and Grania, and Anne have come down to
Monaco to be with us. And then there is a final thing I would like
to say — apart from expressing our appreciation of the generous
hospitality we have received here in Monaco, of the warm-hearted
reception given us by the comité de direction and the great help
we have had from the staff of the Princess Grace Irish Library —
and that is to thank you all for coming, for contributing your
papers, to congratulate you, if I may, on being nice people! Not all
scholars are nice people, as Yeats knew very well. There were so
many discerning things he said so well, among them: 'Always
we'd have the new friend meet the old', and here we have had
some new friends meeting the old. But what is all this about? It's
about humanity, it's about friendly help among scholars, but it is
also about the anti-selves possessed by that fierce competitive-
ness that has increased in modern scholarship over the years.

It is all terrifying to me: I am still an old T Ford jogging along,
happy to have large wheels and a high ground clearance to get
over the ruts since I don't altogether trust too many of the modern

gimmicks. They are very nice when they work. Indeed, at times, they are superb, but they have brought in a slightly unpleasant edge to some aspects of Yeatsian scholarship. At this seminar, however, we have had people — visitors and delegates both — who have remarked on its absence. Somebody said with faint surprise, of the delegates here: 'They are very nice to one another'. I said: 'Of course, because these are very nice people who are not primarily competitive but disinterestedly co-operative in their search for fresh knowledge about a great poet.' So all I would say is thank you all very much for coming, and I suppose I should really add, you lovely people!

A. Norman Jeffares

APPENDIX 1
The Conference Programme

FRIDAY 22

10.00 to 11.15	REGISTRATION. Visit of the Library.
11.15 to 12.30	Private guided tour of the Palace of Monaco.
12.30	Lunch at Castelroc Restaurant (Place du Palais).
16.00 to 16.25	FORMAL OPENING: Address by H.S.H. Princess Caroline. Unveiling of Bust of Yeats made by Sculptor Kees VERKADE. Brief statements by A. Norman JEFFARES and George SANDULESCU.
16.30 to 16.45	INTERMISSION
16.45	Alasdair D. F. MACRAE. 'When Yeats summoned Golden Codgers to His Side.'
17.15	Helen VENDLER. 'The Poetics of Cacophony.'
17.45 to 18.15	DISCUSSIONS
18.15 to 18.30	INTERMISSION
18.30	Patrick RAFROIDI. 'Yeats's France Revisited.'
19.00	Denis DONOGHUE. 'Yeats and European Criticism.'
19.30 to 20.00	DISCUSSIONS. Session ends.
21.15	Private Buffet-Supper, Italian Style, offered by Signora Anne-Marie Sozzani at 3, Place du Palais, Monaco-Ville.

SATURDAY 23

9.30	Jacqueline GENET. 'Villiers de l'Isle-Adam and WBY.'
10.00	Warwick GOULD. 'A Crowded Theatre: Yeats and Balzac.'
10.30 to 11.00	DISCUSSIONS
11.00 to 11.15	INTERMISSION
11.15	Birgit BRAMSBACK. 'WBY and "The Bounty of Sweden" '.
11.45	Peter KUCH. 'A Few Twigs from the Wild Bird's Nest'.

12.15 to 12.45	DISCUSSIONS
13.00 to 15.00	Lunch at Castelroc Restaurant (Place du Palais).
15.00	Declan KIBERD. 'Yeats and the Cost of Art.'
15.30	C. K. STEAD. 'Yeats the European.'
16.00 to 16.30	DISCUSSIONS. (Followed by INTERMISSION.)
16.45	Michael SIDNELL. 'The Presence of the Poet.'
17.15	Ronald SCHUCHARD. 'Yeats, Titian and New French Painting.'
17.45 to 18.15	DISCUSSIONS
18.15 to 18.30	INTERMISSION
18.30 to 19.00	John KELLY. 'Caelum non animum mutant . . .'
19.00 to 19.30	DISCUSSIONS
20.30	Private Buffet-Supper offered by Mr and Mrs P. Taylor at The Sorrento Restaurant, Larvotto Beach.

SUNDAY 24

9.30	William MURPHY. 'Lily Yeats, WBY, and France.'
10.00	Ann SADDLEMYER. 'Georgie Hyde-Lees: More than a poet's wife.'
10.30 to 11.00	DISCUSSIONS
11.00 to 11.15	INTERMISSION
11.15	Michael ALEXANDER. 'Savants and Artists: Pound and Yeats.'
11.45	Bernard HICKEY. 'Lady Gregory: Coole and Ca' Capello Layard.'
12.15 to 12.45	DISCUSSIONS
13.00 to 15.00	Lunch at the Texan Restaurant (La Condamine).
15.00	Coaches depart for Roquebrune.
16.30	Coaches depart for Cap-Martin.
17.00	Hotel Ideal Sejour.
18.00	Reception offered by Mayor of Roquebrune Cap Martin.
19.00	Coaches depart for Monaco (from the Town Hall).
21.00	Dinner and Show offered by S.B.M. at the Cabaret.

MONDAY 25

9.30	Andrew PARKIN. 'W. B. Yeats and Other Europeans.'
10.00	Masaru SEKINE. 'Yeats's Four Plays.'
10.30	George WATSON. 'Yeats, Ibsen, and the New Woman.'
11.00 to 11.30	DISCUSSIONS

11.30 to 11.45	INTERMISSION
11.45 to 13.00	A. Norman JEFFARES. The Summing Up.
13.00 to 15.00	Farewell Lunch at Castelroc Restaurant (Place du Palais).

APPENDIX 2
The Participants

Michael ALEXANDER, University of St. Andrews
Bruce ARNOLD, The *Irish Independent*, Dublin
Massimo BACIGALUPO, University of Genoa
Birgit BRAMSBACK, University of Uppsala
Marcello CAPUZZO, University of Palermo
Toni CERUTTI, University of Turin
Denis DONOGHUE, City University of New York
Roy FOSTER, University of London
Jacqueline GENET, University of Caen
Warwick GOULD, University of London
Bernard HICKEY, University of Venice
A. Norman JEFFARES, University of Stirling
Pierre JOANNON, Princess Grace Irish Library
John KELLY, University of Oxford
Declan KIBERD, University College, Dublin
Heinz KOSOK, University of Wuppertal
Peter KUCH, University of Newcastle, N.S. Wales
Louis LE BROCQUY, France
Colm McGRADY, Irish Embassy, Paris
Wayne McKENNA, University of Toulouse
Alasdair MACRAE, University of Stirling
Jean MALONEY, University of Los Angeles
Carla MARENGO, University of Turin
William M. MURPHY, Union College, Schenectady
Sir David and Lady ORR, The British Council
Andrew PARKIN, University of British Columbia
Stephen M. PARRISH, Cornell University
Patrick RAFROIDI, University of Sorbonne
Ann SADDLEMYER, University of Toronto
George SANDULESCU, Princess Grace Irish Library
Ronald SCHUCHARD, Emory University
Masaru SEKINE, Waseda University, Tokyo
Michael SIDNELL, University of Toronto
Colin SMYTHE, Publisher, Gerrards Cross

Chris SPURR, BBC Belfast
C. K. STEAD, University of Auckland
Richard TAYLOR, University of Bayreuth
Helen VENDLER, University of Harvard
George WATSON, University of Aberdeen
Anne YEATS, Dublin
Michael and Grania YEATS, Dublin
Wolfgang ZACH, University of Graz

NOTES

WHEN YEATS SUMMONED GOLDEN CODGERS TO HIS SIDE
Alasdair D. F. Macrae
All quotations from Yeats's poems are from *Collected Poems* (London: Macmillan, 1952).

1   Donald R. Pearce, ed., *The Senate Speeches of W. B. Yeats*, (Bloomington: Indiana University Press, 1960), pp. 97-98.
2   W. B. Yeats, *Essays and Introductions* (New York: Collier-Macmillan, 1968), p. 192.
3   S. T. Coleridge, *The Poetical Works of S. T. Coleridge*, vol. III (London: William Pickering, 1840), pp. 75-76.
4   W. B. Yeats, *Autobiographies* (London: Macmillan, 1955), p. 116.
5   John Kelly, ed., *The Collected Letters of W. B. Yeats* vol. I (Oxford: Clarendon Press, 1986), p. 502.
6   *Essays and Introductions*, p. 185.
7   *Autobiographies*, pp. 194-95.
8   Richard J. Finneran, ed., *The Poems of W. B. Yeats* (London: Macmillan, 1984), pp. 626-27.
9   Horace Reynolds, ed., *Letters to the New Island by William Butler Yeats* (London: Oxford University Press, 1970), p. 74.
10 W. B. Yeats, *Explorations* (London: Macmillan, 1962), p. 233.
11 Allan Wade, *Letters of W. B. Yeats* (London: Rupert Hart-Davis, 1954), p. 434.
12 Stanislaus Joyce, *My Brother's Keeper* (London: Faber and Faber, 1958), p. 100.
13 *Autobiographies*, pp. 364-65.
14 W. B. Yeats, *A Vision* (New York: Collier-Macmillan, 1966), pp. 132-33.
15 *Autobiographies*, p. 191.
16 *Mythologies*, pp. 359-60.
17 T. S. Eliot, ed., *Literary Essays of Ezra Pound* (London: Faber and Faber, 1954), p. 431.
18 *Essays and Introductions*, pp. 78-79.
19 Edwin Muir, *Collected Poems* (London: Faber and Faber, 1960), pp. 249-50.

YEATS AS A EUROPEAN POET: THE POETICS OF CACOPHONY
Helen Vendler

1   Abbreviations in this essay refer to the following volumes by William Butler Yeats: *CP: Collected Poems* (New York: Macmillan, 1956); *E: Explorations* (New York: Collier Books, 1962); *EI: Essays and Introductions* (New York: Collier Books, 1961); *P: Poems* ed. Richard Finneran (New York: Macmillan, 1983); *V: A Vision*.
    L is the abbreviation for *The Letters of W. B. Yeats*, ed. Allan Wade (London: Rupert Hart-Davis, 1954).
2   *Preoccupations* (London: Faber & Faber, 1980), p. 99.
3   Harold Bloom, *Yeats* (London: Fontana/Collins, 1971) p. 14.
4   *The Vast Design*, quoted in K. G. W. Cross, 'The Fascination of What's Difficult', in *In Excited Reverie*, eds. A. Norman Jeffares and K. G. W. Cross (New York: Macmillan, 1965), p. 332.

5 Richard Ellmann, *Yeats: The Man and the Masks* (New York: Norton, 1979), p. 238.
6 Part I consists of four quatrains each composed of two lines of pentameter
   followed by two lines of trimeter, rhyming abab. Part II consists of eight
   quatrains each composed of two lines of pentameter followed by two lines of
   trimeter, but they rhyme aabb. In Part III, the quatrains resemble those of Part
   II, but there are only five of them. There are several true, but rather self-
   contradictory propositions that can be made about this poem: it is written in
   quatrains; it is written in couplets; it is one poem; it is three poems; it is
   written in pentameter; it is written in trimeter; it is a binary poem (a double
   vision or two visions); it is a ternary poem (with three parts); it affirms
   determinism; it affirms free will; it is European (Sphinx); it is Asian (Buddha);
   it is Irish (Cashel); it is archaic ('Thereon I made my moan'); it is modern
   ('fling into my meat/A crazy juice'). The look of the poem, incidentally and
   appropriately in view of its archaizing tendencies, reminds us of Greek
   meters like the iambic strophe that have stanzas of longer followed by shorter
   lines.
7 This song was unaccountably misread in an early essay by Paul de Man,
   'Image and Emblem in Yeats', printed in Paul de Man, *The Rhetoric of
   Romanticism* (New York: Columbia University Press, 1984). The relevant
   passage appears on p. 227, where de Man argues that Ribh aims his attack 'at
   the doctrine that conceives of earthly and natural things as reflections of a
   divine order'. On the contrary, Ribh supports such a doctrine — derived from
   the Great Smaragdine Tablet — and he attacks the 'absurd' Patrician Trinitarian
   Hellenism that would conceive of a male begetting a male. Ribh says anything
   divine must correspond to what we know of the human.
8 It is for this reason that Harold Bloom's notorious revoicing of 'We Irish' as
   'We Germans', in his *Yeats* (New York: Oxford University Press, 1970), p. 444,
   is mistaken. 'We Germans', as we know it from the 1930s, is uttered in an
   attempt to distinguish Germans from their fellow-Europeans; 'We Irish', as
   Yeats uses it here, is said in order to *ally* the historical predicament of the Irish
   with that of other cultures, including European cultures, which had to
   reinvent 'measurement'. 'Measurement began our might:/Form a stark
   Egyptian thought,/Forms that gentler Phidias wrought', *C.P.*, p. 342. Thus
   does 'Under Ben Bulben' rephrase the conjunction of Ireland and Europe
   which is also the concern of 'The Statues'.
9 In a strange temporal conjunction, Gottfried Benn writes, in his *Novel of the
   Phenotype* (1944), a passage close in feeling to Yeats's 'News for the Delphic
   Oracle'.
      Old age was drawing on, bringing the days of stocktaking . . . Everything
      was brightly illumined, in properly defined relation, the connections
      valid within the framework of their situation — only of their situation:
      for in the background lurked the great disharmony that was the law of
      the universe . . .
         Something immobile entered into him and became manifest, having
      probably been there always; an invisible god, not to be named, who
      belonged to the rustics, for he stayed in the fields, the harvest fell upon
      his shoulders without his stirring, his caverns lay near at hand, and the
      entries to nests and ravines were not inaccessible. And that mythical
      vanishing in streams, the enchantments of naiads, foam-births, tombs
      under water — these, too, he had leisure, had the measure, to reflect on . . .
         Once again he entered into the ambivalence of things that had
      revealed themselves to him so decisively . . . It was an antimony without

end. This gearing of history to the world of the mind was one of the problems to which his age had no answer. *Primal Vision*(New York: New Directions, 1971), pp. 132-133.

YEATS'S FRANCE REVISITED

Patrick Rafroidi

1   George Moore, *Ave* (1911), *Hail and Farewell*, ed. Richard Allen Cave (Gerrards Cross: Colin Smythe, 1976), pp. 247-8.
2   *Ibid.*, pp. 250-4.
3   English text to be found in *The Dublin Magazine*, XXVI, 2, April-June 1951, p. 41.
4   See particularly F. Hugh O'Donnell, *The Stage Irishman of the Pseudo-Celtic Drama* (London: John Long, 1904).
5   George Moore, *Confessions of a Young Man* (1886), (New York: Capricorn Books, 1959), pp. 14-15.
6   W. B. Yeats, *The Speckled Bird*, ed. William H. O'Donnell (Dublin: The Cuala Press, 1973), p. 45
7   This appeared in the *Savoy* in April, 1896. Quoted from *Uncollected Prose by W. B. Yeats I*, ed. John P. Frayne (London: Macmillan, 1970), p. 398.
8   *Essays and Introductions* (London: Macmillan, 1969), pp. 340-1.
9   *A Vision* (London: T. Werner Lowrie, 1925), p. 219.
10 See, for instance, 'Bishop Berkeley', *Essays and Introductions*, pp. 404-5.
11 *Autobiographies* (London: Macmillan, 1966), p. 462.
12 *The Tower. The Poems*, a new edition, ed. Richard J. Finneran (London: Macmillan, 1983), p. 223.
13 J. M. Synge, *Collected Works I. Poems*, ed. Robin Skelton (London: Oxford University Press, 1962), p. 80.
14 Margaret Stanley, *W. B. Yeats et la France* (Doctorat de 3e cycle, Université de Lille 3, 1977).
15 *L'Alphée*, cahier de littérature, (Paris: November 1980). (See *Pleine Lune de Mars*, pp. 103-18.)
16 William Butler Yeats, cahier dirigé par Jacqueline Genet (Paris: Editions de L'Herne, 1981); 'Le Seuil du Palais du Roi', pp. 286-317; 'Le Chat et la Lune', pp. 354-64.
17 *L'Alphée*, op. cit.; 'Sept poemes tardifs 1936-9'; 'An Acre of Grass'; 'What then?'; 'The Great Day'; 'Parnell'; 'What was lost'; 'The Spur'; 'Those Images'; pp. 90-101.
18 *L'Herne*, William Butler Yeats, op. cit., 'Trois poemes' traduits par Raymonde Popot: 'Il invite sa Bien aimée a être passible'; 'Il souhaiterait possèder les voiles du ciel'; 'Petits sous bruns', pp. 37-8; René Frèchet: 'Pas de seconde Troie', p. 40; 'Le Peuple', pp. 40-1; 'Dèmon et bête', pp. 42-3; Patrick Rafroidi: 'The Lake Isle of Innisfree', pp. 63-4; 'Politics', p. 65; 'When You are Old', p. 66; 'Red Hanrahan's Song about Ireland', p. 67; 'Crazy Jane talks with the Bishop', p. 69; ('When You are Old': 'Quand vous serez bien veille', 'Crazy Jane . . .': 'L'entretien de Jeanne La Folle et de l'Évêque' and 'Politics': 'Engagement'), were reprinted by Club 80 with a lithograph by Louis Le Brocquy in 1984; another translation of mine, 'Second Avenement' ('The Second Coming') appeared in 1980 in *Approximations*, Lille, p. 75; Jean Briat 'A l'Irlande Future' pp. 105-6; 'Responsabilites' (introduction), p. 107; 'Les Cygnes sauvages de Coole', p. 108; 'A la memoire du Commandant Robert Gregory', pp. 109-12; 'Le Pêcheur', p. 113; 'Pâques 1916', pp. 114-15; 'Le second avènement', p. 116; 'Prière pour ma Fille', pp. 117-9; 'Méditations du temps de la guerre civile', pp. 120-5; 'Voile vers Byzance', p. 126; 'Byzance',

p. 127; 'Les Spires', p. 128; R. Popot: 'Au coeur des sept Bois', p. 146; 'He Bids his Beloved be at Peace', p. 199: 'He hears the cry of the sedge', p. 202.

19   *Per Amica Silentia Lunae* (Lille: Presses Universitaires, 1979).
      Explorations, ibid., 1981.
      Le Crépuscule Celtique, ibid., 1983.
      La Rose Secrète ibid., 1984.
      La Taille d'une agate (Paris: Klincksieck, 1984).
      Essais et Introductions (Lille: Presses Universitaires, 1985).
      All of these have been undertaken by a team of translators under the direction of Jacqueline Genet.

YEATS AND EUROPEAN CRITICISM
Denis Donoghue

1   W. B. Yeats, *Letters*, ed. A. Wade, p. 379.
2   *Ibid.*, p. 402.
3   *Ibid.*, p. 403.
4   'In the Earth, or in the air?', *Times Literary Supplement*, 17 January, 1986.
5   W. B. Yeats, *Essays and Introductions*, p. 147.
6   W. B. Yeats, *Memoirs*, ed. D. Donoghue, p. 166.
7   W. B. Yeats, *Essays and Introductions*, p. 471.
8   W. B. Yeats, *A Vision*, p. 206.
9   W. B. Yeats, *Autobiographies*, p. 142.
10   W. B. Yeats, *Essays and Introductions*, pp. 106-7.
11   Northrop Frye, *The Stubborn Structure*, p. 277.
12   Northrop Frye, *Fables of Identity*, p. 236.

VILLIERS DE L'ISLE ADAM AND W. B. YEATS
Jacqueline Genet
All quotations from French literature have been translated by the author of the article.

1   *Letters*, Wade, p. 592.
2   Preface to *The Symbolist Movement in Literature* (New York: E. P. Dutton & Co, 1908), p. V.
3   *Ibid.*
4   *Ibid.*, p. VI.
5   Yeats, *Autobiography*, p. 319.
6   *Ibid.*, p. 320.
7   Dorothy Knowles, *La Réaction Idéaliste au Théâtre depuis 1900* (Paris: Droz, 1934), p. 82.
8   Cf. the preface to the English translation of *Axël* by H. P. R. Finberg (London, 1925), p. 7.
9   *Per Amica Silentia Lunae*, Epilogue, *Mythologies* (Macmillan), p. 367.
10   John Charpentier, *Le Symbolisme*, p. 82, quoted by M. H. Pauly: 'Yeats et les Symbolistes français', *Revue de Littérature comparée*, January-March, 1940, p. 25.
11   A. Symons, *The Symbolist Movement in Literature*, op. cit., p. 37.
12   W. B. Yeats, *Collected Plays, The Shadowy Waters* (Macmillan), p. 153.
13   *Ibid.*, p. 147.
14   *Ibid.*, p. 149.
15   Villiers de l'Isle-Adam, *Oeuvres complètes*, Pléiade t.2 *Axël* p. 653.
16   Yeats, *Collected Plays* (Macmillan), op. cit., p. 165.
17   *Ibid.*, pp. 149-150.
18   A. Symons, op. cit., p. 37.

19 Yeats, *Autobiography* (Macmillan), p. 368.
20 Mallarmé, *Oeuvres complètes*, Pléiade 'Le Guignon', p. 28.
21 *Ibid.*, 'Le Sonneur', p. 36.
22 Rémy de Gourmont, *Le livre des Masques*, p. 91, quoted by Guy Michaud, *Message poétique du Symbolisme*, Nizet, p. 84.
23 Mallarmé, op. cit., 'Les Fenêtres', p. 32.
24 *Ibid.*, p. 41.
25 3 June 1863 quoted in J. Genet, W. B. *Yeats: Les fondements et l'évolution de la création poétique*, Publications de l'Université de Lille, III, p. 511.
26 Villiers de l'Isle-Adam, op. cit., p. 672.
27 *Ibid.*, p. 675.
28 Yeats, *Essays and Introductions* (Macmillan), 'The Celtic Element in Literature', p. 51.
29 *Ibid.*, 'Discoveries', p. 285.
30 René Emery, *La Plume*, 15 July 1896.
31 Villiers de l'Isle-Adam, op. cit., p. 577.
32 Guy Michaud, *Message poétique du Symbolisme*, Nizet, p. 371.
33 Yeats, *Mythologies* (Macmillan), p. 367.
34 A. W. Raitt, *Villiers de l'Isle-Adam et le mouvement symboliste* (Corti), p. 185.
35 Mallarmé, op. cit., 'Magie', p. 400.
36 Quoted by V. E. Michelet, *Les Compagnons de la Hiérophanie* (Paris: Dorbon, 1937), p. 67.
37 A. Symons, op. cit., p. 41.
38 Villiers de l'Isle-Adam, op. cit., p. 634.
39 *Ibid.*, p. 635.
40 Yeats, *Autobiography*, op. cit., p. 321.
41 Yeats, *Mythologies*, op. cit., p. 283.
42 *Ibid.*, p. 342.
43 Villiers de l'Isle-Adam, op. cit., p. 644.
44 Yeats, *Mythologies*, op. cit., p. 315.
45 Villiers de l'Isle-Adam, op. cit., p. 653.
46 *Ibid.*, p. 674.
47 *Ibid.*, p. 660.
48 Yeats, *Collected Plays*, op. cit., p. 167.
49 Villiers de l'Isle-Adam, op. cit., p. 669.
50 Yeats, *Collected Plays*, op. cit., p. 147.
51 *Ibid.*, p. 157.
52 M. H. Pauly, *Revue de Littérature Comparée*, Jan-March 1940, p. 28.
53 Yeats, *Collected Plays*, op. cit., p. 147.
54 *Ibid.* p. 150.
55 Quoted in Villiers de l'Isle-Adam, op. cit., p. 1433.
56 Yeats, *Collected Plays*, op. cit., p. 151.
57 *Ibid.*, p. 166.
58 *Ibid.*, p. 167.
59 *Ibid.*, p. 148.
60 *Ibid.*, p. 164.
61 *Villiers de l'Isle-Adam, op. cit., p. 666.*
62 *Yeats, Collected Plays*, op. cit., pp. 152, 154, 158, 162.
63 *Ibid.*, p. 167.
64 Villiers de l'Isle-Adam, op. cit., p. 677.
65 Yeats, *Collected Plays*, op. cit., p. 158.
66 *Ibid.*, p. 165.

67 *Ibid.*, p. 148.
68 Villiers de l'Isle-Adam, op. cit., p. 533.
69 ·Mallarmé, op. cit., 'Proses diverses', p. 663.
70 A. Symons, op. cit., p. 2.
71 Villiers de l'Isle-Adam, op. cit., p. 539.
72 Yeats, *Collected Plays*, op. cit., p. 149.
73 *Ibid.*, p. 156.
74 *Ibid.*, p. 159.
75 *Ibid.*, p. 167.
76 *Ibid.*, p. 156.
77 *Ibid.*, p. 155.
78 *Ibid.*, p. 158.
79 *Letters*, op. cit., p. 425.
80 Yeats, *Collected Plays*, op. cit., p. 148.
81 *Ibid.*
82 *Ibid.*
83 *Ibid.*, p. 149.
84 *Ibid.*, p. 154.
85 *Ibid.*, p. 161.
86 *Ibid.*, p. 165.
87 *Ibid.*, p. 157.
88 *Ibid.*, p. 152.
89 Michel Dufour, *Gaéliana* N° 3, 1981, 'Le Symbole de la Rose dans La Rose Secrète de Yeats'.
90 *Ibid.*
91 Villiers de l'Isle-Adam, op. cit., p. 631.
92 A. Symons, op. cit., p. 44.
93 M. Cazamian, *Le roman et les idées en Angleterre* t. 2 p. 335, quoted by M. H. Pauly in 'W. B. Yeats et les Symbolistes français', *Revue de Littérature comparée*, Jan-March 1940, p. 30.
94 *Revue d'histoire littéraire de la France*, Oct/Dec, 1935.
95 Villiers de l'Isle-Adam, op. cit., p. 1542.
96 Yeats, *The Variorum edition of the Plays*, p. 340.
97 Yeats, *Essays and Introductions*, op. cit., 'Poetry and tradition', p. 225.
98 A. Symons, op. cit., p. 45.
99 Yeats, *Collected Plays*, op. cit., p. 162.
100 *Ibid.*, p. 163.
101 A. Symons, op. cit., p. 47.

A CROWDED THEATRE: YEATS AND BALZAC
Warwick Gould

The following editions of Yeats's work will be cited in the text using these abbreviations: *Autobiographies* (London: Macmillan, 1955) — *Au; A Critical Edition of Yeats's* A Vision (1925), eds. George Mills Harper and Walter Kelly Hood (London: Macmillan, 1978) — *AVA; A Vision* (London: Macmillan, 1962) – *AVB; Essays and Introductions* (London and New York: Macmillan, 1961) — *E&I; Explorations*, sel. Mrs W. B. Yeats (London: Macmillan, 1962; New York: Macmillan, 1963) — *Ex; The Letters of W. B. Yeats*, ed. Allan Wade (London: Rupert Hart-Davis, 1954; New York: Macmillan, 1955) — *L; Letters on Poetry from W. B. Yeats to Dorothy Wellesley*, intro. Kathleen Raine (London and New York: Oxford University Press, 1964) — *LDW; Memoirs*, ed. Denis Donoghue (London: Macmillan, 1972; New York: Macmillan, 1973) — *Mem; Mythologies* (London and New York: Macmillan, 1959) —

Myth; The Variorum Edition of the Poems of W. B. Yeats, eds. Peter Allt and Russell K. Alspach (New York and London: Macmillan, 1957). (To be cited from the corrected 1966 printing) — *VP; The Variorum Edition of the Plays of W. B. Yeats*, ed. Russell K. Alspach (New York and London: Macmillan, 1966). (To be cited from the corrected second printing [1966]) — *VPl.*

1 From 'The Decay of Lying' in Richard Ellmann, ed., *The Artist as Critic. Critical Writings of Oscar Wilde* (London: W. H. Allen, 1970), p. 309. The passage was a favourite of Yeats's. He first heard the essay read by Wilde from proof-sheets at Tite Street on Christmas Day, 1888. See *Au* 135. See attached list of abbreviations for Yeats's works.

2 *AVA*, pp. 171-2. Yeats uses the *theatrum mundi* trope especially in historical contexts, eg., 'History seems to me a human drama, keeping the classical unities by the clear division of its epochs, turning one way or the other because this man hates or that man loves', *Ex* p. 290.

3 Ellmann, op. cit., p. 308.

4 A useful discussion of Yeats and *theatrum mundi* is that of Ruth Nevo, 'Yeats and Schopenhauer', *YA* 3, 1985, pp. 15-32 at pp. 20-7.

5 *L*, p. 588. The thought is carried into 'Ego Dominus Tuus', *VP*, p. 369. See also *L*, p. 575 where Beardsley's 'passion for reality' is shown to include the vision of evil.

6 On 'multitudinousness' in Yeats see W. Gould, 'The "myth in . . . reply to a myth" — Yeats, Balzac, and Joachim of Fiore' in *YA* 5, 1987, pp. 238-51 at pp. 241 & nn; M. Reeves and W. Gould, *Joachim of Fiore and the Myth of the Eternal Evangel in the Nineteenth Century* (Oxford: Clarendon, 1987), Ch. 9, *passim*. Useful discussions of Yeats and Balzac can be found in M. Baron, 'Yeats, Wordsworth and the Communal Sense: the Case of "If I were Four-and-Twenty"', *YA* 5, 1987, pp. 62-82; and in Paul Scott Stanfield's 'W. B. Yeats and Politics in the 1930s' (Ph.D., Northwestern University, 1984), Ch. 4. Older articles include Daphne Fullwood's 'Balzac and Yeats', *Southern Review* 5, (1969), pp. 935-49 and Carl Benson's 'Yeats and Balzac's *Louis Lambert*', *Modern Philology* 49, (1952), pp. 242-7. For Benson, Balzac 'fell into place as the first writer to suggest to Yeats that he might be able to retain the order of a world-view which grew out of his occult study — an order over which the individual artist held control, and yet a view which enabled him to encompass the experiences of "actual men and women".' p. 247.

7 The epitome of Napoleon given by the poet Canalis in *Another Study of Woman* is very similar in style and scope to the epitomes Yeats offers in 'The Twenty-Eight Incarnations' of *A Vision*. Balzac's own admiration for Napoleon extended to promising (on his bust of the Emperor) to finish with the pen what Napoleon had not achieved with the sword. A 'man who could do everything because he willed everything' says Canalis. ' "All despotism and all justice at the right moments. The true king!" ' says de Marsay. See *La Grande Bretêche and Other Stories*, tr. Clara Bell (London: J. M. Dent, 1896), pp. 44-5. Hereafter *LGB*. All quotations from Balzac in this essay will be taken from the edition owned by Yeats from 1905 onwards, unless otherwise indicated. This is an American issue of the 'Dent' *Comedie humaine*, ed. George Saintsbury (London: J. M. Dent, 1895, 40 vols). Yeats's set was published in New York by the Macmillan Company, using Dent's sheets or plates. See *YL* items 76-111, pp. 10-14. Yeats always quotes Balzac in English but with French titles. I shall use the English titles of the Saintsbury edition, the translations for which were provided by Ellen Marriage, James Waring, Clara Bell and R. S. Scott.

8   *E & I,* p. 446. The 'daring and the powerful' inevitably recalls Balzac's descrip-
    tion of the Dévorants, or Thirteen in the preface to the *Histoire de Treize.* Yeats
    would have first encountered this preface in Ernest Dowson's introduction to
    La Fille aux Yeux d'Or by Honoré de Balzac, with six illustrations by Charles Conder
    (London: Leonard Smithers, 1896), pp. v-vii. Yeats was later to deplore the
    decision of Saintsbury or Dent to omit this story from *The Thirteen* tr. Ellen
    Marriage, *YL* item 107.

9   *E & I,* p. 445, also *L,* p. 807: 'How one loves Balzac's audience — great ladies,
    diplomatists, everybody who goes to grand opera, and ourselves' he wrote to
    Olivia Shakespear in 1933, 'think of Tolstoy's — all the bores, not a poor
    sinner amongst them.'

10 Yeats recalls here many favourite tales — Rastignac at the Opéra in *Le Père
    Goriot,* Lucien de Rubempré discovering both the *beau monde* and the back-
    stage in *A Distinguished Provincial at Paris* (London: J. M. Dent, 1897), pp. 22-36;
    108; 146-7; 169-70. Hereafter *DPP.* But the suggestion of closing the book
    identifies the scene as the last page of *The Wild Ass's Skin,* tr. Ellen Marriage
    (London: J. M. Dent, 1895). Foedora, who has presented herself at the opera
    as 'a drama before a drama' p. 137, will 'go to the Opera this evening . . . she
    is Society', p. 288. Hereafter *WAS.*

11 *WAS,* p. 22. For the identification of this passage as the one which 'started'
    Yeats (*VPI,* p. 932), see W. Gould, 'The "myth in . . . reply to a myth" — Yeats,
    Balzac and Joachim of Fiore' in *YA* 5, 1987, pp. 238-51. Raphael Valentin and
    Lucien de Rubempré share this visionary ability with the geologist Cuvier,
    the 'great poet of our Era', according to Balzac.

12 Yeats's first Dante was *The Vision: Or Hell, Purgatory, and Paradise of Dante
    Aligheri,* tr. H. F. Cary (London: Frederick Warne, 1890 edition), which he
    signed in October 1891 (*YL* item 476, p. 73). Cary claimed to have adopted this
    title from earlier translations as 'more comfortable to the genius of our
    language than that of "The Divine Comedy"', observing that Dante himself
    'termed it simply "The Comedy", . . . because the style was of the middle
    kind; and . . . because the story . . . ends happily', *The Vision etc.* (London:
    Taylor and Hessey, 1814), I, p. vii.

13 The phrase is adapted by Paul Bourget from Balzac's own self-description as
    Daniel d'Arthez in his introduction to *Repertoire de la Comédie humaine,* by
    Anatole Cerfberr and Jules Christophe (Paris: Calmann Levy, 1893), p. xi.
    Yeats owned a copy of the work (*YL* item 363, p. 54).

14 André Maurois, *Prometheus The Life of Balzac* tr. Norman Denny (Harmonds-
    worth: Penguin, 1971), p. 285. Hereafter *Maurois.*

15 See eg., *Séraphita,* tr. Clara Bell (London: J. M. Dent 1898), p. 40 where the
    visionary powers of the creative mind are 'enchantments . . . stupendous
    dramas played out between two membranes on the canvas of the brain':
    interestingly the image is phantasmagoric rather than simply theatrical.
    Louis Lambert's mind is a 'camera obscura' where 'natural objects are
    reproduced in purer forms than those under which they first appear . . . to his
    external sense', (*ibid.,* p. 163). Lambert also has 'the gift of summoning to his
    aid . . . the most extraordinary powers, and of concentrating all his forces on
    a given point', (*ibid.,* p. 178). *Séraphita* hereafter *S.*

16 *S* pp. 198 *et seq.* Balzac makes his account of the treatise more 'real' by claiming
    in *Louis Lambert* that the treatment of it in *La Peau de chagrin* is merely 'a work of
    fiction' (*S,* p. 200). For the *Essai sur les forces humaines* see *Maurois* p. 286. In a letter
    to Eve Hanska of 1834 Balzac sketched out the layers of the *Comédie,* the *Études
    de moeurs* beneath the *Études philosophiques,* the former treating individuals as

types, the latter treating types as individuals. After these accounts of effects came that of causes in the *Études analytiques*, in which 'principles must be sought. The *moeurs* are the play itself, the *causes* are the back-stage and the machinery. The *principles* are the author; but as the work spirals upward . . . it tightens and becomes condensed . . . Man, Society and Mankind will be described, judged and analysed without repetitions . . . like a western Thousand and One Nights . . . having composed the poem, the exposition of an entire system, I shall propound its scientific theory in an *Essai sur les forces humaines* . . .'

17 As well as the *Comédie humaine* in Saintsbury's edition, and the *Repertoire*, Yeats owned Mary F. Sandars's *Honoré de Balzac His Life and Writings* (London: John Murray, 1904), (*YL* item 1829, p. 236), Charles Spoelberch de Lovenjoul's *Histoire des Oeuvres de Balzac* 2nd ed. (Paris: Calmann Levy, 1893), (*YL* item 1979, p. 262). His own reordering of the *Comédie* is eccentric and determinedly so; no reason for it has emerged. (See *YL* items 76-111, esp. 76, 78, 81, 86, 106, 108, 111, pp. 10-14, and item 2227, p. 296 for a citation of Balzac in an annotation to Swedenborg.)

18 'Odds and Ends remembered by Lily Yeats', MS. MBY. I am grateful to Michael Yeats for permission to consult this MS.

19 'Avant-propos' to the *Comédie humaine*, 1842, in the translation of George B. Ives, *The Caxton Edition of the Works of Balzac*, I, *Splendors and Miseries etc.* (London: The Caxton Publishing Company, 1895), p. xxiv. In the Dent edition the Avant-propos is found in *About Catherine de Medici*, tr. Clara Bell (London: 1895).

20 See W. Gould, 'The "myth in . . . reply to a myth" etc.', loc. cit., p. 250 n. 14. Parsons compared Balzac's occult thought with that of the Kabbala in his introduction to *The Magic Skin* (Boston: Roberts Bros., 1888), p. xvii. He took seriously Balzac's interest in hypnotism, magnetism and telepathy and updated it in the light of more modern researches. In his introduction to *Louis Lambert* (Boston: Roberts Bros., 1888), he invoked Anna Kingsford, Sweden-borg, Pico della Mirandola, Raymond Lully, Saint-Martin (see *E & I*, p. 440n.), Cornelius Agrippa, Paracelsus and others of Yeats's favourite thinkers, to help him with Balzac's theory of the will. These editions, including *Séraphita*, were reviewed in *Lucifer* 5 (Feb., 1890), pp. 525-30.

21 The incident is used to affirm that 'Great literature . . . is, . . . the Forgiveness of Sin, and when we find it becoming the Accusation of Sin, as in George Eliot . . . [it] has begun to change into something else', (*E & I*, p. 102). The opposition of Balzac to Eliot remained constant in Yeats from 1886 onwards: (see *CL1*, pp. 7-8). 'Our traditions only permit us to bless, for the arts are an extension of the beatitudes . . . blessed be the wise (Balzac)', he wrote in 1935 (*L*, p. 832). The idea develops ' "Blessed are the imperfect, for theirs is the Kingdom of Love" ' which Yeats could not forget from *The Quest of the Absolute*, tr. Ellen Marriage (London: J. M. Dent, 1895), p. 32. See *E & I*, p. 446.

22 *WAS*, pp. 147-8. Later Raphael thinks 'a whole life' lies in Foedora's cry of 'Mon Dieu!' p. 150, but she has forgotten to contact her stockbroker at an opportune moment.

23 The incident might have been recalled by John Butler Yeats. His son recorded that JBY had said ' "A man does not love a woman because he thinks her clever or because he admires her, but because he likes the way she has of scratching her head" ', (*Mem*, p. 144). If so, father and son were very different readers of Balzac.

24 See e.g., *UP* 1, p. 103 for an 1886 interest; also *VSR*, pp. 137, 144, 160 for the 1896 occult romances. On Dec 13, 1908 Yeats considered revising 'The Tables of the Law' and 'The Adoration of the Magi', wondering if in the latter story the

Paris prostitute had revealed to the three Magi 'the doctrine of the Mask' (*Mem*, p. 138).

25 In *Discoveries* (1906), Yeats remarks that 'the cultivated man' will 'disdain a too conscious originality in the arts as in those matters of daily life where, is it not Balzac who says, "we are all conservatives"?' (*E & I*, p. 284). See also *UP* 2, p. 356. Though many passages in Balzac are close I have not discovered the exact wording. Other references of the time turn up in *Samhain*. 'French actresses pay more for attacks than admiring criticism, for "controversy is fame",' (*Ex*, p. 231), says Yeats, citing *A Distinguished Provincial at Paris*, pp. 109-10. In support of 'independence of mind', or 'audacity', Yeats cites the 'great example' of Balzac, and utilises the comic episode from *The Unconscious Mummers and Others Stories* tr. Ellen Marriage (London: Dent, 1897), pp. 44-6, in which the Fourierist sculptor Dubourdieu, creates an allegorical figure of Harmony with six breasts and 'an enormous Savoy cabbage' under its feet (*Ex* pp. 237-8). Yeats partly quotes and partly paraphrases the passage: 'while opinions cannot give talent, they inevitably spoil it; witness this unfortunate being . . . An artist's opinion ought to be a faith in works', p. 46. Yeats transposes Balzac's self-defence in the 1842 *Avant-propos* against the charge of sexual immorality into the Irish context where politics rather than sex is the 'national passion' (*Ex*, pp. 240-1).

26 *L*, p. 513. The recent appearance of Yeats's holograph letter in the salerooms (Christie's, London, December 1987) has allowed me to confirm Wade's reading. Yeats was attending French classes and 'reading Balzac — but in English, for I prefer to read more concentrated French, and I go to the places he speaks of. In my usual way I shall read him all.' Presumably 'more concentrated French' is that of the French lessons which would have lacked the argot found in Balzac. I am most grateful to Ronald Schuchard for providing me with unpublished references to Balzac in the letters of this period.

27 Unpublished letter to JBY. The Scenes of Provincial Life reminded Yeats of Irish life of '60 years ago'. 'Balzac's "social philosophy", though only one half the truth, is even more interesting than his creation.' *Don Quixote* at this point seemed (after the *Odyssey*) 'the best of all stories'. Balzac was 'too much taken up with his worship of the will, which cannot be thoughtless even if it can be happy' (*Mem*, p. 158).

28 Such as John Guinan, unpublished letter, 2 July 1908. Guinan was sentenced to 'six months of Balzac before you write another line', unpub. letter, 28 Aug., 1908.

29 Russell's 'honest heart' saved him from too complete an identity with the 'vagueness' of the pompous poetaster Canalis of *Modeste Mignon* (and elsewhere). (See *L*, p. 536, Oct 10, 1909.) Miss Allgood, having become fashionably dressed at the hands of Mrs Pat Campbell, was compared to the transformed provincials such as Lucien and Mme de Bargeton in *A Distinguished Provincial at Paris*. (See *DPP*, pp. 18-21 and *passim*.) Unpub. letter, 24 Nov., 1908, to Lady Gregory.

30 See above, n. 6.

31 In an unpublished letter of Oct. 16, 1908 to Lady Gregory, Yeats asks for Vols. 21 and 22 or Vols 1 and 2 of his 40 volume set, as renumbered by himself. These would have been *The Thirteen*, *César Birotteau*, *The House of the Cat and Racket* and *La Grande Bretêche*. The second had been read 'long ago' and he would 'soon get through the other' (probably *The Thirteen*), unpub. letter, 24 Oct., 1908. He then asks for Vols 23 and 24 as well, *The Unconscious Mummers* and *A Princess's Secrets*. Missing from his library at present are *La Grande Bretêche* and *A Woman of Thirty* (probably volume 3 in his ordering), and *The Country Doctor* (probably

vol. 32). I deduce the numbers of the missing volumes from Saintsbury's ordering (*WAS*, pp. 1-liii), from contiguous volumes (e.g. *The Country Parson* is No 33), and from Yeats's marginalia in the volumes which remain, which establishes that *A Woman of Thirty* must have been No 3 (*YL* item 94, p. 12). The only volumes now in dispute are Nos 2 and 24, which I suggest should be *La Grande Bretêche* and *A Princess's Secrets*. The latter *is* preserved in Yeats's library, but *YL* item 102 records no renumbering by Yeats.

32   See e.g., *E & I*, p. 444, n. 8 above, n. 25 above.

33   *The Thirteen*, tr. Ellen Marriage (London: J. M. Dent, 1898), p. ix. Yeats condemned the exclusion as 'too prudish', (*YL* item 107, p. 13).

34   *LGB*, p. 17. Vautrin at such critical moments is also a great actor. See *A Harlot's Progress*, tr. James Waring (London: J. M. Dent, 1896), II, p. 259. Hereafter *AHP* I & II. Critical moments (eg Auguste de Maulincour's sighting of Clemence Desmarets in the Rue Soly) are 'those crises . . . when character is modified; and the course of action of the best of men depends upon the first lucky or unlucky step that he chances to take; upon Providence or Fate, whichever you choose' (*The Thirteen*, op. cit., p. 18). Yeats greatly expanded the range of Critical, Initiatory and other moments of crisis in the Automatic Script, see George Mills Harper, *The Making of Yeats's 'A Vision'* (London: The Macmillan Press, 1987), *passim*. Change and Choice in *A Vision* are also suggested by Balzac's thought here, but again, Yeats has abstracted and expanded.

35   *The Thirteen*, op. cit., p. 308.

36   'I recollect telling Yeats, when I was a passionate Balzacian, how Balzac's reward for a writer who had resisted the temptations of social dissipations, to devote himself entirely to his work, was to be the lover of a *highly bred* [my emphasis] and beautiful woman, a countess or even a duchess', recalled William Rothenstein. See E. H. Mikhail, ed., *W. B. Yeats Interviews and Recollections* (London: The Macmillan Press, 1977), II, p. 249, hereafter *I & R*. I am grateful to Omar Pound, and to John Harwood, for the chance to inspect Olivia Shakespear's 1910 diary which contains many quotations (in French) from favourite Balzac novels such as *Illusions perdues* and *Les Secrets de la Princesse de Cadignan* etc. The 16 year old George Hyde Lees is recalled reading Balzac by Grace M. Jaffe in 'Vignettes', *YA* 5 (1987), pp. 139-53 at p. 141.

37   Balzac 'incarnates' de Marsay's theme by awarding to readers of the rest of the *Comédie* awarenesses denied to most of his fictional audience, but available to individual members of it in certain cases. Delphine de Nucingen, de Marsay's 'second' love, ponders her own position in the light of his story, and her husband abstractedly remarks 'How we do forget!' to remind readers of what they have read elsewhere. Lord Dudley, who finds statesmen so rare in France (see above, n. 34), is de Marsay's father, as readers of *La Fille aux yeux d'or* know.

38   *A Princess's Secrets* (London: J. M. Dent, 1898), p. 67. Hereafter *APS*.

39   Yeats's actual behaviour was a little more complex, as it was Lady Gregory who decided not to post Yeats's first letter reproving Gosse's 'insolent' behaviour. Subsequently he seems to have vacillated and the incident, with its conflicting loyalties, left him demoralized. 'Oh masters of life, give me confidence in something, even if it be in my own reason. I can never believe in anything else now, for I have accused the impulses of too many sins' (*Mem*, p. 254). See Denis Donoghue's appendix, pp. 289-91 for all the documents in the case. I am grateful to Deirdre Toomey for alerting me to several qualifications of this comparison.

40   Shelley, *Prometheus Unbound*, IV, pp. 288-9.

41   *WAS*, p. 33. Cf. *VSR*, pp. 127-8, lines 44-7.

42   For John Quinn, JBY's inability to finish his self-portrait was 'a subject worthy
      of Balzac' (LTWBY, p. 414). He doubtless had in mind *Le Chef d'oeuvre inconnu*
      which for Yeats was an apt icon of the 'botch of tone and colour, all *Hodos*
      Chameliontos' which he felt the Cantos to be in 1929 and did not choose to
      revalue before he died (*AVB*, pp. 4-5). But of course, in JBY's endless reworking
      of his portrait there was a talismanic element which recalls *La Peau de chagrin*'s
      grimoire — Quinn was, after all, paying him to stay alive to finish it.
43   *Maurois*, p. 286, and see above n. 16.
44   *Lost Illusions*, tr. Ellen Marriage (London: J. M. Dent, 1897), p. 329. Hereafter *LI*.
45   Richard Ellmann, 'A Late Victorian Love Affair' in *Oscar Wilde: Two Approaches*
      (UCLA: William Andrews Clark Memorial Library, 1977), p. 4. Ellmann
      believes the 'repeated offer of a cigar and Lucien's eventual acceptance of it'
      is the significant detail, though 'nothing is said'.
46   Balzac's use of allusion to the *Arabian Nights* is programmatic. On Yeats's
      perception of the relation between the 'western Thousand and One Nights',
      (*Maurois*, p. 286) and the *Comédie*, see W. Gould, ' "A Lesson for the Circum-
      spect" — W. B. Yeats's two versions of *A Vision* and *The Arabian Nights*' in P. L.
      Caracciolo, ed., *Arabian Nights in English Literature* (London: The Macmillan
      Press, 1988).
47   Balzac's metaphor is drawn from tapestry, its 'wrong side', (*AHP* 2, p. 127).
      Yet 'seamed' side would also not be quite adequate. 'Seamy' now has the
      connotation of 'enseamed' (as in *Hamlet* III: 4, line 92).
48   Any account of the matter would need to deal satisfactorily with some of the
      following: According to Yeats's reading of Swedenborg, sexual intercourse is
      immeasurably inferior to angelic, or 'conjugial' (sic) love, which is 'a single
      conflagration' (*L*, p. 807), the 'incandescence' of which (*Myth*, p. 356) lights
      Ribh's reading of his 'holy book' at the tomb of Baile and Aillinn (*VP*, p. 555).
      Yeats would have found Swedenborg's ideas in *Heaven and Hell* para 382 a &
      b and elsewhere. In 1933 he wrote to Olivia Shakespear that *Louis Lambert* was
      an 'echo' of 'that saying of Swedenborg's that the sexual intercourse of angels
      is a conflagration of the whole being' (*L*, p. 805). The association of Sweden-
      borg with Balzac at the time of writing the essay '*Louis Lambert*' was well-nigh
      complete. The remark to Sparrow dates from 1938. It suggests some regretful
      acceptance of the incompleteness of man (as compared to the angels) discussed
      in *Séraphita*: 'Man himself is not the final creation . . .' p. 19. On the 'three
      degrees of existence', natural, spiritual (angelic) and divine (in which 'the
      angel dwells before bursting its husk'), see p. 59. Man realises his angelic
      potential at death, a point made in *Louis Lambert* (*Séraphita* p. 191). To Lambert,
      'pure love' is the 'coalescence of two angelic natures' p. 192, and unrealizable
      on earth. Hence the 'virginity of the soul'. This conflagration of two separate
      Balzacian themes only leaves aside 'repentance' (except in the limited sense
      of regret). 'Virginity of the soul' is symbolized by Yeats as the Unicorn in *The*
      Unicorn from the Stars (*VPI*, p. 660). Monoceros de Astris, as Yeats writes to his
      sister, was a symbol in his order for 'the soul' (*L*, p. 662). The soul's 'hymen'
      is of course lost to a 'passing bell' (*Myth*, p. 332).
49   Despite Yeats's denial that the instructors were 'dependent on her memory or
      mine', as Harper shows. Yeats is however much nearer the mark in suggesting
      that the 'geometical symbolism' had its source in the automatic writing alone
      (*AVB*, p. 20).
50   David V. Erdman, ed., *The Poetry and Prose of William Blake* (New York: Double-
      day & Co., 1970), p. 544.
51   I use C. S. Lewis's term, as found in Graham Hough, *A Preface to The Faerie*

Queene (London: Gerald Duckworth, 1962), p. 101. Hough cites *The Allegory of Love*, (1936), p. 44 in a chapter all the more obviously derived from Yeats's thought in many of its deeper principles for its exemplary 'wheel' diagram and its account of 'theme simple, image complex' symbolism as 'incarnation' (p. 107). (See also *Ex* p. 369, *Au*, p. 511.)

52 Graham Hough notes that Yeats's 'eternal cosmic drama' has 'no analogue nearer than Dante' but sees the 'contemporary characters who are cited by name in Yeats's later poetry' forming 'a miniature *Comédie Humaine*'. He remembers 'perhaps with surprise, Yeats's lifelong admiration for Balzac' in *The Mystery Religion of W. B. Yeats* (Brighton: The Harvester Press, 1984) p. 85.

53 The *locus classicus* for modern discussion of *theatrum mundi* is Ernst Curtius, *European Literature and the Latin Middle Ages*, tr. Willard R. Trask (Princeton: Princeton University Press, 1953), pp. 138-144 at p. 140. Curtius' studies of Balzac include 'Balzac' in *The Criterion: A Quarterly* 1:2 (Jan. 1933), pp. 127-141; 'New Encounter with Balzac' in *Essays on European Literature*, tr. Michael Kowal (Princeton: Princeton University Press, 1973), pp. 189-210, as well as his classic study, *Balzac* (Bern: Zweite Auflage, 1951).

54 Yeats's favourite of such would be the Duchesse de Langeais (*The Thirteen*, op. cit., esp. pp. 293 *et seq.*) before she slips away to the convent: 'Let us chat and laugh together . . . We will be like two grey-headed philosophers who have learned how to enjoy life to the last moment. I will look my best; I will be very enchanting for you. You perhaps will be the last man to set eyes on the Duchesse de Langeais'. Other examples include the parallel case of Madame de Beauséant in *Le Père Goriot*, and of course Lucien de Rubempré composing rollicking songs to pay for burying his mistress (*DPP*, pp. 363-4).

55 Several of the *Études philosophiques* (1832), including this one, were written at the same time as the first of the *Scènes de la Vie Privée* were being written, and *Les Contes Drolatiques*.

56 Cf. Diane de Cadignan blowing her nose in front of d'Arthez to impress him while maintaining her dignity: she 'tried to do the impossible to confirm d'Arthez' belief in her sensibility' (*APS*, p. 58). See also Richard Ellmann, ed., *The Artist as Critic*, p. 37, for Wilde's view that we 'can believe the impossible, but . . . can never believe the improbable'.

57 Notwithstanding the Swedenborgian *Ursule Mirouët* (1842).

58 In a very different way, and with a local historical focus, Hardy's *The Dynasts* works from a similar perspective, but with a cinematic variety of techniques which render it incomparable. But '*theatrum mundi* is scarcely a metaphor for Hardy: it is a fact', Joan Grundy, *Hardy and the Sister Arts* (London: Macmillan, 1979), p. 70.

59 Which Yeats was certainly alerted to, at least as early as 1926 by Frank Pearce Sturm, via, of course, Macrobius' *Commentary*. See *Frank Pearce Sturm His Life, Letters, and Collected Works* edited and with an introduction by Richard Taylor, (Urbana, Chicago & London: University of Illinois Press, 1969), pp. 59-61 *et passim*.

YEATS AND THE 'BOUNTY OF SWEDEN'
Birgit Bramsbäck

1 *The Bounty of Sweden: A Meditation, and a Lecture Delivered before the Royal Swedish Academy and Certain Notes* (Dublin: The Cuala Press, 1925), p. 7. Yeats's impressions from his Stockholm visit were first published in *The Dial* and the *London Mercury*, Sept. 1924, and were favourably received in Swedish newspapers.

2 The present author's translation here and throughout the paper.

3   *Les Prix Nobel en 1923* (Stockholm: P. A. Norstedt & Söner, 1924), pp. 11-15. In Swedish and French.
4   Gunnar Mascoll Silfverstolpe's translations of 'The Song of Wandering Aengus' and 'The Fiddler of Dooney' appeared in *Stockholmstidningen*, 15 Nov.; Erik Blomberg's translations of 'When you are old' and 'He Wishes for the Cloths of Heaven' in the same paper, 18 Nov.; Karl Asplund's translations of 'The Lake Isle of Innisfree', 'Addressing a Blessed Spirit', 'He Wishes for the Cloths of Heaven', and Hugo Hultenberg's translation of *Cathleen Ni Houlihan* appeared in *Svenska Dagbladet*, 15 Nov.; on 9 Dec. the same paper published Sigrid Lidströmer's translations of 'The Indian upon God' and 'The Sorrow of Love', and *Dagens Nyheter* (Söndagsbilagan) published Ane Randel's translations of 'The Song of the Old Mother', 'The Heart of the Women', 'The Cloak, the Boat and the Shoes', and 'The Travail of Passion'. Another translation by Olof Lagercrantz of 'The Indian upon God' appeared in *Svenska Dagbladet*, 5 September 1943.
        Karl Asplund's translation of 'The Lake Isle of Innisfree' had already appeared in Karl Asplund and Gunnar Mascoll Silfverstolpe's collection *Vers från väster: Modern engelsk och amerikansk lyrik i svensk tolkning (Verse from the West: Swedish Interpretations of Modern English and American Lyrics)*, (Stockholm: Albert Bonniers Förlag, 1922), p. 44. Five more poems in Asplund's sensitive translation appeared in Karl Asplund and Gunnar Mascoll Silfverstolpe's new collection of *Vers Från väster* (Stockholm: Albert Bonniers Förlag, 1924), pp. 45-50. The five poems are: 'Where my Books Go', 'Down by the Salley Gardens', 'Addressing a Blessed Spirit: Cathleen in Paradise', 'The Wind Blows Out of the Gates of the Day', and 'The Song of Wandering Aengus'; Asplund also translated *The Land of Heart's Desire (Längtans Land)*. Margaretha Frölich translated 'Red Hanrahan' and other stories in *The Secret Rose*, under the title, *Röde Hanrahan*, (Stockholm: P. A. Norstedt & Söners Förlag, 1924). For full bibliographical information about plays of Yeats translated into Swedish see Allan Wade, *The Bibliography of the Writings of W. B. Yeats* (1951), and the present writer's *Folklore and W. B. Yeats: the Functions of Folklore Elements in Three Early Plays*, Acta Univ. Ups.: *Studia Anglistica Upsaliensia* 51 (Sweden: Borgströms Tryckeri AB, Motala. Uppsala, 1984), pp. 150, 159-60.
5   (Stockholm: Tidens Förlag, 1950), pp. 242-4.
6   My thanks are due to William Gould for giving me a reference to *New Church Life*, April 1924, (Bryn Athyn, Pa), p. 235, and *ibid.*, Aug. 1924, pp. 504-5, in which there is a mention of Mrs. Nordenskjöld (erroneously spelt Nordenskiöld) inviting the Yeatses to tea.
7   Also separately printed by P. A. Norstedt & Söner, Stockholm, 1924, a very rare item. See Wade's Bibliography, No. 144.
8   In *Les Prix Nobel en 1923*, p. 74, Strindberg's name is replaced by B. Björnson's, but all newspaper reports on 11 December give Strindberg's name in Yeats's speech.
9   At the Monaco Yeats Symposium, George Watson's paper 'Yeats, Ibsen, and the New Woman' threw much new light on Yeats and Ibsen's drama.
10 It may be of interest to recall Yeats's letter to J. C. Grierson, Oct. 21, 1922, in which Yeats tells a gruesome story of how the Black and Tans 'dragged two young men tied alive to a lorry by their heels, till their bodies were rent to pieces. "There was nothing left for the mother but the head" said a countryman and the head he spoke of was found on the roadside'. *The Letters of W. B. Yeats*, ed. Allan Wade (London, 1954), pp. 690-1.
11 As quoted in *The Palatine Chapel in the Norman Palace*, ed. Stefano Giordano, (Palermo: Poligraf, n.d.), p. 7.

12 Giorgio Melchiori, *The Whole Mystery of Art* (London: Routledge & Kegan Paul, 1960), pp. 213-8.
13 The relationship of these poems to the Stockholm City Hall and its Golden Room will be dealt with in another article. Suffice it to say that it is likely that, as Melchiori says, the mosaics in the Golden Room gave Yeats the initial incitement to these poems.
14 Bramsbäck, op. cit., p. 148.
15 *Ibid.*, p. 149.
16 Cf. note 4 above.
17 *The Heart Grown Brutal: The Irish Revolution in Literature from Parnell to the Death of Yeats, 1891-1939* (Dublin: Gill and Macmillan, 1977), p.285.

A FEW TWIGS FROM THE WILD BIRD'S NEST: YEATS THE EUROPEAN
Peter R. Kuch
1 AE., 'Literature and Life', *The Irish Statesman*, 22 January 1927, pp. 477-8. Russell, who figures prominently in Boyd's *Ireland's Literary Renaissance*, reviewed it in *The Irish Homestead* on 18 November 1916. For the review see Henry Summerfield, ed., *Selections from Contributions to the Irish Homestead by G. W. Russell – AE*, 2 vols. (Gerrards Cross: Colin Smythe, 1978), II, pp. 902-4. Several letters exchanged between Russell and Boyd about the writing of the book are deposited at the National Library of Ireland. Russell wrote a foreword to Hugh Law's *Anglo-Irish Literature*. He also reviewed the book in *The Irish Statesman*, 22 January 1927, pp. 477-8. Two significant works that Russell overlooked in his *Statesman* article were Thomas MacDonagh's *Literature in Ireland* (1916) and Daniel Corkery's *The Hidden Ireland* (1924).
2 Johannes Scotus Erigena (?815-?877). Both Russell and Yeats became interested in his writings as early as 1897, as revealed by their comments on William Larminie, 'Johannes Scotus Erigena', *Contemporary Review*, LXXI, pp. 557-72, April 1897. Yeats re-read his works circa 1926. See W. B. Yeats, 'The Need for Audacity of Thought', in John P. Frayne and Colton Johnson, eds., *Uncollected Prose by W. B. Yeats: Reviews, Articles and Other Miscellaneous Prose*, 2 vols. (London: Macmillan, 1970, 1975), II, p. 464. Hereafter Frayne, ed., *Uncollected Prose*.
3 Russell, who could not read Gaelic, obtained his knowledge from secondary sources. Unpub. lettr., Russell to Montagu Powell, n.d., Kenneth Spencer Research Institute, University of Kansas: ' . . . If you are interested in Celtic Mythology you should read Jubainville's *Irish Mythological Cycle* which has been translated by Mr. R. I. Best and is published by O'Donoghue, Dublin. This is on the whole the best book. But you will understand it much better if you read first Lady Gregory's two books of legendary tales *Gods and Fighting Men* and *Cuchulain of Muirthemne* as you could learn from the translations of old tales how the gods appear in the old literature. If you wish to go further into the subject you might read *The Voyage of Bran* published by Nutt which is a translation of an old mystical tale with a long commentary on the Celtic Idea of the Heaven World by Alfred Nutt. O'Curry is out of date and very unreliable . . .'
4 Frank O'Connor, *The Wild Bird's Nest: Poems from the Irish by Frank O'Connor: With an Essay on the Character in Irish Literature by AE* (Dublin: Cuala Press, 1932).
5 Unpub. mss., G. W. Russell, 'The Sunset of Fantasy', Lilly Library, Bloomington, Indiana. Most of this section of the autobiography was published in *The Dublin Magazine*, XIII, pp. 6-11, January 1938. A critical edition of 'The Sunset of Fantasy' has been included in the present writer's forthcoming G. W. Russell (AE), *Writings on Art and Literature*, to be published by Colin Smythe Ltd.

6   W. B. Yeats, *Autobiographies* (1955; rpt. London: Macmillan, 1970), p. 249. Hereafter Yeats, *Autobiographies*.
7   W. B. Yeats, 'The Old Pensioner', in Peter Allt and Russell K. Alspach, eds., *The Variorum Edition of the Poems of W. B. Yeats* (1956; rpt. New York: Macmillan, 1973), pp. 131-2. Hereafter Yeats, *V.P.*
8   *Ibid.*, p. 799.
9   Yeats, 'The Lamentation of the Old Pensioner', op. cit., pp. 131-2. See also Peter Kuch, *Yeats and AE: 'the antagonism that unites dear friends'* (Gerrards Cross: Colin Smythe; New York: Barnes and Noble, 1986), pp. 64-68. Hereafter Kuch, *Yeats and AE.*
10   Alan Denson, ed., *Letters from AE* (London: Abelard-Schuman, 1961), p. xxxviii. Hereafter Denson, ed., *Letters.*
11   Unpub. lettr., James Pond to G. W. Russell, 11 February 1930, VFM 507, Morris Library, University of Southern Illinois at Carbondale, Illinois. Hereafter addressee, date, call number, SIU, Carbondale.
12   Unpub. lettr., Russell to James Pond, 29 April 1930, VFM 507, SIU, Carbondale.
13   Unpub. lettr., Russell to James Pond, 16 May 1930, VFM 507, SIU, Carbondale.
14   Unpub. lettr., Russell to James Pond, 22 May 1930, VFM 507, SIU, Carbondale.
15. National Library of Ireland, MS. 9967-9969, 'Letters from George William Russell (AE), Selected, Transcribed and Edited by Alan Denson.' Hereafter Denson, MS, followed by call number, letter number, name of addressee and date. Denson, MS, 9969, 615, to Harold Macmillan, 30 June 1934.
16   See the present writer's forthcoming, G. W. Russell (AE), *Writings on Art and Literature.*
17   Unpub. mss., G. W. Russell, 'The Sunset of Fantasy', Lilly Library, Blooming-ton, Indiana.
18   G. M. Hopkins to Coventry Patmore, 7 November 1886, in *Further Letters of Gerard Manley Hopkins: Including his Correspondence with Coventry Patmore*, Claude Colleer Abbott, ed., 2nd edn (1938; London: Oxford University Press, 1956), pp. 373-4.
19   Coventry Patmore to G. M. Hopkins, 10 November 1886, op. cit., p. 375. See also George Watson, ed., *Samuel Taylor Coleridge, Biographia Literaria: or Biographical Sketches of my Literary Life and Opinions* (Dent: London, 1975), p. 174: 'good sense is the body of poetic genius'.
20   *Ibid.*, p. 167.
21   See Alexander Preminger, ed., *Princeton Encyclopedia of Poetry and Poetics* enlarged Edition (1965; London: Macmillan, 1975), pp. 270-1.
22   Denson, ed., *Letters*, p. 28 to W. B. Yeats, 10 February 1898.
23   A.E., 'The Poetry of William B. Yeats', *Irish Weekly Independent*, 26 October 1895, p. 9, rpt. in A. N. Jeffares, *W. B. Yeats: The Critical Heritage* (London: Routledge and Kegan Paul, 1977), pp. 91-4. W. B. Yeats, *Poems* (London: T. Fisher Unwin, 1895) reads: 'above them, that He ... go from his dew-cumbered'. See Yeats, *The Wanderings of Oisin*, III, lines 37-44, *V.P.*, pp. 49-50.
24   Yeats, 'Anashuya and Vijaya', *V.P.*, p. 74.
25   Richard Ellmann, *Yeats: The Man and the Masks*(1949; London: Faber, 1961), p. 71.
26   A.E., 'Some Characters of the Irish Literary Movement', quoted in Monk Gibbon, 'The Early Years of George Russell (AE) and His Connection with the Theosophical Movement', Diss., Dublin, 1947-8, p. 67.
27   W. B. Yeats, *Essays and Introductions* (1961; rpt. London: Macmillan, 1971), p. 101.
28   Yeats, *The Wanderings of Oisin*, I, lines 165-87, *V.P.*, pp. 13-14.
29   Harold Bloom, *Yeats* (1970; London: Oxford University Press, 1972), pp. 83-7. Hereafter Bloom, *Yeats.*

30 Yeats, *The Wanderings of Oisin*, III, lines 217-24, *V.P.*, p. 63.
31 A. N. Jeffares, *A Commentary on the Collected Poems of W. B. Yeats* (1968; rpt. London: Macmillan, 1971), p. 521.
32 Bloom, *Yeats*, p. 88.
33. W. B. Yeats to Katherine Tynan, [?22-28 September 1888], in *The Collected Letters of W. B. Yeats*, John Kelly and Eric Domville, eds. (Oxford: Clarendon Press, 1986), p. 98. Hereafter Kelly, ed., *Letters*.
34 John Unterecker, *A Reader's Guide to William Butler Yeats* (1959; rpt. London: Thames and Hudson, 1961), p. 50.
35 Kelly, ed., *Letters*, pp. xii-xiii, *et passim*.
36 Yeats, 'Meru', *V.P.*, p. 563.
37 *O.E.D.*
38 G. W. Russell, 'The Poetry of William Butler Yeats', *The Reader* (New York), August 1903, pp. 249-50, rpt. in A.E., 'A Poet of Shadows', *Imaginations and Reveries* 2nd ed. (1915; London: Macmillan, 1925), pp. 34-8.
39 Yeats, *Autobiographies*, p. 347.
40 *Ibid.*, p. 270.
41 *Ibid.*, p. 254.
42 See Kuch, *Yeats and AE*, pp. 117-25.
43 Yeats, 'Plans and Methods', and 'The Irish Literary Theatre' in Frayne, ed., *Uncollected Prose*, II, pp. 159, 163.
44 Yeats, 'The Irish Literary Theatre', and 'The Acting at St. Teresa's Hall' in Frayne, ed., *Uncollected Prose*, II, pp. 141, 285-6.
45 Yeats, *Autobiographies*, pp. 348-9.
46 *Ibid.*, pp. 101-2. The word 'provincial' occurs frequently throughout the first two sections of the *Autobiographies*.
47 Unpub. lettr., Russell to Lady Gregory, 2 December 1898, Berg Collection, New York Public Library.
48 W. H. Auden, *The Dyer's Hand: and Other Essays* (1963; London: Faber, 1975).
49 Quoted in L. A. G. Strong, 'William Butler Yeats', in *Scattering Branches: Tributes to the Memory of W. B. Yeats*, Stephen Gwynn, ed. (London: Macmillan, 1940), pp. 195-6.
50 I am indebted to Professor John Burrows for directing my attention to this aspect of the late Yeats.

YEATS THE EUROPEAN
C. K. Stead
1 Thomas R. Whitaker, *Swan and Shadow* (Chapel Hill, N.C., 1964), pp. 222-32.
2 The stanza describing the incident is there from the earliest remaining drafts of the poem. See Curtis Bradford, *Yeats at Work* (Carbondale, 1965), pp. 64-80.
3 *The Letters of W. B. Yeats*, ed. Alan Wade (London, 1954), p. 680.
4 *W. B. Yeats* (New York, 1970), p. 356.
5 See Grattan Freyer, *W. B. Yeats and the Anti-Democratic Tradition* (Dublin, 1981), p. 70.
6 *The Letters of W. B. Yeats*, ed. Alan Wade, p. 668.
7 See Elizabeth Cullingford, *Yeats, Ireland and Fascism* (London, 1984), Chapter 6. Cullingford, p. 87, quotes a MS in which Yeats admits he hopes for a German defeat. She explains in some detail why in the context of Irish politics Yeats could not declare this openly.
8 Cullingford, p. 118.
9 Richard Ellmann, *Yeats: The Man and the Masks* (London, 1961), p. 249.
10 See Bloom and Whitaker, for example; also George Unterecker, *A Reader's*

Guide to W. B. Yeats, p. 182: 'For 1919 had brought the end of the First World War and, for the Irish, a time of what seemed deliberate reprisals on England's part for the nationalistic efforts that had gained strength while English attention was focused on Germany. The Black and Tans and the Auxiliaries were recklessly used to frighten the Irish into submission.'

11 By Roy Foster, Yeats's current official biographer; and by Professor A. N. Jeffares.

12 Even if Yeats had noticed this problem when he changed the title in 1928, he might have found it difficult to correct. Simply substituting 'five years ago' would have deprived the line of a syllable.

13 *The Letters of W. B. Yeats*, ed. Alan Wade, p. 656.

14 *The Oxford Book of Modern Verse, 1892-1935*, ed. W. B. Yeats (Oxford, 1936), Introduction, p. xxxiv.

THE PRESENCE OF THE POET: OR WHAT SAT DOWN AT THE BREAKFAST TABLE?
Michael Sidnell

1 *Nobel Lecture, Odcyt w Akademii Szwedzkiej* (New York: Farrar Straus Giroux, 1980), p. 11.

2 *Ibid.*, p. 21. '. . . a few minutes ago I expressed my longing for the end of a contradiction which opposes the poet's need of distance to his feeling of solidarity with his fellow men. And yet, if we take flight *above* the earth as a metaphor of the poet's vocation, it is not difficult to notice that a kind of contradiction is implied, even in those epochs when the poet is relatively free from the snares of history. For how to be *above* and simultaneously to see the Earth in every detail? And yet, in a precarious balance of opposites, a certain equilibrium can be achieved thanks to a distance introduced by the flow of time.' There is an interesting parallelism between this passage and the one in *Discoveries* (*E & I*, pp. 266-7) in which Yeats speaks of the 'two ways before literature — upward into ever-growing subtlety . . . or downward, taking the soul with us until all is simplified and solidified again'.

3 *Poetry in a Divided World: the Clark Lectures 1985* (Cambridge, 1986), pp. x, 11.

4 *The Variorum Edition of the Poems of W. B. Yeats*, eds. Peter Allt and Russell Alspach (New York, 1968), p. 137. Subsequent page references to this edition are given in the text.

5 *Mythologies*, p. 36.

6   O Unquiet heart,
         Why do you praise another, praising her,
         As if there were no tale but your own tale
         Worth knitting to a measure of sweet sound?
         Have I not bid you tell of that great queen
         Who has been buried some two thousand years?
                         (*VP*, p. 181)

7 Letter to J. B. Yeats of 5 August, 1913, *The Letters of W. B. Yeats*, ed. Allan Wade (London, 1954), p. 583.

8 *Essays and Introductions* (London, 1961), p. 509.

9 *Autobiographies*, pp. 299-300.

10 'Estrangement: Extracts from a Diary Kept in 1909', *Autobiographies*, p. 469. The passage is repeated, with some variation, in 'Per Amica Silentia Lunae', *Mythologies*, p. 334.

11 J. M. Synge, 'Preface' to *Poems and Translations*, in *Collected Works*, vol. 1, ed. Robin Skelton (London, 1962), p. xxxvi. Synge and his ideas about poetry

remained, as Yeats made clear, powerful influences on his work and this seems to be particularly evident in those poems in which Yeats attempts a natural or 'brutal' self-image.

12   *Autobiographies*, pp. 6-8.
13   'Yeats', *Selected Prose of T. S. Eliot*, ed. Frank Kermode (New York, 1975), pp. 25-51.
14   *The Birth of Tragedy* and *The Case of Wagner*, translated by Walter Kaufmann (New York, 1967), p. 92. The passage appears at the end of section 5 of *The Birth of Tragedy*.
15   Shirley Neuman, *Some One Myth: Yeats's Autobiographical Prose* (Dublin, 1982), p. 39.
16   The phrase is borrowed from 'The Tables of the Law', *The Secret Rose, Stories by W. B. Yeats: A Variorum Edition*, ed. Phillip Marcus *et al* (Ithaca, 1981), p. 162.
17   Throughout *The Wind Among the Reeds* and notably in 'The Song of Mongan', the poet is doomed with the knowledge of 'all things' p. 177, as is Oisin at the end of his wanderings.
18   Wade, p. 798.
19   Geoffrey Hill, *The Lords of Limit: Essays on Literature and Ideas* (New York, 1984), p. 3.
20   *Autobiographies*, p. 491.

YEATS, TITIAN AND THE NEW FRENCH PAINTING
Ronald Schuchard

1   The *Autobiographies* (London: Macmillan, 1955), p. 82; hereafter cited as *Aut* in the text.
2   The so-called 'Ariosto', once thought to be a portrait of the poet, is Titian's 'Portrait of a Man' (1512), now thought to be a self-portrait (National Gallery, London).
3   This is almost certainly the picture to which Yeats repeatedly refers, though his uncertain memory of Manet's composition is reflected in his various accounts of the painting. In 'Discoveries: Second Series', comprising diary entries written in 1908, he describes it as 'a picture by Manet — a number of people were sitting at little tables drinking in a French café'. See *The Irish Renaissance*, eds. Robin Skelton and David R. Clark (Dublin: The Dolmen Press, 1965), p. 84, hereafter cited as *IR* in the text. In 'The Tragic Theatre' (1910) he remembers it as a 'big picture of *cocottes* sitting at little tables outside a café, by some follower of Manet . . .'. See *Essays and Introductions* (New York: Macmillan, 1961), p. 242, hereafter cited as *E & I* in the text. In 'Reveries Over Childhood and Youth' (1914) he recalls 'a picture at the Hibernian Academy of *cocottes* with yellow faces sitting before a café by some follower of Manet's' (*Aut* p. 82). Finally, it becomes 'a painting by Manet' in *The Oxford Book of Modern Verse* (Oxford: Clarendon Press, 1936), p. xxii, hereafter cited as *OBMV* in the text.
4   *Memoirs*, ed. Denis Donoghue (London: Macmillan, 1972), p. 38; hereafter cited as *Mem* in the text.
5   'Hopes and Fears for Irish Literature', *United Ireland* (15 Oct. 1892), p. 5; rpt. in *The Uncollected Prose of W. B. Yeats*, ed. John P. Frayne, vol. 1 (New York: Columbia Univ. Press, 1970), p. 250; vol. 2, eds. John P. Frayne and Colton Johnson (1976), hereafter cited as *UP1* and *UP2* in the text.
6   See Juliet Wilson Bareau, *The Hidden Face of Manet* (*The Burlington Magazine*, 1986), p. 45.
7   Blake's denunciation of Titian and the Venetians appears in his 'Annotations to Sir Joshua Reynold's "Discourses"' (c. 1808), in which he asks, 'Why should

Titian & the Venetians be Named in a discourse on Art? Such Idiots are not Artists'; in his 'A Descriptive Catalogue' (1809), where he asserts in the Preface: 'The eye that can prefer the Colouring of Titian and Rubens to that of Michael Angelo and Rafael, ought to be modest and to doubt its own powers . . . Till we get rid of Titian and Correggio, Rubens and Rembrandt, We never shall equal Rafael and Albert Durer, Michael Angelo, and Julio Romano'; and in his 'Public Address' (c. 1810), where in an additional passage he explains: 'I do not condemn Rubens, Rembrandt, or Titian because they did not understand drawing, but because they did not Understand Colouring; how long shall I be forced to beat this into Men's Ears?' Blake, *Complete Writings*, ed. Geoffrey Keynes (Oxford and New York: Oxford Univ. Press, 1985), pp. 464, 563-4, 602.

8   Yeats first used the description in a lecture, 'Friends of My Youth', delivered in London on 9 March 1910, published in 'Yeats on Personality: Three Unpublished Lectures', Robert O'Driscoll, *Yeats and the Theatre*, eds. Robert O'Driscoll and Lorna Reynolds (Maclean-Hunter Press: Macmillan of Canada, 1975), pp. 25-41.

9   Yeats was to write to AE on 14 May 1903: 'I am no longer in much sympathy with an essay like "The Autumn of the Body," not that I think that essay untrue. But I think I mistook for a permanent phase of the world what was only a preparation.' *The Letters of W. B. Yeats*, ed. Allan Wade (New York: Macmillan, 1955), p. 402. Hereafter cited as *L* in the text.

10   Letter to the Editor, Dublin *Daily Express*, (14 Sept. 1898) p. 5.

11   The lecture was first published as No. 3 of the Tower Press Booklets, *Reminiscences of the Impressionist Painters* (Dublin: Maunsel, 1906), hereafter cited as *RIP* in the text. It was reprinted as Chapter VI in the first edition of *Vale* (1914) but was heavily revised in subsequent editions.

12   Letter to the Editor, signed 'H. G.' (10 Dec. 1904), p. 5.

13   *The Freeman's Journal* (30 Dec. 1904), p. 7.

14   For a comprehensive discussion of personality and character in Yeats's prose see Edward Engelberg, *The Vast Design* (Toronto: Univ. of Toronto Press, 1964), pp. 151-75.

15. John Butler Yeats, *Letters to His Son W. B. Yeats and Others 1869-1922*, ed. Joseph Hone (London: Faber and Faber, 1944), p. 97.

16   On 13 Oct. 1905, testifying before a Commission of Inquiry into methods of teaching at the Metropolitan School of Art, Yeats stated that 'as regards this question of Modern Pictures, intense interest was excited amongst all the students when a few of Whistler's pictures were brought to Dublin. None of them had seen anything of the kind, and the papers commented on what they thought its too great influence on the students' work. The papers were wrong; a student grows by a series of influences. Really one reason why the student has to go away out of Ireland is that he can't see fine examples here. Every student, at the time I spoke of, was trying to get away. Every student who came to anything did get away.' *Report of the Committee of Inquiry into the Work Carried on by the Royal Hibernian Academy, and the Metropolitan School of Art, Dublin* (Dublin & London: His Majesty's Stationery Office, 1906), p. 61.

17   Yeats read Edmund G. Gardner's *Dukes & Poets in Ferrara* (1904) and his study of Ariosto, *The King of the Court Poets* (1906), copies of which were in his library. See Edward O'Shea, *A Descriptive Catalogue of W. B. Yeats's Library* (London and New York: Garland Publishing, 1985), nos. 728-29, p. 102. Hereafter cited as *YL* in the text. After he returned from Italy Yeats wrote to Professor H. J. C. Grierson on 28 June 1907: 'It was my conversation with you some time ago that sent me to Italy for it started me reading Gardners books

about Ferrara, and in the end sent me to Ferrara.' Unpublished letter, National Library, Scotland.

18 *The Variorum Edition of the Poems of W. B. Yeats,* eds. Peter Allt and Russell K. Alspach (New York: Macmillan, 1973), p. 352; hereafter cited *VP* in the text.

19 *Mythologies* (London: Macmillan, 1959), p. 268; hereafter cited as *Myth* in the text.

20 Yeats later wrote in the Preface to J. P. R. Finberg's translation of *Axël* (London: Jarrolds Publishers, 1925): 'It did not move me because I thought it a great masterpiece, but because it seemed part of a religious rite, the ceremony of some secret Order wherein my generation had been initiated. . . . Even those strange sentences so much in the manner of the time . . . did not seem so important as the symbols: the forest castle, the treasure, the lamp that had burned before Solomon. Now that I have read it all again . . . I can see how those symbols became a part of me, and for years to come dominated my imagination, and when I point out this fault or that . . . I discover there is no escape, that I am still dominated', pp. 7-8.

21 In his 'Notes' for *The Player Queen* Yeats wrote that as early as 1907 'the thought I have set forth in *Per Amica Silentia Lunae* was coming into my head, and I found examples of it everywhere. I wasted the best working months of several years in an attempt to write a poetical play where every character became an example of the finding or not finding of what I have called the Antithetical Self.' *The Variorum Edition of the Plays of W. B. Yeats,* ed. Russell K. Alspach (London: Macmillan, 1979), p. 761.

22 Lady Gregory read to Yeats from the translation (1561) by Sir Thomas Hoby in the Tudor Translations (London: David Nutt, 1900), a copy of which was in his library, *YL,* no. 351, p. 53. He was particularly struck by Peter Bembo's definition of beauty in the Fourth Booke: 'Therfore Beawtie is the true monument and spoile of the victorye of the soule, whan she with heavenlye influence beareth rule over materiall and grosse nature, and with her light overcommeth the darkeness of the bodye', p. 350.

23 Unpublished letter, 7 Feb. 1908, New York Public Library. I am grateful to Senator Michael B. Yeats and Anne Yeats for permission to quote from unpublished letters in this essay. Following the policy of *The Collected Letters of W. B. Yeats,* Yeats's letters are quoted without editorial correction.

24 Unpublished letter, 7 Feb. 1908, Univ. of Kansas Library.

25 Unpublished letter, 22 June 1908, New York Public Library.

26 Unpublished letter, 20 June 1908, Bancroft Library, Univ. of California, Berkeley.

27 *Ibid.* The so-called 'Perseus' is Ingres's 'Roger Freeing Angelica' (1819), Musée du Louvre, Paris. The picture (plate 8), which illustrates an episode from Ariosto's *Orlando Furioso* (1532), was based on the myth of Perseus and Andromeda. In his discussion of Impressionism in 'The Bounty of Sweden' (1925), Yeats identified 'Ingres in the *Perseus*' as one of the 'great myth-makers and mask-makers, the men of aristocratic mind . . . Administrators of tradition, they seem to copy everything, but in reality copy nothing, and not one of them can be mistaken for another, but Impressionism's gift to the world was precisely that it gave, at a moment when all seemed sunk in convention, a method as adaptable as that bow of Renaissance bricks' (*Aut* p. 550).

28 Unpublished letter, undated (July 1908), Bancroft Library, Univ. of California, Berkeley.

29 This letter, conjecturably dated (?1909) by Wade, should be dated 1908.

30   Yeats wrote that his room at Coole was 'hung with Arundel prints, a very large number from Botticelli, Benozzo Gozzoli, Giorgione, Girolamo dai Libri, Melozzo da Forli, Mantegna, the Van Eycks' (*Mem* p. 189). The Bodleian Library possesses a copy of *A Complete List of the Arundel Society Chromos, Engravings, Books, Ivory Casts, etc.*, compiled by R. Richardson (St. Jude's Depot, Birmingham, 1903).

31   Yeats wrote in 'Discoveries: Second Series' (*IR* p. 85) that he had borrowed a copy of Camille Mauclair's pioneering study, *The French Impressionists*, trans. P. G. Konody (London: Duckworth, 1903), and quite apart from the praise of Manet he would have found a passage that brought into sharper focus the irreconcilable difference between his own art and Impressionism: 'Technically Impressionism has brought a complete renewal of pictorial vision, substituting the beauty of character for the beauty of proportions and finding adequate expression for the ideas and feelings of its time' (p. 204).

32   In *The Trembling of the Veil* (1922) Yeats quotes the opening lines of 'The Fascination of What's Difficult' at the close of a passage on his search for Unity of Being (*Aut* p. 355).

33   For a discussion of Yeats's intensive reading of Balzac at this time see Warwick Gould's essay, '"A Crowded Theatre": Yeats and Balzac', on pp. 69-90 of this volume.

34   'Stanzas from the Grande Chartreuse' (1855), lines 85-6. *The Poems of Matthew Arnold*, ed. Kenneth Allott (New York: Norton, 1972), p. 288.

35   Unpublished letter, 1 Feb. 1911, The National Library of Ireland, Dublin.

36   The photograph was evidently of *Ta Matete*(1892; plate 9), and is now in the possession of Anne Yeats. Ironically, the picture may portray five Tahitian prostitutes.

37   Quoted in George Harper, *The Making of Yeats's 'A Vision'*, vol. 2 (London: Macmillan, 1987), p. 212.

38   *A Vision* (London: Macmillan, 1962), p. 294; hereafter cited *AV-B* in the text.

39   (Dublin: Cuala Press, 1939), p. 23.

CAELUM NON ANIMUM MUTANT . . .
John Kelly

 1   W. B. Yeats, *Autobiographies*, p. 189.
 2   Paul de Man, *The Rhetoric of Romanticism* (New York, 1984), p. 146.
 3   Unpublished letter.
 4   *The Letters of W. B. Yeats*, edited by Alan Wade (London: Hart-Davis, 1954), p. 379.
 5   *The Collected Letters of W. B. Yeats*, edited by John Kelly and Eric Domville (Oxford: Oxford U.P., 1986), p. 64.
 6   *Ibid.*, n. 5.
 7   Mallarmé, *Correspondance*, III, p. 235.
 8   *Autobiographies*, p. 320.
 9   Arthur Symons, *The Symbolist Movement in Literature* (1958), p. 69.
10   *Letters*, p. 592.
11   *Uncollected Prose by W. B. Yeats*, edited by John P. Frayne (London: Macmillan, 1970), I, p. 399.
12   *Yeats Annual*, 4, p. 207.
13   *Collected Letters*, p. 379.
14   *Axël*, trans. P. R. Finberg (London: Jarrolds, 1925), pp. 8-9.
15   *Uncollected Prose*, p. 324.
16   Harry Goldgar, 'Axël de Villiers de l'Isle Adam et The Shadowy Waters de W. B. Yeats', *Revue de Littérature Comparée*, 24 (1950), pp. 563-74.

17 Villiers de l'Isle Adam, *Oeuvres Complètes* (Paris, 1914-31), IV, p. 88.
18 Finberg, pp. 8-9.
19 Lady Gregory's unpublished *Diary*, Berg Collection, New York Public Library.
20 *Uncollected Prose*, I, p. 324.
21 *Autobiographies*, p. 321.
22 See *Essays and Introductions*, pp. 56-9, and a discussion of the contemporary poetic treatment of women in *Collected Letters*, pp. 29-30.
23 *Uncollected Prose* I, p. 324.
24 *The Secret Rose. Stories by W. B. Yeats: A Variorum Edition*, edited by Phillip Marcus, Warwick Gould and Michael Sidnell (Ithaca and London: Cornell U.P., 1981) pp. 16-24.
25 *Ibid.*, p. 23.
26 *Druid Craft: The Writing of 'The Shadowy Waters'* edited by Michael Sidnell, George P. Mayhew, and David R. Clark (Dublin: Dolmen, 1972), p. 84.
27 *Uncollected Prose* I, pp. 322-3.
28 *Ibid.*, p. 323.
29 *Collected Letters*, p. 384.
30 *Ibid.*, p. 386.
31 *Irish Daily Independent*, 9 March 1908.
32 *Collected Letters*, p. 421.
33 Unpublished letter. Farquharson was in fact of Spanish, not English, extraction.
34 *Letters*, p. 454.
35 Goldgar, *Revue de Littérature Comparée*, 24 (1950), pp. 572-4.
36 See *Variorum Poems*, p. 768: 'Masters of our dreams,/Why have you cloven me with mortal love?/Pity these weeping eyes'. The idea is retained in the final acting version: see *Variorum Plays*, pp. 325-6.
37 Harold Bloom, *Yeats* (New York, 1970), pp. 138-9.
38 *Letters*, pp. 267-8.
39 *Ibid.*, p. 268.
40 Aurélien Lugné-Poe, *La Parade, II: Acrobaties* (Paris, 1931), pp. 161-2.
41 Arthur Symons, *Studies in Seven Arts* (1906), p. 373.
42 *Ibid.*
43 *L'Evènement*, 11 December 1896, cited in Keith Beaumont, *Alfred Jarry* (Leicester: Leicsester U.P., 1984), p. 101.
44 *Autobiographies*, pp. 348-9.
45 Mallarmé *Correspondance*, VIII, p. 256.
46 Quoted in Beaumont, p. 99.
47 André Breton, *Anthologie de l'humour noir* (Paris, 1941).
48 Guillaume Apollinaire, *Il v a* (Paris, 1949), p. 176.
49 *Essays and Introductions*, p. 249.
50 *Uncollected Prose*, II, p. 46.
51 *Secret Rose: Variorum Edition*, pp. 143-4.
52 Review of *The Treasure of the Humble* in *The Bookman* of July 1897; reprinted in *Uncollected Prose*, II, pp. 45-7.
53 *Collected Letters*, p. 399.
54 *Essays and Introductions*, p. 190.
55 *Ibid.*, pp. 191-2.
56 *Variorum Plays*, p. 1099.
57 *Variorum Poems*, p. 427.
58 *Ibid.*, p. 426.
59 *Variorum Plays*, p. 313.

60 *Explorations,* p. 259. The lines are from the poem 'Michael Robartes and the Dancer'.
61 *Ibid.*
62 *Variorum Poems,* p. 384.
63 *Variorum Plays,* p. 1016; compare Hérodiade's 'The horror of my virginity . . .' op. cit. *Autobiographies,* p. 321; and Sara's 'I am the most mournful of virgins' etc.
64 *Variorum Plays,* p. 1014.
65 *Ibid.,* p. 1021.
66 Unpublished letter.
67 Unpublished letter.
68 See *Essays and Introductions,* p. 159.
69 Unpublished letter.

LILY YEATS, WILLIAM BUTLER YEATS AND FRANCE
William M. Murphy

Unless otherwise indicated, all material is from the collection of Michael B. Yeats, to whom I am indebted for his kindness and generosity.
1   Lily to Ruth Pollexfen Lane-Poole, 4 February 1939.
2   Lily Yeats, Diary, 16 August 1895.
3   I have discussed the subject at length in 'Psychic Daughter, Mystic Son, Sceptic Father', in *Yeats and the Occult,* edited by George Mills Harper (Toronto: Macmillan of Canada, 1975), pp. 11-26.
4   Diary, last entry, but headed 'My fortune told by W. B. Aug 23rd / 95.'
5   Lily to Ruth Pollexfen Lane-Poole, 4 February 1939.
6   Diary, 23 Sept 1895.
7   Diary, 2 October 1895.
8   Diary, 5 October 1895.
9   Diary, 15 October 1895.
10 Lily, Diary, next to last entry, headed '*Told by Willy Sep 18th / 95.*'
11 WBY, 'Reveries Over Childhood and Youth,' *Autobiographies* (London: Macmillan, 1966), p. 10.
12 Lily to John Butler Yeats, 13 July 1916.
13 WBY to Lily, 24 August 1916 (National Library of Ireland). The original of the ode to Alfred is part of the packet which contains the letter.
14 From the MS poem in the National Library of Ireland. See my ' "In Memory of Alfred Pollexfen": W. B. Yeats and the Theme of Family,' *Irish University Review,* Autumn 1970 (Vol. I, No. 1), pp. 30-47.
15 Lily to JBY, 14 August 1916. Her letter to WBY is lost, but she frequently duplicated her comments in letters to different members of the family, and I assume that what she wrote to her father is fairly close to what she wrote her brother.
16 Lollie Yeats to WBY, 25 January 1939.
17 Lily to Ruth Pollexfen Lane-Poole, 4 February 1939.
18 Lily to Ruth Pollexfen Lane-Poole, 27 February 1939.

GEORGIE HYDE LEES: MORE THAN A POET'S WIFE
Ann Saddlemyer

1   See especially George Mills Harper's *Yeats's Golden Dawn* (London: Macmillan, 1974), *Yeats and the Occult* (Toronto: Macmillan, 1975), *A Critical Edition of Yeats's 'A Vision'* (with Walter K. Hood, London: Macmillan, 1978), *W. B. Yeats & W. T. Horton* (London: Macmillan, 1980), his recent impressive two-volume work *The Making of Yeats's 'A Vision'* (Carbondale and Edwardsville: Southern

Illinois University Press, 1987), Robert Anthony Martinich's *W. B. Yeats's 'Sleep and Dream Notebooks'* (Ann Arbor: University Microfilms International, 1986) and Connie Kelly Hood's *A Search for Authority: Prolegomena to a Definitive Critical Edition of W. B. Yeats's 'A Vision'* (1937) (Ann Arbor: University Microfilms International, 1987).

2   Virginia Moore, *The Unicorn: William Butler Yeats' Search for Reality* (New York: Macmillan, 1954), p. 278. This sensitive study, sympathetically assisted and received by George Yeats, deserves more serious attention than it has so far been given.

3   Trinity College Dublin MS. 18104/34. George always spelled her husband's name 'Willy', though his sisters and father seemed to use the 'y' and 'ie' interchangeably. In this paper I will refer to him throughout as 'Willy' and to her as 'Georgie' during her younger years and 'George' once she became accustomed to her married role.

4   Unfortunately another memorialist, George's cousin Grace Jaffe, cheerfully admits that she shares this indecision about dates, a fact to be borne in mind when reading her otherwise helpful autobiography *Years of Grace* (Sunspot, New Mexico: Iroquois House, 1979) and 'Vignettes', *Yeats Annual, No. 5.*

5   According to his will, her father's address in December 1908 was Highshot House, Twickenham, a home for treating habitual drunkards.

6   See Edward O'Shea, *A Descriptive Catalog of W. B. Yeats's Library* (New York: Garland, 1985), especially p. xx, and Moore, *The Unicorn*, p. 315.

7   *Ezra Pound and Dorothy Shakespear Their Letters 1909-1914*, eds. Omar Pound and A. Walton Litz (New York: New Directions, 1984), p. 58. Dorothy, who later did many designs for her husband's publications, published a slim volume of drawings and watercolours, *Etruscan Gate*, ed. Moelwyn Merchant (Exeter: Rougemont Press, 1971), but none of Georgie's artwork apparently survives.

8   *The Unicorn*, p. 229. Unless otherwise indicated, all quotations from letters are in private hands.

9   John Kelly in '"Friendship is all the House I Have": Lady Gregory and W. B. Yeats', *Lady Gregory Fifty Years After*, ed. Ann Saddlemyer and Colin Smythe (Gerrards Cross: Colin Smythe, 1987), quotes from Nelly's letters in 1917, which are in the Berg Collection of the New York Public Library.

10 See Kelly's article, pp. 232-4 and Moore's *The Unicorn*, pp. 251-3 for the most complete discussion of these events. Later, George's first memory of meeting Lady Gregory at the opening of Robert Gregory's exhibition in London, and Lady Gregory's frequent and inconvenient visits to Merrion Square would cloud over the generous and timely help offered during this period and the first years of her marriage.

11 Among George's books is a presentation copy of H. D.'s poems and a letter to Yeats from the author.

LADY GREGORY: COOLE AND CA' CAPPELLO LAYARD
Bernard Hickey

1   Brian Jenkins, *Sir William Gregory of Coole* (Gerrards Cross: Colin Smythe, 1986), p. 243.

2   Lady Gregory, *Seventy Years* (Gerrards Cross: Colin Smythe, 1973), p. 440.

3   Elizabeth Coxhead, *Lady Gregory: A Literary Portrait* (London: Secker and Warburg, 1960), p. 22.

4   Lady Gregory, *Our Irish Theatre; A Chapter of Autobiography* (New York and London: Putnams, 1914), p. 7.

W. B. YEATS AND OTHER EUROPEANS
Andrew Parkin

1 See Alan Wade, ed., *The Letters of W. B. Yeats* (London: Rupert Hart-Davis, 1954) p. 125. Colonel Henry Steel Olcott (1832-1907), was Mme. Blavatsky's associate and co-founder of the Theosophical Society in New York in 1875. He later succeeded Blavatsky as editor of *The Theosophist*.
2 Wade, op. cit., p. 125.
3 Wade, op. cit., p. 93.
4 See Edward O'Shea, *A Descriptive Catalog of W. B. Yeats's Library* (New York and London: Garland, 1985). The books are listed by author, arranged alphabetically.
5 Hugh Hunt, *The Abbey, Ireland's National Theatre 1904-1979* (New York: Columbia University Press, 1979), p. 115.
6 See Lennox Robinson, *Curtain Up* (London: Michael Joseph, 1942), pp. 119-20. Cited by Hunt, p. 115.
7 In her *The Irish Drama of Europe from Yeats to Beckett* (London: Athlone Press, 1986; 1978).
8 This line of thought has been pursued at least since 1965, when Ruby Cohn published her essay, 'The Plays of Yeats through Beckett-Coloured Glasses', in *Threshold* 19, Autumn 1965. See also my essay, '. . . "scraps of an ancient voice in me not mine": Similarities in the Plays of Yeats and Beckett' in *Ariel*, Vol. I, No. 3 (July 1970), pp. 49-58, and Ann Saddlemyer's book, *Synge and Modern Comedy* (Dublin: Dolmen Press, 1968).
9 See Ann Saddlemyer, ed., *Theatre Business* (University Park and London: Pennsylvania State University Press & Colin Smythe Ltd., 1982), p. 83.
10 See Wade, op. cit., pp. 578-9.
11 See Ronald Ayling and Michael J. Durkan, *Sean O'Casey; A Bibliography* (London: Macmillan, 1978).
12 See Konstantin Rudnitsky, *Meyerhold the Director* (Ann Arbor: Ardis, 1981; Moscow, 1969), pp. 173, 217.
13 In *Explorations* (London: Macmillan, 1962), p. 73.
14 *Ibid.*
15 Katharine Worth has brilliantly demonstrated this in her *The Irish Drama of Europe from Yeats to Beckett*.
16 *Explorations*, p. 78.
17 *Explorations*, p. 80.
18 *Explorations*, p. 83.
19 *Explorations*, pp. 86-7.
20 *Explorations*, p. 88.
21 *Explorations*, p. 95.
22 *Explorations*, p. 96.
23 *Explorations*, p. 96.
24 A. P. Chekhov, *The Sea Gull* in *Plays* (Harmondsworth: Penguin, 1986; 1954), pp. 123, 126. See also Paul Schmidt, ed., *Meyerhold at Work* (Austin: University of Texas Press, 1980) p. xi.
25 Schmidt, op. cit., p. xi.
26 *Explorations*, p. 108.
27 *Explorations*, p. 109.
28 *Explorations*, p. 110.
29 *Explorations*, p. 153.
30 Rudnitsky, op. cit, p. 203.
31 Named curiously enough 'A troupe of Russian dramatic artists'.

32 See Alexander Gladkov in 'Meyerhold govorit' in *Tarusskie Stranitsy* (Kaluga, 1961), p. 502. Cited in Edward Braun, *Meyerhold on Theatre* (London: Methuen, 1969), p. 18.
33 Quoted by Meyerhold in *Teatre, Kniga o novom teatre* (Petersburg, 1908). Cited by Braun, p. 50.
34 Rudnitsky, op. cit., p. 33.
35 Braun, op. cit., p. 18.
36 Rudnitsky, op. cit., p. 33.
37 Aleksei Remizov, 'Tovarishchestvo novoi dramy, Pis'mo iz Khersona' in *Vesy*, No. 4, 1904, pp. 36, 37. Cited Rudnitsky, p. 36.
38 Pis'ma Meierkhol'da k Chekhovu, *Literaturnoe nasledstvo*, v. pp. 68, 488. Cited by Rudnitsky, op. cit. p. 44.
39 One deviation was his use of a gong instead of a buzzer to announce the start of a performance. In this, Meyerhold by coincidence used the signal also used at the Abbey, Dublin.
40 Rudnitsky, op. cit., p. 51.
41 K. S. Stanislavsky, *Sobranie Sochinenii*, v. 1, p. 475. Cited by Rudnitsky, op. cit., p. 57.
42 Tsentral'nyi gosudarstvennyi arkhiv literatury i iskusstva, f. 998, ed. khr. 187, 1.42. Cited by Rudnitsky, op. cit., p. 58.
43 Meyerhold, *Teatr, kniga o novom teatre* translated in Braun, op. cit., pp. 35-6.
44 Valery Bryusov in *Vesy* (January 1906) quoted by Meyerhold and translated in Braun, op. cit., p. 45.
45 Cited in Braun, op. cit., p. 49.
46 Braun, op. cit., p. 50.
47 Meyerhold's emphasis. See Braun, op. cit., p. 53.
48 Braun, op. cit., p. 55.
49 Braun, op. cit., p. 55.
50 Braun, op. cit., p. 57.
51 Braun, op. cit., p. 62.
52 Braun, op. cit., p. 63.
53 Jorge Luis Borges, 'The Argentine Writer and Tradition' in *Labyrinths, Selected Stories and Other Writings* (New York: New Directions, 1964), p. 184.
54 Rudnitsky, p. 539. The Meyerhold Theatre was to have been on 'Triumfalnaya Square, where the banner of "Red October" was first raised.' Rudnitsky, op. cit., p. 535.
55 Postanovlenie o likvidatsii Teatra im. Meierkhol'da, *Teatr*, No. 1 (1938), 1. Cited by Rudnitsky, op. cit., p. 540.
56 Wade, op. cit., p. 851.
57 Wade, op. cit., p. 851.
58 *New York Times*, 18 July 1939. Cited by Schmidt, op. cit., p. 231.
59 Mikhail Sadovskij, 'Teatral'nyjcarodej,' *Vstreci s Mejerxol'dom*. Cited in Schmidt, op. cit., pp. 214-5.

YEATS, IBSEN AND THE NEW WOMAN
George Watson
1 See James W. Flannery, *W. B. Yeats and the Idea of a Theatre* (New Haven and London: Yale University Press, 1976), chapter 4; and Katharine Worth, *The Irish Drama of Europe from Yeats to Beckett* (London: Athlone Press, 1978).
2 F. Lapisardi, 'The Same Enemies: Notes on Certain Similarities between Yeats and Strindberg', *Modern Drama* 12 (1969), pp. 146-54.

3   *The Letters of W. B. Yeats*, ed. Allan Wade (London: Rupert Hart-Davis, 1954), pp. 776, 833.

4   *Explorations* (London: Macmillan, 1962), p. 168.

5   *Essays and Introductions* (London: Macmillan, 1961), pp. 274-5.

6   *Autobiographies* (London: Macmillan, 1955), pp. 279-80.

7   *Explorations*, p. 99; Lennox Robinson, '[Yeats] As Man of the Theatre', *The Arrow* (W. B. Yeats Commemoration number, summer 1939), p. 21.

8   Joseph M. Hassett, *Yeats and the Poetics of Hate* (Dublin and New York: Gill and Macmillan, 1986), pp. 20-37.

9   *Explorations*, p. 161.

10 *Uncollected Prose by W. B. Yeats, Volume Two*, eds. John P. Frayne and Colton Johnson (London: Macmillan, 1975), pp. 127-8. In 1899, Yeats speaks of 'the heroic and unadorned sincerity of a play like *Ghosts* or *The Wild Duck*', p. 155.

11 *Explorations*, p. 80.

12 *Ibsen: the Critical Heritage*, ed. Michael Egan (London and Boston: Routledge and Kegan Paul, 1972), p. 84.

13 See *The Variorum Edition of the Plays of W. B. Yeats*, eds. Russell K. Alspach and Catherine Alspach (London: Macmillan, 1966), pp. 160-9. The very difficulty of staging the second version suggests that Yeats had his eye on a book, rather than the stage.

14 *Uncollected Prose by W. B. Yeats, Volume One*, ed. John P. Frayne (London: Macmillan, 1970), pp. 344-5.

15 See Flannery, *Yeats and the Idea of a Theatre*, p. 119; and Leonard E. Nathan, *The Tragic Drama of William Butler Yeats* (New York and London: Columbia University Press, 1965), pp. 273 *n* 33, who argues that Brand may have suggested the somewhat similar character of Paul in *Where There is Nothing*.

16 Holbrook Jackson, *The Eighteen Nineties: A Review of Art and Ideas at the Close of the Nineteenth Century* (Harmondsworth: Penguin, 1939; first published 1913), p. 184.

17 Bernard Shaw, *Our Theatre in the Nineties*(London: Constable, 1948; 3 vols.) III, p. 316.

18 *The Pall Mall Gazette* (5 June, 1890).

19 'The Independent Theatre', *Black and White* (14 March 1891), p. 167.

20 See Flannery, *Yeats and the Idea of a Theatre*, p. 132.

21 *Evening News* (14 April, 1988).

22 *Ibsen: Critical Heritage*, p. 88.

23 *Autobiographies*, p. 279. While Yeats was prepared to have Ibsen on the Abbey stage, Lady Gregory and Synge were more hostile. See Ann Saddlemyer, ed., *Theatre Business: The Correspondence of the first Abbey Directors: W. B. Yeats, Lady Gregory and John M. Synge* (Gerrards Cross: Colin Smythe, 1982), pp. 167-9.

24 *Essays and Introductions*, p. 216.

25 *Ibsen: Critical Heritage*, p. 174.

26 A. B. Walkley *Playhouse Impressions* (London: T. Fisher Unwin, 1892), pp. 62-3.

27 *Ibsen: Critical Heritage*, p. 240.

28 *Uncollected Prose, Volume Two*, p. 45.

29 Maurice Maeterlinck, *The Treasure of the Humble*, trans. Alfred Sutro (London: George Allen, 1897), p. 116.

30 *Essays and Introductions*, pp. 266, 271.

31 *Letters*, p. 469.

32 *Essays and Introductions*, p. 190.

33 *Letters*, pp. 434-5.

34 *Ibsen: Critical Heritage*, p. 270.

35 *Ibsen: Critical Heritage*, p. 6.
36 See G. Bernard Shaw, *The Quintessence of Ibsenism* (London: Walter Scott, 1891), pp. 31-45.
37 Unsigned notice in *Truth* on 5 March, 1891, probably written by Clement Scott. See *Ibsen: Critical Heritage*, pp. 179-80.
38 I am indebted for some of the ideas in what follows to Cassandra Laity, 'W. B. Yeats and Florence Farr: The Influence of the "New Woman" Actress on Yeats's Changing Images of Women', *Modern Drama* 28 (1985), pp. 620-37. Laity concentrates less than I do on Ibsen, and on Farr and the development of Yeats's ideas on the mask; and she mounts a complicated argument that in some way Farr realized through her art Yeats's 'fantasy woman Maud Gonne'. However, I am grateful to her work as evidence of a new interest in the importance of Farr to Yeats. See also Josephine Johnson, *Florence Farr: G. B. Shaw's New Woman* (Gerrards Cross: Colin Smythe, 1975).
39 Clifford Bax, ed. *Florence Farr, Bernard Shaw and W. B. Yeats: Letters* (Dublin: Cuala Press, 1941), p. 43.
40 *Autobiographies*, p. 121. See also pp. 407 and 515, on her voice, elocution and mastery of rhythm, and her Yeatsian love of the intense moment.
41 See Shaw's 'explanatory word' in Bax, *Letters*; and *The Collected Letters of W. B. Yeats, vol. one, 1865-1895*, eds. John Kelly and Eric Domville (Oxford: Clarendon Press, 1986), pp. 485-6.
42 Cited from Hesketh Pearson's biography of Shaw in A. Norman Jeffares, *A New Commentary on the Poems of W. B. Yeats* (London: Macmillan, 1984), pp. 264-5.
43 Shaw, 'Explanatory Word' in Bax, *Letters*.
44 See Josephine Johnson, *Florence Farr*, p. 91; *Ezra Pound and Dorothy Shakespear: Their Letters 1909-1914* eds. Omar Pound and A. Walton Litz (London: Faber and Faber, 1984), pp. 127-30; *Letters*, p. 574.
45 The articles are: 'Man', 19 Sept.; 'Goth and Hun', 26 Sept.; 'Ibsen's Women. No. 1 Hedda Gabler', 17 Oct.; 'No. 2 Rebecca West', 31 Oct.; 'No. 3 Nora Helmer', 14 Nov.; 'No. 4 The Lady from the Sea', 30 Nov.; 'No. 5 Rita Allmers', 21 Dec. I am grateful to Professor Ronald Schuchard for his help in tracing these references.
46 *Modern Woman: Her Intentions* (London: Frank Palmer, 1910), pp. 37, 53, 58, 64, 57.
47 'Another fire has come into the harp,/Fire from beyond the world and wakens it:/It has begun to cry out to the eagles.'
48 The Pre-Raphaelite woman is well described in John Dixon Hunt, *The Pre-Raphaelite Imagination 1848-1900* (London: Routledge and Kegan Paul, 1968), pp. 177-210.
49 *Memoirs*, ed. Denis Donoghue (London: Macmillan, 1972), p. 33.
50 *Memoirs*, pp. 85-8.
51 *Letters*, p. 526; Laity, 'Yeats and Farr' p. 628.
52 Richard Ellmann, *Yeats: The Man and the Masks* (London: Faber and Faber, 1961, revised edn), pp. 182-3.
53 Flannery, *Yeats and the Idea of a Theatre*, p. 165.
54 *Variorum Plays*, pp. 294, 382, 384, 478.
55 *Letters*, p. 511.
56 *Letters*, p. 475.
57 *Variorum Plays*, p. 761.
58 *Letters*, p. 312.
59 In a review (of Binyon's *Attila*) entitled 'Goth and Hun', in *The New Age* (26 Sept. 1907), p. 341, Florence Farr writes: 'Blank verse, which is always apt to run into sing-song inversions and artificial archaisms, will never be the

equal of vigorous prose until some new means are found of vitalising it, such as the German Hofmannsthal has discovered to us in his verse plays.'

60 Of her beauty, sense of rhythm and beautiful voice, Yeats says 'And yet there was scarce another gift that she did not value above those three. We all have our simplifying image, our genius, and such hard burden does it lay upon us that, but for the praise of others, we would deride it and hunt it away'; he also speaks of the anomaly that this woman who reads poems with passion 'spoke of actual things with a cold wit or under the strain of paradox' (*Autobiographies*, pp. 120-1). In *Letters*, p. 394, he bemoans her wilful laziness. His art, however, is absorbed with these kinds of contradictions.

61 Peter Ure, *Yeats the Playwright* (London: Routledge and Kegan Paul, 1963), p. 145. While Mrs Patrick Campbell is the actress referred to in *Per Amica Silentia Lunae*, and as belonging to the assertive Phase Nineteen of *A Vision*, it is clear enough that Yeats saw her as merely histrionic rather than genuinely complex (see *Letters*, pp. 475 and 539). Florence Farr is the prototype. Her variety is much commented on, not least by Yeats himself in 'All Souls' Night', and see also Pound's similar stress in his (somewhat unflattering) 'Portrait d'Une Femme'. See the *Pound-Shakespear Letters*, p. 173.

YEATSIAN STUDIES IN ITALY TODAY
Toni Cerutti

1 G. Melchiori, *The Whole Mystery of Art: Pattern into Poetry in the Work of W. B. Yeats* (London: Routledge and Kegan, 1960); C. Salvadori, *Yeats and Castiglione: Poet and Courtier* (Dublin: Allen Figgis, 1965). Professor De Logu has kindly let me consult his unpublished paper 'The Critical Fortune of W. B. Yeats in Italy', read at the IASAIL International Congress on *Anglo-Irish and Irish Literature: Aspects of Language and Culture*, Uppsala University, 1986, which will be published in the proceedings of the Conference, and allowed me to quote from it.

2 See De Logu on the pre-war critical fortune of Yeats in Italy.

3 *Quaranta Poesie* ed. G. Melchiori (Turin: Einaudi, 1965); *Poesie*, ed. R. Sanesi (Milan: Lerici, 1961); *La torre*, ed. A. Johnson, tr. A. Marianni (Milan: Rizzoli, 1984); *Una visione*, ed. A. Motti (Milan: Adelphi, 1973); *Rosa Alchemica*, ed. R. Oliva (Turin: Einaudi, 1975); *Per Amica Silentia Lunae*, ed. G. Scatasta, (Bologna: Il Cavaliere Azzurro, 1986); *Fiabe Irlandesi*, eds. M. Cataldi, G. Andreolli (Turin: Einaudi, 1982); *Le dodici oche selvatiche*, ed. M. Cataldi (Turin: Einaudi, 1983); *Il crepuscolo celtico*, ed. R. Copioli (Rome: Theoria, 1987); *John Sherman*, ed. P. De Logu, tr. D. Calimano (Turin: Einaudi, 1982); *W. B. Yeats: drammi celtici*, ed. R. Sanesi, tr. F. Vizioli (Milan: Guanda, 1966); *Opere di W. B. Yeats*, ed. S. Rosati (Turin: UTET, 1969).

4 G. Nemi D'Agostino, 'W. B. Yeats: il periodo del sole 1900-1919', *English Miscellany*, 1954; C. Gorlier, 'Maschera a confessore: da Yeats a Spenser', *Paragone*, 1955; G. Cambon, *La lotta con Proteo* (Milano: Bompiani, 1963); G. Melchiori, 'Yeats and Dante', *English Miscellany*, 1968; M. Cappuzzo, 'W. B. Yeats: *The Second Coming* e *Leda and the Swan*', *Teoria e critica*, I, 1972; A. L. Johnson, 'Actantial Modelling of the Love Relationship in W. B. Yeats: from *He wishes for the Cloths of Heaven* to *Leda and the Swan*', *Linguistica e letteratura*, I, 1977; 'Sign, Structure and Self-reference in W. B. Yeats's *Sailing to Byzantium*, *Annali della Scuola Normale Superiore, Classe di Lettere e Filosofia*, Serie III, vol. VIII, 1978; 'Sound and Sense in W. B. Yeats's *Leda and the Swan* and *The Second Coming*', *AION*, XXI, 1-2, 1978; M. Bacigalupo, 'American and Anglo-Irish poetry in Liguria: Pound, Yeats', *Studi di Filologia e Letteratura*, 1981.

5 P. De Logu, 'L'Arcadia di W. B. Yeats', *Annali della Facolta' di Lingue e Letterature Straniere di Ca' Foscari*, XVI 2 1977.

6 T. Cerutti, 'William Butler Yeats', *I Contemporanei, Letteratura Inglese*, vol. I (Rome: Lucarini, 1979).

YEATS IN GERMANY
Heinz Kosok

1 Patrick O'Neill, *Ireland and Germany: A Study in Literary Relations* (New York, Berne, Frankfurt: Peter Lang, 1985), p. 272.

2 *Märchen aus Irlands Gauen*, tr. Eugenie Jacobi (Neuwied: Schupp, 1894).

3 These translations (up to 1967) are surveyed in Susanne Schaup's excellent study, 'William Butler Yeats in deutscher Sicht', unpubl. Ph.D. dissertation, University of Salzburg, 1968, pp. 132-930. See also her bibliography, pp. 195-205.

4 O'Neill, *Ireland and Germany*, p. 272.

5 William Butler Yeats, *Gedichte*, tr. Herbert E. Herlitschka (Zürich: Arche, 1958).

6 On the productions, see Schaup, 'Yeats in deutscher Sicht', pp. 84-131.

7 K. P. S. Jochum, W. B. *Yeats: A Classified Bibliography of Criticism* (Urbana: Illinois U.P.; Folkestone: Dawson, 1978).

8 Leon Kellner, *Die englische Literatur im Zeitalter der Königin Viktoria* (Leipzig: Tauchnitz, 1909), pp. 629-39.

9 Horst Oppel, ed., *Das moderne englische Drama: Interpretationen* (Berlin: Schmidt, 1963, 3rd ed. 1976); Dieter Mehl, *Das englische Drama: Vom Mittelalter bis zur Gegenwart*, 2 vols. (Düsseldorf: Bagel, 1970); Heinz Kosok ed., *Das englische Drama im 18. und 19. Jahrhundert: Interpretationen* (Berlin: Schmidt, 1976); Horst Oppel ed., *Die moderne englische Lyrik: Interpretationen* (Berlin: Schmidt, 1967); Karl Heinz Göller ed., *Die englische Lyrik: Von der Renaissance bis zur Gegenwart*, 2 vols. (Düsseldorf: Bagel, 1968); Horst Meller ed., *Zeitgenössische englische Dichtung* (Frankfurt: Hirschgraben, 1966); Egon Werlich, *Poetry Analysis: Great English Poems Interpreted* (Dortmund: Lensing, 1967); Reinhold Schiffer and Herman J. Weiand eds., *Insight III: Analyses of English and American Poetry* (Frankfurt: Hirschgraben, 1969).

10 *Die Neueren Sprachen*, 9 (1960), pp. 527-39; 10 (1961), pp. 301-13; 14 (1965), pp. 253-68; 16 (1967), pp. 305-11.

11 Johannes Kleinstück, W. B. *Yeats oder der Dichter in der modernen Welt* (Hamburg: Leibniz, 1963); Theodor Klimek, *Symbol und Wirklichkeit bei W. B. Yeats* (Bonn: Bouvier, 1967); Jeannette Lander, *William Butler Yeats: Die Bildersprache seiner Lyrik* (Stuttgart: Kohlhammer, 1967).

12 Hans Joachim Hahn, *Die Krisis des Lyrischen in den Gedichten von W. B. Yeats und W. H. Auden: Eine Untersuchung struktureller Wandlungen moderner Lyrik* (Göppingen: Kümmerle, 1971); Lothar Hönnighausen, *Präraphaeliten und Fin de Siècle: Symbolistische Tendenzen in der englischen Spätromantik* (München: Fink, 1971).

13 Peter Hühn, *Das Verhältnis von Mann und Frau im Werk von William Butler Yeats* (Bonn: Bouvier, 1971); Wulf Künne, *Konzeption und Stil von Yeats' 'Autobiographies'* (Bonn: Bouvier, 1972).

14 Isolde von Bülow, *Der Tanz im Drama: Untersuchungen zu W. B. Yeats' dramatischer Theorie und Praxis* (Bonn: Bouvier, 1969); Klaus Peter Jochum, *Die dramatische Struktur der Spiele von W. B. Yeats* (Frankfurt: Athenäum, 1971); Rudolf Halbritter, *Konzeptionsformen des modernen angloamerikanischen Kurzdramas: Dargestellt an Stücken von W. B. Yeats, Th. Wilder und H. Pinter* (Göttingen: Vandenhoeck & Ruprecht, 1975); Richard Taylor, *A Reader's Guide to the Plays of W. B. Yeats* (London: Macmillan, New York: St. Martin's Press, 1984).

318   Notes to pages 265-267

15   Eitel Friedrich Timm, *William Butler Yeats und Friedrich Nietzsche* (Würzburg: Königshausen & Neumann, 1980); Norbert K. Buchta, *Rezeption und ästhetische Verarbeitung romantischer Poetologie im lyrischen Werk William Butler Yeats'* (Königstein: Athenäum, Hain, Scriptor, Hanstein, 1982).

16   Johannes Kleinstück, 'William Butler Yeats', in: Rudolf Sühnel and Dieter Riesner eds., *Englische Dichter der Moderne* (Berlin: Schmidt, 1971), pp. 193-204; Willi Erzgräber, 'W. B. Yeats als Lyriker', in: Herbert Mainusch and Dietrich Rolle eds., *Studien zur englischen Philologie: Edgar Mertner zum 70. Geburtstag* (Frankfurt etc.: Lang, 1979), pp. 167-88; Manfred Pfister, 'Sailing to Innisfree: Stilwandel und ideologische Entwicklung in der Lyrik von W. B. Yeats', in: W. Welte ed., *Sprachtheorie und angewandte Linguistik — Festschrift für Alfred Wollmann zum 60. Gerburtstag* (Tübingen: Narr, 1982), pp. 113-30; Hans-Heinrich Freitag, 'Die Vision als Form der Wirklichkeitserfahrung bei Mangan und Yeats', in: Freitag and Peter Hühn eds., *Literarische Ansichten der Wirklichkeit: Studien zur Wirklichkeitskonstitution in englischsprachiger Literatur. To honour Johannes Kleinstück* (Frankfurt: Lang, 1980), pp. 173-90; Lothar Hönnighausen, 'Konservative Kulturkritik und Literaturtheorie zwischen den Weltkriegen: Yeats und Eliot', in: Paul Goetsch and Heinz Joachim Müllenbrock eds., *Englische Literatur und Politik im 20. Jahrhundert* (Wiesbaden: Athenaion, 1981), pp. 95-110; Ulrich Schneider, 'Yeats' Byzanz-Bild im Kontext seiner Zeit', *Anglia*, 95 (1977), pp. 426-49; Gerhard Hoffman, 'Die Funktion der Lieder in Yeats' Dramen', *Anglia*, 89 (1971), pp. 87-116; Klaus Peter Jochum, 'Yeats's Sonnets', *Modern Irish Literature*, 4 (1978), pp. 33-43; Joseph T. Swann, ' "Where all the Ladders Start": Language and Experience in Yeats's Later Poetry', in: Heinz Kosok ed., *Studies in Anglo-Irish Literature* (Bonn: Bouvier, 1982), pp. 236-45.

17   William Butler Yeats, *Werke*, ed. by Werner Vordtriede, 6 vols. (Neuwied and Berlin: Luchterhand, 1970-1973).

18   I am indebted to my Wuppertal colleagues Prof Heinz Rölleke, Dr Jutta Rissmann and Dr Werner Bellmann, as well as to Prof Ernst Zinn (Tübingen) for some of the references given here.

19   Rainer Maria Rilke, *Briefe an seinen Verleger* (Wiesbaden: Insel, 1949), vol. II, p. 304.

20   Eudō C. Mason, *Rilke, Europe, and the English-Speaking World* (Cambridge U.P., 1961), pp. 111-13. The best account of the *affinities* (rather than influences) between these two poets is Patricia Merivale's excellent article ' "Ultima Thule": Ghosts and Borderlines In Yeats and Rilke', *Comparative Literature*, 30 (1978), pp. 249-67.

21   See William Rose, 'A Letter from W. B. Yeats on Rilke', *German Life and Letters*, XV (1961), pp. 68-70.

22   Rudolf Kassner, *Sämtliche Werke*, ed. by Ernst Zinn (Pfullingen: Neske, 1969ff.), vol. I, pp. 23-68, vol. III, pp. 518-43; see also the editor's detailed notes, vol. II, pp. 429-39, vol. III, pp. 694-8.

23   Gottfried Benn, *Briefe an F. W. Oelze: 1950-1956*, ed. by Harald Steinhagen (Wiesbaden and München: Limes, 1980), p. 191.

24   Wolfgang Kayser, 'Der europäische Symbolismus', in Viktor Žmegač ed., *Deutsche Literatur der Jahrhundertwende* (Königstein: Athenäum-Hain-Scriptor-Hanstein, 1982), p. 50. For a discussion of the *affinities* (rather than influences) between Yeats and George see Schaup, 'Yeats in deutscher Sicht', pp. 41-4.

25   See O. H. Edwards, 'Dauthendey und Yeats: ihre Begegnungen in den neunziger Jahren', in: Viktor Lange and Hans-Gert Roloff eds., *Dichtung — Sprache*

- Gesselschaft (Frankfurt: Athenäum, 1971), pp. 289-90; Schaup, 'Yeats in deutscher Sicht', pp. 85-6.

26 Stefan Zweig, *Die Welt von Gestern: Erinnerungen eines Europäers* (Berlin and Frankfurt: Fischer, 1965), p. 150. .

27 Henry von Heiseler, *Marginalien, Sämtliche Werke* (Heidelberg: Schneider, 1965), pp. 211-13. Bernt von Heiseler, *Gesammelte Essays zur alten und neuen Literatur*, vol. I (Stuttgart: Steinkopf, 1966), pp. 264-75. Cf. Schaup, 'Yeats in deutscher Sicht', pp. 44-51.

28 Michael Hamburger, 'Hofmannsthals Bibliothek', *Euphorion*, 55 (1961), pp. 15-76, p. 25.

29 Hugo von Hofmannsthal, *Poems and Verse Plays*, and *Selected Plays and Libretti*, ed. by Michael Hamburger (London: Routledge & Kegan Paul, 1961 and 1963). German translation of Hamburger's introductions: Michael Hamburger, *Hugo von Hofmannsthal: Zwei Studien* (Göttingen: Sachse & Pohl, 1964).

30 Hugo von Hofmannsthal, 'Vienna Letter', *The Dial*, 73 (1922), no. 2; German version: *Gesammelte Werke, Reden und Aufsätze II 1914-1924*, ed. by Bernd Schoeller (Frankfurt: Fischer, 1979), p. 278.

31 *Gesammelte Werke, Reden und Aufsätze III 1925-1929 – Buch der Freunde – Aufzeichnungen 1889-1919*, ed. by Bernd Schoeller (Frankfurt: Fischer, 1980), pp. 266-7, 269.

32 See Hugo von Hofmannsthal, *Sämtliche Werke: Kritische Ausgabe, vol. XXVIII, ed. by Ellen Ritter (Frankfurt: Fischer, 1975), p. 281.*

33 *Heinrich Böll, Werke: Romane und Erzählungen 3, 1954-1959* (Köln: Kiepenheuer & Witsch, 1977), pp. 83-4. Further Yeats references pp. 16, 18, 48.

34 Heinrich Böll, *Gruppenbild mit Dame* (Köln: Kiepenheuer & Witsch, 1971), pp. 356-7.

35 Heinrich Böll, *Werke: Essayistische Schriften und Reden, 2, 1964-1972* (Köln: Kiepenheuer & Witsch, n.d.), p. 176.

36 *Ibid.*, pp. 397, 399; *Essayistische Schriften und Reden 1, 1952-1963* (Köln: Kiepenheuer & Witsch, n.d.), pp. 128, 349, 353.

37 Cf. Wolgang Zach and Heinz Kosok eds., *Literary Interrelations: Ireland, England and the World*, 3 vols. (Tübingen: Narr, 1987), especially vol. I, *Reception and Translation*, and vol. II, *Impact and Comparison*, where the reception, in various European countries, of Yeats in particular and Anglo-Irish literature in general is discussed.

NOTES ON CONTRIBUTORS

MICHAEL ALEXANDER was educated at Downside and the Universities of Oxford, Perugia and Princeton. A long-time member of the English Studies Department at Stirling, he is now Berry Professor of English Literature at St. Andrews. He is a poet, whose verse translations of Old English poetry are published by Penguin. Other publications include *The Poetic Achievement of Ezra Pound* (1979) and *Old English Literature* (1983). He is co-editor of the Macmillan Anthologies of English Literature series.

BIRGIT M. H. BRAMSBÄCK (Bjersby) was educated at the University of Uppsala, where she is Professor of English. She has taught at University College, Dublin, and Gothenburgh University as well as holding positions at the University of Uppsala (where she has been in charge of the Irish Institute and the Celtic section of the Department of English). Her publications include *The Interpretation of the Cuchulain Legend in the Works of W. B. Yeats* (1950), *James Stephens: a Bibliographical and Literary Study* (1959), and *Folklore and W. B. Yeats* (1984), as well as a number of articles on other writers. Her forthcoming work will include articles on Yeats and Swedenborg, and Yeats and the Stockholm mosaics; she has co-edited, with Martin Croghan, the proceedings of the IASAIL congress held at Uppsala in 1986.

TONI CERUTTI, Professor of English at the University of Bari, was educated at the Universities of Turin and Cambridge. After teaching Italian at the Universities of Manchester, Cambridge, and Hull, she returned to Turin as Associate Professor of English. Her main area of research is nineteenth century studies with special interest in autobiographical writings. She is the author of *Antonio Gallenga, an Italian Writer in Victorian England* (1974) and *Le vite dei vittoriani: breve storia sell'autobiografia vittoriana* (1981), and of articles on the forms of autobiography, the popular novel, Synge, Yeats, Spenser, Carlyle, Scott, Dickens and Ruskin. Her edition of William Blake's *Selected Poems* is forthcoming, and she is writing on Yeats's autobiographical writings, and style and structure in Ruskin's social writings.

DENIS DONOGHUE, educated at University College, Dublin, holds the Henry James Chair of English and American Letters at New York University. His books include *The Third Voice: A Study of Modern English and American Verse Drama; Connoisseurs of Chaos: Ideas of Order in Modern American Poetry; The Ordinary Universe: Soundings in Modern Literature; Thieves of Fire; The Sovereign Ghost; Ferocious Alphabets; The Arts without Mystery;* and *Yeats.* Three volumes of his selected essays have been published: *We Irish* (1986); *Reading America* (1987); and *England, Their England* (1988). He has also published a book on Jonathan Swift and a Minnesota Pamphlet on Emily Dickinson, and has edited *Jonathan Swift: A Critical Anthology; Memoirs* by W. B. Yeats; *Selected Essays* of R. P. Blackmur; and, with J. R. Mulryne, *An Honoured Guest: New Essays on W. B. Yeats.* He is at present working on a memoir of his early life in Warrenpoint, a small town in Northern Ireland.

JACQUELINE GENET studied at l'Ecole Normale Supérieure de Sèvres. She is Agrégée d'Anglais, Docteur-ès-Lettres, President of the University of Caen and Vice-President of IASAIL. She has published a series of translations into French of Yeats's main prose works, of Patrick Macdonogh's poems, Iris Murdoch's plays, Mary Lavin's stories, *The Penguin Book of Irish Short Stories* and a collection of essays on Blake by Kathleen Raine. She is author of *Contemporary English Novelists,* and *Yeats: Les fondements et l'évolution de la création poétique.* She has edited *Le Cahier de l'Herne* on Yeats, *Collected Studies on Seamus Heaney,* and the review *Gaéliana.* She has written articles on Blake, Yeats, Eliot, Auden, Joyce, Beckett, Iris Murdoch, Heaney and Kathleen Raine.

WARWICK GOULD was educated at the University of Queensland; he is Senior Lecturer in English Language and Literature at Royal Holloway and Bedford New College, University of London. He is co-editor, with Phillip L. Marcus and Michael J. Sidnell, of *The Secret Rose, Stories by W. B. Yeats: A Variorum Edition,* and editor of *Yeats Annual* (Macmillan Press). He has written, with Marjorie Reeves, *Joachim of Fiore and the Myth of Eternal Evangel in the Nineteenth Century* (1987), and is now working on editions of Yeats's *Letters* (Vol. II, 1896-1900) (Oxford University Press), and *The Celtic Twilight & The Secret Rose* and *Early Essays* for the new Macmillan *Collected Edition of the Works of W. B. Yeats.*

BERNARD HICKEY, A.M., educated at the Universities of Queensland, Dublin and Rome, is Professor of English at the University of Venice. He is an Honorary Fellow of Trinity College of Music, London, Chairman of the European Association for Commonwealth Literature and Language Studies, and Vice Chairman of the Italy-India Association. His publications include a critique of Patrick White (1971), an anthology *Da Slessor a Dransfield, Poesia Australiana Moderna, Mito Societa Individuo* (1977), *Incontri Australiani e del Commonwealth* (1983), *Statements* (1984), *Lines of Implication: Australian Short Fiction: Lawson to Palmer* (1984). He has lectured extensively in Europe, the U.S.A., south-east Asia and Australasia, is an Associate of the Australian Studies Centre, Queensland, and of the Centre for Research in New Literature in English, South Australia.

A. NORMAN JEFFARES, A.M., educated at the Universities of Dublin and Oxford, has held teaching posts at the Universities of Dublin, Groningen, Edinburgh, Adelaide, Leeds and Stirling, and is managing director of Academic Advisory Services Ltd., Chairman of Book Trust, Scotland, and President of International P.E.N. Scotland. His recent publications include *A History of Anglo-Irish Literature, A New Commentary on the Poems of W. B. Yeats, Poems of W. B. Yeats, A New Selection*, two collections of his own poems, *Brought Up in Dublin* and *Brought Up to Leave* and his new biography, *W. B. Yeats*. He has edited, with Antony Kamm, *An Irish Childhood*. He is Life President of IASAIL, the International Association for the Study of Anglo-Irish Literature, which he founded with Brendan Kennelly and John Kelly, and is an Honorary Fellow of Trinity College, Dublin.

JOHN S. KELLY, Senior English Fellow at St John's College, Oxford, is Editor of *The Collected Letters of W. B. Yeats*, the first volume of which, covering the years up to the end of 1895, is already published. The next volume to appear will be the third of the series (the second being delayed), covering the years 1904-1910. He has contributed essays to various collections, among the most recent being 'Friendship is All the House I Have: Yeats and Lady Gregory' to *Lady Gregory, Fifty Years After*.

HEINZ KOSOK was educated at the Universities of Marburg and Bristol. He obtained his doctorate for a dissertation on Herman Meville (1960) and his *Habilitation* for a book on Sean O'Casey. He taught in the Universities of Marburg and Stuttgart before becoming Professor of English and American Literature in the new University of Wuppertal in 1972. He was Chairman of

IASAIL (1982-85). He has published widely, both in English and in German, on a variety of topics in English, American and Anglo-Irish Literature, his most recent book being *O'Casey the Dramatist* (1985). He has edited *Studies in Anglo-Irish Literature* (1982) and *Literary Interrelations: Ireland, England and the World* (3 vols., with Wolfgang Zach, 1987).

PETER KUCH was educated at St David's University College, Lampeter, and Jesus College, Oxford. He has held lectureships at the University of Newcastle, Australia, and the Université de Caen, France; he has taught at the Yeats International Summer School in Sligo. He is currently a senior lecturer in the Department of Humanities at Avondale College, New South Wales. He is author of *Yeats and AE: 'the antagonism that unites dear friends'* (1986), of two studies of Somerset Maugham and of various articles as well as radio and television programmes. He is an editor of the Literature volumes of the Collected Edition of the works of AE.

ALASDAIR D. F. MACRAE was educated at the University of Edinburgh. He was a lecturer in the University of Khartoum, Sudan, for five years, and has been a lecturer in English at the University of Stirling since 1969. He has written studies of Shakespeare's *Macbeth*, Shelley's *Selected Poems* and Eliot's *The Waste Land*. He is finishing a contextual biography of Yeats for Macmillan.

WILLIAM M. MURPHY is Thomas Lamont Research Professor of Ancient and Modern Languages at Union College, Schenectady, New York. He was educated at Harvard University and has specialized in the lives of the family of W. B. Yeats. Among his publications are *The Yeats Family and the Pollexfens of Sligo* (1971) and *Prodigal Father: The Life of John Butler Yeats* (1978). He has edited *Letters from Bedford Park* (1972) and, with Richard Finneran and George Mills Harper, *Letters to W. B. Yeats* (2 vols. 1977). In 1979 *Prodigal Father* was one of five works short-listed for the US National Book Award in Biography.

ANDREW PARKIN was educated at Pembroke College Cambridge and Bristol University. He now teaches at the University of British Columbia in Vancouver. Editor of *The Canadian Journal of Irish Studies*, he is also the author of *The Dramatic Imagination of W. B. Yeats, Shaw's Caesar and Cleopatra*, and a volume of poems, *Dancers in a Web*. He chose and introduced *Selected Plays of Dion*

Boucicault, and has published a drama anthology, *Stage One: a Canadian Scenebook*. In 1987 he was a Visiting Fellow at the Humanities Research Centre in Canberra, studying the influence of Japanese theatre on Meyerhold, Eisenstein and Kozintsev.

PATRICK RAFROIDI, educated at the Universities of Paris and Lille, is now a Professor at the University of Paris III (formerly the Sorbonne). He has taught at the Universities of Strasbourg, Lille, Indiana and Canberra. He was President of the University of Lille III (1967-81) and Director of the French Institute in London (1981-84). He has lectured in Canada, Germany, Poland, the UK and Ireland. He founded and directed CERIUL which acts as a centre for French university staff and students working in Anglo-Irish studies. A former Chairman of IASAIL from 1976-79 he has published *L'Irlande et le Romantisme* (1972; English version 1980) and co-edits *Etudes Irlandaises*. He has edited collections of essays and written many articles on Anglo-Irish Literature as well as grammatical and linguistic studies; he has also edited the *Poems* of Shakespeare and various anthologies.

ANN SADDLEMYER, Professor of English and Drama at the University of Toronto and former Chairman of IASAIL, has published and lectured widely on Yeats, Synge, Lady Gregory, the Abbey Theatre, Canadian dramatists, theatre history and modern drama. She is currently preparing a biography of George (Mrs W. B.) Yeats.

RONALD SCHUCHARD, Associate Professor of English at Emory University, has published papers on Yeats in *The Review of English Studies, Yeats Annual*, and *Yeats: An Annual of Critical and Textual Studies*. He is currently co-editing, with John S. Kelly, the third and fourth volumes of *The Collected Letters of W. B. Yeats*.

MASARU SEKINE read English Literature and Drama at Waseda University, Tokyo, and at the Universities of Manchester and Stirling. He is a trained Noh actor and dancer. Formerly a research curator at the Theatre Museum in Waseda University, he now teaches English at that University. He has been a visiting Professor at University College, Dublin and is an Honorary Research Fellow at the University of St Andrews. International Representative of IASAIL-Japan, he has edited two collections of Essays: *Irish Writers and Society at Large* (1985) and *Irish Writers and the Theatre* (1986). His book on the founder of Noh drama was published under the title, *Ze-Ami and his Theories of Noh Drama* in 1985. He is currently working with other scholars on a book on Yeats, Pound and the Noh.

MICHAEL J. SIDNELL is Professor of English at Trinity College, University of Toronto. He is the author of a number of critical articles on Yeats and other subjects, co-editor of *The Secret Rose: A Variorum Edition* (1981), and of *Druid Craft: the Writing of the Shadowy Waters* (1971). His *Dances of Death: the Group Theatre of London in the 'Thirties* appeared in 1984. He is currently working on an edition of Yeats's early prose and a multi-volume collection of dramatic theory.

C. K. STEAD, CBE, was born in Auckland, New Zealand, and educated at the Universities of Auckland (MA, 1955, D.Litt., 1981) and Bristol. He was Professor of English at Auckland 1967-85, when he retired to write full-time. His publications include three critical studies: *The New Poetic* (1964), *In the Glass Case* (1981), and *Pound, Yeats, Eliot and the Modernist Movement* (1986), seven books of poetry and four of fiction, as well as edited works, including the *Letters and Journals of Katherine Mansfield*. His novel *All Visitors Ashore* has recently been re-issued; *Between*, a new collection of poems, is forthcoming and he is completing a new novel.

HELEN VENDLER was educated at Emmanuel College, Boston University and Harvard University. She has taught at Cornell University, Haverford College, Swarthmore College, Smith College, Boston University, the University of Bordeaux, and is William R. Kenan, Jr. Professor of English and American Literature at Harvard University, and poetry critic of the *New Yorker*. She has written books on Yeats, Herbert, Keats, and Stevens (all published by Harvard University Press), and has edited *The Harvard Book of Contemporary American Poetry*. At present she is writing a commentary on Shakespeare's sonnets.

GEORGE J. WATSON was educated at St. Patrick's College, Armagh, Queen's University, Belfast, and Wadham College, Oxford. He is Senior Lecturer in English at the University of Aberdeen and Academic Dean of the Scottish Universities International Summer School. He has edited a comedy by Middleton, *A Trick to Catch the Old One*, and is the author of *Irish Identity and the Literary Revival: Synge, Yeats, Joyce and O'Casey* (1979), and *Drama: An Introduction* (1983); he has written many articles on Irish literature. He is currently working on a book on modern Irish literature.

INDEX